Crashing the Party

Legacies and Lessons
from the RNC 2000

Kris Hermes

Crashing the Party: Legacies and Lessons from the RNC 2000
Kris Hermes

ISBN: 978-1-62963-102-8
Library of Congress Control Number: 2015930883

Cover by John Yates/stealworks.com
Cover photo by R2K Legal Collective
Layout by Jonathan Rowland

PM Press
PO Box 23912
Oakland, CA 94623
www.pmpress.org

10 9 8 7 6 5 4 3 2 1

A portion of the proceeds from this book will be dedicated to a legal support project for the incubation of autonomous law collectives.
CrashingThePartyTheBook.com

Printed by the Employee Owners of Thomson-Shore in Dexter, Michigan.
www.thomsonshore.com

Contents

This book is dedicated to my mother and father, Jeanette and Al Hermes, whose constant encouragement gave me the confidence to attempt all things, to my partner, Erin Stalnaker, whose breadth of support was, and is, invaluable and to Zorra, who sat diligently at my feet for many long hours of writing.

ACKNOWLEDGMENTS

This book is a humble testament to the thousands of people who protested in Philadelphia in the summer of 2000, hundreds of whom were arrested and thereby caught up in the criminal injustice system along with their friends and families. This book is my attempt to chronicle and acknowledge the efforts of a committed group of folks who devoted a significant portion of their lives to build a unified and militant response to state repression of political activity.

In the course of defending themselves against their own criminal charges, several RNC arrestees became core members of the R2K Legal Collective, personifying the DIY ethic of legal strategy by and for those most directly affected. They included: Jacqueline Ambrosini, Caleb Arnold, Alexis Baden-Meyer, Bill Beckler, Christopher Day, Adam Eidinger, Jamie Graham, Jessica Mammarella, Dave Onion, Laura McTighe, Carlos Muños, Danielle Redden, George Ripley, Kate Sorensen, Ethan "Zeke" Spier, Camilo Viveiros, and Chris White.

Movement attorneys were an important part of the R2K Legal Collective and took direction from their dissident clients while ardently defending them against political charges. They included: Paul Hetznecker, Larry Krasner, Paul Messing, David Rudovsky, and Lester Roy Zipris, as well as public defenders Bradley Bridge, Meg Flores, and Shawn Nolan. Some attorneys—such as King Downing from New Jersey, Anastasia Pardalis and Ron McGuire from New York—came regularly to Philadelphia to help defend protesters. Marina Sitrin and Bill Beckler, recent law school graduates at the time, temporarily relocated from New York and, along with others, helped redefine the relationship between defendant and attorney. They also helped to politicize the criminal cases and make that a key element of the legal strategy.

At the heart of the R2K Legal Collective was a group of dedicated activists who did not themselves face charges but fiercely supported RNC arrestees. They included: Jill Benowitz, Kristin Bricker, Amy Dalton, Julie Davids, Jody Dodd, Bull Gervasi, Tim Groves, Christian "xtn" Hansen, Lee James, Katie Krauss, Amy Kwasnicki, Eric Laursen, Bronwyn Lepore, Elena and Elliott Madison, Sara Marcus, Nicole Meyenberg, Rachel Neumann, Clarissa Rogers, April Rosenblum, Matthew Ruben, Curtis Rumrill, Marlene Santoyo, Mac Scott, April Smith, David Webber, Susan Whitaker, and Lesley Wood.

Ezra Berkley Nepon led the charge to raise a near-miraculous $200,000 for bail and legal defense funds.

Suzy Subways was instrumental in creating a multimedia oral history archive of the Student Liberation Action Movement, a group intimately involved in the planning and execution of the August 1 day of direct action against the prison industrial complex. This book draws extensively from the SLAM Herstory Project.

Brad Kayal not only took a number of compelling photographs from the streets, but was also gracious enough to let us include them here.

Much appreciation goes to the National Lawyers Guild members and staff whose work and dedication have been an inspiration. Former Executive Director Heidi Boghosian and national office staff Traci Yoder and Tasha Moro deserve special praise for their steadfast support.

Finally, this book would not have been possible without the skilled and thoughtful editing of AK Thompson to whom I am very grateful.

FOREWORD

PHILADELPHIA, AUGUST 2000: THE REPUBLICAN NATIONAL Convention (RNC) changed the U.S. political landscape. But not how one might imagine.

Hundreds of people were in jail—roughly three to four hundred; the full count had not even come in yet. Those of us on the outside providing legal support were hearing stories of arrestees refusing to comply with the police, demanding that the physical abuse stop, that people not be separated or isolated, and that all arrestees receive the same treatment. There had been reports of people being hog-tied and beaten by police, resulting in broken fingers, concussions, serious contusions, and even sexual assaults. Stories came out of activists piling on top of one another in "puppy piles" to prevent the targeting of certain arrestees, people going limp and removing their clothes as a form of non-cooperation, and holding tight to one another so that the police violence would at least not be individual. While in jail, facing violent and abusive conditions, these activists—led by women—created an atmosphere of support, care, and powerful solidarity: singing, holding assemblies, making demands, and protecting one another. The collective power of the arrestees was incredible and the solidarity, in light of such abuse, was something that sent shivers down our spines.

Of more than four hundred people arrested at the 2000 RNC in Philadelphia, most initially refused to give their names or allow themselves to be fingerprinted, acting in solidarity with their fellow arrestees to avoid selective abuse and excessive charging, especially against the more than three dozen people charged with felonies, ranging from riot and conspiracy to aggravated assault and attempted murder of a police officer. As the police violence against them increased, their solidity increased as well.

But then we got the call. District Attorney Lynne Abraham said that if we thought she would negotiate we should—and I quote, as I was the one to speak with her—"get a life." *Shit.* Silence. Long pause. Now what? What do we tell our friends in jail who are staying so strong in the face of such abuse and who are trying to leverage negotiations on the outside? But there was going to be no negotiation. It was time to revisit our strategy.

The strategy of noncompliance, to achieve the same low-level charges for all people, had been successful in other cities at different times throughout history, including at recent anti-IMF protests in Washington, DC, and famously in Seattle at the anti-WTO protests in 1999. Months before the demonstrations in Philadelphia, the R2K Legal Collective was organized to set up a team of lawyers willing to work with arrested protestors and their allies.

As part of the legal team and one of those who temporarily moved to Philadelphia after the arrests, I can say without a doubt that it was both one of the most frightening and ultimately one of the most inspiring experiences I have ever had. The intention of the legal support effort was to change the political atmosphere so that when those charged with felonies and facing decades in jail went to trial they would do so in a very different political climate—one where the public, and in particular the Philadelphia jury pool—would know that those arrested were targets of a coordinated campaign to criminalize and silence dissent. R2K Legal helped facilitate this process and victory.

After many days of noncompliance and horrible abuse in the jails, and then-unprecedented million-dollar felony bails, most of the lawyers who had agreed to work with the legal team had instead abandoned us. With a growing concern over the safety of arrestees, R2K Legal sent messages to the jails where, after days of assemblies on the inside, the arrestees agreed to shift their tactics from jail to court solidarity.

One of my most powerful memories was when the first group of defendants was called to court. Close to one hundred people from around the U.S. came for their appearances, most wearing silk-screened ties and badges that read "Resist" on their activist formal attire. The DA made an offer to all of them, which meant they would not have to come back to Philadelphia and would not have any serious mark on their records. Offers like that are almost always accepted by activists under these circumstances. But these were not typical, just-arrested activists. These were people who had gone through hell in the jails, many for weeks, and who had protected each other in such powerful ways that there was no turning back. We, the legal support team, not the lawyers, told the prosecutor we would need time to collectively discuss this—in the court room. Reminded of the arrestees' actions in jail, there was a shudder from the court officers concerned by what they might be up against. But the judge agreed and even cleared all court personnel from the courtroom, as we demanded.

Before the assembly began there was a cheer. Not your average cheer, mind you, but a radical cheer that had been used during WTO and IMF protests as well as in the Philadelphia demonstrations. It was "Resist," which begins with "R" for revolution, "E" for everybody, "S" for subvert the system, "I" for ignite debate . . . After the cheer, we were energized to begin the assembly. The vast majority of defendants decided not to accept the offer, but to go back to their cities and towns and help R2K Legal do popular education around the offer so that a critical mass would refuse to accept it and instead organize political trials. This collective strength and decision-making was to set the tone for the hearings and trials that were to take place over the next year. And so it began.

Following the arrestees' release, the legal team had an even greater task than before: to democratically facilitate the discussions and planning of political trials with people from all over the United States. Fortunately, many of those arrested were from the New York area, so after initial strategy meetings in Philadelphia we began with assemblies and trainings in New York. That first assembly at Hunter College will remain forever imprinted in my memory. Together with SLAM (Student Liberation Action Movement), R2K Legal held an assembly for all defendants in the region. The atmosphere was intense, and the trauma from the police abuse was palpable and brought even further to the surface by the discussions. Though the defendants were filled with anxiety and fear, they were also grounded by a deep self-awareness and knowledge of their power.

The legal team used diagrams to help visually explain our attempts at democratic structure and aim to build equal footing among the defendants, lawyers, and supporters. We discussed and debated for hours the structure of the legal team locally, regionally and nationally, as well as the overall political landscape. All decisions were in the hands of the defendants, as they were the ones with their freedom on the line.

Notably, when we began the court solidarity process, mainstream media and the legal system believed that all RNC protesters were there to create mayhem and hurt the police. For defendants to confront this legal and political dynamic and try to change it was a brave move, and one that many did not take lightly. For example, there were teachers and city workers from New York for whom a conviction—even a misdemeanor—would mean never being able to teach or work in a municipal job again. But they still went to trial.

The solidarity shown in jail continued with the legal process in the courts. People took care of one another. The majority of defendants chose to go to trial, some of whom represented themselves, preparing for hours and learning bits of law and then traveling to a city that was not their own on a regular basis in order to show solidarity with others.

After months and then years of organizing we eventually won. *Crashing the Party* tells this story—that of organizing, fighting back, and winning. It goes into crucial detail about how this was done, the coordinated campaigns in different cities and towns, with the media, courts, and public. In the end, after many activists spent over two weeks in jail and then over a year involved in collective and individual court cases, almost all charges were dropped. The ultimate victory in Philadelphia was not only the 98 percent nonconviction rate, although that was tremendous; it was the ongoing acts of solidarity that continued for more than a year, resulting in the system's inability to convict.

In the end, after many activists spent over two weeks in jail and then over a year involved in collective and individual court cases, almost all charges were dropped. Not one person was convicted of a single felony at trial—the ultimate goal of the solidarity actions—and only thirteen were found guilty of misdemeanors. Those arrested were from all over the United States, and these hundreds of people found ways of functioning democratically and collectively to create the solidarity that led to the final equal adjudication of almost all of them.

Since the events in this book took place over a decade ago, there has been a tremendous upsurge in movement organizing and political action, from Occupy to Black Lives Matter. At the same time, we have witnessed an ever-increasing suppression of dissent and protest. While political strategy has become more sophisticated, especially relating to the questions of internal process, prefiguration, and democracy, activists have been slower to develop ways of taking better care of each other before and after political actions in the legal sphere. While there was a flurry of legal collectives organized in the early 2000s around the Global Justice Movement, many of which were modeled on collectives from the 1960s and '70s, most of them petered out.

One of the things I hope this book brings to people is the value of legal collectives in supporting radical actions and supporting solidarity so that no one is left alone to be victimized by the state. While there will continue to be more targeting of specific groups and individuals, we must respond as collectively as we can. To do this will require organizing activist-led legal collectives and similar support groups. Preparing ahead of time, and integrating activists, lawyers and legal workers into ongoing support efforts. While this work is perceived to be less glamorous and unfortunately often goes under the radar of social movements, I hope this book will help change that condition. Keeping people out of jail and unafraid is central to any movement and will be even more important to ours as we deepen our resistance and create alternatives to this system.

What Philadelphia taught us is that by working collectively and democratically we don't have to be forced to behave in one particular way in relationship to the system, particularly the legal system. "Solidarity Rocks!" was the slogan of the R2K Legal Collective. It is only with solidarity that we can protect each other and ourselves. The other huge lesson we must take away from the Philadelphia experience is to always be flexible with out tactics and strategies. There is no recipe—ever. But there are tools. The practice of people listening to one another, working together and being willing and able to change direction were some of the most important tools in our case. Kris has provided a wonderful account of this history as well as a tool for the activists of today and tomorrow.

INTRODUCTION

A MERICANS LIVE IN A NATIONAL SECURITY STATE. WHISTLE-blowers have exposed the breadth of surveillance programs used by the government to maintain control over our lives. Due to their ability to record massive amounts of online communication and the technology to track phone calls and monitor people's geographic positions, our expectations of privacy have been seriously undermined. Spying on dissidents has been part of the U.S. policing apparatus for decades, but now, with virtually no private moment out of reach, the state is more equipped than ever to suppress dissent. According to constitutional attorney and journalist Glenn Greenwald, the government can "literally watch every keystroke that you make." It's enough to make the incredible privacy invasions recounted in Orwell's fictional *1984* seem tame by comparison.[1]

For many activists who have experienced political repression, the hard evidence provided by WikiLeaks, Edward Snowden, and other NSA whistleblowers merely confirmed what they already knew. At the same time, however, such evidence provides greater legitimacy to claims that activists have made for years. From the coordination of local, state, and federal law enforcement working to undermine movements like Occupy Wall Street to the rapid and unchecked increase in government and corporate spending on surveillance and infiltration, Muslims, activists, and other targeted groups are experiencing increased political repression.

For more than a decade, liberals and those to their left have decried the suppression of civil liberties resulting from the "War on Terror," the Patriot Act, and the Department of Homeland Security (DHS). The right has responded by claiming that government encroachment on individual liberties (including privacy) is the "price we pay for our freedom." In truth, this dialogue is largely irrelevant. The roots of contemporary government spying predate 9/11. They can be found in the active repression of social change activists who participated in mass demonstrations during the height of the Global Justice movement. While 9/11 gave the government a convenient pretext to facilitate the rapid growth of the National Security State, both the blueprint and many of its key components—heavy surveillance, infiltration, and disruption of political groups—were already in play before the attacks. The idea that the National Security State predates 9/11 and would have emerged regardless is certainly worthy of investigation, not least because it points to a major focus of this book: the deliberation with which our government has sought to control our struggles and our everyday lives.

Another source for many elements of today's National Security State can of course be found in the counterintelligence tactics the FBI employed against the civil rights, antiwar, and Black liberation movements during the 1960s. Despite COINTELPRO's official end in 1971, J. Edgar Hoover's legacy persisted due to the irresistible and ongoing benefits the state gained by spying on, infiltrating, and disrupting political groups. Similarly, when it came to preserving the financial and political interests of those in power, the benefits of collaboration between law enforcement and other government and corporate actors proved too great for the state to ignore. Shortly after restrictions on politically motivated policing were imposed as a result of the Church Committee findings in the mid-1970s, the Federal Bureau of Investigation (FBI) formed the first Joint Terrorism Task Force (JTTF) in New York City (1980) as a collaboration between FBI and other local, state, and federal agencies. By 2000, there were task forces in more than thirty U.S. cities,[2] an increase that arose in large part from the 1993 bombing of the World Trade Center and the Oklahoma City bombing of 1995. The subsequent passage of President Clinton's 1996 anti-terrorism bill provided further political and financial support for an enhanced policing apparatus. By the late 1990s, however, it became evident that fighting terrorism was only a pretext for the nascent National Security State, which set its sights on political dissidents and other groups that represented a threat to the status quo.

Although numerous movements for social change gained momentum during the 1990s, it was resistance to U.S. trade policy and corporate globalization that ultimately prompted the dramatic change in political policing practices. As a result of their surprising success, the 1999 demonstrations against the World Trade Organization (WTO) in Seattle strengthened political organizing and gave activists new courage to fight back against the state. The anarchist practices of the anticapitalist branch of the Global Justice movement emphasized the importance of mutual aid, decentralized decision-making, and nonhierarchical organizing structures—all of which were, and continue to be, effective tools for confronting political repression. Meanwhile, on the public stage, mainstream media and the state used images of tear gas–filled streets, repeated scenes of black-clad activists breaking corporate storefront windows, and mass arrests to deliberately skew public impressions. Although there's little dispute that militant protest took place in Seattle, it's now clear that most protesters engaged in nonviolent civil disobedience while the police initiated indiscriminate violence. Nevertheless, the manipulated characterization of the events allowed for a new strategy to be developed in reaction to political protest. A discernible shift had taken place.

The dramatic shift in the way the state reacted to WTO protesters becomes evident when situated within the historical development of policing strategies. Following the "escalated force" practices used during the civil rights and antiwar movements of the 1960s and 1970s, a new strategic policing approach developed, which was used until the turn of the century. According to sociologists Clark McPhail, David Schweingruber, and John D. McCarthy, the "negotiated management" strategy of the 1980s and 1990s represented a "softer" approach to dealing with political protest. In particular, it was marked by friendlier relations with dissidents, the increased use of protest permits, less police violence, and fewer arrests.[3] After more than two decades, "negotiated management" came to an abrupt end on the streets of Seattle, where it was replaced with "strategic incapacitation," a designation coined by sociologists Patrick Gilham and John Noakes.[4] Still used today, strategic incapacitation is notable for neutralizing (rather than tolerating) free expression and can easily be recognized by its efforts to undermine demonstrations with a variety of aggressive tactics.

But even as policing efforts were ramping up, the momentum gained from the Seattle WTO protests spilled over into demonstrations against the International Monetary Fund (IMF) and World Bank in Washington, DC, in April 2000, and into the protests at the quadrennial Democratic and Republican conventions that summer. Scheduled to take place in Philadelphia, the Republican National Convention (RNC) represented a national opportunity to oppose U.S.-led policies of trade liberalization, increased privatization, and other domestic and foreign policies. With the neoliberal then-governor George W. Bush being advanced by the Republicans as the next president, heightened attention fell on the City of Brotherly Love. Understanding that activists had many reasons to confront Bush and his political platform, the City of Philadelphia poured vast resources into ensuring an unfettered convention.

With elections held every four years, the dual party system focuses almost exclusively on the Democratic National Convention and Republican National Convention as precursor events wherein each party nominates its presidential candidate. Though Republicans have a long history of hosting conventions in Philadelphia (1856, 1877, 1900, 1940, and 1948), it was a role the city hadn't played for more than fifty years.[5] As a trade union and Democratic Party stronghold, Philadelphia had also not elected a Republican mayor in half a century.[6] Nevertheless, Pennsylvania—and Philadelphia in particular—figured centrally in the Republicans' political strategy. Then-president Clinton had carried Pennsylvania in 1992 and 1996,[7] and the Republicans were anxious to gain ground in the swing state. Having a Republican governor in Pennsylvania to help with fundraising and to lend political clout also surely played a factor in the GOP's choice to make Philadelphia the host city for the RNC 2000.

From the outset, RNC 2000 protesters were vilified by local officials in the mainstream media as "violent anarchists" and "outside agitators," while an expansive policing apparatus was established to spy on and disrupt political activity. In coordination with law enforcement, the city's administrative agencies tried to stifle the demonstrations by denying permits and conducting preemptive raids on activist spaces. For their part, the police and FBI engaged in heavy surveillance and infiltration, and used targeted stops and searches to harass and intimidate protesters. On August 1, the day of direct action against the criminal justice system, police used oppressive crowd control techniques and were indiscriminately brutal. In the end, they arrested more than four hundred people and detained accused protest "ringleaders" on bail as high as $1 million. Throughout, the state's reaction contained initial approximations of many of the elements that have since come to be associated with the National Security State. The story is not solely one of repression, however. Indeed, many of the most noteworthy events occurred in the days and months that followed the Republican convention. While still in jail, activists used solidarity tactics to agitate, achieve demands, and resist the dehumanizing jail experience. The camaraderie and solidarity developed in jail was quickly adapted and used in the courtroom to collectively refuse plea bargains and stage political trials. In the end, hundreds of criminal cases were dismissed or saw their defendants acquitted.

To be sure, the events surrounding the RNC 2000 protests were not entirely unprecedented, nor were they the worst example of political repression the city had ever witnessed. Philadelphia has a longstanding reputation for intolerance to political dissent, with its treatment of MOVE standing out as one of its more shameful episodes.[8] Nevertheless, what took place during the RNC 2000 protests and in the years that followed is important to our social and political history for at least three reasons: (1) the policing model that has now been used by the state to suppress dissent for more than a decade was developed in Philadelphia and honed shortly thereafter by John Timoney, one of the country's most notorious anti–free speech police chiefs; (2) President George W. Bush, who was nominated at the RNC 2000, drew on this experience to expand the "security" apparatus that made Timoney's repressive policing model possible and became crucial to what we now know as the National Security State; and (3) the stunning example of how activists came together in ways that were not only effective but also inspiring and life-changing.

*** *** ***

Law enforcement and public officials from all levels of government learned from the events in Seattle and derived ways to exploit weaknesses in the Global Justice movement.[9] These lessons were applied in Philadelphia with a new level of multi-agency cooperation, which served as a laboratory and training ground for the political policing tactics that have been used ever since. Chip Berlet of Political Research Associates heralded the RNC 2000 protests as a significant turning point. "In Philadelphia, we saw the return of overt government repression of dissent," Berlet told the *Boston Phoenix.* "Which works fine for a police state," he added, "but not at all for the free-speech principles of democracy."[10] The staggering array of repressive tactics used in Philadelphia served as a test run for the policing methods used in today's National Security State. Significantly, these developments would likely have occurred regardless of whether 9/11 had ever happened. For his part, Timoney further refined his policing methods as Miami police chief during the 2003 Free Trade Area of the Americas (FTAA) meetings. Miami Mayor Manny Diaz hailed the notoriously violent reaction as a "model for homeland defense," thereby branding this new approach to policing the "Miami Model."[11]

A confluence of factors, all of which occurred prior to 9/11, made the methods developed on the streets of Philadelphia the preference for crowd control and political policing practices across the U.S. One factor that helped facilitate the multi-agency cooperation at the turn of the century was a new federal designation: National Special Security Event (NSSE). The RNC 2000 protests took place under this new designation, which President Clinton had established two years earlier to help integrate numerous enforcement agencies and to formalize a policing apparatus for political meetings and events of significance in the U.S.[12] Although dozens of different government agencies coordinate responses to mass political demonstrations under the NSSE authority, the U.S. Secret Service is considered the lead agency for the design and implementation of security plans, while the FBI is in charge of counterterrorism and counterintelligence.[13] Examples of NSSEs include the quadrennial Republican and Democratic conventions, presidential inaugurations, and meetings of the FTAA and the North Atlantic Treaty Organization.

Even before passage of the Patriot Act and the creation of DHS (a Cabinet post with the means to more efficiently obtain and share information), the National Security Administration (NSA) and other federal agencies were engaged in large-scale data collection and sorting and the dissemination of political intelligence. According to lauded thirty-two-year NSA veteran Kirk Wiebe, the agency was spying on Americans without probable cause long before 9/11.[14] Meanwhile, a highly secretive, worldwide signals intelligence and analysis network called ECHELON was being run by a U.S.-UK alliance (that also included Canada, Australia, and New Zealand) to gather domestic and international intelligence.[15] Although barely any news on the network appeared in the mainstream media, in July 2000 the BBC reported that ECHELON was using 120 U.S. satellites in geo-stationary orbit and bases in five countries linked directly to the NSA in Fort Mead, Maryland.[16] The network's ability, in the 1990s and early 2000s, to intercept and filter billions of discreet forms of communication based on keywords or word patterns paved the way for even greater invasions of privacy resulting from the U.S. reaction to 9/11. With an ever-increasing budget to spy on Americans and a propensity to criminalize dissidents by intentionally blurring the already nebulous definitions of "activist" and "terrorist," the state has never been more capable of suppressing dissent.

* * *

As grim as that assessment might seem, the events in Philadelphia also contained a number of empowering—yet frequently overlooked—lessons for dissidents. To be sure, the importance of understanding the repressive nature of the state cannot be overemphasized. But the ways in which thousands of RNC 2000 protesters and their supporters came together to resist efforts to neutralize and silence them—in the streets, in the jails, and in the courtrooms—are arguably far more important to movements for social change. The Global Justice movement gained people's attention by renewing interest in collective action and fostering a decentralized approach outside the norms of routine protest. Less frequently noted, however, was the degree to which the movement also inspired forms of collective action like jail and court solidarity and radical legal support.

At the center of most of the action that followed the August 1 arrests was the R2K Legal Collective. The collective was formed in advance of the RNC 2000 protests to provide legal support for activists, but it quickly became a standing organization devoted to long-term legal and political support. Made up of legal workers, lawyers, law students, defendants, and activists, the collective was defendant-driven, with strategic and tactical decisions made by the hundreds of activists most affected.

The first signs of collective action by arrestees occurred on the police buses and were followed by en masse refusals to provide identification to jail authorities. Rarely used but often effective, this tactic aims to leverage the strength of arrestees to achieve demands such as better treatment or release either without charges or with equitable low-level charges. Other forms of collective action were also taken in jail to protect vulnerable or targeted arrestees, but it was this collective spirit that built the camaraderie which, in turn, laid the foundation for what followed. R2K Legal quickly developed ways to interact with arrestees and involve them in decision-making. Because of mistreatment on the streets and in jail, as well as the excessive charges applied to hundreds of protesters, the RNC 2000 arrestees sought vindication in the courtroom, spurring a court solidarity strategy that began with a mass refusal to accept plea bargains and a mass demand for trials.

The stories of activists staging political trials, overcoming charges, exposing widespread surveillance and infiltration, raising unprecedented funds for legal defense, and using media to shift public opinion from contempt for protesters to widespread support are both inspirational and instructional. And, while certain aspects of this legacy have been repeated since 2000 (perhaps most notably following the RNC 2008 protest in the

Twin Cities), all of these elements have never been used together since. In part, this is due to the tendency for activists to underestimate their collective strength against an intimidating criminal legal system.

Seasoned Bay Area criminal defense attorney John Viola believes that legal support is a "necessary evil for social movement activists" and "not an end in and of itself."[17] As a former member of Legal Support to Stop the War (LS2SW), a tight-knit collective formed in advance of the 2003 U.S. invasion of Iraq, Viola emphasized that legal support can also "open up a space where there's more possibility and potential, and where people get a different perspective on the legal system." Consistent with the approach taken by R2K Legal, Viola and other LS2SW members aimed "to have legal support be driven by folks who are taking actions in the street." But the unique, unmediated relationship between LS2SW and the Bay Area antiwar activists organizing mass civil disobedience represented "a very strategic intervention," according to Viola. While LS2SW ultimately took its cue from protest organizers, Viola and his legal support comrades felt that, if the legal system was left to its own devices, "there would be a bad outcome for social activists, especially the most radical among us." By putting itself in the middle of the organizing effort, Viola said LS2SW was able to "encourage people to take steps to protect themselves and make their activism more strategic and effective" without "imposing a model." By using collective legal action to lessen harm to activists and creatively push legal boundaries, LS2SW underscored the importance of legal support as an undesirable but often necessary component of social change.

Arguably, it was this collective desire to push the boundaries of the legal system that sparked a renaissance of legal collectives and the rebirth of a radical legal support movement. The Midnight Special Law Collective, which formed after the 1999 WTO protests, and the R2K Legal Collective formed the following year, inspired a new vision for how activists could engage the legal system. New collectives quickly formed in Austin, Cincinnati, New York, Washington DC, and other locations around the country. This renaissance, however, was relatively short-lived. And though there are more legal collectives today than there were in 2000, many—including Midnight Special—have died off. Unfortunately, the benefits of collective action and radical legal support are often only evident to those who have partaken in them. As a result, they can be difficult to sustain over time. I wrote this book largely to preserve our shared legacy of political and legal resistance so that we can learn from these experiences and challenge ourselves to be more effective in achieving broad-based social change.

* * *

I moved to Philadelphia in 1997 and quickly became involved in AIDS activism. As a member of the AIDS Coalition To Unleash Power (ACT UP) Philadelphia, I had been arrested numerous times for civil disobedience and had become fairly adept at providing legal support. My activism began in the 1980s, but my political perspective took a decided turn in the late 1990s. Along with my exposure to the Global Justice movement, I was irrevocably changed by my engagement with Philadelphia's anarchist community. Antiauthoritarian and antioppression practices, mutual aid and support, and consensus decision-making all made a huge impact on my life and my political organizing. It was in this context that I became eager to support friends and fellow activists mobilizing people to come protest the Republican convention. These factors motivated me to join the R2K Legal Collective and shaped my involvement over the years that followed.

ACT UP banner drop at intersection of I-676 & I-76 during rush hour on the first day of the RNC.

I had no idea that the next four years of my life would become intimately bound to the events stemming from August 1, 2000. I joined the National Lawyers Guild (NLG) the same year I helped set up the legal office to track arrestees and monitor rights violations during the RNC 2000 protests. The NLG had provided legal support for protests in the past, but its intersection with R2K Legal (of which I'd become a core member) created a relatively new dynamic. Since activist-driven legal collectives were a new phenomenon, it made for a sometimes tense—but ultimately empowering—experience. I tell the stories of R2K Legal and its amazing political and legal strength to honor this legacy. My role as an R2K Legal member puts me in a unique position to write about the legal and political events as both a firsthand participant and an objective observer. My involvement in the collective also gave me access to much of the organization's material and to legal documents for the hundreds of prosecutions and various civil lawsuits. While conducting the research for this book, countless hours were spent interviewing dozens of activists directly involved in both the protests and their legal aftermath. I also drew upon hundreds of media articles, editorials, official reports, research papers, and other relevant documents to provide rich anecdotes and varied points of view.

All told, the experience made an indelible mark on me. I stayed an active core member of R2K Legal until its dissolution in 2004. Although I did not become a member of Up Against the Law (the Philly legal collective formed in the ashes of R2K Legal), I went on to do legal work in the Bay Area with the NLG and other legal support groups. I either helped form, staff, or conduct media work for legal support efforts during the FTAA protests in Miami (2003), the RNC protests in New York City (2004) and the Twin Cities (2008), and the more recent NATO protests in Chicago (2012). In 2006, I also helped co-found the Grand Jury Resistance Project, which provided legal support to people subpoenaed to testify before politically motivated grand juries. Over the years, the primary legal-support role I've played has been either in determining where political leverage exists to overcome legal predicaments or in changing the media narrative in favor of dissidents. I was an integral part of R2K Legal's media committee, which was responsible for generating more positive exposure than most summit protests over the past fifteen years have received. A labor of love, this book arose from a genuine desire to share important experiences from our political history. My greatest hope is that we can take these stories to heart and use them to help advance our collective struggles for liberation.

* * *

In order to better understand the influence the RNC 2000 protests had on political policing in the U.S. and the lessons these protests held for activists, I tell this story in three sections. In the first, I explain Philadelphia's rich history of political repression and how various levels of government worked together during the RNC to undermine free expression. Ready to confront the vast resources of the state, the Global Justice movement brought a renewed exuberance to protest with vibrant theatrics and a militant tone that refused acquiescence. I explain how the Global Justice movement struggled to push domestic issues to the foreground and determined to focus its efforts in Philadelphia on resistance to the prison industrial complex, police brutality, and the death penalty. And though the state's immense resources enabled it to neutralize the protests using infiltration, preemptive raids, brutality, and mass arrests, the subsequent stories of solidarity and collective resistance in jail and beyond are at once inspiring and instructive.

In the second section, I detail the unique way that protesters, legal workers, law students, and lawyers came together to fight hundreds of criminal cases in court as well as to raise hundreds of thousands of dollars in legal funds, mobilize allied groups and the public to support the dismissal of criminal cases, and use media to shift public opinion in favor of RNC defendants. Indeed, stories of defendants overcoming a legal system designed to make them powerless became the strongest impetus for me to write this book. From the formation of the defendant-led R2K Legal Collective to the successful use of solidarity tactics in the courtroom, and from staging politicized trials to challenging judicial bias, I recount stories of impropriety by the district attorney and the courts and contrast them with the vindication achieved by dissidents. Perhaps the best examples of ingenuity and courage can be found in the various stories of defendants representing themselves, *pro se*, against intolerant and aggressive prosecutors, state's witnesses, and judges.

The final section is focused on the legacies and lessons of August 1. Such an analysis is not only critical to learning from the successes and failures of our political movements but also relevant to addressing contemporary repressive tactics. Admittedly, some currents of radical political thought assert that the least harm will be sustained by trying to avoid the legal system altogether. But if confrontation with the state is inevitable, as indeed it has proven to be for so many people, then it becomes important to analyze the state's historical progression and current capabilities to better understand countervailing tactics and strategies. In particular, I consider how radical political and legal communities could work more effectively together in the interest of advancing movements for social change and I highlight the legal collective or long-term legal support model as a powerful tool. Notably, the Global Justice movement and the events in

Philadelphia spurred a renaissance of legal collectives that grew substantially through the early-to-mid 2000s—a legacy that remains vital to our political history, and possibly to our future success.

Though I describe the events in Philadelphia mainly from a detached, third-person perspective, I was learning and evolving with everyone else. The lessons taken away from that era are as important to me as they will be to anyone who has decided to be politically active or increase confrontation with the state. We have been deceived into believing that the country's creep toward a National Security State originated in the fight against terrorism; however, the current model of political policing and the increasingly intolerant posture toward free expression was developed in Philadelphia, long before 9/11. Ultimately, and regardless of its motivation, it's crucial that we assess the state's resources, strategies, and tactics, as well as its limitations and vulnerabilities if we are to be effective in advancing social change. We must therefore learn the ways in which we might gain collective strength against the state. If we're going to come together on the streets to oppose our government's policies, we should also be prepared to build on and use that collective strength to confront the state in the jail and the courts.

Gone is the expectation of privacy. Neither lawsuits challenging civil liberties violations yielding unprecedented monetary awards nor strict consent decrees limiting police behavior have significantly changed U.S. political policing practices. If you dare to organize political demonstrations that are effective at advancing social change, you can expect to face the full force of the state. Edward Snowden may have exposed the NSA's sweeping surveillance program, but we had already glimpsed the vast law enforcement apparatus when hundreds of Occupy encampments were raided and dismantled city by city. Nevertheless, the state's seemingly unlimited access to information and unprecedented resources should not discourage us. Instead, it should enjoin us to be more clever, more imaginative, more diligent, and even more militant in our opposition. Which is why a better understanding of our history is so instructive, and why the stories woven through this book remain so important.

SECTION I
IN THE STREETS

Photo © Brad Kayal

CHAPTER 1:
PREPARATION AND PROTEST

Political Repression in Philadelphia

P
HILADELPHIA HAS A LONG HISTORY OF POLITICAL REPRESSION. IN 1894, Philadelphia police worked undercover to monitor a local contingent of "Coxey's Army" (a historic labor and employment rights march, named after Jacob Coxey of Ohio), which passed through Philadelphia on its way to Washington, DC.[1] Seven years later, they prevented anarchist lecturer Emma Goldman from speaking in the city. More recent examples of intolerance include the 1978 and 1985 city-led attacks on the west Philadelphia home of the MOVE organization,[2] as well as the 1981 shooting of former Black Panther and journalist Mumia Abu-Jamal, who was convicted and sentenced to death for supposedly having killed officer Daniel Faulkner.[3]

By 1981, it was common knowledge that the federal government had been spying on and disrupting movements like the Black Panther Party (BPP). In Abu-Jamal's murder trial, it was revealed that the FBI had been surveilling him since he was fourteen years old. For their part, and with a counterintelligence repertoire similar to that of the FBI, Philadelphia's Civil Affairs Unit (CAU) has long been known as the city's "political police." Under the authority of the Philadelphia Police Department (PPD), the CAU started in the early 1960s as the Civil Disobedience Unit (CDU), and partook in the surveillance, covert operations, and disruption of the COINTELPRO era. During the 1960s and 1970s, the CDU worked with the FBI and other law enforcement agencies to spy on, infiltrate, and suppress Black liberation movements like the BPP and MOVE. In the 1980s, the CDU became the CAU and appeared to temper its aggressive tactics. Nevertheless, the organization was still actively gathering political intelligence right up until and during the RNC 2000 protests.[4]

In 1987, Philadelphia activists gained a modest advantage against counterintelligence efforts when they sued the city, as well as local and federal law enforcement, for spying on them and obstructing their efforts to demonstrate at an event celebrating the bicentennial of the U.S. Constitution.[5] The lawsuit resulted in an injunction that prohibited Philadelphia police from infiltration except with the approval of the mayor, the managing director, and the police commissioner.[6] Then, in 1991, protests against the AIDS policies of then-president George H.W. Bush resulted in another lawsuit when activists were violently attacked by police.[7] The combined effect of a monetary settlement from the lawsuit and the earlier injunction-inspired mayoral directive against infiltration helped mitigate aggressive police behavior toward activists for nearly ten years—until the RNC 2000.

The history of political repression in Philadelphia cannot be properly evaluated without recognizing the much broader and longstanding problem of police brutality. For people of color, police violence is a daily reality.[8] Less than three weeks before the RNC 2000, about a dozen police officers were filmed beating Thomas Jones, an unarmed African American man. Jones was seriously injured after being shot five times by police prior to the beating.[9] Further evidence of the city's racist legal system can be found in the disproportionate incarceration rate for Black Philadelphians—an astonishing 70 percent of people jailed in the city[10]—and a death-row population with the highest percentage of African Americans in the country.[11] For their part, the Philadelphia district attorney's office has proven to be reluctant to prosecute police accused of brutality and murder. At the time of the RNC 2000, District Attorney Lynne Abraham had come under fire for her lackluster effort to prosecute officer Christopher DiPasquale for the 1998 shooting death of Donta Dawson, a nineteen-year-old unarmed Black man.[12] Abraham also refused to prosecute officer John Salkowski for the January 2000 murder of twenty-six-year-old African American activist and student Erin Forbes. But it was in her role as a Philadelphia Common Pleas Court judge (a post she held from 1980 to 1991) that brought Abraham notoriety for signing the 1985 warrant that enabled the police bombing of the MOVE house. After becoming district attorney in 1991, Abraham quickly became known for her "tough on crime" attitude and her extensive use of the death penalty. It was enough to compel the *New York Times Magazine* to call her the "Deadliest D.A."[13] These links between police brutality, the city's racist legal system, and its history of political repression were not lost on activists planning to protest the RNC 2000.

Citywide Effort to Chill Dissent

In addition to law enforcement, Philadelphia's history of political repression was made possible through the full cooperation of municipal agencies and, commonly, the tacit approval of mainstream media. All of these factors came into play during the RNC 2000, and it was within this context that Philadelphia embraced the role of host city.

Before becoming mayor just months prior to the convention, John Street had been a City Council member in North Philadelphia and Center City for nearly twenty years and was previously well regarded as a community organizer working on housing issues.[14] Despite these dubious activist roots, however, Mayor Street was under pressure to pull off a seamless convention in order to attract tourist dollars. Displaying his contempt for RNC protesters, Street publicly characterized them as "idiots" and threatened "a very ugly response" for those aiming to "disrupt" or "make a spectacle" of the city.[15] In a similar fashion, Philadelphia police commissioner John Timoney told Reuters that, while he didn't mind "taking the first punch," he would surely "retaliate."[16] As far as Timoney was concerned, "nobody is going to disrupt the convention." Moreover, he was prepared to use "fisticuffs" if necessary.

Sworn in as Philadelphia's police commissioner in 1998 after working for the New York Police Department (NYPD) for nearly thirty years, Timoney had already policed three political party conventions, including the Democratic National Convention in 1992.[17] Nevertheless, Timoney's defining moment with the NYPD came during the Tompkins Square Park riot, which he led in August 1988. During the riot, police attacked homeless people, housing activists, and their supporters.[18] Timoney left the NYPD as deputy commissioner, but his legacy gave dissidents cause for concern as he took over a beleaguered PPD.[19] Initially hired to address criticism that the PPD was ineffective and corrupt, the Police Advisory Commission received more reports of misconduct by Timoney's police force during the year of the convention than in any previous year of the commission's existence.[20]

While Timoney and his PPD were the most culpable for abuses perpetrated against activists during the RNC 2000 protests,[21] the effort to chill dissent also included a wide range of city agencies and departments. These included the Department of Human Services (DHS), the Fire Department, the Law Department, Licenses and Inspection (L&I), and the Managing Director's Office (MDO) (which, according to the City of Philadelphia's website, is "the Cabinet-level office that directly supervises the [City's] thirteen operating departments").[22] The MDO was also the city agency tasked with issuing permits for political demonstrations, a role it abused on multiple occasions.

One of the most egregious examples of predemonstration harassment was carried out by DHS against organizers of the "March for Economic Human Rights," planned for the opening day of the convention. The march had been organized by KWRU, a people of color–led organization of poor and homeless families based in North Philadelphia, and the Poor People's Economic Human Rights Campaign (PPEHRC), a national network of grassroots anti-poverty organizations. The city was well aware that poor families from these organizations would populate the march; however, rather than designing ways to accommodate them, they refused to issue a demonstration permit and announced plans for taking children into custody if their parents got arrested. With less than two weeks before the march, DHS used the threat of arrest and the removal of children to stifle participation.[23]

With less than a week before the RNC 2000 protests, and with too little time for activists to mount an effective legal challenge, the Philadelphia City Council adopted a ban on wearing masks, including gas masks and bandanas.[24] Introduced by Council member Rick Mariano, the anti-mask legislation was modeled after a Georgia law designed by the Anti-Defamation League to help identify rallying members of the Ku Klux Klan.[25] A similar measure was adopted by Detroit in advance of the June 2000 protests against the Organization of American States meeting in nearby Windsor, Ontario. Detroit police used the ordinance to arrest thirteen people.[26] Despite vocal opposition from some members of the Philadelphia City Council, the bill passed 11–5 and was signed by Mayor Street.[27]

Meanwhile, the Philadelphia courts took action by announcing a scheduling change to accommodate anticipated mass arrests. According to the *Legal Intelligencer*, Common Pleas Court president Judge Alex Bonavitacola said prior to the protests that "all trials involving persons in custody, police officer witnesses, the use of sheriffs and jurors will be postponed to free up law enforcement authorities at the request of Philadelphia Police Commissioner John Timoney."[28] The courts seemed untroubled by the likelihood that postponement of routine criminal cases would adversely affect the rights of those already imprisoned and awaiting trial. Nevertheless, the diversion of regular court business allowed the judicial branch to focus disproportionate attention on the expected mass arrest of protesters.

In the Beginning

By November 1998, more than a year after then-mayor Ed Rendell formed "Philadelphia 2000," the nonprofit Republican convention host committee, the city had been officially selected as the site for the RNC 2000.[29] Philadelphia 2000 was set up to raise funds, negotiate public and private contracts, facilitate the convention, and absorb any liability for the Republican Party and the City of Philadelphia. Pennsylvania governor Tom Ridge, one of Philadelphia 2000's co-chairs and a leading contender for the vice-presidential nomination, was an enthusiastic cheerleader for the convention and its accompanying security apparatus.[30] By the time the RNC 2000 occurred, Ridge had achieved a reputation for carrying out the first execution in a Northeastern state since 1967 and signing two execution warrants for Mumia Abu-Jamal.[31] Another co-chair and the driving force behind Philadelphia 2000 was David L. Cohen, chief of staff for Ed Rendell and a partner at Ballard Spahr Andrews & Ingersoll, one of the hundred largest law firms in the country.[32] For his part, City Solicitor Kenneth Trujillo negotiated between Philadelphia 2000 and the city for labor and service contracts, including convention security, emergency medical services, and telecommunications.[33] It was Trujillo's office that negotiated the insurance policy purchased by Philadelphia 2000, which covered the city against liability for violating people's civil rights.[34]

In August 1999, a full year prior to thousands of people protesting in the streets, Philadelphia 2000 and the city's Law Department drafted agreements that gave the Republicans both "right of first refusal" on more than a hundred city venues and an "Omnibus Special Events Permit."[35] Signed in the shadows away from public scrutiny, these agreements came to embody the hubris of the GOP and the city, and their complete contempt for dissent. This contempt would reveal itself in other ways later, but the path had been paved for ultimate deference to the RNC and the Republican Party.

On the surface, the space grab was meant to allow free rein in event planning; however, it was also a thinly veiled attempt to prohibit protest activity and limit the ability to hold demonstrations. And while the arrangement included provisions for a "protest pit"—an officially designated "free speech zone"—to pacify any outcry over the exclusion of protest, few were fooled.

The "pit" was to be 40 by 190 feet in size and located at FDR Park, far away from the convention site. Free speech was further curtailed by a requirement that groups apply for one of seventy-two protest-pit time slots—with each slot representing fifty minutes of so-called protest[36]—in a police-run lottery.[37] Meanwhile, Republicans were to have full use of all ten blocks surrounding the First Union Center where the convention was being held.[38]

Two of the first organizations to apply for—and be denied—permits were Unity 2000, a coalition of more than a hundred groups planning what was expected to be the convention's largest march and rally on July 30, and the Ad Hoc Committee to Defend Health Care, which was planning a smaller march and rally for July 29. Unity 2000 applied for a permit in February 2000 and was twice rejected with the explanation that the Republicans had previously reserved the space.[39] The Ad Hoc Committee's permit application was pending at the time, but it too was expecting to be rejected. On April 6, 2000, Unity 2000 and the committee filed a federal lawsuit with the help of the American Civil Liberties Union (ACLU) of Pennsylvania. The plaintiffs accused the city of viewpoint discrimination and argued that "while the First Amendment clearly guarantees the right of the Republican Party to convene, the same amendment protects the right of those with competing views."[40] The suit further argued, "Philadelphia cannot prefer Republican over dissenting speech, and cannot abrogate its responsibility to accommodate protesting speech by handing over the entire public space to one side of the political spectrum."

Under threat of a federal ruling that it was violating the U.S. Constitution by denying permits to protest groups, the city agreed to a settlement on April 28, 2000.[41] As a result of the agreement, the city made significant legal, political, and financial concessions. With the publicity that was generated from the lawsuit, Philadelphia suffered a political defeat that threatened its historical status as the "cradle of liberty." The biggest hit taken by the city, however, was a financial one. While Unity 2000 agreed to pay a $10,000 permit fee as part of the settlement, the city agreed to provide all services to the protesters at no charge. This included a stage and sound system, portable toilets, medical services, security, and cleanup services, totaling an estimated $75,000.[42] Yet, despite its political loss, the city continued to deny permits to other protest groups including the Kensington Welfare Rights Union (KWRU), which was organizing the March for Economic Human Rights on July 31.[43] KWRU would have ongoing difficulty around its permit application and other matters right up until the time of the march.

Police Training and Protest Observation

The large turnout of protesters in Seattle against the WTO may have surprised many people in the U.S., but the Philadelphia police department had the forethought to travel there to observe the demonstrations.[44] It was around six months before the Republican convention, and Philadelphia police were anxious to analyze protester tactics. Looking back on Seattle in February 2000, Timoney stated that there would be "a whole host of training for police" in the lead-up to the convention that summer.[45] That same month, a conference was held at the FBI Academy in Virginia for police commanders from around the country—including Las Vegas, San Diego, Minneapolis, Tulsa, and Washington, DC, to study the Seattle protests and prepare for similar events.[46] Around that time, the International Association of Chiefs of Police noted that attendance had doubled for its "critical situation" courses on crowd control.[47] Philadelphia took full advantage of this heightened concern by demanding more money for RNC security. By March 2000, Timoney had requested an additional $5 million for police overtime, training, and expenses. For their part, the Pennsylvania State Police asked for $1.9 million to purchase new riot gear.[48]

In April 2000, hundreds of FBI and other law enforcement agents from Pennsylvania, New York, and New Jersey gathered at a former Philadelphia Naval Base with the supposed aim of being trained in counterterrorism and crowd control techniques.[49] Ironically called "Stolen Liberty," the training included a fictional hostage scenario. Normally of little interest to the general public, trainings like this can serve to intimidate would-be protesters if strategically placed in the mainstream media. In another pre-RNC training, police practiced crowd dispersal and mass arrests at the Naval Air Warfare Center just north of Philadelphia.[50] They were also trained in the use of riot gear and vehicle formations to break up crowds. Undercover police were also spotted in Philadelphia conducting surveillance months before the convention. At a well-attended Philadelphia teach-in preceding the April 2000 IMF/World Bank protests scheduled to take place in Washington, DC, plainclothes police filmed a crowd of people watching the "Insurrection Landscapers" puppet show in Rittenhouse Square, which is adjacent to the Philadelphia Ethical Society where the teach-in was held.[51] By this time, police were also routinely harassing activists by asking them if they lived in a particular neighborhood, taking pictures of their houses, and even rummaging through their trash.

Hundreds of Philadelphia activists went to Washington, DC, on April 16, 2000, to protest the IMF and World Bank. The April 15 police raid on an activist convergence space in DC should have given warning of what to expect in Philadelphia. The signs, however, were largely ignored. As they had done previously in Seattle, Philadelphia police traveled to DC to observe the protests and conduct surveillance. Days after the IMF/World Bank protests, Timoney commended the DC police for having done an "outstanding job" despite evidence of political suppression and the indiscriminate, unlawful arrest of hundreds of people, not to mention rampant police violence. Timoney was quoted by the *Philadelphia Inquirer* saying, "We've learned another lesson, if you will, from Washington on top of the lessons from Seattle. We will incorporate all of that into our thinking, into our training. And we think we'll be fully prepared for any eventualities [during] the Republican convention."[52]

Less than two weeks after the Philadelphia police returned from their field trip to DC, another contingent was dispatched by Timoney to New York to observe that city's May Day protests. Undercover Philadelphia police were seen taking pictures of an anarchist demonstration on May 1, 2000, with the apparent cooperation of the NYPD,[53] despite a prohibition on political spying in the city.[54] Center for Constitutional Rights attorney Franklin Siegel stated in a letter to then–NYPD commissioner Howard Safir and Corporation Counsel Michael Hess that the city's consent decree had been violated when the NYPD "cooperated, facilitated and supported activities" of the Philadelphia police.[55] In no way concerned with impropriety, Timoney stated publicly that the surveillance was part of Philadelphia police strategy to identify troublemakers planning to attend the RNC 2000 protests.

In addition to the Philadelphia police surveillance, the FBI admitted to its own long-term planning and surveillance. Robert S. Conforti, the FBI agent in charge of the Philadelphia office, said that the Bureau had "been planning for the Republican National Convention for a year and a half" and had sent agents to Washington, DC, and Seattle—ostensibly to observe the protests, but undoubtedly also to profile people by means of questioning, photographing, and videotaping.[56] Conforti also admitted to "a 16-member executive committee made up of local and state police, and federal agencies such as the FBI, Secret Service, and the bureau of Alcohol Tobacco and Firearms," that had "devised" a strategy on dealing with the RNC protests.

Surveillance, Intelligence Gathering, and Political Profiling

Unity 2000 organizer Michael Morrill noted the existence of electronic surveillance as early as August 1999 when Pennsylvania State Police (PSP) appeared on an activist listserv. In June 2000, undercover police were seen on at least five separate occasions photographing activists coming and going from the Women's International League for Peace and Freedom (WILPF), a well-known organizing location.[57] Because WILPF is across the street from the Philadelphia Convention Center, the loading docks made a convenient location from which to photograph people. Eventually, the *Philadelphia Inquirer* was alerted and reporters confronted two men on June 29. The undercover officers refused to answer questions and refused to say which law enforcement agency they were with. When the *Inquirer* asked the FBI about it, a spokesperson would neither confirm nor deny any involvement, though the Bureau had already admitted to electronic surveillance.[58]

When the police were asked about their involvement in the photographic surveillance, PPD spokesperson Lt. Susan Slawson flatly denied the allegations. According to the *Inquirer*, "None of the officials would speculate on how such photographs might be used, how the targets might be picked, and what behavior could provoke surveillance." Yet they noted that a "tip sheet" had been distributed by the PPD in recent weeks to "Philadelphia-area security officials." The tip sheet requested that the PPD be notified if there was "a significant increase in the population of predominantly young white males and females in a particular area, especially those who dress in rag-tag clothing and dye their hair in multi-colors."

The people being targeted didn't need this kind of proof that police were profiling them. Nevertheless, the evidence helped to vindicate activist allegations. By the time mainstream media began exposing the surveillance, there had been multiple reports of harassment, politically motivated questioning, and frivolous arrests. On May 18, two people were approached by police while checking e-mail at the University of Pennsylvania. The two were detained, asked questions about the upcoming convention and their political beliefs, and eventually arrested for trespassing.[59] They were taken to two separate precincts, grilled, and abused for not "cooperating." One of the arrestees was released after four hours. The other was further questioned by the Organized Crime Division about whether he had been in Seattle or DC and if he knew anyone organizing anti-RNC protests. After refusing to answer questions about Mumia Abu-Jamal, the male arrestee was threatened with anal rape using a nightstick and had ice water poured down his back before being released.[60] In another University of Pennsylvania episode, police arrested a group of five young activists watching Fourth of July fireworks from a parking garage and charged them with trespassing and conspiracy.[61] Just as with the other arrestees in May, the police questioned this group about where they came from, the locations of any meetings, and their plans for the convention.[62] During their twenty-four hours in detention, the arrestees were also questioned about their political beliefs, whether they were "anarchists," and urged to provide the names of anarchists they knew.

With just over a week before the convention, the PPD was forced to admit to the politically motivated surveillance of activists. The admission came on July 20, 2000, after the *Inquirer* traced registration records from the license plate of the car used by the plainclothes officers taking photographs.[63] Lt. Slawson took full responsibility for her earlier denial, claiming that she "didn't check into it before [making] the comment." But the *Inquirer* noted that, in the two weeks following Slawson's original statement, "Neither [Police Chief] Timoney . . . nor any other senior police official publicly corrected Slawson's denial."

Law Enforcement Preparations

Well before the exposure of Philadelphia police surveillance, the FBI and other federal agencies including the U.S. Secret Service and FEMA had set up shop and were busy coordinating the security effort. The RNC 2000 had been designated a National Special Security Event, assigning the FBI, Secret Service, and FEMA as the lead agencies for the convention. In May 2000, the FBI told the *Inquirer* that "virtually every resource that the FBI has available will be put into play," and that protesters had "become more of a focus." Nevertheless, it failed to justify either the investment or the reasons that greater attention was being paid to political activists.[64] Expansion of the law enforcement dragnet was underscored by *Inquirer* revelations concerning a twenty-four-hour "command center" where the Secret Service coordinated "the work of dozens of federal, state, and local agencies employing thousands of officers—some of whom will be dressed like tourists to mix with their surroundings."

According to Reuters, the division of labor among law enforcement agencies included the Secret Service "running security inside the convention and at main hotels"; the FBI handling intelligence gathering; state police "providing escorts for dignitaries" such as two former presidents

(George H.W. Bush and Gerald R. Ford), former first lady Nancy Reagan, then–presidential candidate George W. Bush, and dozens of diplomats; and the Philadelphia police enforcing local laws.[65] Yet this compartmentalized account failed to properly illustrate the breadth of their collaboration. In the months leading up to the protests, the FBI stated publicly that it was using undercover agents to gather intelligence, but the Bureau also brought computers to Philadelphia to link to its Special Intelligence Operations Center in Washington to assist local and federal law enforcement in gathering intelligence on convention protesters.[66]

Before 9/11 and the formation of the Department of Homeland Security, FEMA was under the Department of Defense and in charge of preparing for and reacting to natural disasters and "civil disturbances." Based on its finances, however, FEMA was much more geared to "civil disturbances," which included civil unrest in poor Black communities and mass political protest, as well as developing plans for "Martial Law." A 1992 study found that, over the prior ten years, FEMA budgets included only $243 million for disaster relief but $2.9 billion for classified operations.[67] In its operational plan leaked around the time of the convention, FEMA observed that the RNC would "dominate national headlines" and admitted that its goal was to "preclude" an event "that would reflect negatively on Philadelphia, the Commonwealth of Pennsylvania, or the United States."[68] In what was officially referred to as the Operations Supplement to the Federal Response Plan (FRP), FEMA noted that any response to "civil disturbances" would be under the authority of "Operation Garden Plot," a military plan known for its objectionable surveillance practices.

Housed in its regional office at 615 Chestnut Street, the FEMA Regional Operations Center (ROC) was established to anticipate an event that may require federal assistance under the FRP. The Multi-Agency Communications Center (MACC), referred to by the *Inquirer* as a "command center," was established by the Secret Service in a Pentagon-owned building, centrally located at 20th and Johnson Streets in South Philadelphia, "to manage the coordinated [federal] operational activities . . . in conjunction with State and local agencies." From this location, the Secret Service coordinated the law enforcement activity of neighboring cities, counties and states, as well as the thirty-five states from which Republican governors were expected.[69] In addition to collocating its command post at the MACC, the FBI also used its field office at 600 Arch Street to conduct intelligence-gathering operations. Meanwhile, the city's Emergency

Operations Center (EOC) located at 240 Spring Garden Street was "the primary command and control location for Philadelphia operations" and served as a backup location for the MACC.[70] According to the FRP, at least eighteen other local and state Emergency Operations Centers were deployed for the RNC 2000.

Financing Suppression

While much of the funds the RNC host committee raised were spent on constructing the convention site and paying for staging the event, significant sums were also spent on a massive security apparatus and a PR campaign aimed at convincing Philadelphians that the RNC was going to bring jobs, business, and tourism to the city. The financing behind Philadelphia 2000 was largely revealed in a postconvention report filed with the Federal Election Commission (FEC) in October 2000. Between March 1997 and September 2000, Philadelphia 2000 raised and spent $66 million—nearly triple the amount spent on the prior 1996 Republican convention in San Diego, and nearly double the original projection of $35 million.[71] According to the 180-page FEC report, the money came from 473 business and government entities. Despite predictions that the private sector would pick up more than half of the bill, taxpayers became the largest donors to the host committee, albeit without their informed consent. In the end, taxpayers funded $38.9 million, or about 59 percent of the convention's cost.

Contributing $19 million, the City of Philadelphia was the largest single donor to the convention, $7 million of which was in cash, with the rest as "in-kind" services, including police, telecommunications, and computer support. Pennsylvania taxpayers contributed $9.4 million, seven million of which was in cash. Exchanging such large sums in a city that was struggling financially was not lost on Philadelphians. The *Philadelphia Inquirer* even commented that the costs borne by taxpayers might have been better used if the city had put the money into social services like housing, public education, or public transportation. Philadelphia 2000 co-chair David L. Cohen dismissed the *Inquirer*'s assertion, claiming a need to enhance "the region's image."

Of the more than $27 million raised from the private sector, much of it came with favors. The scheme referred to by the *Inquirer* as "pay-to-play" resulted in about 30 percent of the corporate donors becoming suppliers to the convention. As an example, PECO Energy Company, the largest utility in Pennsylvania, donated more than $600,000 and was paid $1.6 million for supplying power to the convention complex. The largest private investor was Bell Atlantic Corporation (now Verizon Communications Inc.), which leveraged its more-than-$3 million "donation" to become the convention's official telecommunications provider. Philadelphia 2000 paid about $166,000 for this service, in addition to the $6–$8 million in revenues expected from people needing services at the convention. Other high-level corporate donors included the TV cable giant Comcast at $1.4 million, AT&T at $1.2 million, and General Motors and Motorola at $1 million each.[72] As early as April 2000, Philadelphia Newspapers Inc. (PNI), which publishes the *Inquirer* and the *Daily News* (the two largest daily newspapers in the city), had pledged $50,000 in cash and free advertising space. But Federal Election Commission (FEC) filings later revealed that PNI actually donated at least $288,000 to the RNC host committee.[73]

Besides reaping direct or indirect financial benefit, another aspect of the "pay-to-play" scheme was the opportunity for corporate executives to curry political favor with decision-makers. Although corruption by the Nixon administration caused Congress to ban corporate underwriting of political conventions, by 1984 the law was relaxed enough to allow "nonpartisan" host committees to accept unlimited tax-deductible gifts from corporations.[74] Exploiting this relaxation were companies like Microsoft, DaimlerChrysler, and Lockheed Martin. At the time, Microsoft was embroiled in an antitrust lawsuit, pursued by the federal government. According to the *Philadelphia Inquirer*, both Microsoft and Lockheed Martin, which contributed $500,000 and $100,000 respectively, had "a slew of issues before Congress and the administration." DaimlerChrysler, which contributed $250,000, benefited from its investment by being able to host parties and set up vehicle displays for delegates and politicians at the convention center. Insurance company Ace INA Group, which contributed $100,000 to the convention, hosted a golf tournament at its lodge in suburban Philadelphia for the thirty-one Republican governors in attendance.

The FEC report also helped to identify what the RNC host committee spent its money on. The $66 million price tag included: $13.2 million for police and security systems, $10.8 million for constructing the convention complex and building a tent city for reporters in the parking lot, $2.7 million for free transportation of delegates, $1 million for loaner cars, $148,615 for portable toilets, and $3,500 per month for fifteen months to rent a three-story, roof-decked apartment in one of Philadelphia's most expensive downtown districts for a "top Republican convention official."[75] The money spent by the host committee was also not always dispersed locally or regionally. For example, the three businesses employed by Philadelphia 2000 that received the most money (totaling nearly $12 million, or about 20 percent of the host committee's budget) were a general contractor from Louisiana, a production company from California, and a transportation-management company from Virginia. The Louisiana-based Freeman Decorating Company, which earned $5.4 million for building the convention complex, also held the contract for the 1996 Republican convention in San Diego and was chosen for the RNC 2000 over local Philadelphia bidders.

The most rewarding investment made by the host committee, however, was a little-known insurance policy purchased behind closed doors many months prior to the convention. While it was suspected that the city had taken out a policy to protect itself from liability, confirmation of that policy—as well as the cost and extent of its protection—was not known until many months after the convention. In a February 2001 *Philadelphia Daily News* article,[76] Federal Election Commission filings for the RNC host committee were revealed that outlined the city's protection from liability for: false arrest; wrongful detention or imprisonment; malicious prosecution; assault and battery; discrimination; humiliation; violation of property rights; violation of civil rights; wrongful eviction or entry; and defamation, slander, or libel of persons or organizations.[77] "Knowing that they weren't liable," remarked Danielle Redden after the policy became public, "the City of Philadelphia and its police conspired to suspend the rights of thousands of people during the convention."

Protest Groups Unite

A weeklong preprotest "convergence" was held in Philadelphia from July 24 to 30. The event focused on trainings and workshops, as well as puppet-making and the opportunity to participate in evening spokescouncils.[78] In an attempt to give equal voice to a wide array of issues, organizers planned for different political themes on each day of the convention protests. One day was dedicated to universal health care, another to protesting the influence of capital on government, another to economic rights, and yet another to direct action against the criminal justice system and the death penalty. In the end, a diverse coalition of local, regional, and national groups came together to help with the mobilization.[79]

Activists in Philadelphia and surrounding areas formed four main coalitions. The Poor People's Economic Human Rights Campaign, the Ad Hoc Committee to Defend Health Care, and Unity 2000 sought permits to march. As part of the larger continental Direct Action Network, the Philadelphia Direct Action Group (PDAG) focused instead on mobilizing for mass civil disobedience. Along with other groups, these coalitions came together under the umbrella of the R2K Network to protest the Republicans, their convention, U.S. domestic and foreign policies, and the harmful influence of capital on our daily lives.[80] The R2K Network operated under a set of guidelines designed to avoid marginalizing more militant activists.

Although various coalitions and organizations planning to protest often had their own calls to action, the R2K and D2K Networks also issued a joint statement calling for "celebration and action for global, social, economic, racial and environmental justice."[81] Declaring "No more business as usual," organizers focused on an array of issues, including: growing economic inequality, corporate takeover of politics, failing health care and educational systems, homelessness, as well as unprecedented rates of incarceration and executions disproportionately affecting youth and people

DIRECT ACTION

CHALLENGE THE REPUBLICAN & DEMOCRATIC PARTIES THIS SUMMER IN PHILADELPHIA & LOS ANGELES

TAKE ACTION FOR GLOBAL & NATIONAL JUSTICE! ABOLISH THE PRISON INDUSTRIAL COMPLEX

of color. The call also emphasized solidarity with people of the global south "suffocating under structural adjustment policies, third world debt and U.S. intervention under the guise of the 'war on drugs.'" Penned in 2000, the unified call could have been written yesterday—a fact that underscores the ongoing need for fundamental change in several areas of U.S. society.

One of the first protests preceding the RNC 2000 occurred for a captive audience in an upscale department store in downtown Philadelphia on Friday, July 28. A group of about sixty activists organized by United Students Against Sweatshops (USAS) surreptitiously entered Lord & Taylor. Many of the activists began shouting "No more sweatshops!" and chanting, "What's outrageous? Sweatshop wages! What's disgusting? Union Busting!" Other USAS activists dropped banners from the second and third-floor balconies, including one that read: "Just Say No to Nike."[82] After leaving the store, USAS activists held an impromptu rally on Market Street before marching to City Hall.[83] That same day, a Silent March was staged with eighteen thousand shoes lining the area around Independence Hall.[84] The shoes represented the people lost to gun violence in the U.S. but, according to organizers, the number of actual deaths was closer to thirty thousand per year at the time.[85]

On July 29, the Ad Hoc Committee to Defend Health Care organized the first mass demonstration in advance of the RNC 2000 as nearly three thousand people rallied at Love Park to demand affordable, universal health care. The demonstration was endorsed by several health care organizations, including the local chapters of Physicians for Social Responsibility and Physicians for a National Health Program, American Medical Students Association, ACT UP Philadelphia, and District 1199C of the Hospital and Healthcare Employees Union. Speaking at the rally, presidential candidate Ralph Nader addressed the failing state of the U.S. health care system.

Sunday, July 30, was the last day before the convention. On that day, people were expected to demonstrate against U.S. domestic and foreign policies and the corporate domination of everyday life. The day's events were dubbed "Unity 2000" by its founder, the Pennsylvania Consumer Action Network (PCAN). PCAN had envisioned a feisty but feel-good march and rally down Ben Franklin Parkway in Center City with as many as one hundred thousand people, representing an array of issues. After successfully suing the city over a permit, Unity 2000 grew to be a coalition of more than two hundred local, national, and international social justice, civil rights, religious, peace, environmental, and labor groups. In the end, twenty-five thousand people marched in what was a colorful display of resistance. Although riot cops lined the route, the attempt to intimidate was diffused by countless signs, banners, and puppets, which brought the political issues to life. Neither did the scorching heat stifle the playful antics of Billionaires for Bush or Gore, the Radical Cheerleaders, or "Corpzilla"—a democracy-devouring monster fashioned on an eighteen-wheeler with the flatbed doubling as a mud-wrestling ring for the presidential candidates.[86]

The rally on Ben Franklin Parkway boasted thirty speakers on as many issues. Although the day of mass direct action against the prison industrial complex was slated for Tuesday, many people came to the Unity 2000 march ready to speak out against Bush's death penalty record. Groups like Pennsylvania Abolitionists United Against the Death Penalty and Campaign to End the Death Penalty joined the protest to demand a new trial for Pennsylvania death row prisoner Mumia Abu-Jamal. Rally speakers also included representatives from United Students Against Sweatshops and Students for a Free Tibet. Then-ninety-year-old social justice activist "Granny D" spoke about campaign finance reform and her recently completed fourteen-month walk across the country to draw attention to the issue. Father Roy Bourgeois spoke about the U.S. Army "School of the Americas," as hundreds marched behind banners calling for its closure. Some of the more militant activists branching off of the Unity 2000 march and rally—including a black bloc and an anti–death penalty contingent— were able to express themselves without much incident. While the police attempted to assert their authority, no arrests were made.

The first Shadow Convention was held during the RNC 2000 at the University of Pennsylvania's Annenberg Center and was geared toward disaffected RNC delegates and right-of-center activists concerned with U.S. policies. The four-day event was organized by United for a Fair Economy, Common Cause, Public Campaign, the Lindesmith Center-Drug Policy Foundation, Call to Renewal, the National Campaign for Jobs and Income Support, and author Arianna Huffington.[87] John McCain's opening address was followed by three days of presentations covering issues including campaign finance reform, growing economic inequality, and the failed war on drugs. Holding large photos of their loved ones incarcerated for nonviolent drug offenses, scores of family members spoke out against the drug war.[88] The mostly Black and Latino wives, mothers, and sisters of imprisoned young men came to Philadelphia from New York, Massachusetts, Virginia, Maryland, Minnesota, and Washington, DC, along with the children they were struggling to raise.

On Monday, July 31, before the sun had completely risen on the first day of the convention, ACT UP Philadelphia pulled off an attention-grabbing stunt, which greeted Republican delegates and local rush-hour drivers alike.[89] It wasn't yet 7:00 A.M. when four indistinguishable figures scaled the ladder attached to a tall billboard at the freeway junction of I-76 and I-676. With stealth and precision, they reached the top of the structure looking down on the maze of intersecting freeways. Pulling a thirty-by-seventy-five-foot banner from a backpack, they unfurled a message of gigantic proportions: "Bush + Drug Company Greed Kills. Generic AIDS Drugs for Africa Now! ACT UP" As one of the activists scouting the area on the ground, I was relieved to not see any police. Once the banner was affixed to the billboard, the four activists got themselves safely to the ground and fled without capture. Immediately thereafter, a press release was issued and calls were made to mainstream media outlets.[90] Within minutes, other members of ACT UP Philadelphia were conducting interviews, explaining their message, and making public demands of Governor Bush. Far surpassing expectations of how long their "welcoming reception" would last, the banner was left hanging for several hours before it was removed.

Between the ACT UP banner drop and the beginning of the March for Economic Human Rights, several School of the Americas (SOA) Watch activists orchestrated a "die-in" in front of City Hall. According to IMC reporter John Tarleton, about fifty SOA protesters gathered across from City Hall at 8:00 A.M. to call attention to Republican support for the School of the Americas, an organization that has conducted combat training for thousands of Latin American soldiers implicated in human rights abuses.[91] Gathered in front of the First Union Bank, activists dramatized the impact of the SOA by enacting a military massacre of farm workers. Tarleton described the scene: "Red paint splattered the sidewalk as the soldiers dragged the campesinos into the intersection of 15th and Market where they were eventually buried." Eight SOA Watch activists were arrested after police arrived and cordoned off the intersection.

Later that day, KWRU, a multiracial organization of poor and homeless families fighting for an end to poverty and homelessness, joined forces with the Poor People's Economic Human Rights Campaign to launch the March for Economic Human Rights.[92] The PPEHRC was a national network of over fifty grassroots antipoverty organizations including migrant workers in Florida, welfare moms in Idaho, public housing tenants in Chicago, and downsized workers in Ohio.[93] By addressing poverty as an economic human rights violation, the PPEHRC used the Universal Declaration of Human Rights to fight for the right to food, clothing, housing, health care, education, and a living wage.[94] In 2000, 250,000 families were living

below the poverty line in Philadelphia; meanwhile 40,000 uninhabited houses had been boarded up by the city.[95]

Prior to the march, KWRU worked to get poor people into the mainstream media. In order to provide shelter for people participating in the march and to draw attention to the issue of poverty, KWRU erected "Bushville," a four-day tent city in North Philadelphia, one of the poorest sections of the city. Bushville was an allusion to the Hooverville shanty-towns of the 1930s erected in response to President Herbert Hoover's failure to address the economic hardships of the Great Depression.[96] According to KWRU Education Director Willie Baptist, Bushville "had over 300 residents," with "theater, music, songs, and workshops."[97] Co-chair of the KWRU Organizing Committee Liz Ortiz was mayor of Bushville. "To carry out my task I had to view Bushville as part of a larger whole, part of a bigger picture," she stated. "The bigger picture was that Bushville was to serve not just as a place where people can stay. It was a 'base of operations' to house and help the marchers to become messengers. It was set up to ensure that the poor were not disappeared or hidden before the Republican National Convention and 15,000 news reporters from around the world. It was an important opportunity to have our message heard." KWRU also conducted "reality tours," which bused people into poor areas of Philadelphia. This

method of organizing made lasting impressions on its participants. Over four days, the reality tours took hundreds of people by yellow school bus from the opulence of Center City to quickly immerse them in some of the poorest areas of the country.

Unlike Unity 2000 and the Ad Hoc Committee to Defend Healthcare, the March for Economic Human Rights was never able to obtain a permit from the city. Right up to the point of marching, organizers and participants were being threatened and intimidated. The scene was "tense" according to *In These Times* reporter Dave Lindorff.[98] "Several thousand activists assembled without a permit," and as they "spilled into the street around City Hall, police kept pressing them back toward the sidewalk and insisting there would be no march." Lindorff emphasized the "brilliant tactical move" of KWRU organizers who "suddenly pulled a rope across the street, blocking all traffic," which allowed "an advance contingent of small children and disabled people in wheelchairs" to start marching. The nearly four-mile march was a straight shot down Broad Street from City Hall to the First Union Center, where the convention was being held. But while police failed to prevent the march from starting, they certainly attempted to derail it. "At several points along the route, police tried to stop the marchers or turn them away from Broad Street, the city's main north-south artery," recounted Lindorff. "But having backed down the first time, they were unable to stop the marchers' forward momentum." Ending within a block of the convention site at the city-designated "First Amendment Zone," the march slowly dispersed. Despite police threats, no arrests were reported.

In the weeks before the RNC protests, New York–based groups like the Student Liberation Action Movement (SLAM) heavily influenced the decision to emphasize issues vital to communities of color during the actions planned for August 1.[99] "It was a good political struggle," said SLAM member Kai Lumumba Barrow, "because a lot of the comrades who were organizing these actions were really focused on dealing with anti-globalization."[100] Barrow and other activists felt that the best way to connect struggles in the global south with the struggles in Philadelphia was to focus on the prison industrial complex (PIC), "because you couldn't talk about racism, white supremacy, capitalism, and not talk about PIC." Philadelphia activist Amadee Braxton agreed: "The political work that has most galvanized people organizing for racial justice has been the fight against the racist criminal in-justice system." As governor of Texas, George W. Bush epitomized the injustice of the criminal legal system. He was notorious for having signed execution warrants for 138 people and executing 152 people—more than any other governor in the history of Texas up to that point.[101] The State of Texas had thus far been responsible for one third of U.S. executions since the death penalty was resumed in 1977.[102] Joining Texas in its enthusiasm for killing prisoners, Pennsylvania boasted the country's fourth-largest death row.

Not everyone agreed with Barrow and Braxton. Some complained that the PIC theme diluted the broader message and that the focus was "too narrow."[103] For Braxton, however, a more focused theme was a conscious choice "to build this movement in a particular direction—the direction of more involvement of activists of color, and by extension, communities of color." Heated discussions around sovereignty, self-determination, and colonialism ensued. Barrow couldn't understand how they could not focus on Mumia's case "when the Republicans were pushing for more law and order." Recounting the dynamic, Barrow insisted: "We are bringing what this movement does not have, which is people of color, predominantly young people of color, predominantly female-bodied and queer and poor people of color, who are coming to this action from our own particular experiences, our own analysis, which is completely different from the analysis that is currently existing. And that has value."

The flyer distributed by the August 1st Direct Action Coalition read, "This August we are calling for direct action at the Republican National Convention to confront the U.S. criminal justice system."[104] Protest organizers had planned on "hundreds of people risking arrest and reflecting the diversity of groups and communities affected by the policies of the Republicans and Democrats." Their efforts were directed toward making connections between international institutions and the domestic institutions that oppress people in the U.S. "While U.S.-dominated institutions like the WTO, the IMF and the World Bank wage war on the global poor . . . a parallel war is waged daily on the poor and people of color in the U.S. by a criminal justice system that enforces racial and economic injustice. It is time for the different currents in this movement to stand together against this system of criminal injustice and for real democracy." The demands of the August 1 Direct Action Coalition were to free Mumia Abu-Jamal and all political prisoners, abolish the prison industrial complex and the death penalty, stop police violence, and end the corporate war on the poor.

On August 1, 2000, direct action paralyzed the downtown with street theater, satire, and civil disobedience.

CHAPTER 2:
August 1

Opposition to the Criminal Justice System

P EOPLE TOOK TO THE STREETS ON AUGUST 1, 2000, TO DEMON-
strate against the prison industrial complex, police brutality, the
death penalty, and for the release of Mumia Abu-Jamal and all
political prisoners. In addition to the mass civil disobedience and street
blockades, people also engaged in permitted and nonpermitted rallies and
marches. The American Friends Service Committee hosted a discussion on
the morality of the death penalty, the social causes of crime, the failings of
the justice system, and strategies for building the movement to stop executions. Leading a crowd at UPenn's Annenberg Center in booming chants of
"Schools, not jails!," Jesse Jackson and Al Franken were joined by others at
the Shadow Convention to speak out against the war on drugs.

Having signed execution warrants for more than 130 death
row prisoners up to that point, Texas governor, George W. Bush was
basically "known . . . for killing people," said Jeffrey Garis, then-director of Pennsylvania Abolitionists United Against the Death Penalty
(PAUADP).[1] Garis and fellow death penalty opponents dubbed the RNC
2000 the "Executioner's Ball," and called for people to "crash the party."
PAUADP and other anti–death penalty groups organized a speak-out
and rally at City Hall, which drew a crowd of more than two thousand
people. The Free Mumia Abu-Jamal Coalition also organized a march
through Center City to call attention to his case and demand an end to
the death penalty.

In addition to these actions, a lively march of puppets, banners, and street performances had been planned for August 1. A spiraling march of resistance was supposed to wind its way through downtown Philadelphia, ending up at City Hall, but by seizing the instruments of protest—including puppets, signs, banners, and leaflets—in a raid, the police prevented the march from happening. But while the raid curtailed activists' plans, a strong commitment to disrupting "business as usual" persisted and fueled mass direct action that afternoon. Refusing to be intimidated by police actions, thousands of activists stuck to their plan and conducted civil disobedience throughout the downtown area. Some of these protests were theatrical, but most involved street blockades, something the city hadn't seen in decades.

Bike police make an arrest at City Hall. Photo © Brad Kayal

The intent of the civil disobedience was never to shut down the Republican convention. The First Union Center, where the convention was being held, was several miles from downtown and had never really been a focus. Instead, activists chose to obstruct the flow of delegates traveling to the convention from their hotels. This confrontational tactic was quite effective at bringing traffic to a standstill in many parts of the city. It also drew attention to the prison industrial complex.

For most of the afternoon and into the night, a cacophony of wailing sirens and thumping helicopters pervaded Center City," reported the

Philadelphia Inquirer somewhat dramatically.[2] Groups "as small as 30 and as large as 300 paralyzed intersections" and "created near-gridlock" conditions.[3] One of the largest actions began at approximately 4:00 P.M. at the on-ramp to I-676, close to the intersection of 16th and Callowhill Streets. According to the *Inquirer*, "Hundreds of protesters dressed as clowns or adorned in the finery of 'billionaires'" blocked a key traffic artery by weaving "wire and police tape around posts." Protesters chanted and danced to drums as dozens of activists linked arms in a "soft block" to encircle a smaller group using lockboxes in a "hard block."[4] The confrontation lasted for nearly an hour, ending around 6:00 P.M. with the arrest of forty-eight people.[5]

Soon after the on-ramp blockade began, hundreds of protesters flooded the intersection of Broad and Spruce Streets near the Doubletree Hotel where many delegates were staying. Having blockaded the intersection, activists occupied the space by playing soccer, drumming, dancing, singing and chanting. Dumpsters were hauled into the intersection and overturned. Eventually, eight protesters sat down in the intersection and formed a "hard block," while three-dozen others formed a "soft block" around them. As Sheriff's buses sped down Broad Street, police began breaking up the blockade. According to independent reporters Josie Foo and John Tarleton, police "broke apart the soft block by forcing the ends of billy-clubs into the protesters' backs" while other officers "arrested or pushed away protesters and media."[6] In anticipation of the confrontation, some of the approximately seventy-five protesters arrested at the blockade prepared a statement outlining why they were in the streets risking arrest.

> We apologize for the inconvenience and know that this unexpected delay in your afternoon might appear as a malicious attack on the city and the Republicans. We need to convince you that this is FAR from the truth . . .
>
> We each employ the tools at our disposal: they have money and an established base of power. We have our bodies, a $20 budget at Home Depot, and some moral conviction. We replace chiseled jingles with a cacophony of makeshift drums. Professional camera crews are replaced by the documentation of our peers. Special effects give way to cardboard puppets, advertising is replaced by handwritten slogans on our tee-shirts and bodies.[7]

The Black Bloc

"They were purposeful and courageous," recalled SLAM member Kai Lumumba Barrow.[8] "One thing I dug about the black bloc was . . . their fearlessness," he said; they moved "as if they had nothing to lose." While not all activists agreed with property destruction, RNC 2000 protest organizers explicitly supported a "diversity of tactics," including use of the black bloc. Starting at approximately 4:00 P.M., a large black bloc converged on the Four Seasons Hotel at Logan Circle, close to downtown Philadelphia.[9] Waving anarchist flags, dozens of black-clad, masked protesters confronted Republican delegates in front of one of the city's most expensive hotels. The group began to barricade an adjacent street but headed south at the sound of police sirens. Weaving through the downtown core, upending newspaper boxes and pushing dumpsters into the street. The bloc was trailed by more than twenty cops as it snaked through Center City. At one point, police pinned several people against a building on 17th Street and arrested six, including a journalist with *U.S. News and World Report.*

As police were breaking up a bicycle blockade at 17th and Samson, a red paint bomb splattered at their feet and a thick cloud from a smoke bomb filled the air. Soon after, near 16th and Market, the black bloc merged

Members of the black bloc moving a dumpster. Photo © Brad Kayal

with remnants of the Mumia and anti–death penalty demonstration and the colorful Clown Bloc. Near City Hall, protesters spray-painted "Free Mumia" and other slogans on the Municipal Services Building while others threw red paint at the Frank Rizzo statue and the district attorney's office.[10]

Now more than two hundred strong, the black bloc marched down Ben Franklin Parkway as some protesters targeted police cars and other city vehicles. According to the *Philadelphia Inquirer*, "several city cars had been spray-painted and doused with orange paint, tires had been slashed," and the "windows of at least 20 police cars had been smashed." Independent journalist Amy Hammersmith, who was covering the black bloc march and the police reaction, recalled what happened next: "In a matter of minutes, hundreds of officers pursued the crowd across the park and onto Cherry Street. Pandemonium broke out as bike cops flung their bikes down and wrestled protesters to the ground. A medic was attacked in the melee, and three others were arrested. Journalists, bystanders, and protesters alike were shoved back from the arrestees, and several people were clubbed in the process."[11]

Police-Instigated Riots

Meanwhile, back at City Hall, police surrounded a permitted rally against the death penalty. According to one report, they "made repeated forays into the crowd to harass people."[12] Nearby, police on horseback and motor-cycles attacked a large contingent of Mumia supporters near 15th and JFK, beating them with clubs and chasing them down 15th Street through the anti–death penalty rally.[13] In an attempt to hold the area, hundreds of protesters sat down along JFK between 15th and 18th Streets. As police began attacking two protesters holding a "Stop the Texas Killing Machine" banner, the crowd chanted: "The whole world is watching!" One of the pro-testers with the banner, Jamie Loughner (also known as "Bork") was inter-viewed on *Democracy Now!* a couple of days later. While admitting that she took to the streets to commit civil disobedience, she was unprepared for the violent reaction. One cop tried to cut the banner while others threw her to the ground. Reflecting on the scene, Bork recalled police "wrapping me in the banner and dragging me and kicking me."[14] After cuffing her with the banner still wrapped around her body, Bork was thrown into a police van and taken to the hospital where she was "diagnosed with a minor con-cussion and 'deep bruises and contusions' to her right eye, forearm, thigh, and hip."[15] Another demonstrator, who was standing on the curb and not violating any orders, was "yanked into the street and thrown face down onto the pavement, where five police officers jumped on him, wrenching his arms behind his back while his head was pressed into the macadam by one officer's knee."[16]

A Quaker and president of the Mental Health Association of Southeast Pennsylvania, Joseph Rogers had volunteered on August 1 to monitor police reaction to the protests.[17] "I found myself in the middle of a sit-in at the intersection of 15th and JFK," recounted Rogers, who said the protesters were blocking the intersection "as a way of making a statement." Yet Rogers also noted that protesters were not the only people in the streets. "Aside from the protesters, other people, including police and reporters, were milling about on the road preventing the flow of traffic." In fact, at one point "there were a lot more police and reporters blocking the road than there were protesters." Without warning, Rogers found himself in front of a line of police who were "sweeping the area," and "using their bikes as sort of a moving barricade." One of the cops took his bicycle and "shoved it hard into my back," said Rogers. "Several other officers behind him were grabbing people and arresting them." Police eventually arrested at least fifty-two people, including Rogers, in the vicinity of 15th and JFK.

"As you looked down 15th Street," recalled local activist Danielle Redden, "you could see buses full of people who had just been arrested and more buses were pulling in."[18] Redden was part of one of several roving flying squads that blocked intersections until receiving dispersal orders. By the time Redden and her group got to 15th and JFK, word finally reached them that the giant march through Center City would not happen as planned because of a preemptive police raid. Instead of blockading the intersections around the downtown hotels housing delegates, Redden's group decided to blockade the busloads of arrestees to prevent them from leaving the area. Eventually, Redden and the others were arrested and put on the same buses they had tried to stop.

A few blocks away, near Rittenhouse Square, police were hemming in a group of protesters in front of the Warwick Hotel at 17th and Spruce Streets. According to the *Philadelphia Inquirer*, police rammed them with bicycles before arresting about ten.[19] Other protesters at the scene were chased by police on horseback. About a block away, at 17th and Latimer, a melee ensued as police on bicycles—including Police Commissioner Timoney—rushed a group of protesters leaving the permitted rally against the death penalty.[20] In their subsequent incident report, police claimed that protesters had attacked them with bikes; however, all evidence pointed to the police using their bikes to attack protesters instead.[21] After all was said and done, Camilo Viveiros, Darby Landy, and Eric Steinberg were arrested and charged with a total of nineteen misdemeanors and seven felonies including riot and assault. One cop purportedly suffered a concussion, and Timoney apparently received some bruises. Viveiros, Landy, and Steinberg came to be known as the "Timoney 3." And, because it involved the police commissioner, their trial would become the most high-profile RNC felony case.

Police at a barricade near City Hall. Photo © Brad Kayal

Many of the arrests on August 1 stemmed from the downtown blockades; however, large groups of protesters were also arrested for doing nothing more than dispersing. Known organizers and activists talking on cell phones were particularly vulnerable to being targeted for arrest, and police accused the cell phone users of coordinating illegal activity.[22] Several members of ACT UP Philadelphia were singled out despite not doing anything illegal. One of the most notorious targeted arrests was that of AIDS activist Kate Sorensen, who was "nabbed" while walking through Love Park talking on her cell phone. Despite her assigned task of de-escalating tension in the streets, Sorensen was accused of being a protest "ringleader." Ruckus Society director John Sellers and local Philly activist Terrence McGuckin were also targeted as "ringleaders" and arrested on August 2 while talking on their cell phones. Along with many other activists using cell phones at the time of their arrest, Sellers, McGuckin, and Sorensen were charged with possession of an instrument of crime.[23] All three were blamed for everything that occurred on August 1. As in the Timoney 3 case, their bail was set at then-unprecedented levels for political protest cases. Sellers and Sorensen were initially held on $1 million bail. McGuckin was held on $500,000 bail, and the Timoney 3 had bail set at $450,000 apiece.

The police also targeted other known organizers. According to local activist Jody Dodd, the police "fostered a sense of paranoia that at any moment, at any time, anyone who was in the streets could be arrested."[24] Dodd pointed to the arrest of fellow Philadelphia activist Jacqueline Ambrosini, who was on her bicycle riding to a meeting in Center City— "then no one heard from her." Ambrosini had been "picked off" by the police, who left her bicycle at the scene. Several other people were "plucked off the street" as well. According to Dodd, "we would get calls on the hotline that they were missing and assumed arrested even though they were not engaging in civil disobedience." People being "snatched" like that created "pandemonium for activists" and added to the city's effort to "thwart the strategic day of action."

Police also profiled legal observers. Jamie Graham was acting as an NLG legal observer on August 2 when he witnessed police arresting a protester on Race Street, just blocks away from the legal office. Doing as he was trained, Graham pulled out his camera and began taking pictures. Noticing that they were being photographed, the police turned on Graham, tackled him, and proceeded to kick him repeatedly. After sustaining a concussion and a cracked rib, Graham was taken to Hahnemann Hospital before being held in jail for three days.[25] Before she went missing, Ambrosini witnessed a similarly aggressive arrest in the same vicinity.[26] Riding her bike down Race Street, she saw a well-dressed man with a video camera get off the bus to head to a nearby Ralph Nader rally. She stopped long enough to observe police pepper-spraying and then aggressively arresting the man for no apparent reason. Once police recognized Ambrosini as a protest organizer, she too was arrested without cause. She later found out she was charged with a couple of misdemeanors and accused of locking arms with other protesters and spitting on a police officer.

Removing the Veil of Mystification

Although there were many other instances of police violence and unlawful mass arrests, Timoney was skilled at keeping that violence from the public eye. Many months after the protests, he would unabashedly reveal that "the paramount goal for the Philadelphia Police Department" was "not to be seen on the six o'clock news beating the living daylights out of protesters."[27] One might assume from such comments that the police had been motivated by a desire not to engage in violence at all. Protesters were keenly aware, however, that Timoney's PR statement meant that—as long as police assaulted them off-camera—they could do so without reprisal. "Police decided not to be open about beating up people in the streets," explained RNC protester Alex Rae to the *Boston Phoenix*. Nevertheless, "they were just as aggressive behind the scenes."[28] Timoney also cleverly touted police restraint by avoiding the use of tear gas and rubber bullets, but these were just replaced by more proximate forms of violence like pepper spray, nightsticks, bicycles, and brute force.

In the end, the police used unrestrained force against hundreds of people. Many who endured or witnessed that violence reported their experience to the R2K Legal Collective. Although the extent of police-instigated violence on August 1 was never completely known, reports filed with R2K Legal provided a telling snapshot.[29] According to hundreds of accounts compiled by the law collective, police indiscriminately punched, choked, and clubbed people. Police jumped and kneeled on people and kicked them in the groin, ribs, and head. Protesters were dragged across pavement and thrown into walls. Sometimes their heads were slammed into the street and held down by police boots. Police used bicycles to herd, charge, and strike protesters. Police horses chased and entrapped activists, injuring at least one person in the process. In addition to this violence, disturbing reports came from people those who had been pepper-sprayed. Police routinely targeted people's faces, directly pepper-spraying inside their mouths, noses, and eyes. Pepper spray was also used on unventilated police buses in excruciatingly hot temperatures. Police also overtightened the cuffs on scores of arrestees. In several cases, this caused bleeding, circulation problems, and nerve damage. While in transit to jail facilities, police slammed bus doors on people and threw numerous arrestees down bus stairs.[30]

According to independent journalist Ana Nogueira, reporters took "at least ten video witness accounts of police brutality directed at specific individuals on random streets and hidden alleyways."[31] Meanwhile, undercover police were also brutalizing protesters. Nogueira pointed to an Independent Media Center (IMC) video report detailing "an incident of police disguised as anarchists beating a demonstrator while radioing uniformed officers for assistance." According to one IMC reporter, "There were about five or six [undercover agents] amid the protesters and once the marching group started to thin out, they turned around and jumped one man and threw him to the ground." The police proceeded to assault this person and many others. Nogueira noted that the violent police behavior "escalated dramatically starting around 6:00 P.M., after the city was emptied of its workforce."

Police on bikes making more arrests near City Hall. Photo © Brad Kayal

While the vast majority of protesters were charged with misdemeanors, most were charged with several offenses and held on unreasonably high bails. More than forty protesters—most accused of assaulting police—were charged with felonies.[32] One such "assault" occurred when local Philly activist Dave Onion instinctively threw an empty water bottle in the hope of distracting a group of bike cops who were brutally arresting a protester. Although Onion's attempt was successful—the cops turned on him and beat him unconscious—in the end, he was charged with three misdemeanors and three felonies including causing a catastrophe, failure to avoid causing a catastrophe, and assault on a police officer.[33] Onion and several others who were charged with assault on a police officer were themselves brutalized by police.

After tallying reports from legal observers, attorneys, and other witnesses, R2K Legal estimated that a total of 420 people were arrested on August 1. According to the collective, at least 300 were charged with misdemeanors and as many as forty-three were charged with felonies. More than half of those charged with misdemeanors were charged with several offenses. Previously, acts of civil disobedience such as those practiced on August 1 in Philadelphia tended to be met by summary citations and a small fine. Reflecting on her previous twenty years as a political organizer, Jody Dodd recalled how the consequences of previous experiments in civil disobedience "were so different than what the RNC 2000 brought us."[34] Dodd pointed to the historically common practice of detaining activists for a few hours before citing and releasing them as Jane and John Does.

By contrast, Mayor Street took a hard line and claimed that such a practice would be "terrible public policy."[35] Street lamented that "people were allowed to just walk away" after mass protests in other cities. This time, he pledged, "That will not be the case." Street's claim that prosecutorial punishment could prevent activists from committing civil disobedience in the future was especially frustrating given the prior agreement made with R2K Legal attorneys that civil disobedient protesters would be charged with summary offenses. Unsurprisingly, the city denied ever making such an agreement, and PPD attorney Brad Richman dismissed R2K Legal's accusations of overcharging, claiming that "people were charged with whatever crime they committed."[36]

After the arrests, mainstream media ridiculed the activists who took to the streets but seemed unwilling to go to jail for what they believed in. A *Philadelphia Inquirer* editorial even scoffed that protesters "acted as if they didn't realize that breaking a law meant going to jail."[37] In fact, most activists were fully willing to go to jail for their actions; however, the physical and mental abuse endured by many while in custody, the denial of access to an attorney and to an arraignment (*habeas corpus*), the excessive charges, and the exorbitantly high bails went far beyond legal and ethical standards. According to Dodd, antinuclear and native-rights activists from the 1980s and 1990s expected to have to go back to court; however, "there was this general understanding that civil disobedience had a different standard in the courts, a recognition that people were not engaging in criminal acts for selfish purposes."[38] It was an altruistic action, said Dodd, "to make the world better, and the legal system responded accordingly." Admitting that people have faced serious charges and long jail terms for political actions over the last several decades, Dodd pointed out that "most of those were plowshares, where people went in and destroyed nuclear weapons or computers."

According to Sorensen, local activists wanted to use the momentum of the Global Justice movement to pull off a similar kind of protest against the Republican Convention in Philadelphia; however, she explained, "we didn't think about how differently the police would react," or what lessons they had learned from activists undermining the WTO in Seattle.[39] Sorensen also noted an important distinction between protests against international trade organizations and protests against domestic political conventions. "Protesting a party that's about a presidential election is really different than protesting the IMF," she said, "because it's so personal to the president and the United States itself." Pointing to the increased use of federal resources during the RNC 2000 protests, Sorensen recounted how "we saw a different type of reaction." According to Dodd, this reaction came from a preplanned strategy and a preset narrative: "We will not let them interrupt this process."

Because the City of Philadelphia has never admitted to its aggressive reaction to RNC protesters, it has never felt compelled to explain its motivations. While some local officials said publicly they wanted to avoid another "Seattle," this could and did have several different meanings. One interpretation is that the state did not want to be embarrassed again by the shutdown of a major event. Another is that the state was not going to let activists gain the upper logistical hand by having too few police to quell dissent. Yet another is that the police were going to use heavy-handed tactics to avoid the few occurrences of property destruction common to contemporary political protests.

The decision by protest organizers to focus on the criminal justice system also surely played a part in angering the police. Demands like "freedom for Mumia Abu-Jamal" and "an end to the death penalty" likely agitated a police force that views Abu-Jamal as a "cop killer." This polarity was made explicit by a counterdemonstration held on August 1 by the Fraternal Order of Police, which called for his immediate execution. At the same time that police were assaulting and arresting people for blocking traffic in Center City, three to four hundred police and their supporters occupied multiple city blocks in a busy part of South Philadelphia less than two miles away without a permit and without incident.[40] Dodd noted "an anger amongst the police," which she hadn't seen before.

The likeliest reason for mass arrests on August 1 was the city's desire to eliminate threats to the convention's ability to attract tourists and "consumers." Too much capital was at risk to let a rag-tag group of activists disrupt "business as usual" and embarrass those in power. It didn't seem to matter that Philadelphia was a "blue-collar" city, under Democratic control. Advancing the city's business interests was more important than the rights of dissidents. The money spent by the "Grand Old Party" and the potential for future financial returns on that "investment" was enough to incite a widespread conspiracy to suppress dissent.

CHAPTER 3:
THE GREAT PUPPET CAPER[1]

Spiral Q Puppet Theater

ATTHEW "MATTYBOY" HART WAS A YOUNG QUEER ARTIST from Philadelphia making puppets with the Radical Faerie community when he discovered Bread and Puppet and had a "truly life-changing moment."[2] He formed the Spiral Q Puppet Theater in 1996 to use parades, pageantry, and puppets "to build an urban arts democracy rooted in principles of accessibility, inclusion, self-determination, collaboration, sustainability, and lifelong learning."[3] According to Hart, Spiral Q was a convergence of everyone who didn't quite fit. "The Spiral is a universally recognized symbol of energy, a destination or source," said Hart.[4] The Q, he explained, "is the queer, it's the other, it's the ghost in the back of the bus." According to its mission statement, Spiral Q uses art "to connect people, actions, values, neighborhoods, organizations, and movements to each other and to their collective creative force for change." The project began as a place to create protest props with groups like ACT UP Philadelphia and KWRU before going on to include local schools and community groups.

On July 21, less than two weeks before the RNC protests, Hart saw two men on a nearby rooftop taking pictures of the Spiral Q building.[5] Later that afternoon, while Hart was conducting workshops with single moms from KWRU and teenagers from Asian Americans United, police and Philadelphia's Department of Licenses & Inspection (L&I) raided and temporarily shuttered Spiral Q's downtown studios. Because police could not obtain a search warrant for the raid, they did what they routinely do, which is to use a city agency—in this case L&I—to gain entrance. Although the U.S. Supreme Court has held that administrative searches, like fire and building inspections, cannot be used as pretexts for criminal investigations, the police continue to use such methods.[6]

Indeed, it was at the request of the Philadelphia Police Department that L&I Deputy Commissioner Dominic Verdi arrived at the art studio claiming that "something . . . came off the roof of the building and went through a police car window."[7] Though this claim was never substantiated, L&I inspected the building's exterior as well as its interior, where it focused most of its attention on the Spiral Q studios. Although the building had been inspected by L&I six months earlier and given a "statement of certification," this time the agency declared the building uninhabitable, shut it down, and cited Spiral Q for twenty-five code violations. Activists were thus forced to quickly remove and relocate a large amount of artwork, including puppets, signs, posters, and banners.[8]

After the city received threats of litigation, the studio was promptly reopened a few hours later, but the damage had been done. "It should never have happened," commented Hart. "People were totally terrified and disrupted, not knowing if we were going to be arrested, not knowing anything, and I'm sure it's not over."[9] According to the mayor's spokesperson, Barbara Grant, they reopened the Spiral Q studios in an effort to "dispel the notion that that the city doesn't want the protestors."[10] Trying to appear congenial, the city's statement proved to be nothing more than an effort to deflect criticism.

Refusing to be intimidated by the raid, KWRU issued a press release declaring, "Poor and homeless people . . . will not be silenced, nor will we disappear—with or without our signs. Their attempt to silence us and to make us afraid will not work. We will continue to march." KWRU's defiant statements were tempered, however, by the unsettling feeling that more was just around the corner. The raid on Spiral Q should have alerted the legal community to the need to protect other activist spaces in the city, including the Independent Media Center (IMC) and the puppet warehouse in West Philadelphia. Unfortunately, the R2K Legal Collective was not yet capable of exerting pressure to seek injunctions against the rights violations the city would soon commit.

The Ministry of Puppetganda

Known as the "Ministry of Puppetganda," the puppet warehouse was another activist space used in the lead-up to the Republican convention protests. Located at 4100 Haverford Avenue, the twelve-thousand-square-foot Victorian trolley and bus barn was an unassuming place. Nevertheless, it had previously been owned by the predecessor of Southeastern Pennsylvania Transportation Authority (SEPTA) and, in the 1950s had been picketed by African American workers because the company refused to hire them.[11]

The building was purchased by Michael Graves in 1991 for his flooring business and as a space to make art.[12] The union floor-layer and artist cherished the 120-year-old warehouse and its cathedral ceiling. In keeping with his dream to use it as an art space, Graves and his wife Susan Ciccantelli rented the warehouse to protesters for $500 to allow them to construct street theater props, puppets, and other political art. Prior to the demonstrations, scores of activists and artists calling themselves "puppetistas" spent two weeks creating giant puppets and other props from cardboard and papier mâché. Some identified strongly with the name. "It has a sort of revolutionary flair to it," said Argentinean puppeteer Graciela Monteagudo, "like 'anarquista' or 'Zapatista.'"[13]

Facade of the puppet warehouse.

Inside the warehouse, the puppetistas set to work storyboarding five days of public pageantry. According to movement chronicler Morgan Andrews, "July 28th centered around health care, July 29th focused on militarism and gun control, July 30th would highlight the shortcomings of the two-party system, July 31st featured a massive anti-poverty march, and August 1st was a day focusing on the prison industrial complex and the death penalty."[14] According to Jodi Netzer, one of the artists who helped to organize the effort, "We made over 300 puppets."[15] One of the largest projects in the warehouse was a semi-trailer float called "Corpzilla," a corporate monster with the head of Godzilla attached to a giant wrestling ring featuring personifications of Bush and Gore slinging mud at each other. Different rounds in the wrestling ring correlated to different issues like war, health care, and the environment. Satirical puppets Anti-Sam (the spoiler of democracy) and Elephonkey (the mongrel that exhibited no distinction between political parties) were also created in the warehouse, along with 138 eight-foot-tall cardboard and bamboo skeletons, each bearing the name of a person executed by then-governor G.W. Bush. Netzer grimly recalled that "we had to add skeletons that week (before the protests) because more people were getting executed." Meanwhile, numerous other props were being made to poke fun at the Republicans, including mouse heads (to scare the elephants), peanuts (to feed the elephants), and cockroaches (to clean up the mess).[16] At any given time, several art projects—as well as workshops on direct action, legal rights, and on political issues like the death penalty and the corporate takeover of media and politics—were taking place inside the warehouse.

The puppetistas. Photo © Jodi Netzer

Police Surveillance

For at least a week before the August 1 raid on the puppet warehouse, the Pennsylvania State Police engaged in surveillance of the building and of people going in and out of it. Official reports filed by state troopers would subsequently reveal some of the details of that surveillance. With little hard evidence of illegal activity, the police reports resorted to hyperbole. One report from July 26 referred to an individual standing in the warehouse doorway as a "'Charles Manson' type."[17] Another described a pick-up truck that had arrived at the warehouse as being "heavily loaded with anarchists."[18] Making much of people's appearance, still another referenced "unidentified individuals wearing grunge style clothes," possibly implying that they came from Seattle or elsewhere in the Northwest.[19] One report from August 1 even mentioned surveillance occurring more than a mile from the warehouse at the homes of known organizers, which were referred to by state troopers as "significant protester locations."[20] The report ominously read, "48th and Baltimore is quiet no lights on two people on the front porch."

About the same time that state troopers began infiltrating the warehouse, Jodi Netzer described an unsettling experience. "I was alone in the warehouse at about 10 o'clock at night when a helicopter came by with a spotlight, scoping out the building."[21] "The helicopter was loud and only about 20 feet from the top of the building." A bright beam of light from the helicopter pierced the building's skylight and could be seen on the floor of the warehouse. The spotlight shifted and moved erratically around in an apparent search for activity inside. Although she was not doing anything illegal, Netzer said the experience was "really intense" and she "started panicking, going to the sides of the building so they couldn't see me." Netzer recounted that for months afterward, every time she heard a helicopter, even in the distance, she would have a panic attack. Yet, despite the intense police surveillance of press conferences, the warehouse, and activist homes, no incriminating evidence was ever found.

Nevertheless, at approximately 2:30 P.M. on August 1, police began to surround the warehouse. Inside, an activist going by the action name "Stripling" and dozens of others were putting the finishing touches on the signs, puppets, and banners that would be taken to Center City where most of the direct actions would occur. The idea was to stage a magnificent spiraling march through the streets of downtown Philadelphia with puppetry and other protest regalia displaying the issues of the day. It was a vision that would go unfulfilled.

The noisy bustle in the warehouse was abruptly interrupted by shouts: "Police, police are surrounding the building!"[22] The warning was quickly confirmed as cops began trying to force their way in, but activists inside the warehouse refused them entry and demanded to see a search warrant. The cops retaliated by pepper-spraying at least one person in the face before those inside could close and lock the door. With only the warehouse walls separating them from dozens of cops outside, a standoff began.

According to Stripling, the large group inside the warehouse gathered to discuss the situation. The police were attempting to get a search warrant to enter the warehouse, claiming that there were weapons on the premises. The knowledge that no such weapons existed, however, did little to subdue the activists' fears of being arrested or pepper-sprayed while attempting to leave. Coming to grips with their predicament, the puppetistas became frustrated, frightened, and angry. Still, the group needed to decide what to do. Unsure that legal help would arrive in time, the group decided to test the reaction of police by sending a handful of volunteers outside to see whether they would be detained.

Before the plan could be implemented, however, the puppetistas inside received word that more than a hundred cops had surrounded the building and that some were scaling the roof. Just then, activists peered up through a large skylight to see two cops crawling around and trying to look inside. One of them spat through a hole in the skylight trying to hit people below. One of the puppetistas called "Lovebug" peeked through a mail slot to ask the police why they were there only to be pepper-sprayed by a cop lingering in front of the door.

Designated a police liaison in advance of the protests, local activist Jody Dodd had met previously with the top cops and was told to be in touch in the event of problems on the street. At the time of the raid, Dodd had two cell phones and both were buzzing. On one phone, she was desperately trying to reach ACLU attorney Stefan Presser to urge him to head to the warehouse. On the other, Dodd was screaming at Deputy Police Commissioner Sylvester Johnson who told her that police had received a report of a weapon in the warehouse. "There is no weapon in the warehouse," Dodd yelled.[23] "Well, if I'm wrong," said Johnson light-heartedly, "I guess I'm going to have to eat some crow." To which Dodd replied, "Well, you better decide now whether you like it baked or fried."

A few minutes after 3:00 p.m., public defender Bradley Bridge got out of a cab on Haverford Avenue to view what looked like a scene from a movie.[24] More than two dozen police cruisers lined the avenue and scores of cops—many without visible identification—had surrounded the warehouse. At least three helicopters hovered loudly above. A handful of cops were on the roof and many had formed a barricade to prevent people from approaching the building. Two large Sheriff's buses were parked out front waiting to transport activists to jail. The city had staged an elaborate drama full of hysteria and allegations to justify what it was about to do. A crime scene had been created. Observing the raid from outside the warehouse, Jodi Netzer overheard one news reporter say: "We're getting reports that they might be building bombs inside."[25] The city faced a problem, however. Not only were no bombs being made, no crime at all had been committed. In response, the puppetistas raised a banner for all to see: "Puppeteering is not a crime! Free the Haverford 70!" The words would go on to become a slogan for the legal battles ahead.[26]

Bradley Bridge, a senior attorney with the Philadelphia Defender Association, was shocked by what he saw. The *Philadelphia City Paper* reported that Bridge was denied access to the warehouse. He attempted to explain to law enforcement that it was illegal to hold protesters against their will, trapped in a building, without access to legal counsel and without a search warrant or probable cause. Ignoring Bridge's warnings, police attempted to enter the warehouse by force. According to Pennsylvania State Trooper Karina Betz of the Bureau of Criminal Investigation, at 3:36 P.M. police started "using a chainsaw to get inside."[27]

At some point between 3:45 and 4:30 P.M., police obtained the search warrant they needed.[28] Municipal Court president Judge Louis J. Presenza signed the puppet warehouse warrant and, unbeknownst to many, also signed warrants to search three vehicles that police connected to the warehouse. At the request of District Attorney Lynne Abraham, Judge Presenza also agreed to seal the affidavit for thirty days. The city thus provided no immediate evidence to justify the raid. Even when the affidavit was unsealed a month later, it failed to provide any concrete details of criminal activity. But the delay conveniently allowed the city to allege wrongdoing while avoiding public and judicial criticism for its lack of evidence.

Back at the warehouse, and for no other reason than to add dramatic effect, Deputy Police Commissioner Johnson and Commissioner Timoney's legal adviser John Gallagher pulled Bridge aside to warn him that the activists inside were manufacturing poisonous acid and that "all of the violent activities" taking place in the city at the time were being orchestrated from the warehouse. Likely quoting the police, *ABC News* called the warehouse a "nerve center of criminal activity."[29]

Soon enough, revving chain saws could be heard from inside the warehouse. Under threat of forced entry, the puppetistas agreed to leave peacefully. Before they did, however, they issued some demands. According to the *City Paper*, Bridge eventually declared that the activists "would surrender, on three conditions: that he be allowed to accompany law enforcement officials when they searched the warehouse; that everyone would be released if nothing illegal was found; and that two activists be permitted access to the media camped out across the street." Johnson apparently agreed to the terms.

Seventy-nine puppetistas began to line up at the door. Once outside, they held up signs and puppets before being handcuffed, photographed, and put on police buses. Everyone was arrested, including warehouse owner Michael Graves and many others who were just checking out the schedule of protest activity. Agitated for being arrested without cause, the puppetistas began rocking the buses into which they'd been placed back and forth, causing the large vehicles to sway precariously in the hot afternoon sun. After everyone had been "processed," they began the brief journey to the "Roundhouse," Philadelphia's police headquarters, where the buses remained parked for hours on end. Though they were again trapped, this time in tighter and hotter confines, the puppetistas were still in fairly good spirits. Many were optimistic that, once the warehouse was searched and no weapons were found, they would be released.

As time dragged on, however, optimism turned into resignation. With no food, water, or access to toilets, and with intense heat and no ability to lower the windows, police had created fairly dangerous conditions for those on the buses. As a result, numerous people suffered from nausea, heat exhaustion, and dehydration. According to more than one activist, they were held under these conditions for as long as nine hours before police brought them into the Roundhouse.[30]

"Harry" and the Vanload of Activists

In a related incident, a smaller group of activists who left the warehouse just prior to the raid drove a van from the Ministry of Puppetganda toward Center City to engage in the protests scheduled to occur that afternoon. Most of the people in the group had previously worked at the warehouse in preparation for the action. In fact, just that morning, some had gathered there for a rehearsal. The plan was to drive to 12th and Arch Streets, near a few of the hotels where delegates were staying and near the Philadelphia Convention Center where some of the convention programs were taking place. The people in the van intended to strategically position themselves in the intersection to block the flow of traffic. This act of civil disobedience was meant to occur in concert with other similar actions happening downtown that afternoon.

Caleb "Curry" Arnold was one of the activists in the van. A few weeks before coming to Philadelphia, she had attended a Ruckus Society training camp in California in preparation for protests against the DNC 2000. Along with a few other activists at the camp who were planning to protest the RNC, she joined an affinity group committed to reconvening once they arrived in Philadelphia. Curry and her affinity group became one of three groups among the eighteen people arrested in the van. The other two groups were recruited later in the planning process.

Curry's affinity group put together the plan for a blockade at the entrance to a tunnel below the Convention Center at 12th and Arch Streets. The group made the lockboxes and other props necessary to pull off the action and scouted the area to determine the type of blockade and the number of people required. In planning the action, care was taken to separate "risk-taking" from "no-risk" roles. People preferring "low-risk" and "no-risk" roles would act as the "soft-block." Other lower risk roles included occupying the intersection or adjacent sidewalks holding signs, puppets, and banners. People playing support roles planned to find their own way to the protest site, where they would meet up with the activists risking arrest. After realizing that they needed more people to pull off the action, Curry's affinity group found two other groups working in the puppet warehouse that were interested in participating. One of these groups had been working on protest props with someone named "Harry," who was thus invited to be part of the action.

On the morning of August 1, a small group from the three affinity groups met to iron out logistics. A short time later, the three affinity groups met to practice their action in the back of the puppet warehouse. By early afternoon, the helicopters hovering overhead were making everyone nervous. Wanting to leave the area quickly, they all piled into the van to head downtown. In addition to the activists, the cramped van also included an independent videographer and a Reuters reporter from Washington, DC, who wanted to cover the action up close.

Because the owners of the van—Scott Crow and his wife Ann Harkness—wanted to take part in the protest activity downtown, they decided to give the keys to Harry, the one person who said he was not able to risk arrest. George Ripley, who was more familiar with Philadelphia than most of the activists in the van, sat up front to provide Harry with directions to the protest site. After stopping to pick up more lockboxes, the van began heading toward Center City. Within a matter of minutes, the activists noticed that they were being followed.

Harry later testified that he had placed his baseball cap on the dashboard as a signal for the police to pull them over. Responding to the flashing police lights, he pulled the van over at the 8th Street exit on the Vine Street Expressway. At the activists' request, Harry refused at first to roll down the window for Corporal James Heins, the state trooper who had pulled them over. Heins later testified that he stopped the van for not having a registration tag on the back plate.[31] He also testified that he had been instructed by the state police commander of organized crime to pull the van over regardless.[32] After Heins asked Harry to get out of the van, the person whose role had been integral to the group's plan was never seen again. That is, until they all met up in court.

After Harry left the van, those willing to comply with police orders got out first. In a show of defiance, others used noncompliance tactics to force the cops to remove their limp bodies from the van. Once outside, they waited on the side of the road with no indication of why they were being detained. During this time, they spoke with R2K Legal over the phone and learned that the puppet warehouse had been raided. Eventually, a police bus arrived. They were arrested, cuffed, and taken to the Roundhouse (the Reuters reporter was not arrested). Once there, the protesters joined their comrades who had been arrested at the puppet warehouse and other locations throughout the day.

Puppet Warehouse Infiltrators Exposed

Though some were suspicious of Harry and the other "union carpenters" who were helping out at the warehouse, police infiltration would not be confirmed until the search warrant affidavit was unsealed on September 6, 2000. While activists were still in jail in the days following the protest, Timoney made sweeping allegations about the puppet warehouse while refusing to discuss what led police to the site.[33] He knew that police had infiltrated the warehouse and that the affidavit made outlandish claims against political organizers in jail at the time. But he also knew that divulging such information would be politically inconvenient.

Once unsealed, the affidavit explained how undercover state police operatives came to the warehouse to "assist in the construction of props to be used during protest." Harry, George, Tom, and Joe claimed to be "union carpenters from Wilkes-Barre who built stages."[34] To many at the warehouse, the four "stagehands" stood out. They were older and fairly muscular. Just striking up a conversation with them immediately raised the next red flag: they were not very political or well informed. The "carpenters" continued to raise suspicion with their insistence on drinking beer despite its ban in the warehouse.

Maria Danielson came to Philadelphia in July 2000 to take part in the RNC protests. Like hundreds of others, she spent time in the puppet warehouse. On July 28, she attended a workshop called "Action Basics," which was also attended by the four infiltrators. Once it became public knowledge that the warehouse was infiltrated, Danielson issued a statement hoping to shed light on the agents' conduct and to raise issues of police provocation.[35] Recounting the workshop experience, she wrote: "Four heavyset men identified themselves as stage-building union members who had come to Philadelphia as part of a strike and were presently assisting in the construction of a float called 'Corpzilla' at the puppet warehouse."

"The men purporting to be union members freely contributed suggestions for action." In one prescient moment, the workshop facilitators led the group in a role-play where "police were knocking on the front door and demanding to come in." Since raids had already occurred in Philadelphia and other cities, educating activists on their rights was an important part of preparing for the protests. But Danielson remembered that one of the "stagehands" deviated from the rights-based discussion to provocatively suggest "opening the back door so those wishing to leave could escape."

At one point in the workshop, the issue of property destruction was raised and, in an effort to give time to differing perspectives, facilitators divided the room into those who agreed with the idea and those who did not. According to Danielson, "the undercover officers moved to that side of the room assigned for individuals who believed it acceptable to destroy property." The entire group then discussed the issue. "Not having moved to that side of the room, I specifically engaged them during the discussion about this issue. The officers, in support of their position, argued, supposedly from their union background, that it would be perfectly acceptable to destroy a bus if it was being used to carry strikebreakers." The infiltrators even went so far as to demonstrate how to form a human barricade, to avoid or prevent arrest, and use defensive tactics to protect someone being beaten by police. On avoiding arrest, one officer volunteered to do a role-play on "un-arresting" by "showing how one could reach out an arm to nearby demonstrators and be pulled away from policemen trying to make an arrest." At least one workshop participant was impressed. Referring to the infiltrators, they said, "You guys are good. I'm going to stick near you."

Whether such eyewitness accounts could be used as evidence of provocation remained unclear. Even after it became known that undercover police were used extensively during the protests and that provocation was an issue, virtually no investigation occurred. But regardless of what the undercover Pennsylvania state troopers might have done while spying on activists, the mere act of infiltration raised important ethical questions about the city's actions. Unlike virtually every other municipal force in the country, Philadelphia cops are prohibited from engaging in infiltration without formal consent. Even though the U.S. Supreme Court[36] and the vast majority of state and local governments across the country condone infiltration, Philadelphia police had been forced to abide by a mayoral directive, adopted in 1987, prohibiting them from infiltrating political groups.[37]

Although the City of Philadelphia could have easily authorized the infiltration of political groups, it likely wanted to avoid public relations problems resulting from that strategy. Instead, the city chose to obfuscate by using state police to do its dirty work. After the infiltration was exposed, the realization caused many to accuse Timoney and the PPD of unethical and illegal behavior. It was not long, however, before mainstream media lost interest and the story was dropped.

Destroying the Evidence

To justify the raid on the warehouse, the police accused protesters of planning violent activity and housing illegal materials. At one point, they said activists "were storing C4 explosives" and "preparing weapons in the form of acid-filled balloons."[38] These accusations were made to demonize activists, strike fear into the public, and place sympathy on the side of law enforcement. They also provided probable cause to search the premises and preemptively arrest dozens. After the warehouse search had concluded, the police came out publicly with their find. According to the *New York Times*, "the best evidence police could cite was that chicken wire and plastic tubing . . . were the ingredients of illegal protest material."[39] Despite the fact that such items are commonly used for making puppets, signs, and banners, Deputy Police Commissioner Sylvester Johnson claimed that they were "instruments of crime." He declined to elaborate further.[40]

A day after the raid, the police began destroying the crime scene. Without any chance for experts to determine whether the city's allegations were true, the contents of the warehouse were displaced. In a shocking display of contempt, the police even ordered L&I to destroy much of the warehouse contents, including all the protest material—puppets, signs, banners, leaflets, and other political props—as well as personal possessions left behind by activists. If the raid had been designed to intimidate protesters and limit their activity, the destruction of evidence, personal property, and First Amendment material helped to prevent scrutiny of the city's actions.[41]

On August 2, police held back an angry crowd outside the warehouse as three L&I garbage trucks approached the scene. People were outraged that the city would destroy both evidence and personal property—including tools, paint, silkscreen equipment, a sewing machine, musical instruments, identification, and clothing. Activist and RNC arrestee Adam Eidinger had an estimated $10,000 worth of personal property taken in the raid, including a cell phone that he said was used while he was in jail.[42] A student who was in jail for eleven days and had her backpack taken in the police sweep found out after she was released that her credit cards had been used at four Philadelphia gas stations.

In a last-ditch effort to resist the destruction, three volunteers from a local community garden sat down in front of the garbage trucks.[43] After a brief standoff, police arrested them and allowed L&I to continue the unlawful seizure and destruction of evidence. "The grinding sound of a trash compactor could be heard from inside the former 'Ministry of Puppetganda' for over four hours," reported independent journalist John Tarleton, "as the police destroyed hundreds of paper mache puppets and sent them away in garbage trucks." As far as L&I Commissioner Ed McLaughlin was concerned, however, "We're just taking the trash out. We're responding to a police request."[44] Having witnessed the destruction, Jodi Netzer said, "They compacted everything. When I went back to the warehouse it was swept clean."[45]

That police could accomplish this illegal activity without consequences was unlikely. Still, the advantages made it worth the risk. When asked what was in the warehouse at the time of the raid, they could conveniently shrug their shoulders. Moreover, without the political props from the warehouse, the city could use protesters' apparent lack of message to undermine their credibility. The strategy paid off. Philadelphia resident Erik Lipson told the *New York Times* that the protesters were "just rebels without a cause."[46] On the same day, Timoney was quoted in the *Philadelphia Inquirer* claiming that protesters were "not interested, even slightly in . . . the right to free speech."[47] With fewer visible signs and banners, mainstream reporters were more apt to sensationalize the activity of protesters than to cover their issues. On August 1, activist Morgan Andrews was performing street theater with the puppet troupe "Goats with a Vote" when he was knocked off his bicycle by a cop.[48] Wearing a cardboard goat head at the time, Andrews could not help but comment on the police's deliberate effort to target puppets. "That was our voice," he said. "Yesterday when the media was saying that there was no clear message; that's because our clear messages were being destroyed."

In order to deflect scrutiny of the raid and the subsequent destruction of evidence, the city zealously prosecuted the puppetistas. They were charged with several misdemeanors each and faced bails between $10,000 and $15,000. The city used an even heavier hand against warehouse co-owner Michael Graves who, in addition to being locked up for fifty-four hours and charged with nine misdemeanors, was released to find his warehouse condemned. It would cost Graves about $50,000 to fix the problems cited by L&I, which only gave him four months to accomplish the "repairs." Since the warehouse was the site of his floor-laying business, he had little choice but to comply.

The Affidavit

When the court unsealed the search warrant affidavit a month after the protests, both the activist community and the general public wanted answers.[49] By that time, the city had begun vigorously prosecuting the puppetistas and the hundreds of others arrested on August 1. It was no surprise that the affidavit lacked evidence to justify the raid, but the resulting egg on the city's face was an unexpected bonus.

The superficial reason for sealing the affidavit was described in a "Request for Sealing Order." State police claimed "disclosure of [the] affidavit could endanger the lives and well being of these law enforcement officers" due to "an ongoing criminal investigation into several activist groups planning to engage in illegal [activity] in connection with [the RNC]." But by waiting more than a month to unseal the affidavit—long after any investigation would have concluded—the police only weakened their claims of endangerment.

The more substantive reasons for sealing the affidavit lay just beneath the surface. The affidavit revealed two things that hurt the city's attempt to prosecute activists and win public favor. The first concerned acts of infiltration. The PPD was already in hot water for surveillance it had conducted prior to and during the protests. This revelation would prove difficult for Timoney because of Philadelphia's limitations on the infiltration of political groups. As a result, he was forced to finesse his "well-coordinated, multi-agency operation" line so that it would not seem like city police "used" state troopers to do what they could not. The infiltration was not limited to the puppet warehouse either. State police eventually admitted in court to additional acts of infiltration. And though their identities were kept concealed, police efforts to deny people their rights were becoming increasingly exposed.[50] Philadelphia's blue-collar *Daily News* found it all too hard to swallow. In a November 15, 2000, editorial, they opined: "A contingent of 'secret police,' no matter how well-intentioned, is disturbing."[51]

The second revelation was that the affidavit presented nothing more than empty claims made by the Maldon Institute, a right-wing think tank dredged up from the Cold War. Lacking credible evidence of illegal activity to convince the court to sign the search warrant, the Pennsylvania State Police used Maldon and its director, John Rees, for something the longtime FBI informant was skilled at: red-baiting. Although it is unclear how long the relationship between the state police and Rees lasted or how much spying Rees himself had done, he claimed to have discreetly visited the puppet warehouse displaying media credentials a day before the raid. Rees was interviewed by the *Philadelphia Inquirer* nearly three months after the protests and remained resolute in his stance that "elements of communism still exist and are advanced internationally and in America by groups such as those that tried to disrupt the GOP convention."[52] He would later use the same baseless claims he provided to police in a postaction report.

The "Affidavit of Probable Cause in Support of Search and Seizure Warrant #97823" listed numerous organizations, some of which had direct involvement in the protests on August 1 and others that did not. All of the organizations listed, however, were directly or indirectly accused of objectionable politics and using violent tactics. The police officers who compiled the information for the affidavit (the "co-affiants") were Corporal Howard W. Sheppard, assigned to the Bureau of Criminal Investigation (BCI) to "oversee and conduct behavioral analysis of violent crimes committed in the Commonwealth of Pennsylvania" and Trooper Gregg J. Kravitsky, also assigned to the BCI. Kravitsky worked under the BCI's Organized Crime Division Eastern Task Force and was responsible for "undercover and covert investigations of corrupt organizations relating to illegal narcotic, vice, gambling, traditional and nontraditional organized crime." At the time, Sheppard and Kravitsky were also part of a "joint task force consisting of various operational units within the Pennsylvania State Police assigned to the RNC."

Co-affiants Sheppard and Kravitsky included many individuals along with the list of targeted groups, but only the organizations are provided below. The rationale for the list allegedly stemmed from the co-affiants' belief that the groups were simply "going to be present and active in . . . the upcoming [RNC]." Organizations listed in the Affidavit included (in order of appearance):

- Revolutionary Anti-Capitalist Bloc anarchists, a.k.a. the "Black Bloc"
- Pennsylvania Consumer Action Network
- Direct Action Network (DAN), a.k.a. Philadelphia Direct Action Group
- Kensington Welfare Rights Union
- Anarchists
- Ruckus Society
- AIDS Coalition To Unleash Power
- International Concerned Friends and Family of Mumia Abu-Jamal
- International Action Center
- Independent Media Center

Defense motions later used by the puppetistas attacked the affidavit as being "replete with McCarthyite allegations," and argued that "such statements have no role in a probable-cause affidavit, except to smear the defendants as subversives." Accused of being responsible for "the agitation and violence which occurred during protests at IMF/World Bank meetings in Washington, D.C.," the inclusion of the black bloc set the tone. Pennsylvania Consumer Action Network (PCAN), the main organizer of the Unity 2000 march and rally, was the second group listed in the affidavit. Maldon's April 7, 2000, report *Spring Rites Return: Protests against the IMF/World Bank* was cited in order to make a link between PCAN and People's Global Action (PGA), a "self-styled 'leaderless' international network of groups opposed to the global market economy."[53] The affidavit went on to say that "[PGA] funds allegedly originate with Communist and leftist parties and from sympathetic trade unions," implying that it was somehow illegal or illegitimate to receive such funds even if the allegations had merit. "Other funds," continued the report, "come from the former Soviet-allied World Federation of Trade Unions."

The affidavit made a further attempt to play up the likelihood of violence by stating that "major media sources report that violent acts committed during the WTO in Seattle and the IMF in Washington, D.C. were committed by anarchists."[54] Presentation of this sensationalized information was followed by the uncanny finding that "anarchists in the Philadelphia area have announced that they will protest during the RNC." It was on the basis of such weak links that the raid on the warehouse was justified. Notably, while most of the protest organizers named in the affidavit were arrested on August 1 or 2 and maliciously prosecuted, none of them were arrested in the puppet warehouse. Other than that, the affidavit made vague assertions about groups that were known, historically, for engaging in nonviolent demonstrations and "civil disobedience." Although the information on dissidents and protest groups was largely irrelevant and failed to provide police with probable cause, unsubstantiated allegations of violence and property destruction allowed the city to conjure it into a credible threat.

Red-Baiting

According to the *Philadelphia Inquirer*, at the time of RNC 2000, John Rees had been tracking protest and dissent for four decades, "from antiwar demonstrators in the 1960s to today's anti-globalization movement." A one-time editor for the John Birch Society, Rees gained a reputation over the years for providing "intelligence" to law enforcement. But while Rees worked extensively with law enforcement, some agencies considered his methods inauspicious. The *Inquirer* reported that "a confidential FBI memo written in 1968, made public later through a civil lawsuit, urged agents not to deal with him." According to the memo, "Rees is an unscrupulous unethical individual and an opportunist who operates with a self-serving interest. Information from him cannot be considered reliable."

In 1976, a scandal broke out in New York around Rees's mimeographed *Information Digest*. It was found that New York State Police, with help from Rees, kept files with information on at least a million residents. That same year, the New York state legislature formed an investigative committee and found that material reported in *Information Digest* was "casually used to create dossiers on a wide spectrum of Americans whose only crime was to dissent." The committee further found that "*Information Digest* was the string that held together a network of hidden informants whose information was recorded by police departments throughout the nation without the individual involved knowing of the process and without independent checking by the police as to the validity and source of this derogatory information." Soon afterward, New York State Police abandoned that system of intelligence gathering.

In 1985, Rees formed the Maldon Institute, which took its name from the Battle of Maldon where Vikings surprised the Britons in 991 A.D.[55] According to the *Philadelphia Inquirer*, Maldon had received as much as $2 million from the conservative billionaire philanthropist Richard Mellon Scaife. The *Inquirer* further reported that Rees and the Maldon Institute "churned out monographs on everything from protests against the World Bank to rebel movements in Colombia and Uzbekistan."[56] Maldon Board members included D. James Kennedy, a Florida televangelist who co-founded the Moral Majority with Jerry Falwell, and Robert Moss, a journalist and novelist who in the 1980s wrote that the KGB used Western media to manipulate public opinion.[57] Although Rees considered his Maldon-style information gathering to be superior to the FBI's methods, he admitted to the *Inquirer* that "much of the time he draws upon already-published information from newspapers or public petitions and the like," and "of late, he has been relying heavily on the Internet."[58]

Responding to "the naiveté of those who think the communist threat is gone," Rees tried to set matters straight in Maldon's postprotest R2K report.[59] Several things are revealed in the document's appendices, not the least of which was Rees's propensity to treat political thought like a disease. In Appendix I, titled "People's Global Action," Rees described the activities of PGA using his characteristically distorted filter. He also took the liberty to editorialize: "Though the Cold War is over, it is important to recognize that communist-trained thinkers, policy advisers and officials remain active in many parts of the world, reorganizing under new and often imaginative names and adopting new issues, especially environmentalism and the rights of indigenous peoples." In Appendix II, Rees attacked the National Lawyers Guild for its role in providing legal support during countless demonstrations over the years. Similar to the red-baiting found in Appendix I, the National Lawyers Guild (NLG) is portrayed as being "in lockstep with the Communists" and "defending the organizers of riots . . . and virtually all the leftist domestic terrorist groups of the 1970s and 1980s."

Yet despite the sensational information provided to the Pennsylvania State Police and used in the affidavit that gave them the warrant they needed to raid the warehouse, during Rees's personal tour of the warehouse a day prior to the raid, he "saw nothing extraordinary," he explained to the *Inquirer*. "Nothing to write about. Not at all."

CHAPTER 4:
Jail Solidarity

Jail Solidarity and Reasons for Its Use

THROUGHOUT HISTORY, DISSIDENTS HAVE BEEN JAILED, BRUTAL-ized, and murdered by the state. And while this repression inten-tionally restricts both individual activism and the progress of entire movements, it has often been met with effective resistance. One form of resistance is the use of jail solidarity, which has a long rich history in the U.S. When used effectively, it can even make the incarceration pro-cess unbearable for the state. From the free speech fights of the Industrial Workers of the World in the early 1900s to the student desegregation movement of the early 1960s and the antinuclear protests of the late 1970s and early '80s, jail solidarity has been used to respond to political impris-onment while undermining the state's effort to silence dissent.

Jails are designed to coerce and oppress individuals, and guards gen-erally maintain tight control. Nevertheless, they function less than opti-mally when prisoners work together. By acting in unison and refusing to cooperate, prisoners can make jailers feel an unusual lack of control. By facing the prison system as a group, those engaged in jail solidarity can remove much of the fear from the jail experience and exert much greater political leverage. "Through jail solidarity we can take power in a situation designed to make us powerless," read a flyer used to organize the WTO protests in Seattle. According to its author, jail solidarity was "the name for a variety of tactics by which direct action arrestees influence the legal process and take care of each other through collective action."[1]

Integral to the success of jail solidarity is the ability to exploit vulnerabilities in the system, namely that: (1) the authorities need the cooperation of arrestees to process them, (2) it's expensive to detain large numbers of people, and (3) many jails are beyond capacity and unable to deal with heavy influxes. Jail solidarity is typically used with the aim of achieving certain goals, such as: gaining equal treatment for all arrestees, protecting targeted individuals and groups, helping to negotiate the widespread dismissal or reduction of charges, making collective political statements, or simply resisting the criminal justice system. The prison and legal system have a history of discriminating against known organizers, so-called "leaders," people of color, immigrants, and queer people—often through the use of violence, intimidation, and isolation. One of the most common reasons to take collective action in jail is to ensure equal treatment for all arrestees and to protect those who are being singled out.

By refusing bail, arrestees can stay in jail together, in communication, and at great expense to the state.[2] But this can sometimes involve a serious time commitment. While negotiations for uniform low-level offenses can eliminate the need to go to court later, it can also take many days to achieve the desired aim. Therefore, as many arrestees as possible must stay in jail for as long as necessary to achieve equal and minimal punishment. Jail solidarity need not be coercive, however. Activists who for whatever reason cannot stay in jail are not betraying the group. Other activists forsake jail solidarity claiming that they are better off in the streets than in jail. Given that there are many ways to maintain solidarity without staying in jail, there is no need for coercion. According to the War Resisters League *Nonviolent Action Handbook*, "the strength of our solidarity comes from the free agreement of all who take part in it."[3]

Noncooperation tactics can vary dramatically and can be as creative as the arrestees employing them. The mass refusal to provide identification is the foundation of contemporary jail solidarity and the tactic most associated with such efforts. By agreeing not to carry identification, to use aliases or "action names," and refuse to cooperate during processing, activists can severely hamper jail authorities[4] and ensure that arrestees are processed together to prevent the targeting of individuals for political reasons, as well as those with a criminal record or at risk of deportation. At the same time, jail solidarity helps create a singular, collective identity that builds strength and fosters selflessness. The refusal to be fingerprinted is another noncompliance tactic used by dissidents to avoid identification and obstruct the incarceration process.

Other noncooperation tactics include not responding when called, refusing to get on or off police buses, collectively sitting or lying down, refusing to walk or move, surrounding or piling on top of people at risk of being taken away, refusing to get dressed, changing clothes with other arrestees, and refusing to eat. Singing, chanting, and making loud noises are also common tactics used to strengthen solidarity, meet a demand, divert attention, or generally disrupt the jail process. All of these tactics risk being met with retaliation. Many arrestees have been brutalized for their refusal to cooperate, underscoring the significance of deciding when, how, and how long to engage in noncooperation tactics. The appropriate use and escalation of tactics can also make the difference between the success and failure of jail solidarity. Activists who initiate hunger strikes too quickly, for example, can undermine the effect of less serious tactics and can cause the public and key officials to question their judgment and credibility.

Jail Solidarity in Philadelphia

Inspired by the successful use of jail solidarity in Washington, DC,[5] activists prepared to engage in jail solidarity with the expectation of mass arrests in Philadelphia. But they were not only confronted by a heightened level of police violence but their solidarity efforts put them at odds with a city that refused to negotiate. Resistance by the state was so strong that jail solidarity, which was still effective on many levels, had the appearance of failure. In addition to the intractability of key city officials, activists had lost the element of surprise. As dissidents honed their use of jail solidarity tactics, law enforcement began implementing contingency measures. According to Jamie Graham, authorities were not going to allow a repeat of what happened in DC, where arrestees clogged the jails and negotiated the terms of their release. "The authorities in Philadelphia were set on not having to negotiate."[6]

In order to offset a shortage of space in the jails, Graham, who was also a prison case manager with Action AIDS at the time, said the courts were releasing people at a greater rate than normal. "A lot of people who were turning themselves in for probation violations were being told that their sentences would be delayed and that they could stay out for a couple of more months." Graham confirmed this with prison guards who said they "were getting ready for the Republican convention" and "trying to make room" for protesters. The City of Philadelphia also reopened Holmesburg Prison—a notorious century-old dungeon—to help deal with the expected surge. Officially closed in 1995, Holmesburg was the site of a 1973 prison riot in which the warden and deputy warden were killed. It was also home to chilling "medical experiments" that took place between 1951 and 1974 in which the primarily African American prisoners were exposed to "doses of radiation, carcinogenic pesticides such as dioxin, psychotropic drugs and an assortment of infectious diseases."[7]

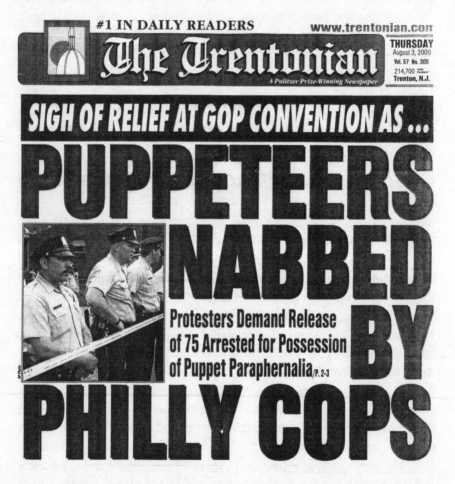

#1 IN DAILY READERS   www.trentonian.com

The Trentonian

THURSDAY
August 3, 2000
Vol. 57 No. 305
214,700 Daily Readers
Trenton, N.J.

A Pulitzer Prize-Winning Newspaper

SIGH OF RELIEF AT GOP CONVENTION AS ...

PUPPETEERS NABBED BY PHILLY COPS

Protesters Demand Release of 75 Arrested for Possession of Puppet Paraphernalia /P. 2-3

Despite these warning signs, activists and protest organizers remained determined to engage in jail solidarity. PDAG, Training for Change, and other groups conducted several direct action, civil disobedience, and legal trainings, which included discussions about jail solidarity. "People talked about the procedure for enacting demands and role-played some of the jail solidarity tactics," said Graham, who was trained and then led trainings himself. These tactics included "withholding identity, refusing to move under your own power, locking arms with fellow prisoners, and so on." Graham also noted that "people role-played the tactic of collectively refusing to move and chanting a demand over and over and over again." As important as training can be, however, Graham concluded that "one of the limitations of any train- ing situation is that it merely simulates the jail experience and often does not convey the harsh reality."[8] According to some activists who were part of affinity groups that had planned street actions, the decisions of whether and how jail solidarity should be employed was a critical component of their overall plan and discussed at length during spokescouncil meetings.

Working together in the lead-up to the protests, National Lawyers Guild and ACLU attorneys, public defenders, and other private attorneys thought they knew what to expect. But despite knowing about jail solidar- ity and having a reasonable expectation that such tactics would be used, it was unclear whether the R2K legal team adequately investigated whether negotiations would be plausible and, if so, which local officials might be in a position to negotiate. More difficult to assess but also critically important was the degree to which police and jail guards might be prone to violence when reacting to jail solidarity tactics. Instead of focusing on these issues, the R2K legal team found comfort in the informal agreement it made with the city and the courts in advance of the protests—an agreement the city ignored and later denied.[9]

As part of the agreement, RNC arrestees charged with summary offenses were supposed to be held and processed over a few hours at Holmesburg Prison.[10] Instead, over two dozen arrestees with more serious charges were held at Holmesburg for longer than two days in squalid condi- tions, without running water, functional toilets, or access to legal counsel.[11] "Its lead-laden pipes and elevated level of airborne asbestos rendered the building and its four-foot thick stone walls, uninhabitable," said Dave Bailey of RPM Puppet Conspiracy, an arrestee taken by bus to Holmesburg.[12] "But apparently not so uninhabitable as to preclude it from being used for activ- ists and protesters." Resisting detention at Holmesburg, Bailey and other arrestees joined together "in an uncanny display of solidarity" and refused to get off the bus, forcing the police to take them elsewhere. Other protest- ers, however, had to spend multiple days in the condemned prison before being sent to other detention facilities. According to independent jour- nalist John Tarleton, "male prisoners fashioned chess pieces out of bits of chipped lead paint and made a deck of cards out of their police citations."[13]

Though the number of RNC protesters held at Holmesburg was rel- atively small compared to the total number of people arrested on August

1, they still chose to engage in jail solidarity and noncooperation tactics. Activist Joshua Stephens, for example, was "completely uncooperative" from the moment he was arrested. As fellow Holmesburg arrestees were booked and interrogated, Stephens refused to say anything. Even after four cops held him down, flex-cuffed him from ankle-to-wrist, and kicked him a few times, Stephens still refused to say anything. "Go ahead, stay like that," said one of the cops; "I hope you shit on yourself and die." They eventually threw him into a cell with three other RNC arrestees and left him hog-tied for twelve hours. Long before others took up the tactic, Stephens and some of his fellow Holmesburg arrestees refused to eat or drink fluids in protest of their detention. When they were finally moved from Holmesburg, Stephens collapsed in transit and had to be taken to the emergency room.

The city's intake of arrested RNC protesters occurred mainly at police headquarters, otherwise known as the "Roundhouse." Hundreds of arrestees spent their first few days of detention in the basement jail of the Roundhouse before being arraigned and then taken to longer-term jail facilities in the northeast part of the city. Once photographed and fingerprinted, most were transferred to the Curran-Fromhold Correctional Facility (CFCF) or the Philadelphia Industrial Correctional Center (PICC) based mainly on police perceptions of gender. But because so many arrests were made on August 1, people were also held for many hours on the streets, in local precincts, and on various police buses before setting foot in the Roundhouse. One of the first forms of widespread abuse against protesters involved keeping them trapped and handcuffed for hours on unventilated buses in the brutal afternoon sun without water or access to toilets.

This abuse, however, was met with some of the first acts of protester solidarity. Arrestees comforted each other, shared what little water they had, and yelled to get the attention of police. Some activists refused to be photographed before getting onto the buses, and others switched their clothing to add confusion to the arrest process. Protesters also pounded on the floors, walls, and seats of the buses, and vigorously rocked the vehicles from side-to-side to stop police assaults, to get tight handcuffs loosened, or to get water, medical attention, or access to toilets. Student Liberation Action Movement (SLAM) member Kazembe Balagun recalled that it was hotter than 100 degrees in Philly that day. "They had us in a school bus for hours," Balagun told the SLAM Herstory Project.[14] "I passed out." When Balagun lost consciousness, other activists yelled for medical attention. Dragged off of the bus by his arm, shirt and hair, Balagun was taken to the hospital before being sent to the Roundhouse.

In another example of early solidarity, arrestees came to the aid of Jamie Graham, who had been brutally arrested before being thrown into a police van with other protesters. Graham was bleeding badly and had sustained a concussion and cracked rib; however, police ignored his requests for medical attention. By pounding incessantly on the walls of the van, Graham's comrades forced the police to take him to Hahnemann Hospital. Despite his injuries, Graham was later transported to the Twenty-Third Precinct and then to the Roundhouse, where he spent three days in jail.

One protester who became radicalized by her brutal arrest and incarceration used her time on the bus to discuss plans for jail solidarity. Raised in a very conservative Catholic family, Danielle Redden was a twenty-two-year-old Villanova student when the Republican convention came to Philadelphia. In the lead-up to the protests, she worked with the Kensington Welfare Rights Union (KWRU) to organize a tent city and the March for Economic Human Rights on July 31. While she knew about the concept of jail solidarity, the elements of noncooperation, and the victory in DC a few months earlier, Redden had never been arrested herself. Jail solidarity was discussed in trainings, at spokescouncil meetings, and among affinity group members, but nothing could have prepared her for the experience.

Redden had decided to get arrested, thinking it would happen during the KWRU march. But since no arrests took place that day, she joined the protests against the criminal justice system on August 1. In fact, Redden was arrested with her affinity group while obstructing the intersection at Fifteenth and JFK during an anti–death penalty demonstration. After being arrested and handcuffed in a routine manner, she was unexpectedly assaulted. As she was lying on the ground waiting to be put on a bus, a plainclothes cop picked her up by her handcuffs, slammed her into the ground, pulled her hair, and then walked away. "By the time I got on the bus I was really upset," she said. "I was pissed."[15] Almost immediately, arrestees on the bus started demanding that police loosen their cuffs.[16] Everybody was discussing jail solidarity—explaining what it was, sharing stories about Seattle and DC, and asking one another if they planned on withholding their identity. Redden took comfort in the level of interaction between arrestees. "We were meeting instantly," she said. "It was like a spokescouncil right on the bus. I was really into that because the whole thing was scary, and new, and weird. I felt very comfortable in meetings."

After spending a few hours on the bus, Redden and her comrades were taken to the Roundhouse for processing. Elements of jail solidarity were quickly put into action. According to Redden, "Everybody was doing the same thing—not saying anything." Consistent with the trainings and preprotest discussions, people simply stated: "I'm going to remain silent. I want to talk to my attorney." According to Redden, there wasn't a moment when she wondered "Am I going to do this or not?" The advice given to those who were "out of the loop" was, "Just don't tell them who you are. . . . We'll clog up the system and then we'll get all our charges dropped."

Mali Lorenz was arrested at the puppet warehouse and held on a police bus for at least seven hours. After hours of chanting, banging, and rocking the bus to demand water, she and her fellow arrestees were given only a sip each. Not to be deterred, they adopted a more subtle form of solidarity while taking advantage of some timely precipitation. "Thankfully, it started raining while we were parked at the Roundhouse," recalled Lorenz in a postprotest statement.[17] "We stuck our fingers out the cracked windows and let water run down our arms so that we could drink and wet our heads under streams coming off each other's elbows." The implications were obvious: "We were ready to practice 'jail solidarity.'"

Arrestees Hold Meetings at the Roundhouse

Once at the Roundhouse, arrestees immediately began meeting in their gender-separated cellblocks. Yet such communication remained difficult. On the women's side, there was only one pay phone for a row of fourteen cells and the arrestees were prevented from using it for at least the first day. Redden recounted the jail layout: "You look out your cell and all you can see is a wall. You can kind of peek out a little bit, and maybe see down the hallway, but you couldn't see each other except for the people in your cell." Each cell seemed to contain its own affinity group. "There was always one person in the cell who was 'spoking,'" said Redden. "We were in an almost constant spokescouncil. My overwhelming memory is that we were in a meeting for three days straight." Redden also reflected on the challenges of engaging in a cellblock-wide meeting: "It was hard to hear down either end. I had a hard time hearing cell 14, because I was in cell 3. So, someone from the middle cell was always facilitating. A lot of times they were repeating what folks were saying from down at the end so everybody could hear. People were trying to yell really loud."

Other unconventional methods of communication were used as well. Lorenz recalled, "The holding cell didn't have a toilet, so occasionally we had to be let out and taken to . . . use the toilet in Uncle Mike's cell."[18] By allowing the exchange of information among arrestees through Uncle Mike, the jail unwittingly created a scenario that, as far as Lorenz was concerned, became "instrumental [to] our information dissemination." Uncle Mike, also known as Kate Sorensen, described the experience from her perspective. "As someone was shitting or pissing, they would tell me information because they had a phone in their cell"[19] From there, Sorensen would "get on the floor next to the neighboring cell and tell them what I had just learned, and they would relay that down the line of cells." Questions were also asked of Sorensen from the women in nearby cells so she could relay those questions to the next person who needed to use the toilet. Once back in the holding cell, that person would make a call to people on the outside in order to get an answer. For Sorensen, the process was both "pretty intense" and "beautiful."

One of the first things determined by the cellblock was a list of demands and how to communicate those demands to the outside world. Another thing determined early on was how many arrestees were choosing to engage in jail solidarity. Though the cellblock was able to reach consensus on the demands, Redden said the process was really exhausting and bewildering:

> In the course of all of this constant spokescounciling, you had people getting taken out and questioned; you had people getting taken out for their arraignment; you had people moving around; an investigator would come and ask people questions. So, in the middle of all of this, there was just chaos. At the same time, it was totally interesting, and this fascinating thing. It's hard for me to even imagine it happening. . . . We said, "We're going to try and be as empowered as possible within this really disempowering and awful situation."

Meeting constantly had its drawbacks too. "After two or three days of it, it kind of started to break down and didn't make any sense," recalled Redden. Activity in the women's cellblock was about more than just meetings, though. For Joshua Stephens, their zeal and resourcefulness was "fiercely contagious."[20] From another part of the cellblock, he recalled hearing the women chant, sing, and beat on walls "to stay connected to each other and keep their spirits up." They also engaged in "creative and often hilarious forms of resistance according to Stephens. Periodically, when male guards would make the rounds, they would fake orgasms in unison to make the guards uncomfortable. Lorenz recounted how, on August 3, both the women and men's cellblocks flushed all of their toilets in unison during Bush's coronation.[21]

Although all of the protesters arrested on August 1 should have been arraigned by August 4, only a fraction even knew what they had been charged with by that date. Most, in fact, had yet to see an attorney. Nevertheless, enough people had been arraigned to get a sense of the gravity of the charges and the release conditions. Many had been charged with several misdemeanors, including resisting arrest, disorderly conduct, failure to disperse, obstructing a highway, obstruction of justice, possessing an instrument of crime, reckless endangerment, and conspiracy. It was rare for an RNC protester to have only one charge. Typical felony charges included assault on a police officer, riot, and conspiracy. In unprecedented fashion, scores of protesters charged with simple misdemeanors were being held on bail amounts ranging from $10,000 to $50,000.[22] Numerous activists had their bail set between $100,000 to $1 million. John Sellers of the Ruckus Society was charged with fourteen misdemeanors and accused in a bail hearing by Philadelphia Assistant District Attorney Cindy Martelli of "facilitating the more radical elements to accomplish [the] objective of violence and mayhem."[23] More than seventy activists arrested inside the puppet warehouse were absurdly charged with "obstructing the highway."

In an effort to justify the city's actions and ensure the public's disfavor toward the jailed protesters, Mayor Street and Police Commissioner Timoney held multiple press conferences denouncing the actions of dissidents. Street equated acts of civil disobedience with "guerilla warfare" and "terrorism,"[24] and portrayed protesters as "out-of-town troublemakers."[25] Timoney labeled protesters as "a cadre . . . of criminal conspirators," causing "mayhem," "property damage," and "violence," which was "targeting cities around the nation."[26]

Noncompliance

Most of the jailhouse abuse inflicted on protesters occurred at the Roundhouse during the first few days of incarceration. It coincided with a refusal by many activists to cooperate with authorities—both as a result of the abuse and as a means to make it stop. The solidarity tactic that most frustrated the city involved the widespread refusal to be identified, but many other tactics were used as well. People refused to be fingerprinted to resist being processed. Protesters also refused to cooperate by locking arms or by stripping naked to prevent undesired movement within the jail or to prevent people from being placed in isolation. Chanting, singing in unison, or banging on cell bars and walls were probably the most widely used tactics to achieve short-term goals like access to toilets, water, medical attention, or legal counsel. Incessant noise was also used to deter jailers from assaulting arrestees.

Unfortunately, though not unexpectedly, some noncompliance tactics resulted in extensive abuse by jail authorities. Guards in the Roundhouse repeatedly retaliated against protesters for their refusal to be identified. According to RNC arrestee Dave Bailey, a hulking Roundhouse guard "smashed my head into the wall, over and over."[27] "Goddamn," said the guard, "I could do this shit to you John-Doe motherfuckers all day." While at the Roundhouse, Redden was in a cell with multiple arrestees that resisted fingerprinting. "The first people that were taken out to get fingerprinted would just go limp," said Redden. "They got really hurt." One woman in Redden's cell had a broken arm, which was twisted by police when she went limp to resist fingerprinting.

In response, another of Redden's cellmates escalated the resistance by taking her clothes off to avoid fingerprinting. Many activists were under the impression that there were rules against handling naked arrestees; however, even if such rules existed, the police and jail guards did not care. According to Redden, her cellmate was "dragged around by her hair and her arms" until she was "covered in bruises." Eventually, people stopped resisting the fingerprinting process. "There was no point in doing it if people were going to get hurt," said Redden. "It also wasn't a group decision about whether to go limp or not; it was a personal thing." Amethyst, an RNC arrestee who wrote about her experience at the Roundhouse, claiming she witnessed several episodes of "people being dragged, cuffed wrist to ankle and being slammed into walls, doors and file cabinets."[28] She also saw several people who "were having their fingers and arms twisted, were being choked and were having their toes stomped on by guards."

Just as some of the tactics used by protesters were met with violence, some of that violence was met in turn by new rounds of noncompliance. Graham recalled that guards would commonly raid a cell by "grabbing somebody . . . beating them up, and dragging them out." As intimidating as that was, some arrestees put themselves between the guards and those they targeted. If someone got singled out for abuse, Graham said, they would suddenly have to deal with "everybody coming at them, or everybody locking arms, or everybody screaming at them." Redden agreed that arrestees "tried very physically to not have people taken out by themselves." According to SLAM member Kazembe Balagun, when four guards attempted to remove him from his cell, "this anarchist brother locked arms with me" and made it more difficult to move him. "To me, that was the spirit of solidarity. . . . This was someone I didn't even know." Graham noted that, while tactics of resistance often resulted in violence against arrestees, they also "prevented police from using normal methods to deal with non-compliant arrestees, like locking them up in solitary confinement."

Reports from arrestees during and after the jail experience indicated that abuse by guards was significant and widespread. Some of these abuses were highlighted in an August 10 letter to the editor drafted by members of PDAG, which cited fifty-nine counts of excessive force including multiple beatings (sometimes to unconsciousness), twenty-two counts of denying essential needs, six counts of sexual abuse, and threats of rape by corrections officers.[29] Examples of excessive force included punching, kicking, and throwing activists forcefully against walls. Protesters were dragged naked across the floor, sometimes through broken glass, doused with pepper spray, hogtied hand-to-ankle, and handcuffed tightly enough to cause bleeding. Several witnesses saw a guard rip body hair from a man's arms, chest and pubic area; another arrestee was handcuffed to his cell bars crucifixion-style.

The denial of needs is a serious problem in the Philadelphia jails, and protesters were feeling the brunt of it. One activist recalled that her Roundhouse cellmate "had an untreated concussion from getting her head slammed in the police bus door" and "was merely told not to sleep."[30] In addition to denying medical attention to those who needed it, jail authorities also withheld much-needed medication. Numerous arrestees who had been badly assaulted by police were denied pain medicine. Others, including an HIV-positive activist and people with asthma, diabetes, epilepsy, and hypoglycemia, were denied important prescription drugs.[31] Scores of arrestees were denied access to food, water, and toilets for more than twenty-four hours at a time. In the end, a number of protesters required hospitalization as a direct result of the jail experience.[32] Jail guards also engaged in sexual abuse. On the male side of the Roundhouse, guards were seen "wrenching a man's penis" and violently twisting someone's nipples.[33] On the female side, multiple guards sexually assaulted an arrestee by pulling her clothing off and forcefully inserting fingers into her vagina and anus.[34]

Sensitive to the fact that these types of abuses routinely occurred in the criminal justice system, activists tried to draw attention to that reality whenever possible. They also understood that there was a risk of trivializing such abuse by exaggerating their own claims. What they could not have expected, however, was to be accused of exaggeration by the very people purporting to be defending them. In a shocking rebuke to claims of abuse, the ACLU of Pennsylvania made sweeping statements that undermined activists and caused a rift that would last for years. After negotiating a "tour" of the jails, ACLU legal director Stefan Presser conducted interviews with numerous mainstream news outlets, including the *Associated Press* and the *New York Times*. Presser said that legal monitors inside the detention area had received no complaints of brutality[35] and that activists' claims of abuse were "highly unlikely."[36] Predictably, these statements diminished protester credibility. As a result, it took far longer to garner the support of media and the general public.

Public Solidarity

Although the solidarity tactics used by arrestees had important effects, the work of those on the outside must be acknowledged as well. One of the first forms of support came from e-mail alerts requesting that people call key officials and send money for bail.[37] Updates on how many people were arrested, how many had felony charges, and how many were engaged in jail solidarity were accompanied by accounts of brutality in the jails. R2K Legal and protest organizers urged people to call, fax, and e-mail the offices of Mayor John Street, District Attorney Lynne Abraham, City Solicitor Ken Trujillo, and City Council members. The idea was that, if people could put enough pressure on key decision makers, the combined effort of arrestees and their supporters might force them to capitulate. Whether or not that expectation was realistic, the protesters' demands were straightforward: (1) immediately and unconditionally release all arrestees on their own recognizance, (2) drop all charges—both misdemeanors and felonies—and, in the meantime, (3) end the isolation of arrestees, and (4) meet all health and medical needs of arrestees.[38]

During the first week of incarceration, several marches, rallies, vigils, and press conferences were organized in support of the RNC arrestees. One of the focal points was Franklin Square, a large park across the street from the Roundhouse where people would coalesce to demand the release of friends and comrades. Activists held a press conference on August 2 to highlight the harsh treatment of protesters on the streets and in jail. People carried signs and chanted "Free the political prisoners!" while passing out leaflets.

The police response was characteristically repressive. At one point, a band of at least twenty bicycle cops rode out of the Roundhouse at

breakneck speed, heading straight for the park and the hundreds of
people gathered there. One cop rode up to a sign hanging from a large
tree at the corner of 7th and Race and yanked it down, claiming that it
was unlawful to hang signs from trees. At another point, about thirty
cops surrounded a puppet show, which was taking place in the park.[39]
Refusing to be intimidated, the puppeteers continued their show as officers threw their props around. Eventually, the police withdrew to watch
the show as a puppet cop arrested the other puppets for conspiring to
commit a crime. After hours of tense confrontation between police and
protesters, the park was eventually declared off-limits until R2K Legal
member Jody Dodd was able to convince the city to allow the crowd to
remain overnight.[40]

Confrontation at Spruce and Broad. Photo © Brad Kayal

By August 3, the crowd in Franklin Square had expanded to hundreds
of people. Correspondingly, the police deployed bike patrols and dozens
of officers in riot gear to surround the park.[41] Another press conference
featuring Pam Africa from MOVE and New York civil rights advocate Al
Sharpton was held that day. Amid signs demanding freedom for the RNC
420 and an end to the prison industrial complex, Sharpton decried the jail-
ing of protesters. "I came in solidarity because the holding of protesters in
jail is an outright shame and disgrace," he said. "People have the right to
protest; people have the right to dissent; people have the right to challenge

you on your racist and killing policies." Sharpton subsequently joined activists as they marched around police headquarters.

The vigil outside of the Roundhouse continued the following day, as did the tension between police and activists. According to Dodd, the ACLU called the police in response to activist requests for help in securing their actions against police violence, but the police told Stefan Presser that they were not planning on arresting anyone. "He believed the police and the city before he believed us," lamented Dodd.[42] Finally, on August 4, too late to do much good, the ACLU sent a letter to City Solicitor Ken Trujillo asking the police to "refrain from interfering with [protesters'] use of Franklin Park." The letter cited a federal permanent injunction from 1987 that prohibited the "Police Commissioner of the City of Philadelphia . . . from preventing . . . individuals or groups from . . . assembling . . . on the streets, sidewalks, parks, or other areas open to the public."[43]

After days of inaction by the city and continuing reports of abuse inside the jails, activists took their demands directly to the mayor's office. Four protesters intent on conducting a "sit-in" entered City Hall on the afternoon of August 4 and made their way to the second floor. In front of the mayor's office, the four were confronted by two-dozen police officers. Nevertheless, they refused to leave unless R2K Legal attorneys were allowed into the jails and that adequate medical attention was provided to the arrested activists. Soon after City Hall closed for the day, the four were arrested for refusing to leave. And while the action was covered by both Philadelphia daily newspapers the next day, Mayor Street showed no signs of capitulation. In fact, he publicly characterized the jailed RNC protesters as "out-of-town troublemakers hell-bent on bringing Philadelphia to its knees." Vowing they wouldn't get off easy, he proclaimed, "each person that has been arrested and that is charged will be fully prosecuted."[44]

Despite Street's resistance, activists continued to pressure the city by holding rallies. On August 6, coordinated solidarity rallies were held in Philly, New York, Boston, and California to draw attention to the demands of protesters and to the abuse in jail.[45] Another local rally was held the following day at the courthouse, where bail reduction hearings were scheduled for the more high-profile arrestees. Inside the courtroom, the agitated crowd was threatened with removal on more than one occasion during the two-hour hearing. Though the *Philadelphia Inquirer* accurately conveyed the anger expressed toward Mayor Street and Police Commissioner Timoney's actions, it failed to report the ongoing abuse in jail—unquestionably due to the ACLU's damaging comments.[46]

Hunger Strikes

Seeing little progress on the inside, arrestees began to step up their jail solidarity efforts by staging a mass hunger strike. By August 6, approximately 150 of the jailed protesters were refusing to eat. Communicated through R2K Legal, their demand was for the city to enter into negotiations with the legal team. If the city failed to do so by August 8, the arrestees threatened to expand the hunger strike. In order to bring that message to the public, several attorneys, legal workers, and activists held a press conference. R2K Legal attorneys also wanted to confront the city for failing to keep its preconvention agreement to charge civil disobedient protesters with summary offenses.[47] The city had further angered R2K Legal attorneys by refusing to provide them with access to their clients in jail—another broken promise. Legal counsel for the PPD Bradford Richman maintained the city's posture of denial. "We would not agree in advance to charges with lawyers," he claimed.[48] By the time of the press conference, more than four dozen lawyers and legal organizations had signed a statement of solidarity with arrestees, promising to "help litigate these gross violations to the fullest extent of the law."[49] The National Lawyers Guild condemned "the police overreaction to Republican National Convention demonstrations," citing the targeting of organizers, overcharging, excessive and extraordinary bail, and the mistreatment of protesters in jail.

In response, District Attorney Lynne Abraham told R2K lawyers seeking to negotiate with her to "Get a life. It's not going to happen."[50] Yet the protesters stuck to their promise and, on August 9, the number of hunger strikers climbed to 250. That same day, more than a dozen people began a much more serious liquid fast,[51] with forty more arrestees on the women's side threatening to join in unless the district attorney agreed to demands including negotiating in good faith with R2K Legal, releasing all misdemeanor arrestees on their own recognizance, reducing the bail of felony arrestees to 1 percent of current levels, and providing adequate medical attention.[52]

While supportive of the arrestees' demands, the legal team remained concerned about the ongoing hunger strike and the possible effects of a water strike. Local activist and protest organizer Dan Murphy said he was "deeply worried about my friends at the PICC, but I know they understand the risks and hopefully the city does too." Jail authorities reacted to the food and water fasts with even greater hostility by placing all the male arrestees on twenty-four-hour lockdown and prohibiting them from leaving their cells at any time.[53] Neither the water strike nor the lockdown lasted, but both were stark examples of the lengths to which both sides were willing to go.

The Faith Community

The continued reports of abuse compelled R2K Legal to seek help from the local faith community to monitor what was happening in the jails. The first to respond was author and Shalom Center director Rabbi Arthur Waskow, who issued a statement of support for the RNC protesters and urged others to help. In an August 7 public plea to "help jailed & brutalized protesters in Philadelphia," Waskow condemned the mistreatment of political activists.[54] "Arrestees have been . . . punched, kicked, thrown against walls, bloodied, dragged naked across floors," read his statement. Meanwhile, throughout the "extremely slow" processing, "diabetics, epileptics, and asthmatics continue to be denied medication." He accused the city of attempting to "break the back of the most promising new protest movement to emerge in the U.S. since [the 1970s]" and urged people to "call local officials to demand that prisoners be released on recognizance at once, and charges be dropped."

Rabbi Waskow's plea was quickly followed by "A Progressive Jewish Response to the City of Philadelphia," a statement signed by dozens of rabbis and leaders from the Jewish community who held a press conference on August 9 at the National Museum of American Jewish History denouncing the arrests of political protesters.[55] On the morning of Friday, August 11, a delegation of religious leaders visited the Curran-Fromhold Correctional Facility, where most of the RNC protesters were being detained. Reverend Benjamin Maucere of the First Unitarian Church of Philadelphia, David Watt of the Society of Friends, Rabbi Mordechai Liebling, and two other rabbis explained in a press advisory that they intended "to visit the prisoners to check on their health and welfare and to relay greetings and prayers from family members."[56] After speaking with a number of arrestees, members of the religious delegation publicly upheld the claims of abuse. "We're fairly sure, from the stories we've heard, that there were abuses," said Reverend Maucere.[57] Rabbi Liebling concurred: "I don't think, in the Roundhouse, we can doubt there was police brutality. There's no way those people could coordinate their stories."

Jail Solidarity versus Preventive Detention

By denying jailed protesters access to lawyers, failing to hold timely arraignments, imposing excessively high bails, and refusing to negotiate with R2K attorneys, the city and the courts unlawfully extended the incarceration period for hundreds of people. District Attorney Abraham's refusal to negotiate with the protesters or their lawyers was unwavering. According to arrestee Jamie Graham, Abraham viewed jail solidarity as a direct assault on her authority. "She needed to demonstrate that she was in control."

Meanwhile, the city maintained that any delay in releasing protesters was due to their refusal to identify themselves.[58] Mayor Street publicly blamed the protesters for their incarceration because they "did virtually everything they could to stymie, to slow and to defeat the process."[59] City Solicitor Ken Trujillo said that if the protesters had only "given their names when they were arrested, they would have been released from jail."[60] Senior Common Pleas Court Judge Lisa A. Richette agreed and refused to grant bail reduction hearings for approximately 150 arrestees.[61] "We cannot grant hearings to Jane and John Does," said Richette. "If they don't give their names, they'll have to sit in jail."[62]

The city's pretext appeared less tenable in light of the prohibitively high bails imposed on scores of protesters, however. Another flaw in the city's argument was that dozens of people who had provided identification when arrested had been held along with the hundreds engaged in jail solidarity.[63] Graham, who never expected to get arrested, was carrying ID when taken into custody. "Even though I had my ID and provided it to the guards," said Graham, "I was still identified in jail as a John Doe." By his account, "a lot of people . . . were kept in jail even though they had identified themselves." The mother of one RNC arrestee, who later sued the city, confirmed in a deposition that "the police were not willing to take Tamara's identification and, therefore, didn't acknowledge that she was in jail when I called them directly."[64]

Although some protesters were arraigned soon after their arrest, most were held without an arraignment for up to six days. This delay stood in violation of the Sixth Amendment and prevailing case law, which makes clear that preliminary arraignments in Philadelphia must occur within forty-eight hours of arrest.[65] Delays of more than six days were also reported, with some protesters being denied an arraignment altogether.[66] Those who were arraigned were lucky if they got to hear brief comments from a public defender while packed in a cell with other arrestees. Many never got to see a lawyer before being arraigned, another due process violation. Meanwhile, most arraignments were held inside the jail by closed-circuit television. As a result, arrestees had trouble hearing the magistrates, prosecutors, and public defenders in the courtroom, thus making it difficult to ascertain their rights or determine what plea to enter.

Lawyers Try to Break Solidarity

After RNC arrestees had been processed through the Roundhouse, they were moved to either PICC or CFCF, two detention facilities differentiated by gender. The experience in these jails was vastly better than the violence endured at the Roundhouse. But while RNC arrestees at both facilities were more able to shower, eat, and sleep, those held at CFCF were still kept on twenty-three-hour lockdown.[67] By contrast, Redden recalled that arrestees at PICC "felt kind of reinvigorated or rejuvenated." Internal and external communication was also better at PICC. Telephones were more accessible and people were able to meet in large groups outside their cells.

Despite efforts by jail authorities—and even the attorneys—to get the arrestees to reconsider, jail solidarity continued at both PICC and CFCF. The attorneys who were eventually permitted to visit with protesters in jail had not told about the purpose and tactics of jail solidarity. Activists with no intention of breaking solidarity were instructed to abandon the tactic. This led to considerable confusion and mistrust between the arrestees and attorneys ostensibly there to help them. R2K attorney Paul Hetznecker went to PICC soon after Redden was placed there. "He walked into this holding room and said to the group of us, 'Listen, jail solidarity is not work-ing. You've got to stop this right now.'" Although they later became friends, at the time Redden could not take Hetznecker's advice to heart. "I literally grabbed him by his shirt and shoved him up against the wall and said, 'Get the fuck out of here.'" For Redden and others, jail solidarity had become "something that made us willing to just about die for each other."

The public defenders who ended up working closely with the R2K Legal team also visited arrestees at PICC to convince them to abandon the jail solidarity effort. But Redden recalled that the public defenders handled the jail visits a bit better by letting arrestees know that they understood why they were doing it. After validating the solidarity effort, however, the public defenders also said it wasn't going to work. "It was really upsetting for people," recalled Redden. "We didn't want to keep doing something that wasn't going to work, but at the same time we were all so committed. It was so weird. I was with all these people, and I didn't even know what their names were, but we were really committed to jail solidarity working. We were ready to sit there for weeks."

General Population

Possibly the biggest risk for jailers in detaining dissidents arises when political arrestees are integrated with a jail's general population. Being confronted by the sheer number of people imprisoned, their racial composition, the reasons for their imprisonment, and the inhumane way in which they're treated commonly radicalizes activists. At the same time, the political camaraderie and solidarity brought into the jail by political activists has its own contagious effect. Under such circumstances, general population arrestees can gain a better understanding of their collective power. For these reasons, jail authorities attempt to keep activists and the general population separated for as long as possible—even though guards, for dramatic effect, may threaten otherwise. Eventual integration is inevitable, however, especially after several days of detention in an overcrowded system. Recalling an interaction between political arrestees and the general jail population in Los Angeles, DNC 2000 arrestee Vanessa described how "such positive connections were exactly what the authorities feared."[68]

> One general population prisoner stated that this was the first time she had witnessed all the women holding a centralized conversation. It became a group event, they collectively sang spirituals and shared stories. The activists pounded on the glass door, requesting pen and paper to write down the contact information and situations of the general prisoners. Authorities gathered outside the cell, watching the interaction with bewilderment. . . . The interactions provided the activists with a concrete connection with a population hard hit with class and race oppression. The general population prisoners were reinvigorated with hope.

Drawing out the stark disparity between general population prisoners and detained dissidents, anti-IMF/World Bank arrestee Mary Caroline Cummins underscored the difference in privilege between the two groups. "Our experience was not like having to be there for real," she said, "not being able to get out, not having people bringing you food upon release, and no television cameras documenting your arrest and release."[69] Nevertheless, it's important for activists who are predominantly young, middle-class, and mostly white to have those firsthand experiences. RNC arrestee Mali Lorenz observed that such experiences show the "hard realities to a lot of relatively privileged people who don't usually directly suffer from police brutality."

This sentiment was captured by the experience of the male RNC arrestees at CFCF. At one point, a group of twenty-four arrestees wrote an open letter about their jail experience and urged readers to contact key public officials in support of their demands. "From the moment of our arrest we have experienced and witnessed the workings of a system designed to dehumanize people," read the letter. "Many of us were brutalized. . . . Some of us were beaten or pepper-sprayed after we were handcuffed."[70] The arrestees recognized that this behavior was routinely perpetrated against the people of Philadelphia.

> We believe that our experiences so far strongly vindicate us in our decision to take powerful action to expose the brutality and injustice of the so-called criminal justice system. As we go through this process we are learning personally of the mistreatment people experience every day in this country. As a group of mainly white and mainly middle class men we know full well that the treatment routinely received by poor people, people of color, and other marginalized people is much worse than what we have received.

Like many political arrestees of the past, the RNC arrestees also had an empowering and transformative experience interacting with the jails' general population. The letter from CFCF continued by describing some of that experience:

> While we have had little contact with other prisoners, that contact has been overwhelmingly positive, they know why we are here and they let us know in many ways that they support our actions and respect our commitment and solidarity. In turn we are learning from them about the workings of the prison and their own traditions of resistance. They have our respect, admiration and solidarity. So far the efforts of some personnel to cultivate distrust and antagonism between us and the other prisoners have failed.

According to Lorenz, "The best time of my 10-day jail stay was the last three nights, in Alternative and Special Detention (ASD)." During this time, Lorenz and other arrestees "had extensive contact with the general prison population there, which was wonderful." Hearing their stories was a "vital part of the jail experience," Lorenz claimed. "Most of them were in on drug charges. . . . Many had families. None were intimidating to us. They were the only people we encountered in jail who consistently treated us with love and could give us a straight answer about how anything worked."

Another notable outcome of integrating dissidents with the general jail population is a genuine sense of solidarity across race and class lines. The two groups have often collaborated to demand changes to the deplorable conditions inside the jails. In the CFCF, prisoners narrated accounts of their abuse and RNC arrestees used their connections with media, public officials, and activists on the outside to help highlight what was going on in the jails. "Some of the protestors collaborated on a list of prisoners' demands and released it into the mainstream media," said David Bailey.[71] On August 11, a group of male RNC arrestees issued a statement with several general population demands, including "the right to a speedy trial; the right to prompt medical care and decent food; an end to overcrowding; an end to abuse by guards; an end to arbitrary lockdowns; access to phones, showers, and visits; prompt credit of monies sent from outside; reasonable commissary prices; prompt response to sanitary problems; and real rehabilitation programs."[72]

The Last Protesters to Be Released

Some arrestees were released after a week, some after ten days, but many were held a full two weeks for what should have been minor charges. Danielle Redden was prepared to engage in jail solidarity for as long as it took. "I was going to be the last one out," she said emphatically. "Once everybody was out and everybody was okay, then I would leave." But Redden's solidarity effort was cut short not by the police or the courts, but by her parents who bailed her out against her will, eight days after she was arrested. Redden's father had found her by poring over more than two hundred mug shots at police headquarters. With tears streaming down her face, clutching a list of the employers, parents, and loved ones her cellmates had asked her to call, Redden listened as her comrades sang her a song she had taught them. Wanting desperately to remain in solidarity with her fellow arrestees, Redden joined the R2K Legal Collective. Little did she know that, in addition to fighting her own charges, she would spend years helping to fight the charges against hundreds of others.

One of the last protesters to be released was Clay Hinson, otherwise known as "Proudhon the Clown." Hinson's "action name" was taken from author Pierre-Joseph Proudhon, the French anarchist intellectual most famous for the assertion that "property is theft." As Proudhon the Clown, Hinson was part of the Clown Bloc, whose purpose was to bring comedy, theatrics, and de-escalation to the Republican convention protests. After being arrested on August 1 for no apparent reason, Hinson was taken to the Roundhouse in full clown garb. Before he was released, his long and circuitous journey involved being moved numerous times, getting arraigned twice, and being questioned by the FBI.

Hinson was first arraigned in the Roundhouse a couple of days after August 1, but he was arraigned twice on different charges and at different times, many days apart. At his first arraignment, he was allowed about five minutes beforehand with a public defender who explained the process and what he was being charged with. The attorney also told him, "I can't really do anything on your behalf." Once in the "arraignment room" inside the jail facility, Hinson was brought before someone acting as a magistrate. Although he pleaded "not guilty" to two misdemeanor charges of spreading debris and disorderly conduct, he was neither released nor granted bail.

After nearly two weeks, much of which was spent on hunger strike and being moved between different jails and cells no less than seven times, Hinson was taken to a small precinct-like building called "Major Crimes Division." Once inside, someone wearing a polo shirt with an FBI insignia on it questioned him about his politics. Soon after, Hinson was told he was being charged with felonies and went through another arraignment process. This time, he was taken to a small room and arraigned by closed-circuit TV. The screen was split into four sections, three of which displayed people. One was a judge, one was a prosecutor, and the other was a public defender that Hinson had never seen before. Once again, he pleaded "not guilty." In addition to his original misdemeanors, this time he was charged with several felonies including aggravated assault against a police officer. Hinson's public defender said nothing on his behalf, the vapid TV image a visceral reminder of the dysfunctional justice system. He was released on bail following his second arraignment, fifteen days after he was arrested.

"Of the 420 people that got arrested, I was actually the last one out," recalled Darby Landy, one of the Timoney 3 defendants.[73] The severity of Landy's charges and his bail of $450,000 had kept him in jail longer than other protesters. Still, the city was hard-pressed to justify his seventeen-day incarceration. Because they were still in jail, both Landy and Hinson missed the final jail-focused press conference, which was held in Philadelphia on August 15. Like previous press conferences, this one highlighted the experiences of recently released protesters while focusing exclusively on women arrestees. At the press conference, Kate Sorensen recounted her time in jail, much of which was spent in solitary confinement. "I've never seen anything like that," she said. "It was a very formative moment for me."[74]

Assessing the Effects of Jail Solidarity

Many people saw the R2K jail solidarity experience as a failure and a blow to the movement that had been gaining momentum since Seattle. The widespread brutality was startling enough, but the length of the incarceration period was also uncharacteristically punitive. The excessive charges and the exorbitantly high bails forced activists to pay thousands of dollars in fees. Some protesters no longer had jobs to return to when they got out of jail. If success was to be based on the timely release of protesters with minimal penalty, then jail solidarity in Philadelphia failed miserably. At the same time, the ways in which hundreds of arrestees resisted abuse from the police, jail guards, prosecutors, judges, and other city officials was admirable and illustrated how collective action can have a powerful effect. Their efforts gained the support and solidarity of countless people in Philadelphia, across the country, and around the world.

According to Jamie Graham, activists in Philadelphia set more difficult goals for jail solidarity than had been set at prior demonstrations. In DC during the IMF/World Bank protests, activists were able to negotiate a "post and forfeit" deal that excluded people charged with felonies. In contrast, Graham noted, "we based our support on the idea that everyone is included in the demands of jail solidarity and we didn't sever those with felonies." Although local officials may not have given arrestees the opportunity to negotiate the terms of their release, solidarity tactics were still used to great effect. "We did manage to achieve some goals," argued Graham. Not only were many of the felony bails reduced as a result of the solidarity effort, "having hundreds of people in jail after two weeks put some pressure on the city to release people without bail on their own recognizance." Overall, Graham declared the jail solidarity effort in Philadelphia "a victory." Still, he admitted that "it was kind of an ugly victory."

SECTION II
IN THE COURTS

Photo © Brad Kayal

CHAPTER 5:
R2K LEGAL

Into the Fire

THE PHONES AT THE R2K LEGAL OFFICE BEGAN RINGING OFF THE hook the moment mass arrests began on August 1 and didn't stop ringing for days. The plan had been to staff the office and a twenty-four-hour hotline for a couple of days but, because of the city's intransigence, round-the-clock support lasted for more than two weeks. Initially, people called with legal questions, requests for support, and to provide incident reports from the streets. Protest organizers, medics, and other activists also called to request legal observers when police were amassing, brutalizing dissidents, or making arrests.

"Each person that has been arrested and is charged will be fully prosecuted by the district attorney," proclaimed Mayor John Street, working hard to legitimize the mass arrests and justify the city's aggressive response.[1] R2K Legal thus became a thorn in the city's side. On August 2, several police cars surrounded the building that housed R2K Legal in what was surely an attempt to intimidate those inside. Multiple cops entered the building without a warrant. In response, legal workers initiated security measures to prevent the seizure of privileged and sensitive information. The police left soon thereafter without ever entering the legal office.

Despite regular communication between the city and attorneys working with R2K Legal in the lead-up to the days of action, their calls went unanswered once the mass arrests occurred. Repeated attempts to contact the police department and the district attorney's office by local, well-known attorneys Jules Epstein and David Rudovsky failed to elicit a response. To make matters worse, attorneys working with R2K Legal were also refused entry into the jails and were prevented from making contact with the hundreds of detained activists. A refusal by jail authorities to allow arrestees to make phone calls further hampered communication. In addition to making the task of tracking arrestees extremely difficult, these restrictions on communication also hindered potential collective bargaining efforts.

During the detention period, R2K Legal acted as an intermediary between arrestees and the outside world. Once R2K Legal began receiving regular calls from arrestees, legal workers staffing the hotline listened intently and recorded relevant information. Many of the calls were about coordinating bail funds, but most were from arrestees describing the effects of solidarity tactics and the abusive conditions inside the jails. Legal workers also provided arrestees with updates on community support efforts and efforts to get the city to negotiate. Because R2K Legal was often the only means by which friends and family members could communicate with arrestees, the collective had to deal with an array of emotions—from concern and frustration to anger and confusion. Many didn't understand why their loved ones were still in jail and failed to understand that important decisions were ultimately up to the arrestees themselves. Legal workers commonly fielded questions such as, "What is jail solidarity and why are they refusing to eat?" When some of the female prisoners decided to begin a water strike, people expressed dismay that the collective couldn't prevent the arrestees from taking such dangerous measures. Both arrestees and legal workers agreed, however, that decision-making authority rested with those in jail.

R2K Legal Transforms Itself

By overcharging dissidents, imposing excessive bails, and obstructing attorneys from entering the jails, the city helped catalyze R2K Legal and enabled the collective to turn frustration into opportunity. What was originally a fairly small collective became, through necessity, a much larger group of people. The rights violations on the streets and in jail also compelled a number of attorneys from Philadelphia and other parts of the Northeast to get involved. Although broadening the size and scope of the collective forced its members to grapple with unwieldy problems, R2K Legal became a model for legal support efforts.

Many activists who had committed to providing legal support during the Republican convention were incapable of extending that support indefinitely. Attrition was mitigated, however, by the arrival of new recruits ready to devote energy to the fight. "Very few people were left over from the pre-convention planning group focused on legal support," recalled R2K Legal member Jamie Graham.[2] Quickly, the R2K Legal Collective reshaped itself into a larger group of students, law graduates, legal activists, and released arrestees that had been radicalized by the jail experience. "A lot of people were getting involved because they had friends that were still in jail," said Graham. "People were coming out after spending a week in jail to join the legal support effort."

One of the inherent problems with such a large collective was maintaining an effective security culture. "People had been so traumatized by the police crackdown," reflected Jody Dodd, "that it created a climate of paranoia."[3] Immediately after the arrests, people didn't trust anybody they didn't know. According to Dodd, "people felt so violated by infiltrators and undercover agents" that an unhealthy level of suspicion pervaded the collective for weeks. People knew that infiltration had occurred, but before the puppet warehouse affidavit was unsealed only the police and certain city officials knew who was involved. At one point, R2K Legal brought in

State troopers who infiltrated the puppet warehouse © Jodi Netzer

an expert on counterintelligence and COINTELPRO to address collective members on security culture issues. RNC arrestee and new R2K Legal member Kate Sorensen recalled the value of knowing how such tactics were used against dissidents and being reminded that "we were actually doing the right thing" by leveraging collective strength.[4]

The R2K Legal attorneys who had expected to assist in the arraignment of summary defendants were quickly replaced with public defenders who were less knowledgeable about jail solidarity tactics but had access to the jails. It was public defenders that arraigned most of the arrestees. The newly composed R2K Legal Collective was more prepared for the long-term legal and political battles that lay ahead, and it quickly switched from trying to directly negotiate with the city to generating public support to drop the charges.

One way the collective began to play its new role was by taking detailed notes in the courtroom. R2K Legal considered note taking to be critical to the overall effort by enabling legal workers to convey information and legal dispositions to defendants, the media, political allies, and the general public. R2K Legal members also took notes to inform future courtroom tactics and legal strategies. Invariably, the volunteers who took notes were themselves impacted by the experience. Kate Sorensen recalled learning a lot about the justice system by sitting through all the other cases on the docket. "We learned how unjust the system was and how people were just sitting in jail," she said. "The majority of them were people of color sitting in jail waiting for a trial." Although disheartening, Sorensen also noted that "the more we did it, the more we felt strongly about what we were doing."

Other important tasks included matching up defendants with attorneys; providing legal status reports to defendants, the media, and the public; searching for evidence and helping to find witnesses; coordinating bail payments and refunds; paying for travel expenses[5] and facilitating housing for defendants returning to Philly; and investigating patterns of police brutality associated with the felony cases. Over its nearly four-year existence, R2K Legal moved offices four times, raised more than $200,000, organized numerous press conferences, filed multiple lawsuits, and mobilized the support of dozens of local and national organizations.

Exposing the Abuse

Several emergencies forced R2K Legal to quickly broaden its scope beyond staffing a round-the-clock office, gathering evidence, and serving as a communication hub. One of these emergencies involved highlighting the abuses that occurred against protesters on the streets and in jail. RNC arrestees calling from jail reported that they had been abused or had witnessed abuse, and those released from jail were debriefed in an effort to record as many instances as possible. Because the abuse was so widespread, a database was eventually created to sort the details. With the help of the Midnight Special Law Collective, this type of cataloging has become common practice for legal teams supporting arrestees from mass demonstrations.

E-mail alerts outlining the harsh treatment of protesters and providing the means to take action were widely distributed. Examples of police brutality, excessive charges, and unprecedented bail were used to compel people to donate to the legal defense fund and to contact the offices of relevant city officials to demand that the charges be dropped. A frequently asked questions document (FAQ) was created to educate more mainstream individuals and groups. Activists had to explain, for example, that their messages appeared difficult to discern not because of a lack of preparedness or naïveté—reasons asserted by the mainstream media—but because of the police raid on the puppet warehouse and the destruction of countless posters, signs, banners, and leaflets. Activists also explained that the hundreds of arrestees were not simply out-of-town troublemakers charged with violent acts, but were in fact arrested for engaging in nonviolent civil disobedience for which they were being detained on excessive charges and unreasonably high bail.

E-mail helped to educate the activist community; however, it was not as helpful in reaching the general public. To accomplish this goal, activists had to overpower the city's lies by broadcasting the truth as loudly as possible. Fortunately, there was still a large contingent of activists with whom R2K Legal could work in the first few days after the protests. This transient but committed group of people used press conferences and media stunts to tell their stories. Even though the effort to publicize abuse was met with resistance, activists succeeded in getting stories into the *New York Times*, the *Washington Post*, and Philadelphia's *Inquirer* and *Daily News*.[6]

Meanwhile, R2K Legal worked with PDAG and organizers from the greater R2K Network to solicit help from religious and human rights groups to expose the city's abuse of protesters. Philadelphia's faith community took the first supportive actions by making public statements in the initial days after the arrests, and by pushing the city to allow them access to the Curran-Fromhold Correctional Facility. After getting firsthand accounts of abuse, the contingent of Jewish, Quaker, and Unitarian leadership worked with R2K Legal to publicize their findings. This effort helped to counter the official line and gained further traction with the help of human rights groups such as Amnesty International and Human Rights Watch (HRW).

On August 14, Amnesty International sent a letter to Mayor Street, Police Commissioner Timoney, and District Attorney Abraham.[7] The human rights group voiced concern over the reported treatment of activists in the streets, at the time of mass arrests on August 1, and subsequently in the jails. Amnesty International's U.S. program director Javier Zúñiga urged Mayor Street "to establish a full and impartial investigation into all allegations of ill treatment and to ensure that those still detained are treated humanely." The letter pointed to reports of "people being pepper sprayed while handcuffed," as well as people in jail "being kicked, jumped on, [and] dragged across the floor." The letter stated that, in one case, "a woman was reportedly dragged naked and bleeding" and, in another case, a man "reportedly had his genitals pulled and twisted" by a corrections officer. The letter also cited instances of protesters being denied "essential medication" as well as "food, water and use of the bathroom." Such abuse, according to Amnesty International, would amount to violations of the International Covenant on Civil and Political Rights, the United Nations Convention against Torture, and the United Nations Code of Conduct for Law Enforcement Officials.

A week after Amnesty International sent its letter to city officials, HRW also publicly condemned the treatment of protesters in Philadelphia. In an August 22 letter addressed to Mayor Street and Police Commissioner Timoney, HRW requested a "prompt and thorough investigation" into allegations of abuse.[8] After speaking with several people who were arrested and detained and reading the accounts of others, HRW called on Street and Timoney "to investigate all allegations of excessive force promptly and fairly, and to hold those officers responsible accountable." The HRW letter also urged the Police Advisory Commission (PAC) "to review individual cases of alleged abuse and to examine the police policies and practices surrounding actions against [RNC 2000] protesters."[9]

Raising Bail Funds

Another emergency during the first week involved tracking and publicizing bail hearings. Most of the activists with bails above $100,000 were subjected to multiple hearings before their bails were reduced to more reasonable levels. Some bails had been reduced by August 7, but the judge indicated that no bail would be reduced for those who refused to reveal their identity.[10] The bail of accused "ringleader" John Sellers was lowered from $1 million to $100,000. Camilo Viveiros, one of the three protesters accused of assaulting Police Commissioner Timoney, had his bail reduced from $450,000 to $150,000 on August 9.[11] Likewise, Terrence McGuckin—who the city called "one of the leaders"—had his bail reduced from $500,000 to $100,000.[12] The next day, Kate Sorensen had her bail reduced from $1 million to $100,000. The publicity R2K Legal generated around bail hearings helped to reduce bail amounts and highlight the city's use of preventive detention. Nevertheless, many people's bail remained absurdly high.

As a result, the legal office was a chaotic maelstrom during the first week after mass arrests. Phones rang off the hook, a constant flow of people came through the office, and updates were routinely shouted out above the din as collective members scrambled to hold strategy meetings. Among the urgent legal tasks was the need to coordinate bails and sureties. In order to bail someone out of jail, R2K Legal had to gather funds and a local resident had to take that money to the courthouse, often signing on as a surety.[13] Although activists had expected the need to raise bail funds, they had not anticipated the sums involved. Weeks before the protests, the R2K Network assumed that a modest $2,000 would cover legal support.[14] The need to quickly raise money and the complicated logistical process for arranging bail made it difficult to ensure the timely release of scores of protesters.

Meanwhile, not everyone wanted to get out of jail as solidarity and resistance remained strong. Among those who did, however, many were prevented from doing so because of excessively high bails. The courts required arrestees without assets to post 10 percent of the bail (plus a nominal $10 fee) before they could be released. For someone with a $20,000 bail (commonly imposed on RNC 2000 protesters), $2,010 had to be posted. Provided the defendant appeared in court, 70 percent of the $2,000 ($1,400) was returned. This financial burden did not go over well with either the arrestees or their supporters. Nevertheless, the need to coordinate the process was still pressing. Moreover, the logistical complications involved made R2K Legal vulnerable. Belying the fairly high level of paranoia at the time, the collective was undiscerning with one particular individual who later ran off with hundreds of dollars in bail funds. Though a modest financial setback for the collective, the incident shed light on issues of race, favoritism, and trust.

Soon after the mass arrests, Emily Nepon needed to step back from her role in coordinating the bail effort for a brief period. Consequently, "as soon as somebody came up for bail," recalled Nepon, "R2K Legal would send whoever was around."[15] Into this environment walked "TJ," an African American man in his twenties who was willing and eager to help out. Instead of applying a rigorous security protocol, the mainly white R2K Legal activists sought instead to include TJ as best they could. In retrospect, Nepon said this unconditional acceptance lacked "a deep anti-racist commitment" and attributed it to "liberal racism" or "an unwillingness to notice that a person of color could be sketchy." Others defended TJ, who was ultimately entrusted with thousands of dollars for payment to the courts.

R2K Legal members would not find out about the financial loss until it became evident that TJ had signed as a surety for several protesters. Soon after all the bail had been posted, TJ disappeared. To be fair, Nepon admitted that it was "a really hard call to make in a crisis," given how racism can lead people to overcompensate when making quick decisions. "We never knew if TJ was a cop or just plain sketchy," said Nepon, "but he caused a huge amount of chaos and was responsible for a lot of missing money." Attempts to get records of TJ's transactions were mostly in vain. According to Nepon, "a lot of energy went into trying to track him down." Such credulity became the subject of several R2K Legal meetings, which forced people to examine the ways that racism manifests in society and establish tighter security protocols. "The lesson learned is to figure out ahead of time a system of accountability, what the checks and balances are," said Nepon. "Don't do it in total chaos, and work with people you trust."

The Lawyers Speak

As R2K Legal began expanding its focus, lawyers working with the collective began speaking out to help counter the city's PR campaign. In addition to staging rallies in support of the arrested protesters, R2K Legal organized attorneys to speak at press conferences decrying the city's criminalization of dissent. Given the outrage over constitutional rights violations, mobilizing attorneys wasn't a problem. In an August 4 press release issued by the R2K Network, New York attorney Ron McGuire called Philadelphia's response to the protests "a civil rights catastrophe of the first order," symbolizing "a systematic political effort to undermine and destroy the momentum of a growing movement for social and environmental justice."[16] Helpful comments by other R2K Legal–affiliated attorneys like Larry Krasner—who called John Sellers's $1 million bail "absolutely ludicrous"[17]—helped to undo the damage caused by Stefan Presser's earlier comments.

Ostensibly working with other R2K Legal attorneys to protect the rights of protesters, Presser had made several comments that effectively undermined hundreds of activists. The same day that the R2K Network issued its attorney-focused press release, Presser was quoted in the *Philadelphia Inquirer* calling the targeting of known political organizers a "smart tactic" while praising "the speed at which the city resumed to normalcy."[18] Then, as if to seal his endorsement of the police response to the protests, Presser proclaimed, "I don't see that there's a constitutional question here. It just makes good sense." The effects of these statements were further compounded when, days later, Presser undermined protesters' claims of abuse.[19]

After facing an outcry from R2K Legal and internal pressure from its board, ACLU-PA issued a press release on August 7 that was critical of Timoney and Abraham for "overreacting to the disruptions and vandalism that occurred in Philadelphia on August 1, 2000."[20] ACLU-PA Executive Director Larry Frankel (and not Stefan Presser) issued the carefully worded press release, which touched on Timoney's call for a federal investigation, "artificially high" bails, the questionable seizure of the puppet warehouse, and the city's lack of transparency regarding the search warrant affidavit. He also raised the still-sensitive issue of abuse in jail. "Over the weekend," wrote Frankel, "credible stories concerning serious injuries inflicted upon those who were arrested last week have been reported to the ACLU."[21] Although the release promised further investigation into the claims, nothing was ever reported to R2K Legal. Neither Presser nor Frankel made any retractions or apologies for the earlier statements.

R2K Legal later found out that Human Rights Watch had contacted the ACLU-PA about conducting an investigation but was discouraged by Presser from doing so. And while the ACLU-PA publicly issued supportive follow-up statements and tightened its leash on Presser by forbidding him from conducting RNC-related interviews, it was too little too late. R2K Legal member Jamie Graham said, "It's clear that we can't stick a camera anywhere near [Presser's] face without him turning around and stabbing us in the back!" That sentiment eventually caused R2K Legal to send the ACLU-PA a stern letter, cutting off relations with Presser and explaining that the collective refused to work with the ACLU-PA as long as Presser was involved.[22] "It is regretful that activists in Philadelphia cannot work with a representative of the ACLU on a case that specifically upholds civil rights," read the letter. After numerous meetings, many RNC defendants concluded that Presser had played "a major role in the media black out . . . as we worked to get our message of police misconduct to the press" and, as a result, had worked against the interests of people he should have been supporting. "We also asked him not to speak on our behalf," said Danielle Redden, coauthor of the letter and member of R2K Legal. "We wanted to make sure he didn't feel that he was in any way any kind of spokesperson for our group." Although an agreement was eventually reached whereby R2K Legal attorney David Rudovsky—who also wore the hat of ACLU-PA General Counsel—would litigate on behalf of the group in any cooperative legal matters, the bitterness remained for some time.[23]

Despite the difficulty with Presser and the ACLU-PA, R2K Legal continued to mobilize attorneys and legal organizations from across the country. Another press conference was held on August 8, projecting a unified call to drop the charges and release the hundreds of protesters still in jail. A number of well-known attorneys and organizations like the National Lawyers Guild (NLG), the Center for Constitutional Rights (CCR), and the National Conference of Black Lawyers "join[ed] together with the current Philadelphia legal defense committee to help litigate these gross violations to the fullest extent of the law."[24] In a prepared statement, the NLG condemned the official response to the protests as "a blatant attempt to silence dissent and seriously curtail First, Fifth and Eighth Amendment rights."[25] In a separate statement, CCR called the response "frightening and disturbing" and accused the City of Philadelphia of "arresting hundreds, often without a reasonable basis; of holding those people for long periods of time without arraignment or access to their attorneys; of requesting, and too often obtaining, expropriatory bonds; of terrorizing and brutalizing those being held in jails and lockups; and, worst of all, doing these things as a way of punishing those who merely want to express [dissent]."[26] By highlighting support from the legal community, the collective hoped to exert pressure on the city to compel negotiations. "We have just begun to fight here in Philadelphia,"[27] insisted SLAM attorney Ron McGuire. The rallying cry failed to intimidate Mayor Street or District Attorney Abraham. Nevertheless, it did convey how perseverance would eventually prevail against the city's intractability.

Effective Form and Function

Once the last protester had been released from jail and many of the core activists had returned to previous commitments, the responsibility to turn things around fell largely on the nascent R2K Legal Collective. Although the collective provided invaluable support during the mass arrests and the subsequent detention period, its biggest impact would be made in the following weeks and months. Whereas legal support had historically been set up to conduct trainings, staff an office, coordinate bail, and monitor the release of arrestees, R2K Legal became engaged in long-term efforts such as fundraising, community outreach, and media.

Once reorganized, R2K Legal was composed of activists, defendants, and their attorneys. The collective understood the limitations of attorney-led groups and worked to ensure that their efforts were defendant-driven. Because R2K Legal was composed primarily of RNC arrestees, those with the most at stake became active participants in the development of their own legal strategies. Because people had been so impacted by the arrests and the jail experience, a new cadre of legal activists was born.

As a defendant-led collective, R2K Legal connected movement principles with legal defense efforts. R2K Legal also established a greater level of trust than is often the case with attorney-led defense teams. Its unique structure better enabled R2K Legal to: (1) organize defendants strewn across the country, (2) hold large group meetings to reach consensus on important strategic decisions, and (3) facilitate communication between defendants and their attorneys. Although the coordination needed to develop legal and political strategies while bringing hundreds of cases to trial was relatively uncharted territory, the infusion of political energy resulted in highly charged court proceedings and politicized trials.

Because R2K Legal knew that success would require transparent group decision-making, the collective employed these principles as it channeled its members into working groups focused on outreach, media, fundraising, and evidence collection. Some of the collective's most exciting achievements were made through these groups, which were open to the public. The organizational structure also called for a "legal strategy" working group that uncharacteristically included both attorneys and activists.

The legal strategy working group was made up of R2K legal-affiliated attorneys, as well as law school graduates (6) and a limited number of defendants (3) and supporters (4), all chosen by the larger collective. R2K Legal felt it was important to have a working group that brought lawyers and activists together in order to bring accountability to the legal team and ensure that the defendants' political interests were understood and respected. Local activist and RNC defendant Dave Onion described defendants involved in the legal collective as being "really conscious about our own interests."[28] Usually, Onion argued, "people give lawyers or their ideas so much weight, and end up kind of losing themselves in the context the lawyers set up for them." This context, according to Onion, "is often extremely at odds with people who are trying to do political work, especially people involved in direct action." Fortunately, as a defendant-led collective, R2K Legal was able to bring balance to that dynamic. Onion pointed to the effort of prioritizing felony cases and of "trying to create solidarity between the people with lower charges and those with higher charges" as an example of how the interests of RNC defendants were different from those of nonpolitical defendants.

The purpose of the legal strategy working group was to discuss various legal options and design strategic and tactical proposals to be taken to the larger group. For security reasons, the legal strategy group was "closed" and represented an exception to the collective's principle of full transparency. But to address the potential power imbalance, this group was not authorized to make decisions on its own, and any proposals developed by the legal strategy group had to gain the consent of the larger collective. Although this aspect of the structure worked well, it also represented a barrier to the development and discussion of legal strategies generated by people outside of the working group.

Despite the collective's defendant-driven approach, the team of attorneys was still integral to its structure. R2K Legal sought to foster collaboration among attorneys, but it was not always easy. For the most part, individual attorneys maintained their own autonomy. Some attorneys were paid for certain criminal defense cases, but most volunteered their time and defended protesters on a pro bono basis.

Meanwhile, maintaining defendant participation proved to be a significant challenge. For R2K Legal to remain true to its democratic principles, it was important to address the communication dilemma, which was partly resolved by using multiple e-mail listservs and teleconference calls, and by holding regularly scheduled working group meetings. R2K Legal also used volunteer phone banking for everything from court appearance reminders to fundraising, and from reaching consensus on important group decisions to soliciting participation in the various working groups. Although many decisions were made in committees and among people working on particular projects, much of the communication, education, and decision-making happened online.

Simultaneous with this impressive coordination, another complicated effort was underway. In the background, the evidence working group was collecting, sorting through, and categorizing photographic and video documentation, along with scores of written and audio-taped accounts of police brutality. Jody Dodd recalled that the activity of the evidence working group was intentionally kept secret because of concerns about information leaks. While the members of the evidence working group collaborated with the attorneys, Dodd said, "There was a wall between the lawyers, the folks working on evidence and everyone else, including some of the legal workers like myself."[29]

In an effort to acquire video footage of the protests, R2K Legal issued a letter on August 14 in an effort to reach out to known videographers in order to begin "collecting evidence for the many trials to come."[30] With considerable help from the R2K Medic Collective, R2K Legal created a database of evidence for the criminal cases and a database of police abuses for both criminal and civil cases. Because of the extensive physical abuse against protesters, trained medics were responsible for interviewing most of the arrestees after they were released from jail. With the eventual dissolution of the medic collective, however, R2K Legal took over the process and began assisting the team of attorneys in collecting and compiling evidence.

From a few weeks before the protests, until a few weeks afterward, R2K Legal had an office in a ten-story, mostly unoccupied, industrial building from a bygone era, located at 12th and Pearl Streets just outside of Center City. Soon after the last protester was released from jail, however, the collective began looking for another office location. Conveniently, a three-story Center City office space owned by the American Friends Service Committee (AFSC) became available. The space had been occupied by the R2K Medic Collective, which was disbanding at the time. "An array of bicycles sits in one corner of the first floor," explained the *Philadelphia Daily News* as it affectionately described the offices of R2K Legal.[31] "In another [corner] are foot-high cardboard skeletons on sticks, reminders of the six- to eight-foot puppets police confiscated and destroyed after the Aug. 1 raid on the puppet warehouse." The space was conveniently located near a number of important landmarks (such as the courthouse, City Hall, and the district attorney's office) and was an optimal size for the activity going on. As the months dragged on, however, the collective was unable to afford the rent. Eventually, in March 2001, it moved to an office in the headquarters of the Industrial Workers of the World (IWW) at Spring Garden and 11th Streets. The legal office remained at this location until June 2002, when R2K Legal decided to stop staffing an office, despite continuing to work on legal cases and hold public meetings.

Building a Movement to "Drop the Charges"

In the weeks following the protests, R2K Legal began mobilizing support to pressure the city to abandon its RNC-related prosecutions. Complemented by Stefan Presser's harmful statements, the mainstream media's allegiance to the official line made changing public opinion difficult. Serious doubt had been cast on the credibility of RNC protesters.

Jody Dodd experienced this challenge firsthand at a meeting that took place shortly after people were released from jail. Many of Philadelphia's "old guard" leftists were in attendance, people who had been organizing civil disobedience actions for years. New to Philadelphia at the time, Dodd didn't know most of them—though she considered them her peers. At any rate, she was better acquainted with the younger activists in the room, including Kate Sorensen, who spoke about how activists had been targeted. Dodd recalled how most of the older activists "had accepted, hook, line, and sinker, what was being told to them by the police about what happened."[32] Her blood began to boil when they told Kate and others that the RNC protesters "should apologize for what happened." Dodd said she "found it stunning that people with a long history of critiquing government" would trust the police version of events over that of the activists. Indeed, the success of the city's PR campaign underscored "how much work we had to get done." It was in this context that R2K Legal began building a movement to drop the charges.

By late August, all of the R2K Legal working groups were in full swing. Besides the obvious emphasis on legal strategy, most of the collective's initial work went into correcting public misperceptions. The outreach effort consisted mainly of public education and securing organizational, labor, clergy, and political support. One of the first public education events was held on August 23 at Temple University in North Philadelphia.[33] Organized by ACT UP Philadelphia, the Brown Collective,[34] and other community leaders, the event focused on the city's reaction to the RNC protests and the everyday experience of police abuse endured by people of color.

During subsequent meetings at the A-Space (an anarchist community center and art gallery[35]), the White Dog Café (a restaurant and meeting space well known for its social activism[36]), and other locations, the public gathered to discuss how the city had reacted and what people could do about it. Educational events also occurred in Boston, Chicago, Detroit, Washington, DC, and various cities throughout California, New Jersey, and New York. Throughout, R2K Legal shared stories about the RNC 2000 and the subsequent arrests and prosecutions. Such events also provided opportunities to raise money for legal defense.

Along with its various outreach and educational projects, R2K Legal also put pressure on the Philadelphia City Council to investigate police misconduct during the RNC and urged the district attorney to drop the charges. This was done by holding individual meetings with City Council members and by voicing outrage during public hearings. On September 14, activists gathered in City Hall to demand action at the first City Council meeting since the beginning of its summer recess. Advanced notice of a Council resolution introduced by Rick Mariano in support of the police response to RNC protests drew a large dissenting crowd. While activists and much of the public had voiced opposition to law enforcement's repressive conduct, some public officials were claiming that the police deserved commendation for their "restrained" behavior during the RNC.

Signs filled the council chambers, deploring police brutality and calling for an end to the prosecution of RNC protesters. Along with others, Julie Davids of ACT UP Philadelphia had developed a briefing paper that provided all the hard-hitting information the Council needed to justify an investigation with hearings and corrective action.[37] Unfortunately, impassioned colloquies by Council members David Cohen and Angel Ortiz on the history and importance of free speech and civil disobedience fell on deaf ears.[38] Despite the chamber full of supporters and plenty of evidence, City Council could muster only enough political vigor to adopt a resolution "memorializing the conduct of both uniformed and civilian employees of the City of Philadelphia, the citizens of the City," and snidely referring to "those protestors who managed to deliver their messages without damaging property and unduly interfering with the rights of others during the year 2000 Republican National Convention held in the City of Philadelphia."[39] Further attempts to get the Council to investigate fell flat due to resignation and reluctance on the part of most Council members and a legitimate concern that the testimony of activists provided to the Council could be used against them in their upcoming criminal cases.

Shifting Public Opinion

Exploiting the mainstream media was yet another method R2K Legal used to engage the public. By shifting the emphasis of the outreach working group to garnering mainstream media attention, the collective used the media to highlight the treatment of protesters and influence how legal cases would be covered. During its lifespan, R2K Legal issued more than thirty media releases and organized numerous press conferences, which were used to draw attention to important court hearings, trials, and legal victories, as well as to lively rallies outside the courthouse. By highlighting criminal cases involving abusive cops, well-known defendants, or activists defending themselves, legal workers used the media to embarrass the state for its actions and to undermine its prosecutorial efforts. R2K Legal also worked to educate reporters about calls for independent investigations by human rights organizations and the support RNC arrestees had from the legal, labor, and faith communities.

At first, R2K Legal was uncertain how it would accomplish its long-term media goals. It took considerable time debating whether to hire a public relations firm on its modest budget. Concerned that a PR firm might not focus on the harder stories surrounding the felony cases or address the issues that compelled people to protest on August 1, the collective ultimately decided to undertake the media effort itself.[40] With sustained activity lasting longer than that of any other working group, the media working group of R2K Legal carried out a very effective campaign over time. It became the primary vehicle for drawing attention to the plight of RNC arrestees and their political issues.

Even before the criminal trials got started, R2K Legal set out to change public opinion by promoting dissident voices in several opinion pieces and editorials generated by activists. One of the media working group's first efforts was to coordinate multiple opinion pieces calling on the city to "drop the charges." In September, local activists, community leaders, and members of R2K Legal met with the *Philadelphia Inquirer* and *Philadelphia Daily News* editorial boards. Over the next three months, a series of commentary and op-ed pieces were published in both daily newspapers. These included "An Attempt to Criminalize Dissent," an early October *Inquirer* op-ed and one of the first mainstream pieces to convey an activist perspective,[41] followed by four more op-ed pieces in December penned by local Philly activist Sara Marcus,[42] local activist and White Dog Café owner Judy Wicks, Unity 2000 organizer and Pennsylvania Consumer Action Network (PCAN) director Michael Morrill, and local activist, graduate student, and teacher Matt Ruben.[43]

While emphasis was placed on getting coverage in the mainstream media, R2K Legal also worked closely with independent media sources including the Philadelphia Independent Media Center (IMC), which was formed in anticipation of the RNC 2000 protests.[44] In addition to its online newswire, the Philly IMC incorporated video, radio, and print media into its decentralized, grassroots journalism. Other independent media outlets such as *Democracy Now!* and *Free Speech Radio News* were integral to ensuring coverage. By late 2000, the IMC video collective had released an hour-long documentary called *Crashing the Party* as well as a shorter version that was useful as a community-organizing tool. The IMC radio collective Radio Volta also broadcasted frequent updates. For its part, the IMC print collective spread news about postprotest legal issues in its print periodical *The Unconvention*. Other independent media outlets also regularly focused on RNC protest-related stories, including the Philadelphia anarchist periodical *the defenestrator, 2600: The Hacker Quarterly*, Pacifica's WBAI, and *Free Speech Radio News*.[45] These were joined by a Bridgeport,

Connecticut radio show called *Between the Lines*, which broadcasted several stories from listener-supported *WPKN*.[46]

Statements of Support

In an effort to better educate the public on the history of civil disobedience and to explain why such a tactic was used on August 1, R2K Legal sought and obtained a statement from historian and activist Howard Zinn. On September 26, Zinn sent the legal collective a previously issued statement titled "The Role of Civil Disobedience in Promoting US Democracy," to be used in any way they saw fit.[47] Used in outreach efforts, Zinn's statement started by recognizing the long and honorable tradition of civil disobedience in the United States. Zinn described civil disobedience acts as "technical violations of law to serve important social values." Zinn concluded by charging that "American history sustains the idea that civil disobedience . . . should be distinguished from criminal disobedience, where a law is violated for individual gain."

October 2000 was an especially active outreach month for R2K Legal. With momentum continuing to build from the previous month's exposure of police infiltration, R2K Legal achieved several political gains that underscored the strong community support for RNC protesters. One of the most significant political achievements was obtaining a congressional letter of support that urged the City of Philadelphia to "end its campaign to cast non-violent, peaceful protesters as violent criminals" while calling on the district attorney "to drop all charges against those who were arrested while exercising their rights to free expression during the Republican convention."[48] The October 19 letter was authored by U.S. Representative Cynthia McKinney (D-GA), and co-authored by Barbara Lee (D-CA) and ranking House Judiciary Committee member John Conyers (D-MI). It was the result of collaboration between the R2K Legal Collective and an RNC protester from McKinney's district in Atlanta. Together, the congressional members expressed "grave concern at the treatment of activists who exercised . . . dissent . . . through the time-honored tradition of civil disobedience," and called the police response "disproportionately harsh, and apparently aimed at preventing free expression." The letter went even further by calling the continued prosecution of dozens of RNC felony defendants "disturbing" and based on "charges whose veracity is dubious at best." Refusing to sidestep difficult issues, the letter made the connection between protesters being in the streets "to draw attention to injustices within the criminal justice system" and how "they experienced first-hand some of the routine cruelty and unaccountability of that system." Although the letter failed to convince the district attorney to drop the charges, it undoubtedly had an impact on public opinion.

In addition to the congressional letter of support, R2K Legal also sought similar letters from local religious and labor leadership. Through its work with the Philadelphia Progressive Roundtable, a local coalition of progressive groups, R2K Legal was able to obtain a letter of support co-authored by several local unions. On October 5, AFSCME District Council 47 president Thomas Paine Cronin, United Food and Commercial Workers president Wendell W. Young III, Brotherhood of Maintenance of Way Employees chair Jed Dodd, Philadelphia Coalition of Labor Union Women president Katherine Black, and Lynne P. Fox of UNITE, all signed a letter calling on the district attorney to "reduce to the lowest possible level the fines and punishments of [the RNC protesters]."[49] Another separate letter was sent the following day by Arthur T. Doherty, president of the Philadelphia Area Local of the American Postal Workers Union, AFL-CIO.[50] Doherty's letter went even further by calling on the district attorney to "drop all charges."

The authors of the October 5 letter also signed on to a joint clergy-labor letter sent to the district attorney on October 10.[51] In addition to the labor leaders, co-signers included Reverend Beverly Dale of the Christian Association and the University of Pennsylvania (UPenn), Reverend Will Gespin, Chaplain at UPenn, Rabbi Rebecca Alpert, assistant professor of religion at Temple University, Rabbi Brian Walt of the Congregation Mishkan Shalom, Reverend Benjamin Maucere of the First Unitarian Church of Philadelphia, Reverend Patricia Pearce of the Tabernacle United Church, and David Watt of the Central Philadelphia Monthly Meeting. Cosigners of the clergy-labor letter expressed "deep concern and a sense of obligation" and requested a meeting to address "the city's treatment of the Republican Convention protesters." Their narrative was compelling:

> We watched our city intimidate the people who planned to protest—taking pictures of them, infiltrating their groups and interrogating suspected participants. Our local churches were harassed by L&I simply because we offered shelter and sanctuary to out-of-town participants. We watched in dismay as our city arrested dozens of people in a puppet-making

workshop, singled out supposed ringleaders for pre-emptive arrests, detained hundreds of people without arraignment to keep them off the streets during the Convention, physically mistreated protesters in jail, and declared a willingness to prosecute protesters to the fullest extent of the law. Many activists still face serious charges, including felony charges for conspiracy and assault. They say the charges are trumped-up, and we take them seriously.[52]

Despite the letter's compelling tone, however, District Attorney Abraham refused to meet with them. Not to be deterred, R2K Legal continued mobilizing community support. Probably the greatest outreach effort involved gathering local and national organizational co-signers on a "Drop the Charges" letter to Mayor Street and District Attorney Abraham.[53] Over a period of many weeks, hundreds of individuals and organizations were contacted to obtain the maximum number of organizational co-signers. By the end of October, less than three months after the protests, more than eighty organizations had signed on to the mostly symbolic letter calling for an end to the RNC prosecutions.

Boasting multiple letters of support, R2K Legal staged a press event at the offices of District Attorney Abraham on October 24.[54] The first RNC protester trial was scheduled for the next day. At the press conference, various community leaders spoke out at the press conference against the city's treatment of protesters and urged the district attorney to "drop the charges."[55] Speakers included National Organization for Women (NOW) Pennsylvania chapter president Barbara DiTullio, KWRU director Cheri Honkala, Kathy Black, Reverend Beverly Dale, and Rosita Johnson of the Philadelphia Federation of Teachers. Prevented from holding their press conference on the steps of the district attorney's office, members of R2K Legal and the reputable group of community leaders were forced onto the sidewalk by a solid row of security guards. The same guards also prevented the group from entering the office in order to deliver the letters. Finally, with help the help of City Council member Angel Ortiz, the letters made it to their destination.

A Tremendous Success

Although R2K Legal had its share of failures, it was in many ways a tremendous success. In turning the tide of public opinion and overcoming difficult legal obstacles, the innovative structure of R2K Legal proved invaluable. The jail experience had radicalized hundreds of activists and the subsequent years of legal work—though frustrating and time-consuming—served as an example for legal support efforts to come. By bringing attention to what happened on the streets and in the jails, by building support in various communities, by pushing the boundaries of the legal system, and by successfully raising funds to sustain long-term support, R2K Legal broke new ground for legal collectives. "I really think we created a model for how to support people," said R2K Legal member Jody Dodd.[56] "The one thing I really wished we had figured out was how to translate that to the larger community."

The first two weeks after the RNC 2000 protests were tense and frightening. Yet, what happened in the following months and years was inspiring. R2K Legal set out to raise more than $200,000 and, for the most part, accomplished that goal. The collective published several newspaper opinion pieces, flyers, brochures, newsletters, and even ran an ad in *Z Magazine*. In February 2001, the collective disseminated a timeline of events highlighting law enforcement's conspiracy to suppress dissent.[57] They also organized a coordinated "week of solidarity" with RNC defendants to educate the public on what happened to protesters and how to urge the city to drop the charges.[58] Activists from several U.S. cities took part by targeting city officials with letters, calls, and faxes, and by hosting local legal defense fundraisers. In May and September of 2001, R2K Legal issued newsletters updating defendants, supporters, the public, and the media on the status of criminal and civil cases, and the effort to get the charges dropped.

Many collective members worked full-time at strengthening the legal support effort, with more than ten people often working fifty hours per week. R2K Legal member Bill Beckler and at least two others moved to Philadelphia to support their comrades and work full time with the collective. In his estimation, tens of thousands of hours were spent on legal support stemming from the RNC 2000 protests. "It's overwhelming," reflected Beckler, "to think how many lives have been changed and how much time has been spent on this project."[59] In the end, R2K Legal was relegated to a box of papers, tucked away in the basement of a secure building. Nevertheless, it was the lessons it passed on that have become its legacy.

CHAPTER 6:
COURT SOLIDARITY

Building Court Solidarity in Philadelphia

D ISTRICT ATTORNEY LYNNE ABRAHAM AND MAYOR JOHN STREET stood firm on their threat to "fully prosecute" each person who was arrested and charged.[1] Consistent with her unwillingness to negotiate while activists were still in jail, Abraham was also unrelenting in court. Not only did the district attorney refuse to reduce what were clearly excessive charges against hundreds of activists, she also appealed judicial decision resulting in the dismissal of many of the more egregious charges. She even assigned homicide attorneys—the "city's A-list of lawyers"—to prosecute misdemeanor protest cases.[2] In the face of political pressure, Abraham obstinately endured countless legal battles. Yet it was the city's unreasonable approach that compelled RNC arrestees to continue using solidarity tactics to achieve their goals.

To do this, R2K Legal drew on the lessons of historical court solidarity efforts like those that were used by Seattle anti-WTO protesters and the anti-nuke demonstrators of the 1980s. They also drew on the lessons of the Chicago 8 trial, which stemmed from the 1968 Democratic National Convention protests. While not "court solidarity" in the typical sense, many of the antics used by Chicago 8 defendants and their attorneys were reprised during the RNC 2000 cases. What most differentiated Philadelphia from its historical antecedents, however, was the prolonged legal support, which lasted for more than two years and had a huge impact on activists, politicians, media, and the public.

As postprotest discussions about court solidarity began in different cities, events were still unfolding in Philadelphia that would have a direct impact on the legal options available to hundreds of RNC defendants. On August 14, seven members of the R2K Medic Collective filed a lawsuit, accusing the police of illegal stops, searches, harassment, and destruction of property, including medical supplies.[3] Then, on September 6, the search warrant used by the police to enter the puppet warehouse was finally unsealed.[4] The city's problems were compounded by the search warrant's Red Scare allegations that Communists had funded the RNC protests. Once unsealed, the search warrant quickly became a focus for mainstream media, which began to question the city's use of surveillance, infiltration, and preemptive mass arrests.[5]

Just as the city was dealing with this bad publicity, R2K Legal ramped up its organizing efforts. In addition to informing attorneys about court solidarity and the unique interests of RNC defendants, the collective struggled to ensure that defendants knew their legal options and were able to participate in group decision-making about case strategies and tactics. To facilitate this process, the New York–based working group of the August 1st Coalition along with R2K Legal developed an in-depth frequently asked questions document (FAQ).[6] The FAQ was intentionally prepared to maintain political context and to explain certain aspects of the legal system in political, as well as legal, terms. It defined court solidarity in the following way:

> Court solidarity is a strategy and ideology of defendants working together and making consensus decisions. Like jail solidarity, it has been effective in ensuring that those who are traditionally singled out (long-time activists, people of color, queers, anarchists, etc.) are treated equally. It may mean committing, as a group, not to take individual plea deals that don't address the question of equal treatment. It may mean going to trial, which is a long-term investment of time, energy, and resources. It may mean that people charged with misdemeanors accept a deal that will allow them to focus resources on the felony cases. Because it involves a long-term commitment (working, in some way, until all charges are cleared for everyone), it is often seen as upping the ante from jail solidarity—staying strong and unified in the long run.[7]

Dissemination of the FAQ was timed to coincide with the first misdemeanor hearings on September 16, 23, and 30. Because there wasn't much time to coordinate with hundreds of RNC defendants about whether to refuse plea bargains and demand trials, R2K Legal used the FAQ to educate activists about court solidarity, and to urge defendants to participate in meetings scheduled for the day before and evening after each of the three September hearings. In addition to facilitating strategy discussions, these meetings trained defendants in court solidarity. In addition to meetings in Philadelphia, clusters of RNC defendants met in Boston, New York, Washington, DC, and elsewhere to contemplate the decisions that needed to be made.[8]

Arrests at Spruce and Broad with legal observers present. Photo © Brad Kayal

The misdemeanor defendants were split up into approximately twenty blocs (cases) and assigned to one of the three initial court hearings in September. Each group was supposed to represent a different time and location of arrest. Philadelphia provides misdemeanor defendants the right to a bench trial (before a judge); however, the city is somewhat unique in that, if convicted, defendants have a right to a second "appeal" trial with either a judge or a jury. Although travel was still an issue for activists outside of Philadelphia, having two chances made it less risky for misdemeanants to fight their charges. Practically speaking, this made it easier to stand in solidarity with the RNC felony defendants. The threat of appeals also played well with the objective of clogging up the courts to frustrate an overloaded legal system.

Because the misdemeanor cases were expected to get resolved more quickly than the felony cases, and because the felony defendants needed to develop different case strategies, a separate R2K Legal felony working group was eventually formed. This working group also developed ways for misdemeanor defendants to use court solidarity to support felony defendants. Although risks were inherent in just about all of the strategies, the biggest step for misdemeanor defendants in showing their support was to refuse plea bargains, plead not guilty, and proceed to trial. It was expected that the city would offer many misdemeanor defendants something called "Accelerated Rehabilitative Disposition" (ARD). As an alternative to pleading "guilty" or "not guilty," ARD suspends a defendant's court case for six months and, if the defendant has not been found guilty of a criminal act during that time, the charges are dropped and expunged. A fine is typically associated with ARD and for RNC defendants that fine was $300. If all of the defendants had agreed to ARD, the city would have accumulated approximately $100,000 in fines—an unsettling price to pay.

The ARD option appealed to many activists who didn't live in Philadelphia or didn't have the time or money to deal with a lengthy legal battle. Nevertheless, a large number of RNC defendants were angered enough to want to fight their charges. The added motivation of court solidarity compelled most RNC defendants to continue doing what they could to support those facing serious charges and jail time.

Having misdemeanants use their cases as leverage to protect those with more serious charges was a fairly untested form of court solidarity. By all accounts, the strategy demanded a huge legal and political effort and had a strong chance of failure. Yet, support for felony defendants and others singled out with high-level charges remained strong. In the anarchist Philly periodical *the defenestrator*, Dave Onion issued the following plea regarding the importance of maintaining solidarity with the high-risk defendants:

> Those accused with felonies are the ones looking at doing serious time and the ones under a real attack by the State. We need to have their backs. This is where the new movement fucked up after N30 (the 1999 WTO protests) in Seattle, when the felonies were basically left to fend for themselves

when everyone else was off scot-free. The felony cases are our
potential future political prisoners. And that's something we
don't ever need. Numerous accused felons are seasoned and
valuable activists, organizers, and important souls we can't
afford not to have with us on the street.[9]

As efforts to seek equal treatment for all RNC defendants were
building momentum, a group of about seventy-five defendants met in
Philadelphia on August 22 to discuss court solidarity, their legal options,
and next steps.[10] After the Radical Cheerleaders opened the meeting with
a raucous cheer, R2K Legal members began explaining the collective's
history, structure, and newfound purpose: supporting hundreds of defendants through the legal system. From there, the bulk of the meeting dealt
with court solidarity. Attorneys answered questions about the criminal
cases, the expected consequences, and the commitment required to go to
trial. The meeting was wildly successful. An overwhelming majority of misdemeanor defendants chose to use their cases as leverage to support the
felony defendants.

On August 24, another group of approximately forty defendants met
in Washington, DC, and drafted a statement of support for court solidarity.[11] Within a couple of weeks, the August 1st Coalition from New York
and a smaller contingent from Ithaca had agreed to join Philadelphia and
DC in their stand for court solidarity. On September 6, a joint statement
was issued outlining the goals of court solidarity: (1) equal treatment in
the court system; (2) support for defendants facing felony charges; (3) solidarity with all prisoners in the Philadelphia prison-industrial complex;
(4) raise awareness of the city's civil rights violations; (5) a refusal to pay
any further penalties (no jail time, fines, restitution, probation, community
service, or any other punitive measure); (6) protect activists from any prec-
edent that would have the effect of stifling dissent; and (7) retain the right
to sue the City of Philadelphia, the police, the Department of Corrections
and any other city agency found to be responsible for rights violations.[12]

On September 16, a crowd rallied outside of the Philadelphia courthouse in support of more than one hundred RNC defendants appearing
that day. It quickly became apparent that the district attorney's offer of ARD
would not be extended to all of the misdemeanor defendants. Although the
ARD plea offers represented a considerable change in the city's posture,[13]
many defendants were unwilling to pay a fine. With activists in high spirits,
the mainstream media took note of the mass rejection of ARD deals.[14]

At the September 23 hearing, fifty-four more defendants refused ARD deals and addressed the court in what the *Philadelphia Inquirer* called "a spirited display of solidarity." RNC defendant John Harris, a high school history teacher from Los Angeles, read from a statement drafted by a group of defendants: "The vast majority of RNC defendants . . . demand our rights to a full trial because good-faith negotiations have not been made for the reduction of charges of all RNC accused felons and high-level misdemeanors."[15] Once Harris completed the statement, the courtroom erupted in applause and was quieted only by the bailiff's stern demand. As additional cases were called, more statements were made and, despite the suppression of vocal support, fists were raised in solidarity with fellow defendants.

Massive police presence at Spruce and Broad. Photo © Brad Kayal

The September 30 hearing played out in similar fashion, with statements made to the court and fists raised in solidarity. In response, a frustrated Trial Commissioner James Thorpe said, "I'm not putting up with this for the rest of the afternoon." After cutting the activists' statements short and calling a recess, he forced the remaining defendants to jointly decide whether to accept the ARD offer or proceed to trial.[16] Upon returning to the courtroom, many defendants and supporters had covered their mouths with duct tape in defiance of the commissioner's censorship. Afterward, defendants and their supporters rallied outside the courthouse and reveled in their resistance. An additional 128 protesters had refused ARD and demanded a trial.

In total, 237 defendants refused the district attorney's offer, which represented a significant short-term victory for R2K Legal and the dozens facing felony or serious misdemeanor charges. It also meant that the city now had the burden of proof at trial, and was obligated to quickly amass sufficient evidence against more than 200 RNC defendants.

Preparing for Political Trials

The first set of trials were scheduled for October 25, which didn't leave much time for defendants to develop their legal strategies. Multiple trial trainings in Philadelphia, New York, and elsewhere helped to foster the development of effective legal strategies. Once RNC defendants had been grouped together by time and location of alleged violation, group meetings became much more evidence-based and case-focused. Typically, they included only defendants who were, or were thought to have been, arrested together. As important as the details of each case were, however, the meeting also covered the history of political trials, self-representation, and the material aspects of criminal trials in Philadelphia.

The first trial training for RNC defendants was organized by the August 1st Coalition in New York and held on October 18 at Hunter College. The training described how some political trials have been theatrical, based on the actions and attire of defendants and their supporters. The training also detailed how and why defendants might represent themselves. Much time was spent reviewing trial procedures and when certain events or legal actions could be expected to occur. Organizers explained that, if a misdemeanor defendant was convicted at her first trial before a judge in Municipal Court, she could exercise her right to another trial in the Court of Common Pleas. While the disposition from the first trial is ignored on appeal, prior testimony can be used in the second trial. Defendants learned how their testimony could be politically compelling but also how it could become incriminating for themselves and even for felony defendants. Activists were warned that the city could use the misdemeanor cases as a fishing expedition to find evidence against those more seriously charged. Finally, while political trials could allow defendants to make political statements, prosecutors and judges generally try to prohibit politically motivated testimony.

The trial trainings heavily emphasized good communication between defendants and attorneys. They also explained that defendants could represent themselves *in propria persona*, otherwise known as *pro per* or *pro se*. The *pro se* defense was covered in the trainings mainly because of its use in staging politically charged trials. This owed to the greater opportunity for *pro se* defendants to talk, to slow down trials for judges to properly instruct defendants, to make opening and closing statements oneself, and to gain greater jury sympathy by calling attention to the law's unjust elitism. The court typically gives *pro se* defendants the benefit of the doubt when it comes to technicalities like local rules of procedure. And, if a *pro se* defendant puts herself on the stand, she is uniquely poised to make statements that would be inadmissible if expressed by a criminal defense attorney.[17] The disadvantages of a *pro se* defense, according to the trial trainings, included the alienating and foreign aspect of legal proceedings, the potential lack of rapport between judge and defendant, and the possibility of being taken less seriously by the court.

Once RNC defendants determined that they wanted political trials, they were encouraged to push their attorneys in that direction. A couple of strategic political defenses were discussed: necessity defense and *de minimis* defense. The necessity defense can be used to describe how the "criminal" act (civil disobedience, in the case of most RNC defendants) was necessary to prevent a greater harm. This theoretically allowed the defense to include information about why activists took to the streets on August 1. The *de minimis* defense has been used when the alleged crime is so trivial (each civil disobedience act inconvenienced a small number of people for a limited amount of time) as to not warrant the court's time or money. These defenses and others can be used to compel jury nullification, whereby jurors vote their conscience and acquit despite a possible crime having been committed. Although jury nullification is not a goal commonly sought by criminal defense attorneys, it is often a desired outcome in political trials. It is not a crime for a juror to ignore the court's instructions by voting their conscience, and they cannot be punished for it.[18] But because jury nullification tends to disregard judicial instructions and can result in the acquittal of people the court considers guilty, it's strongly discouraged by the criminal justice system.

Because character witnesses were an important option for defendants, they were covered independently in the trial trainings. Character witnesses are typically used at the end of a trial to make statements about a defendant's reputation in the "community" and can often influence a judge's ruling. But since some RNC defendants had greater access than others to witnesses perceived to be favorable by the court (i.e., clergy, professors, etc.), there was a potential for unequal treatment and thus greater harm for defendants without such access. The trainers suggested that co-defendants discuss the issue before trial and reach consensus on whether to use character witnesses and, if so, how. Character witnesses do not have to rely on the court's standard of ethics and values and, as such, defendants were encouraged to be creative about how they used them. If defendants decided to put character witnesses on the stand, it was explained that the prosecutor then had the right to cross-examine them and ask questions about a defendant's past, including political activity and criminal history. Letters from character witnesses were not admissible at trial, but could be used to achieve a lighter sentence after conviction.

The final focus of the trial trainings was on court support, courtroom conduct, and the attire of defendants and supporters. Court support was strongly encouraged to show that the world was watching by packing the courtroom with supporters, friends, and family, and by ensuring that journalists reported on the cases. Having supporters in the courtroom also enabled RNC defendants to take advantage of coordinated attire or actions that send a visual message. This was tricky since there could never be certainty as to whether the attire or antics would anger the judge or alienate the jury rather than appeal to their sympathies. It was important for defendants to understand that the conduct of supporters could help or hinder their goals, and could also affect the cases of their co-defendants.

The initial trial training was so successful that a second one was held in New York on November 15. By this time, a number of trials and pretrial appearances had occurred, giving R2K Legal solid experience in the courtroom. The collective had a better feel for the judges hearing RNC-related cases and what could be expected from them. This knowledge helped to guide the remaining defendants as their goals and options came into better focus.

Beyond the goal of equal treatment, the legal goals of activists varied considerably. For some, the goal was simply to get acquitted. For others, it was to discredit the police and seek accountability. For most, it was to advance the issues that brought them to the streets in the first place. The training acknowledged that a defendant's goals need not exist in isolation and that the differing goals of defendants could still be compatible. The collective goal of using misdemeanor trials to pursue equal treatment for those with high-level charges remained a priority, but it was still unclear what impact misdemeanor trials would have on the rest of the cases.

Court Solidarity Wins the Day

What RNC arrestees and their supporters were unable to achieve through jail solidarity was eventually achieved through court solidarity. That it took years and an unbelievable amount of work is a testament not only to the strength of solidarity and the perseverance of countless activists but also to the effect it had on movements for social change. "They've taken 400 people and put them through hell," said RNC defendant Alex Rae of the city's prosecutions.[19] Calling the experience "a real wake-up call," he still had no regrets. For Rae and many others, the Philadelphia story helped illustrate the powerful impact that solidarity can have on a movement. According to the March 2001 issue of *the defenestrator*, "Solidarity for defendants has been strong, unlike anarchists living in the States have seen in years."[20] Unfortunately, the Philadelphia experience also diminished the resolve to use the collective leverage of solidarity to resist the state and achieve common goals at subsequent protests.

CHAPTER 7:
POLITICAL TRIALS AND EARLY VICTORIES

Pretrial Dismissals

BEFORE THE FIRST RNC TRIAL EVEN TOOK PLACE, R2K LEGAL HAD already achieved several important victories. As pretrial hearings occurred in the felony cases, charges were routinely dismissed or remanded (reduced) to misdemeanors.[1] In a pretrial hearing on October 12, Philadelphia Common Pleas Court Judge Pamela J. Dembe threw out dozens of charges—including felonies—against three young men accused of assaulting police officers including Police Commissioner John Timoney.[2] By October 20, the number of RNC protesters with felony charges had been reduced through pretrial hearings from forty-three to twenty-five.[3]

As the RNC trials approached, numerous R2K Legal attorneys filed several sweeping "omnibus" motions in the cases of many misdemeanor defendants.[4] Some of the motions were aimed at obtaining further evidence and others were aimed at having charges dismissed in advance of trial. The Defender Association of Philadelphia's motion for a bill of particulars argued that "the discovery is substantially incomplete and fails to provide with sufficient specificity, information regarding the circumstances of arrest and the allegations against" the defendant. Because of "incomplete" and "inadequate" evidence supplied by the city to back up its criminal allegations, the defense also demanded a large amount of undisclosed documentation with a motion for discovery. The puppet warehouse search warrant affidavit revealed the use of infiltrators and surveillance but provided little detail about those operations or who was involved. The motion to disclose the identity of undercover informants was aimed at bringing this information to the surface so that it could be used in the criminal cases. Some of the motions to dismiss argued against certain charges, such as resisting arrest, reckless endangerment, and possession of an instrument of crime (PIC). The motion to dismiss the PIC charge argued that defendants were in "possession of non-criminal instruments, e.g., chicken wire, pvc pipe, concrete, rope, chain or even a cell phone," and, "To the extent that the PIC statute might encompass such common household items, [it] is unconstitutionally overbroad and prosecution under such a statute would be a denial of due process under the Pennsylvania and United States Constitutions." Other motions to dismiss argued more broadly for the dismissal of entire cases, such as the motion to dismiss based on outrageous police misconduct and selective prosecution. The legal team called the police infiltration and reports of provocation "outrageous" and argued that by "encouraging or facilitating lawless behavior, such actions by police agents would violate due process and taint the entire prosecution."

Some of the motions were politically motivated and strategic, but most were similar to motions routinely filed in criminal defense cases. Nevertheless, as routine as most of the motions were to a normal legal defense strategy, the effort to dismiss cases was controversial and not really consistent with the court solidarity strategy adopted by the defendants. In fact, the mass filing of motions caused a stir among defendants who wanted their cases to remain active to clog the courts. As it happened, R2K Legal did not really expect the motions to be granted. The legal team felt that, by filing them, the defense was able to act "offensively" and, in doing so, attract public attention to the excessive nature of the charges. Meanwhile, dismissal of some of a defendant's charges would still enable that defendant to go to trial on their remaining charges, and thereby continue their solidarity effort.[5] After discussing the matter at length, defendants reached consensus on filing the motions, which indeed helped to politicize the cases.

As expected, the various judges hearing RNC-related cases denied almost all the motions. Still, they did compel the city and other government agencies to turn over valuable information. On October 13, one judge gave the district attorney's office seventy-two hours to comply with an order to turn over hundreds of hours of police video footage.[6] On October 19, another judge ordered the district attorney to provide the public defender's office forty-two separate police videos—forty-one local and state police tapes, and one FBI tape—filmed on August 1.[7] Notably, although the discovery-related documents received by the defense repeatedly referenced the involvement of numerous federal agencies—including ATF, FBI, Secret Service, and state police—only one FBI tape was turned over, thus indicating how reticent the federal government was to reveal its surveillance and infiltration programs.

The court also ordered the disclosure of information on infiltrators and undercover police, such as their identity and any reports or communication they generated. Eventually, the identities of the four state troopers who infiltrated the puppet warehouse—Harry Keffer III, Joseph Thompson, George Garris, and Thomas Bachman—were publicly revealed.[8] Court-ordered interviews with the four troopers conducted on October 11 by the city's Homicide Division were shallow and provided little meaningful evidence for either the defense or the prosecution. Nevertheless, the troopers' identities and the subsequent testimony provided in the puppet warehouse cases would become fodder for the media and create considerable controversy.

On October 30, Municipal Court Judge James M. DeLeon dismissed all of the charges against five School of the Americas (SOA) Watch activists.[9] In a rare published ruling, the judge granted one of the only pretrial motions to dismiss filed by R2K Legal attorneys working with the public defender's office. The defense motion had argued that the city selectively arrested and prosecuted SOA Watch activists based on their political beliefs and not on their actions. Staged on the street in front of City Hall, the July 31 SOA Watch "die-in" was contrasted with another nonpermitted rally of hundreds of people in South Philadelphia calling for the immediate execution of Mumia Abu-Jamal. The rally in South Philadelphia blocked several streets for at least three hours, but because the Fraternal Order of Police (FOP) supported the demonstration no arrests were made.

The Philadelphia judiciary thus found itself reiterating leftist dissident messages in a published criminal court opinion. "The protest consisted of defendant's [sic] lying on the ground, circled in white chalk, posing as corpses strewn with makeshift blood and placards stating the names of various Central and south American countries adorning their bodies," read Judge DeLeon's decision.[10] "When the defendants [refused to move], they were arrested" and "charged with a variety of misdemeanor offenses, including obstructing a highway and conspiracy to obstruct a highway, resisting arrest, obstructing justice and disorderly conduct."

Ultimately, Judge DeLeon saw no difference between the SOA Watch protest and the anti-Mumia demonstration in South Philly or the routine demonstrations held by local Philadelphia unions. AFSCME District Council 47 president Thomas Paine Cronin testified during the motions hearing that his local had held numerous spontaneous nonpermitted rallies and protests that obstructed traffic near City Hall, which didn't result in arrests. Judge DeLeon dismissed the case based on his finding that the defendants "met both prongs of the selective prosecution doctrine analysis," which states that "(1) others who are similarly situated to the defendant are not generally prosecuted for similar conduct; and (2) the defendant has been intentionally and purposefully singled out for prosecution for an invidious reason." No other RNC-related cases were dismissed on the similar basis of selective prosecution, yet the city's blatant political favoritism and double standards had been exposed.

Misdemeanor Trials Begin

The pretrial dismissals were having a significant impact on the legitimacy of the charges levied against protesters. That credibility was further undermined when the RNC misdemeanor trials, which began on October 25, resulted in more dismissals and acquittals.[11] Within a week, ten misdemeanor trials had occurred. Two cases were dismissed at trial after the arresting officers failed to appear. The prosecution dismissed three cases after police were unable to positively identify the defendants (one of whom was Christopher White of West Philadelphia, charged with no less than ten misdemeanors). Only two trials resulted in conviction and both defendants immediately appealed the ruling. Activists, supporters, and family members packed the courtrooms wearing white flowers to show solidarity. The defendants who were found guilty made eloquent political statements to the court before they were sentenced. One stated that he stood in solidarity with felony defendants and that he and others would continue to fight for the freedom of Mumia Abu-Jamal and an end to the prison industrial complex.

By early November, police failures to properly identify defendants had become a pattern. In a November 7 trial involving activists arrested while blockading the intersection of 12th and Arch Streets, several bike patrol cops testified.[12] Their testimonies were weak and contradictory. One officer identified a defendant in the courtroom as the person he arrested, only to be shown a Polaroid in which the person he was arresting was clearly not the defendant on trial. Notably, some of the solidarity tactics used in jail made positive identification difficult for the prosecution. According to R2K Legal, one of the prosecutors complained that "because we did not give our names and made their job so difficult, they were confused and making mistakes and having generally a hard time with our cases."

The next day, members of the Student Liberation Action Movement (SLAM) were tried. Patches and ties emblazoned with the letters "R-E-S-I-S-T" were made beforehand so that defendants and their supporters could wear them to court.[13] Minutes before the trial, the prosecution withdrew the cases of two defendants for lack of evidence. While on the stand, another defendant skillfully incorporated political issues into his testimony. The attorneys also wove politics into the trial and argued that the defendants were being selectively prosecuted because of their message. Three defendants were found guilty of summary offenses, but all of them appealed and ultimately overturned their convictions.

The high proportion of cases thrown out before or at trial did not come as a surprise to activists. It spoke to the city's failure to provide evidence to justify its fervent prosecutions. The disparity between convictions and dismissals or acquittals grew with each passing week. Despite an embarrassing prosecutorial record, the city refused to negotiate with R2K Legal for a reasonable settlement on the remaining cases. Instead, the district attorney began using homicide attorneys to try the RNC misdemeanor cases.[14] This strategy had little effect on the outcome of the trials, which continued to go badly for the city. In the face of failure, the city's prosecutorial persistence and the vast outlay of public funds became a source of great irritation for defendants, their supporters, and eventually much of the public.[15]

The first "high profile" trials were on November 14 against Ruckus Society director John Sellers (accused of being a protest "ringleader," charged with fourteen misdemeanors) and Terrence McGuckin (also singled out as a "ringleader," charged with seven misdemeanors). At Sellers's bail hearing, Assistant District Attorney Cynthia Martelli had referred ominously to a "massive dossier" that federal and local authorities had built against him.[16] Yet, despite this alleged dossier, the number of charges, the outrageous bail, and the serious accusations, the city meekly withdrew all of Sellers's charges on the first day of trial. That should have been embarrassing enough, but police records later revealed that an officer videotaping Sellers said he never saw him "direct or instruct anyone." Nonchalantly and without apology, district attorney spokesperson Cathie Abookire commented that "after we reviewed the case, interviewed people and looked at many, many hours of videotape, the evidence was not there" to prosecute, "so we withdrew the charges."[17]

The McGuckin case was tried by Municipal Court Judge Lydia Y. Kirkland and was based mainly on evidence from key prosecution witness Angelo Parisi, a Washington, DC, police detective who apparently followed McGuckin around filming him on August 1. Parisi tried to convince Judge Kirkland that McGuckin, who was arrested on August 2 by about twelve cops (including Deputy Police Commissioner Robert Mitchell), had led groups of people around Center City the previous day and directed them to blockade certain intersections.[18] The story, however, lacked sufficient evidence and wasn't plausible enough to persuade Kirkland. The judge acquitted McGuckin of all but two misdemeanor charges of disorderly conduct and obstructing the highway, which were later thrown out on appeal.

In a press conference organized by R2K Legal to follow that day's trials,[19] Sellers asserted that "activists were given fraudulent charges not for the tactics that they employed, but for the message that they brought to the street."[20] Attempting to shed light on the state's true motivations, Sellers further remarked, "Questioning the institutional racism of the US justice system is more of a threat than non-violently blocking a street." McGuckin's attorney, UPenn law professor David Rudovsky, called the acquittal "a damning indictment of the Police Department and of the District Attorney's Office."[21] Commenting on his client's "unprecedented" bail, Rudovsky told the *Washington Post* that "you don't get that for murder in this city" and that "it was pure preventive detention for political purposes."[22] The *Boston Phoenix* aptly noted that Sellers's bail was "$500,000 more than the bail recently set for Nathaniel Bar-Jonah," a man accused at the time of cannibalizing a ten-year-old boy.[23] "That they would lock him up on $1 million bail, and then come to court without any evidence, tells me that the police and DA have gone way overboard," said Sellers's attorney Larry Krasner to the *Phoenix*. Krasner called the case against Sellers so weak that police resorted to "making stuff up."

In response, the two Philadelphia dailies published editorials condemning the arrests and failed prosecutions.[24] Referring to Sellers, the *Philadelphia Inquirer* opined, "It's a rare feat to go from the status of Public Enemy No. 1—mug shot posted on the Police Department Web site—to someone who doesn't even face jaywalking charges." After noting that Sellers's arrest took on "all the hallmarks of preventive detention," the *Inquirer* called for a "thorough post-mortem" and inquiry by the city's Police Advisory Commission.

Additional Infiltration Revealed

Around the same time, R2K Legal was able to exploit new, previously undisclosed, and controversial information. Unexpectedly, during a pre-trial hearing in a case against a group of defendants charged with obstructing an on-ramp to the I-676 Vine Street Expressway, the prosecution's witness accidentally revealed that additional infiltrators had been used by the Pennsylvania State Police (PSP).[25] Apparently, while reviewing surveillance video of the arrests in preparation for trial, a Philadelphia police officer pointed out four undercover state troopers being arrested along with the protesters. Hundreds of protesters had gathered to block the freeway on-ramp and eventually forty-eight were arrested, including the four troopers who had linked arms with others to obstruct traffic.[26] Assistant District Attorney Trevan Borum downplayed the issue and flippantly said police "decided to join along rather than blow their cover."[27]

The disclosure of additional undercover agents was a significant revelation, since the police and prosecution had so far only admitted to the use of four infiltrators at the puppet warehouse. The failure by prosecutors to come clean about the level and type of infiltration delayed the trials as more information was sought and further eroded the city's credibility. Serious questions remained about whether troopers were used by local police to sidestep a directive that restricted the infiltration of political groups. In early September 2000, after the puppet warehouse search warrant was unsealed and the identities of four undercover state troopers were revealed, police made a series of contradictory statements. Initially, in what appeared to be an effort to shield local police from any liability around infiltration, the PSP said, "We did not give the Philadelphia Police Department advance notice of our specific intelligence operations."[28] But given Philadelphia Police Commissioner Timoney's "prime responsibility" for the "control and coordination of [multiple] law enforcement groups,"[29] the PSP later contradicted itself by admitting that "we told [the Philadelphia Police Department] in advance that we would be infiltrating certain groups."[30]

In addition to the four officers arrested while engaged in civil disobedience at the on-ramp to the Vine Street Expressway, the PSP and prosecutors admitted to the arrest of another two infiltrators elsewhere in the city, bringing the total number of known infiltrators to ten.[31] According to a PSP spokesperson interviewed by the *Philadelphia Inquirer*, the other two arrested undercover officers were engaged in "passive resistance-type" demonstrations, though he would not reveal where. According to prosecutors, the six arrested infiltrators were quickly released once police realized who they were. Defense attorneys demanded to know the identity of the additional infiltrators so that they could be questioned. "It's outrageous that only now, this late in the game, and with trials under way, we are getting new facts on the extent of infiltration," said public defender Shawn Nolan—"especially in light of Police Commissioner John Timoney's unequivocal public denial that this was happening."[32] According to R2K Legal, the criminal cases of nearly half the RNC defendants going to trial were affected by police infiltration. Also concerned by this revelation, Judge DeLeon asked PSP legal counsel Joanna Reynolds, "How far were they to go?" and "What limits were there?" Then, under a "Rule to Show Cause" for withholding evidence, DeLeon issued what the *Philadelphia Inquirer* called "a sweeping order" for information on the state's undercover operations.[33]

The November 8 order in *Re: Walter Stanezack* (one of the puppet warehouse defendants) forced the PSP to turn over "Any and all written communication including memorandum and documents & notebooks, generated by the PA police," in connection with the puppet warehouse operation.[34] The court also demanded police orders "given to confidential agents and officers of PA State Police regarding scope and limits of their undercover activities." And, because of the incredible, unsubstantiated "Red Scare" accusations made in the puppet warehouse affidavit, Judge DeLeon ordered the PSP to produce copies of "all information from public and non-public domain" used by state police in its preparation. According to the *Philadelphia Inquirer*, Reynolds was "worried that some of the disclosure might reveal police infiltration methods or names of informants." Nevertheless, she said the agency would comply with his order.[35]

The PSP got off virtually scot-free. Apart from meager photographic and videotape documentation of the outside of the puppet warehouse, the only information the state police ever provided was a three-page memorandum issued on November 13 by PSP Organized Crime Commander Lt. George L. Bivens to the PSP Office of Chief Counsel on the "Orders/Directions Given to Undercover Intelligence Officers—Republican National Convention."[36] R2K Legal attorney and public defender Bradley Bridge accused the PSP of manufacturing evidence by writing "a report four months afterwards to justify what happened."[37] The other problem was that the PSP response to the order was superficial and entirely inadequate, especially given how many cases were impacted by infiltration and the serious nature of the charges. Lt. Bivens stated in his memo that he had searched but apparently couldn't find, nor did he recall, "any specific written orders given to undercover officers regarding the methods they were to employ, or limitations placed on their ability to gather criminal intelligence." According to Bivens, undercover officers were only provided with "verbal direction." Without writing any of it down, "Supervisors would provide UC (undercover) officers with initial assignments" and the "UC officers would then carry out their assignments while maintaining contact with supervisors." Despite "constant interaction between undercover officers and supervisors," the PSP wanted the court to believe that no written documentation existed.

Lt. Bivens feigned helpfulness by providing the court with the basic outline of a preassignment briefing for undercover officers on PSP responsibilities during the convention. Topping the list was "Protection of our Governor, Lt. Governor, visiting Governors, and various dignitaries." Second, and far less credible, was "Protection of the citizens of Philadelphia . . . from harm resulting from violent protests." That Bivens also claimed the PSP was responsible for "Protection of the rights of protesters lawfully exercising their First Amendment rights" was a particular affront to the activists currently defending themselves in court. The Bivens memo went on to paint a sensational pretext for infiltration; how the PSP was "monitoring" groups it "had reason to believe may be promoting an agenda of unlawful activities," and "groups advocating harm to police officers . . . assaulting dignitaries or attendees at the convention."

A November 21 motions hearing before Judge DeLeon focused on the Bivens memo and various issues concerned with infiltrators and communication between the PSP and the Philadelphia Police Department (PPD). The hearing addressed several RNC-related cases being heard by DeLeon. Attorney Bradley Bridge argued strenuously that "we're entitled . . . to know who [the infiltrators] were."[38] They're eyewitnesses, noted Bridge. In the context of the motion to dismiss based on "outrageous police misconduct" then before the court, Bridge further argued that "what these specific police officers did and what it was they said is incredibly relevant." Nevertheless, the PSP successfully dodged orders to divulge this information and the names of the additional PSP infiltrators were never disclosed. Judge DeLeon was ultimately persuaded by the prosecution's argument that the undercover officers would be put at risk if their identities were revealed.

The other main issue at the motions hearing was communication between the PSP and the PPD. According to the Bivens memo, the PSP "Task Force" mission included "Assist[ing] the Philadelphia Police Department, if necessary, in the event of civil disturbance." But neither the PSP nor the PPD turned over any communication between the two departments to the defense. "If there's an undercover operation involving state police, there should have been contact [with] the Philadelphia Police Department," argued Bridge. Furthermore, the PSP information was used by the PPD to develop the search warrant affidavit to raid the warehouse, so they had to be communicating to some extent. But Bridge complained to the court, "We've been given none of that."

Appearing to understand the need for this information, Judge DeLeon ordered the city police to turn over any communication it received from the PSP. Yet the city managed to dodge that bullet too. In fact, because so much attention was put on state trooper infiltration, the city's complicity and culpability in benefiting from that "intelligence" was never fully addressed. But before the issue could be swept completely under the rug, R2K Legal worked to draw attention to the conspiratorial nature of the infiltration. In a press release issued by the collective, Bridge asked, "What have the State Police taught us, other than that the government fears the messages of its citizens and that it will go to great lengths to infiltrate and then arrest members of peaceful groups?"[39] According to R2K Legal member and RNC defendant Bill Beckler, "Various law enforcement agencies can continue to deny working in collaboration with each other, but at the end of the day, we were still heavily infiltrated in a city that is prohibited from engaging in such practices."

Putting on a *Pro Se* Defense

The largest RNC-related trial took place on November 27 against forty-two defendants arrested during a demonstration at Broad and Spruce Streets. The defendants were being tried for their alleged part in obstructing one of the main traffic arteries from Center City to the convention site a few miles away. Activists blocked the transport of Republican delegates by playing soccer and engaging in street theater in the middle of the huge intersection. It was a lively and politicized trial, with three defendants representing themselves *pro se*.[40] As they made impassioned statements about the right to free speech and standing in solidarity with RNC felony defendants, the other defendants stood behind them with fists raised, displaying political messages on their bodies in defiance of court rules.

Meanwhile, an overly confident district attorney failed to offer sufficient evidence to try the cases and, after the prosecution rested, the defense moved to dismiss. Before granting the motion to dismiss charges against thirty-eight of the defendants, Municipal Court Judge James DeLeon told prosecutors, "You're going to have to have somebody come in here and testify that somebody did something wrong."[41] Initially, the three *pro se* defendants had planned not to join the motion to dismiss so that they could proceed to trial and stand in solidarity with the felony defendants. But as the courtroom proceedings played out, only one of the *pro se* defendants, Peter Cantrell, refused to go along with the motion.[42] This caused quite a stir in the courtroom. In a desperate attempt to maintain control, Judge DeLeon fired Cantrell as his own legal counsel and appointed his back-up attorney to take over. But Cantrell then instructed his lawyer not to move for dismissal. Now fairly frustrated, Judge DeLeon pleaded with the prosecution to just drop the charges against Cantrell so he could move on.

A selective prosecution motion was filed on behalf of the remaining defendants, but was denied on the basis that the activists "had no message" despite overwhelming evidence and testimony to the contrary. One of the activists still being tried, Ethan "Zeke" Spier, was a *pro se* defendant and an active member of the R2K Legal Collective. At trial, Spier argued that the charge of obstructing a highway was not an "unreasonable inconvenience" in this situation.[43] According to Spier, the First Amendment protected their actions. "It is not unreasonable for people to have to go a little out of their way to preserve the ability of citizens to speak out in the streets," Spier continued. Of the four that proceeded to trial, one was dismissed for lack of proper identification, one was found guilty of a summary offense, and two (including Spier) were found guilty of misdemeanors. All three appealed and later had their convictions overturned.

The Three-Day Motions Hearing

Between November 28 and 30, Municipal Court Judge James DeLeon heard from what the *Philadelphia City Paper* called a "small army of defense attorneys"[44] (public defenders, private attorneys, law professors, and *pro se* defendants, all working with the R2K Legal Collective) as they squared off against two assistant district attorneys for what was to be the longest and most exhaustive motions hearing connected to the RNC pros-ecutions. The hearing affected the cases of forty-six defendants arrested in the puppet warehouse and the van. Five puppet warehouse defendants who felt that seeking pretrial dismissals might jeopardize court solidarity chose not to join the defense motions and instead invoked their right to a trial.[45]

The political nature of the motions to dismiss allowed the RNC defendants to adopt offensive postures. Prior restraint motions indi-cated the police did not have probable cause to arrest everyone in the warehouse, since their intent was simply to engage in First Amendment activity. Motions to dismiss based on outrageous police misconduct were aimed at revealing the politically motivated nature of the infiltration, as well as possible police involvement in illegal activity. According to the motions to dismiss based on destruction of exculpatory evidence, police not only destroyed the protesters' property, but also unlawfully destroyed First Amendment material like signs, banners, leaflets, and puppets. Even the statutory challenge to the vague and overreaching nature of "posses-sion of an instrument of crime" (PIC), a charge sustained by most of the puppet warehouse defendants, was politically based. The defense took the opportunity to argue that a lockbox—PVC pipe often used by pro-testers to lock themselves together in blockades—is not necessarily a tool for committing crimes and can bring attention to political speech and even de-escalate conflict by focusing attention on an inanimate object. During the three-day hearing, the court heard testimony from numerous witnesses. At times, there were as many as four defendants representing themselves *pro se* and thus animating what would otherwise have been a boring set of hearings.

In deciding whether to grant the motions, the court heard from the head of intelligence for the state police, four state troopers involved in the infiltration operation, counsel for the Philadelphia Police Department, and the deputy commissioner for the city's Department of Licenses & Inspection (L&I). Most of the hearing focused on trying to show how the level and type of infiltration amounted to "outrageous police misconduct," and how the destruction of evidence by L&I was not just unconstitutional but ultimately orchestrated by the police.

The motions hearing began the morning of Tuesday, November 28, with the prosecution trying to introduce as evidence a videotaped TV news segment of the Seattle WTO protests. The city asserted that the tape was one of the things the state police considered when they made the decision to infiltrate. But besides the inaccurate and sensationalized representation of the events in Seattle, those protests were totally irrelevant to the cases being litigated. Trying to rationalize this introduction of irrelevant information, Judge DeLeon claimed that showing the tape wouldn't prejudice the puppet warehouse defendants.

State Police Intelligence Chief Testifies about Infiltration

Lieutenant George Bivens took the stand on Wednesday morning and testified that he "had been assigned . . . to oversee intelligence operations for the state police."[46] Bivens called the Seattle WTO protests "an eye opener" that supposedly caused him and others to "look into some of these groups" and travel to Washington, DC, to "witness what occurred down there firsthand." R2K Legal attorney David Rudovsky countered that "until the Commonwealth ties any of these defendants as having been in Seattle, what's the connection if there were lockboxes or not?" Rudovsky continued his argument:

> If somebody had a gun in Seattle, so what? If somebody had a baseball bat in Seattle, so what? . . . What's the relevance? Can we [argue] outrageous police misconduct [in] that the police beat up a Mr. Jones in July in this city? That's not relevant. Do police do that? Sure they do it. It's no connection to this case. . . . In the same way what happened in Seattle what may have happened in Birmingham, Alabama 35 years ago, what happened in Mississippi, what happened in Washington is irrelevant unless they can tie any particular person or group that they're investigating to those activities. Without it, it is not only not relevant, but of course it's prejudicial.

Bivens was also grilled by the defense about the presence of another state trooper who was part of the infiltration operation. The previous day, Trooper Harry Keffer testified that he saw Trooper William Donohue working security outside the warehouse.[47] Bivens admitted to R2K Legal attorney and public defender Meg Flores that he knew Donohue—now the eleventh known infiltrator—was there at the warehouse. "So, when the judge had asked you were there any other undercover informants aside from the four," Flores questioned Bivens, "you lied to the judge?" At this point, the prosecution's objection was sustained, but the judge was clearly unhappy. "If there's a guy that infiltrated himself into such a condition that he ended up being security for the people that you were going after anyway," declared Judge DeLeon, "I mean it seems like you should of [sic] let me know that." Bivens sidestepped the judge's admonition by claiming Donohue was just "passing through" and that his real assignment was to "interact with a group of anarchists" at the A-Space. Flustered, DeLeon asked Bivens "Out of the cases that are left . . . ready to go to trial . . . don't we need to know whether or not there was [sic] any undercover state troopers in those groups? I mean isn't that a legitimate question to ask?" Flores followed up by asking Bivens if there were any more infiltrators the defense should know about, but the question went unanswered.

Bivens was then pressed on the lack of documented communication between the state police, the Philadelphia Police Department, and other law enforcement agencies. Bivens denied keeping any surveillance logs and answered "no" when asked by R2K Legal attorney Paul Hetznecker whether records existed for "anything done by the troopers . . . during the time of surveillance that kept . . . you and others from the state police abreast of what was going on."[48] Later that afternoon, Rudovsky summarized the situation for the court. "We've been told by the city . . . there was literally no communication" with the state police and "the city didn't even know that there would be undercover officers in the warehouse."[49] Rudovsky underscored the claim that the Philadelphia police didn't know details about the infiltration until the warrant was filed. The defense should be able to test "the credibility of that assertion," argued Rudovsky, but Bivens continued to deny anything other than superficial and infrequent verbal communication between him and his officers. Hetznecker then picked up where Rudovsky left off and asked Bivens point blank whether he was "aware during the coordination of this operation that . . . the Philadelphia Police Department was prohibited by an injunction from infiltrating protest organizations in Philadelphia?" An objection was sustained and the question went unanswered.

Bivens was also unapologetically vague about how his "research" on activists and political groups—including the Maldon Report with its Red Scare hysteria—made its way into the hands of the Philadelphia Police Department and onto the search warrant affidavit. "Did you supply the information to the Philadelphia police?" asked Hetznecker. "I did not personally supply it, but I did direct that it be supplied," Bivens obstinately replied. Though he admitted to having "discussions with the Philadelphia police" about the possibility of a raid on the warehouse, Bivens denied directing them to conduct a search. "I had no input on what would be done at 4100 Haverford (the puppet warehouse)," he said. "We provided that information at the request of the police department."

Testimony about the destruction of evidence began on Tuesday and took up most of Wednesday morning as the court heard from the deputy commissioner of L&I, who was present when puppets, political literature, and personal property seized from the warehouse were put in a trash compacter and destroyed. "We [are] taking the position that both the infiltration and then the seizure of any evidence that resulted from that infiltration is barred by the 1st and 4th amendment," argued Rudovsky.[50] "It was illegal for the police to send in undercover agents without authority, without search warrant and without probable cause."

> The Supreme Court of United States has said because of the threat to 1st amendment freedoms that might result from the seizure of raw materials, which is exactly what we are alleging here, not only do you need a search warrant of probable cause before you go into [sic] seize, but there has to be an adversary hearing among the parties before the seizure can take place so the judge can determine in the first place what can be seized and what can't be seized.

Before L&I testified, legal counsel for the police department Karen Simmons was called to appear. The defense attempted to elicit a connection between the actions of the police and L&I, but Simmons told the court that the police "did not confiscate any evidence from the warehouse and no evidence was destroyed by the police department." Attempting to undermine the city's argument that the police had nothing to do with the destruction of property, R2K Legal attorney and public defender Shawn Nolan pointed out that "the police were there (at the scene of the property destruction) enough to arrest our two clients who were trying to guard that evidence." Two of the defendants in court that day had been arrested for lying down in the road to block the removal of property. Judge DeLeon, wanting to cut through the morass of obfuscation, demanded to know from the city "under what authority did L&I come in there and destroy that property and why." The question would go unanswered throughout the hearing.

L&I Testifies

L&I Deputy Commissioner Dominic Verdi began his testimony Wednesday by explaining his involvement in the destruction of property.[51] Verdi said that he was directed by the Fire Department "to some flammable liquids," consisting of "gasoline cans and propane tanks," which were removed from the warehouse by a private company called Clean Venture. It was apparently these "flammable liquids" that gave L&I cause to destroy puppets, banners, posters, political literature, and a significant amount of personal property belonging to both protesters and warehouse owner Michael Graves. In the process, L&I also declared the building to be unsafe due to electrical violations like improperly installed lighting fixtures and missing cover plates.

R2K Legal attorney and public defender Karl Baker started direct examination by asking if it was common practice to destroy property in such a manner. "If there was a violation at the Forrest Theater and it was necessary for you to close that property, would you remove from that building all of the material, including props and costumes, and . . . cart them off in sanitation trucks?" Verdi responded tersely, "If they posed a threat to public safety and if they were piled in a heap next to flammables, yes, we would remove them." Judge DeLeon interjected by drawing an analogy for Verdi, "If you're at a property that you're getting ready to basically condemn and the owner is there and they're asking for permission to take their property out, would you allow them to do so?" Verdi responded, "Yes, if the owner of the property was there." Graves, of course, was in jail at the time with the rest of the people arrested at the warehouse. DeLeon then distinguished between real estate and the property or goods contained within. "If the owner of the real estate was not the owner of the goods but the owner of the goods was there to receive their goods," posed DeLeon, "would that person be allowed to take their goods out of the property?" "In some cases," Verdi replied, but followed by stating he could not just give property to people off the street. "I have no way of knowing if that is in fact their property." Yet if the material was no longer an apparent threat, and destined to be destroyed anyway, why not give it to people off the street? In fact, Judge DeLeon wondered aloud, "why not call a flat truck so that the stuff could be dumped on top for any owner to come at a later time to recoupe [sic]?"

The defense then showed a videotape of the scene at the warehouse on August 2, which included L&I, Philly police, and a group of angry protesters. The tape was obtained from a California TV station, whose reporters had filmed the destruction of puppets and police preventing protesters from approaching the building. Verdi featured prominently in the video. Although he initially denied that there were people protesting the destruction of their property, he later admitted to "people protesting against, or yelling at us for taking items or throwing them in the trash." When Baker asked if Verdi recalled "the three demonstrators who actually laid down in front of the garbage truck . . . and refused to get up," he said yes but apparently had no idea why they were there. Two of those protesters were tried that day before Judge DeLeon. Although both had the same defense, one was acquitted and the other was found guilty and given a $100 fine. The convicted activist immediately appealed and was eventually acquitted as well.

Referring to the video, Baker asked Verdi if the person who he was ordering behind the police line was protesting. "What do you mean by protesting?" he flippantly replied. Paradoxically, Verdi had the expectation that those with property interests would approach him despite the fact that he was ordering them to get back. Pointing again to the video footage, Baker asked Verdi "What was being loaded into the back of that garbage truck?" To which he responded, "Trash." Efforts by multiple R2K Legal attorneys to get Verdi to admit he was destroying First Amendment material helped politicize the proceedings; however, they failed to deter Verdi from his narrow responses. Asked to review photographs of a giant pig's head and skeletons, Verdi feigned ignorance. At one point, Hetznecker called Verdi a "hostile witness" and later asked him if "the skeletons, posters or placards that you viewed both on the video tape and photographs" could have been "part of . . . a demonstration?" But Verdi just responded sarcastically that "it could have been left over from Halloween for all I know."

Lightening the mood somewhat, *pro se* defendant Alexis Baden-Meyer asked Verdi if he recalled seeing a set of shelves in the warehouse, which held "our backpacks and our shoes," as well as other items such as "cameras and, you know, your plane tickets, your wallet." Before Verdi could answer, Assistant DA Joseph Labar objected, explaining that Baden-Meyer had the option to pursue civil remedies. In an attempt to underscore the absurdity of destroying art and personal property on the pretext that it was flammable, Baden-Meyer blurted out, "Are leather high-heels flammable?" DeLeon, however, struck the question, prompting a response from R2K Legal attorney Larry Krasner. "If in fact they were basically destroying everything that belonged to the protesters regardless of whether it was flammable," argued Krasner, "then that's a credibility determination for the court to make as to whether or not this gentleman has testified truthfully about the motivation for having destroyed various puppets and things of that sort." Tiring of this line of questioning, Labar noted that "the motion goes to the destruction of physical evidence, not fashion items." The issue actually pertained to the veracity of the witness, argued Krasner, "as to whether or not his explanation matches what they really did."

"The Commonwealth is taking the position that L&I acted on its own independent of the police," Hetznecker argued to the court. "And I think I have a right to establish through cross-examination that they were not acting alone, that they were acting in conjunction with one another." Honing in on the interaction between L&I and the police, Hetznecker got Verdi to admit that L&I consultations between the two departments did occur, so as not to violate the parameters of the search warrant. Verdi told the court that local police had the final say about which articles should be removed or destroyed, but he never recollected which supervising police officer at the scene instructed him on August 2 to destroy certain property. Still, Hetznecker was able to point out that the flammable material had been taken away long before the property was destroyed, that the property no longer posed a hazardous risk, and that police sorted through the property before "handing it over" to L&I for destruction. As long as the city could maintain the suspension of disbelief—that what was turned over to L&I was "trash" and not First Amendment material, personal property, or exculpatory evidence—then the city could continue the specious cover for its destruction. And, for the most part, the city succeeded.

At one point during Verdi's testimony, Meg Flores leaped out of her chair to point out that Deputy City Solicitor Cheryl Gaston was sitting behind the prosecutors "shaking her head yes or no" each time a defense lawyer questioned the witness.[52] Verdi would then answer correspondingly. As egregious as these actions were, the city went unpunished by the court. Near the end of Verdi's testimony, Hetznecker questioned him about the raid on Spiral Q Puppet Theater a couple of weeks before the convention. "It was not a raid," Verdi shot back.[53] Yet, Hetznecker got Verdi to admit that the police called L&I to the site because "something . . . came off the roof of the building and went through a police car window," a claim that was never substantiated when L&I showed up at the scene. Verdi's testimony concluded with Krasner pushing him on the appearance of a conspiracy between the police and L&I to shut down locations of dissident activity. "Sir, do you have any explanation," asked Krasner, "for why it is that within a ten day period around the Republican National Convention that L&I was called into both Spiral Q Puppet Theater, where you had never been, and into [the puppet warehouse], two places that have a direct relation to the production of puppets for . . ." But Krasner was cut off by a sustained objection.

Later that afternoon, Hetznecker attempted to probe the basis for the intelligence operation and the necessity of coordination between the Philadelphia police and other law enforcement agencies. Hetznecker said the defense was trying to uncover "whether or not this was a legitimate criminal investigation or whether this was an investigation of political activities that was fishing for criminal activity."[54] The crux of the case, according to Hetznecker, was whether "there was illegitimate surveillance and intelligence gathering upon legitimate First Amendment activities."

> Without laying the groundwork there's no way for the court
> to adequately determine the issues of prior restraint, on the
> destruction of evidence. What the . . . Commonwealth has
> done in this case is compartmentalize. They've said here we
> have the state troopers, here we have the police department.
> There's very little communication and whatever communi-
> cation there was we've been thwarted in trying to establish
> them as witnesses; L&I is operating on its own. I mean that's
> essentially what they've argued. Now, I want to be able [to]
> establish that they're all linked. . . .
>
> All I'm asking is that in fact this was not done in isola-
> tion. . . . They certainly had coordinated activities. They can't
> come into court and say state troopers . . . had no coordina-
> tion with the Philadelphia police; Philadelphia police had no
> coordination with L&I. That's ludicrous. I think I have a right
> to probe that.

Before the hearing came to a close on Wednesday, the city had dropped all charges against warehouse owner Michael Graves.[55] Despite being arrested with everyone else in the warehouse on August 1, and spending three days in jail, Graves was provided no explanation for his treatment or the abrupt dismissal of his charges. On Tuesday, the first day of the motions hearing, Keffer revealed on the stand that Graves had not done anything illegal, but the district attorney was reluctant to dismiss the charges right away. "I don't want to put the cart before the horse," said prosecutor Borum to the court. "I understand," replied DeLeon, "but a bag just fell of the cart." The city's approach to Graves's case was odd to say the least. Graves was never offered the same probationary deal (Accelerated Rehabilitative Disposition) as his fellow arrestees, and while the case was still active, Assistant District Attorney Charles Ehrlich outrageously claimed that Graves's "involvement was more intense than the others."[56] On the one hand, Graves was pleased that the dismissal paved the way for a lawsuit against the city, a chance to recoup his losses and seek some form of justice for violations of his civil rights. On the other hand, however, he continued to face hard times. Not only did he lose thousands of dollars when L&I wantonly destroyed his tools and other property, he also had to spend at least $50,000 in repairs after L&I condemned his warehouse.[57] These costs and the temporary closure of the warehouse had a measurable impact on Graves and his flooring business.[58]

The Infiltrators Testify

During the course of the three-day motions hearing, all four of the named state troopers who infiltrated the puppet warehouse—Thomas Bachman, George Garris, Harry Keffer, and Joseph Thompson—testified in court. Despite spending a week in the warehouse and other activist spaces, taking part in building political props, attending workshops, and speaking with numerous RNC protest organizers, the troopers' testimonies remained underwhelming. Two things became quickly apparent: (a) all of them rarely, if ever, took notes about anything they did, saw, or heard; and (b) none of them could decipher a political message or a point to the protests. Besides these two suppositions being highly implausible, their testimonies seemed coordinated and contrived so as to prove that no political message existed. The only trooper who admitted to taking any notes at all was Keffer, who said, "We would relay [everything] verbally to the supervisor" with the exception of taking notes "when we got a chance."[59] Keffer apparently put some notes onto 3 ½–inch floppy disks, and hard copies were "faxed to command post." But neither Keffer's notes nor those of any other troopers were ever provided to the defense. Even Corporal James Heins of the state police, who was instructed by Lt. Bivens to pull over the vanload full of activists headed to Center City, failed to provide a report of the incident. Either it was PSP policy to not leave any trace of their operation or, more likely, the agency simply evaded disclosing relevant documentation that was, in fact, recorded.

Each trooper testified about their participation in preprotest trainings for activists, with particular emphasis on direct action trainings. As with their other testimony, however, that too revealed very little—that is, with the exception of Keffer's testimony. Offering a moment of levity, Keffer explained that the nonviolent direct action training in which he participated "was violent." Puzzled, Shawn Nolan reconfirmed, "It was violent training?" Keffer explained that he considered it violent "to get locked down and the police have to take a chance to arrest you and drag you away." With a combination of seriousness and sarcasm, Nolan responded, "That's if the police gets [sic] violent and drag you away, right?" Keffer, not realizing the hole he'd dug for himself, pushed the point by claiming that officers would endure "violence" if they have to bend over and pick up protesters. Nolan asked incredulously, "You might throw your back out?" At which point, the defendants and the large group of supporters in the courtroom erupted into laughter. "Exactly," Keffer unwittingly responded. The prosecutor tried to appeal to the judge, claiming not to "understand what [was] so funny," but Nolan wasn't going to let that one go by. "If Martin Luther King is sitting on the ground and you [pick him up]," asked the defense attorney, "that's violent?" An objection was sustained, but the point was clearly made.

At the prompting of prosecutors, all four troopers tried to convince the court that the protesters lacked a message. When asked why they thought activists were taking to the streets, Keffer replied, "No one gave me a reason,"[60] Bachman claimed he "did not hear any message,"[61] and Thompson had a similar but much more contrived response. "I thought about this over and over again," recounted Thompson, "and from day one I never particularly heard anybody say that they had some type of direct message other than just doing lock downs and blocking traffic and causing mayhem." Thompson added that he never heard "a message of what any of them stood for, what the particular argument or what their view was." In response to Garris's claim that he "never observed a banner or sign . . . with any message," Meg Flores challenged the veracity of the troopers. "For the court to listen to this witness saying, hey, there was no message, is like the court listening and saying, hey, the skeletons, which we all know were puppets, were trash."

The troopers continued to feign ignorance when asked about the large table with numerous pamphlets inside the warehouse and the anti–death penalty and prison industrial complex posters at the William Way Center, an activist convergence space and where the infiltration operation began. Garris allegedly did not recall seeing political propaganda at any of the spaces and Thompson said he "saw materials" but "did not know . . . what they stood for." Adding to the surreal nature of the proceedings, Judge DeLeon interrupted Bachman's testimony to chastise the defendants for not effectively getting their message across. "You are supposed to indoctrinate a person why it is necessary, what the cause is," coached the judge. "That's why there were signs and pamphlets all . . . over the puppet warehouse," explained Nolan. But, according to Judge DeLeon, "Signs and pamphlets by itself are not good enough."

Brushing off Judge DeLeon's ridiculous assertions, *pro se* defendant Alexis Baden-Meyer attempted to jog Bachman's memory about actual events. She asked if he recalled having conversations about the use of puppets and street theater to project political messages. "Do you remember us talking about the reason why we were using puppets throughout the blockade?" Yes, Bachman responded, "in order to lead in the protesters," implying that the puppets were Trojan horses. In response, Baden-Meyer reminded him that the reason "was so we could get [the symbolic message] out once the street had been taken, right?" Bachman testified that the only goal he knew of "was to block the buses." To which Baden-Meyer shot back: "Maybe you should have stayed for the whole meeting."

Puppets under Examination

The troopers were also asked specific questions about puppets made in the warehouse—some of which they themselves had worked on—including "Corpzilla," "Anti-Sam (a caricature of Uncle Sam)," a mash-up of the Republican elephant and Democratic donkey called "Elephonkey," and a giant pink pig representing corporate excesses. Given attempts by the prosecution to deny its existence, it was important for the defense to give life to some of the political art and propaganda that had been destroyed. Pushing the infiltrators to talk about the puppets and their symbolic meaning also helped politicize the trial. Keffer had been intimate enough with Anti-Sam to know it was "made out of papier-mache," and "probably nine to 10 feet tall and nine feet wide."[62] He also described Corpzilla as a "float on a tractor trailer" meant "to look like Godzilla," with "a wrestling ring where they were going to have . . . George Bush and Al Gore wrestling in mud." Not all of the troopers were as observant, however. Thompson, for instance, saw skeletons in the warehouse but "had no clue" why they were being made.[63] When asked if he noticed the name "Ricky Blackman" written on a skeleton head depicted in a photograph taken at the warehouse, Bachman said he "never noticed names." Assistant DA Borum cynically proffered, "I would guess he probably killed someone." To which defense attorney Meg Flores responded, "Or he got murdered."

The troopers testified that they thought some of the puppets would be used to block intersections on August 1 but failed to back up their assertion with evidence. Puppets like Anti-Sam and the giant pig were made out of papier mâché and lightweight enough for police to quickly move out of the way. Other large puppets had wheels attached to them, making a stationary or immobile blockade impossible. Nevertheless, the troopers maintained their position. The defense was forced to rely on photographs to make their point since the city had destroyed the evidence.

Although Keffer had helped to make some of the skeletons and had a better recollection than Thompson and Bachman, he still didn't think they represented a "specific cause."[64] Defense attorney Shawn Nolan started to say, "There were a hundred skeletons . . ." but Keffer interrupted to correct him: "149, I think." Nolan continued, "Representing all of the people that George Bush had executed, right?" Keffer affirmed. Actually, the number of skeletons was 138, but the point was well made.[65] "You took that to mean anti–death penalty, didn't you?" asked Nolan.[66] "I didn't really think about it, to be honest with you," responded Keffer. "It wasn't illegal so I didn't care." Keffer also claimed not to know about the symbolism of large moneybags made at the warehouse and depicted in photos. In response, *pro se* defendant Baden-Meyer tried to remind him by asking if he recollected being told they symbolized "corporate influences on politics?" Failing to recall, Keffer claimed, "You could have said something like that. I wasn't paying attention."

Even Corporal Heins, the state trooper who pulled over the van, deflected questions about the protest message. Pointing to a video that depicted the inside of the van, *pro se* defendant Baden-Meyer asked if he could "see the . . . masks of Al Gore and . . . George Bush?"[67] After Heins affirmed, Baden-Meyer asked if they were put on a property receipt. "I didn't do it," responded Heins. In fact, none of the masks, posters,

leaflets, or other political material in the van were put on a police property receipt. It appeared that police had destroyed this evidence too.[68]
Baden-Meyer continued, "Do you see another sign here . . . and more
leaflets . . . advertising The Day of Direct Action Against the Criminal
Justice System?"[69] Possibly, replied Heins. Further infusing politics into
the hearing, Baden-Meyer asked if Heins was aware that "George Bush is
pro death penalty, yes?"

While she had him on the stand, Baden-Meyer grilled Heins about
police mistreatment of her and other protesters during the arrest process. Referring to her own abusive arrest, Baden-Meyer asked if the
trooper had observed an officer "grab me in the crotch?" Heins didn't
recall, but Judge DeLeon followed up by asking whether any female officers were present to conduct searches. Again, Heins did not recall. He
did remember people being dragged to the police bus; however, when
Baden-Meyer asked him about protesters "dumped in a heap at the front
of the bus," he once again could not recall. "Did you hear the other anti–
death penalty protesters scream that my wrists were bleeding because of
the way I was being handled by your officers?" asked Baden-Meyer. "No,"
answered Heins.

On December 1, Judge DeLeon ruled on the motions argued over
the previous three days and, unsurprisingly, denied almost all of them. By
ruling that there was sufficient probable cause to raid the warehouse, no
prior restraint of free speech, no improper police conduct, and no destruction of evidence by police, DeLeon had dealt the defendants a political
blow. In response to the ruling, public defender Bradley Bridge accused
the police of making arrests based on the possibility that people might
do something illegal. "That's possible cause," Bridge exclaimed. "That's not
probable cause, and that's not a reason to go to trial."[70] Rudovsky argued
that the police were obligated to wait until protesters had actually broken
the law before arresting them. The one redeeming outcome of the motions
hearing was a dismissal of the "possession of an instrument of crime"
(PIC) charge.[71] Even though DeLeon failed to hold the police responsible
for the destruction of property and First Amendment material seized in
the raid, he was troubled enough by the circumstances to suppress all of
the evidence confiscated from the warehouse. The practical effect of this
was a blanket dismissal of the PIC charge levied against puppet warehouse
defendants.

Nevertheless, defendants and their supporters were tired of the
repeated slander against their tactics and message. For this reason, they

attempted to "take back some of the power and dignity [the] court had been trying to take from [them] all week" by engaging in resistant and disruptive activity in the courtroom.[72] A report-back from the legal collective described what happened next:

> After one of the pro-se defendants gave his closing statement, beautifully articulating our message and our passion, we stood up in court, covered our mouths with tape that had written across it "Silenced Again." We held up banners that read "Criminal INjustice: Alive and Well in this courtroom," "Dissent is a Right," "We must fight injustice wherever it may be." As we left the courtroom another pro-se defendant made her closing statement about how the injustice in this courtroom is exactly what we were out protesting against. She exited the courtroom chanting "No Justice, No Peace."

Failure to Identify

Within two weeks of Judge DeLeon's denial of the defense motions, the charges against most of the warehouse defendants were dismissed for lack of identification.[73] The activists arrested in the van driven by Keffer were unfortunately not included in those dismissals, however, and some were forced to endure years of prosecution. Nevertheless, the mass dismissals were a huge short-term victory. On December 7, the state troopers who had alleged criminal activity in the search warrant affidavit and throughout the pretrial hearing just days earlier, spent hours at the district attorney's office poring over police "photo spreads" of activist mug shots. In the end, they were only able to recognize three people and could not tie even them to any criminal activity. As a result, charges against thirty-one puppetistas were dismissed. The district attorney's office and the police commissioner refused to comment to the media, but R2K Legal took full advantage of the city's failure. "This is not a matter of misidentification," explained Larry Krasner to the *New York Times*.[74] He accused the city of preventive detention and said: "These people never should have been arrested in the first place." Public defender Bradley Bridge similarly told the *Philadelphia Inquirer* that "the whole process shows again how completely baseless the arrests were."[75] The mass dismissals compelled the *Inquirer* to publish an editorial titled "Tyranny's Puppets," which characterized the raid and arrests as an "embarrassment" to the city.[76] Condemning the police actions, the *Inquirer* wisely opined that "the arrests were an end in themselves" and called for the dismissal of the rest of the puppet warehouse defendants.

Another thirty-three puppetistas had their charges dropped on December 13 after the troopers failed to identify the remaining warehouse defendants.[77] R2K Legal held a press conference outside City Hall to coincide with the dismissals. Despite the chilly late fall day, the press conference advisory boasted street theater and pageantry, defendants and attorneys, and a puppetry reenactment of the warehouse raid, including scaled-down versions of the 138 skeletons destroyed by the city.[78] Although a full reenactment didn't happen, there were plenty of colorful visuals for media—including a blown-up map showing the route of the puppet march through downtown Philadelphia that was foiled by the raid. In an effort to connect the short-term victory with the longer-term court solidarity strategy, puppetista Rebecca Tennison said, "People with high-level misdemeanor and felony charges were singled out by a system that is attempting to over-prosecute all of the RNC defendants."[79] An R2K Legal press release quoted Bradley Bridge who said, "The facts clearly demonstrate that no one was doing anything but making puppets." Bridge also emphasized how the case raised "very troubling questions of why a search warrant was issued when nothing was found in the warehouse, why people were arrested when they were doing nothing wrong, and why it took over four months to get to this point when there was no basis for prosecution."

Shift in Public Opinion

As R2K Legal publicized the ongoing dismissals and acquittals and drew attention to the extensive infiltration,[80] a discernable shift in public opinion took place. In addition to stories published in regional and national media outlets, multiple editorials appeared in the *Philadelphia Inquirer* and *Daily News*. A November 15 *Daily News* editorial titled "Rock-a-Bye, Constitutional Rights" questioned whether evidence against Sellers ever existed, calling the price of improperly arresting activists "too high" for either "good PR" or any professed forthcoming "tourist boom."[81] The editors also railed against what they called a "contingent of 'secret police,' no matter how well intentioned." The *Inquirer* similarly concluded in a November 16 editorial that the cost of peaceful streets during the convention was "a tarnished justice system."

THE PRAXIS ORGANIZING COLLECTIVE PRESENTS

A NIGHT OF SOLIDARITY WITH THE RNC 420

A DINNER CAFE TO BENEFIT THE RNC 420
WEDNESDAY, DEC. 6TH, 6:30-9:00
@ THE MARSH COMMONS IN ARCATA
$5 - $10, SLIDING SCALE

On December 8, the *Philadelphia Inquirer* published another editorial pointing out that the puppet warehouse arrests were "a major embarrassment."[82] Three days later, the *Daily News* published yet another editorial, titled "'Enhanced Image' or a City's Shame?" This time, they focused on a report from the RNC host committee, which claimed that the convention produced $345 million in sales, a ridiculously inflated value. Referring to the host committee's feel-good rhetoric, the paper dismissed it as "hollow" and "self-congratulatory." This was especially true in light of the collapsing cases against RNC protesters who the editors said were held on bails "befitting Osama Bin Laden."[83]

The editorializing was not contained to Philadelphia either. In cities as far away as St. Petersburg, Florida, newspapers were weighing in on the

RNC legal predicament. "While acts of civil disobedience and vandalism clearly occurred," wrote the *St. Petersburg Times* in a January 6, 2001, editorial, "it is equally apparent that police overreacted and interfered with the First Amendment rights of hundreds of political protesters by engaging in street-sweeping arrests without legitimate cause."[84] The editorial board called the arrest of Sellers, "a pretext, intended not to respond to a criminal act but to interfere with planned demonstrations." In conclusion, they called for "a Justice Department investigation" into the "disturbing, unconstitutional tactic" of preemptive arrests.

Underscoring the discernable shift in public perception, Beckler noted, "The arrestees were no longer 'violent protesters' but rather 'victims of preventive detention.'"[85] More than a year after the RNC protests, he emphasized that "this change was a result of our victories and our intense media and outreach campaign." Concurring with Beckler, R2K Legal member Jody Dodd said that, in the aftermath of the protests, "turning the message around was one of the things the legal collective and people working on media can be really proud of."[86] In many ways, the success of R2K Legal's media campaign was unprecedented. It's unusual for legal support teams to engage in proactive media efforts to help achieve their goals; however, to garner such favorable coverage was virtually unheard of.

By mid-January 2001, only sixty misdemeanor cases remained and the forty-two felony cases had dwindled to fourteen as a result of dismissals and judicial rulings.[87] It was around this time that one RNC felony defendant who could no longer pursue his case took a plea bargain and was sentenced to two years probation with no jail time. This ended up being the *only* felony conviction the city ever successfully pinned against an RNC 2000 protester.

By all accounts, the court solidarity and political trial strategy had been wildly successful. Combining resistance, theatrics, and repeated legal victories with an effective PR campaign did more than vindicate the hundreds of defendants. It also served to embarrass the city for its role in silencing dissent. Most important to the R2K Legal Collective and all of the RNC defendants, however, was safeguarding those accused of felonies. For the time being, it seemed that the decreasing number of felony cases indicated that the political trials and court solidarity strategy were working.

CHAPTER 8:
JUDGE McCAFFERY

LESS THAN TWO WEEKS BEFORE THE RNC 2000, THE UNIVERSITY OF Pennsylvania (UPenn) held an event that—at the time—seemed to have little relevance to the protests about to happen. On July 19, 2000, a class on "The Effects of Violence, Crime, and Delinquency on Community Health" took place in the main dining room of the Children's Hospital at UPenn. Approximately forty students from the schools of social work, dentistry, medicine, and law were in attendance. The class featured a panel of speakers including Dr. Jonathan Pletcher, director of the Adolescent Care Center at the Children's Hospital of Philadelphia; Professor Anthony Rostain from UPenn's Department of Psychiatry; Kevin Vaughan, executive director of the Philadelphia Commission on Human Relations; and Philadelphia Municipal Court Judge Seamus (pronounced "shame-us") McCaffery.

A day before the class, an Amtrak police officer at Philadelphia's 30th Street Station shot and killed an unarmed homeless man with a history of mental health problems. Given the relevance to "community health," the class spent time discussing the police response to such incidences. The conversation eventually led to the upcoming RNC protests and what the police response to that activity might be. According to Vaughan, McCaffery said, "The judges had met and made a plan. What they planned on doing was [to] hold the protesters who were arrested for three days until the convention was over."[1] Startled, Vaughan replied, "You can't do that. That's illegal." To which McCaffery responded, "Yes we can. It's within the law. The law gives us the ability to do that." Vaughan claimed that the students were so upset by McCaffery's comments that the judge was compelled to leave the class before the end of the discussion.

At the time, the activists who would make up the RNC legal support effort knew next to nothing about McCaffery, let alone the "plan" he announced in July of 2000. It would be many months before R2K Legal would learn about McCaffery's scandalous comments. Nevertheless, the discovery compelled activists to shine a spotlight on both his character and an abusiveness of the system he represented.

The Legendary Judge

In just seven years on the bench, McCaffery had made quite a name for himself at Philadelphia's Criminal Justice Center (CJC). In January 2001, the *Philadelphia Inquirer* summed up McCaffery's brief judicial career, giving him the dubious distinction of being "Philadelphia's most famous, and sometimes most outlandish, judge."[2] McCaffery seemed to enjoy making a spectacle of himself, causing the *Inquirer* to call him a "media star," who exploited the forums like "talk radio, TV magazine shows, the nightly news, the morning news, the noon news, the Internet, and the front pages of daily newspapers large and small." Host of the self-proclaimed "Seamus Show," McCaffery set his judicial sights high. "My ultimate goal," he told the *Inquirer*, would be "the Pennsylvania Supreme Court," a goal he eventually reached in 2007.[3]

In 2000, McCaffery was fifty years old and had already completed a twenty-year career as a "decorated" officer in the Philadelphia Police Department. At that time, McCaffery lived in the Bustleton area of northeast Philadelphia, a working-class neighborhood considered very conservative with plenty of racial tension brewing just beneath the surface. Known for riding his Harley-Davidson to work with a pistol on his hip, McCaffery consciously shaped his cavalier, pro-cop persona. A thirty-three-year military veteran at the time, McCaffery served as an active colonel in the U.S. Air Force.[4]

Once it became clear that McCaffery would hear many of the RNC protest cases, legal support activists quickly brought themselves up to speed on how he conducted his courtroom. Attorneys working with R2K Legal gave historical accounts of McCaffery's tenure on the bench, and direct experience in his courtroom more than filled in the gaps. An early example of McCaffery's "kangaroo court" occurred on October 25, 2000, when he swiftly convicted activist Scott Matthews of simple assault, resisting arrest, disorderly conduct, failure to disperse, and obstruction of the highway. Before sentencing Matthews, McCaffery delivered a heartfelt speech about how he and his friends served in the Vietnam War and "put our lives on the line" to defend Matthews's and others' constitutional rights.[5] McCaffery referred to the officer who claimed to have been struck by Matthews as "a victim," and explained to his "audience" how police put their lives on the line every day to protect our rights. The police, according to McCaffery "used real restraint" during the RNC protests. "When I was out there [as a cop]," McCaffery said to a courtroom filled with police and activists alike, "that man right there (pointing to Matthews), he'd still be in the hospital." Over strenuous objections from Matthews's attorney Shawn Nolan, McCaffery asked Officer Sulpizio, who said he was struck during the arrest, whether the defendant deserved "jail or probation."[6] Although Sulpizio refused to choose, McCaffery wasted no time in handing down what would be one of the harshest sentences delivered to an RNC protester: thirty to sixty days' incarceration followed by two years' probation, and a $300 fine.[7]

One of McCaffery's roles as a Municipal Court judge was to hear all of the cases remanded (downgraded) by the Court of Common Pleas from felonies to misdemeanors. In other words, all of the felony defendants whose charges got reduced to misdemeanors were sent to McCaffery's courtroom. As it turned out, almost all of the forty-three defendants charged with felonies during the RNC protests had their charges reduced to misdemeanors. To make matters worse, McCaffery was also scheduled to try some of the larger group cases.[8] Troubled by the prospect of numerous convictions and jail time, R2K Legal began investigating ways to avoid such an outcome. By November 2000, however, McCaffery had convicted several RNC misdemeanor defendants, handing down months-long jail sentences for what was clearly First Amendment activity. His decisions stood in stark contrast to the dismissals occurring in other courtrooms.

The Plan to Recuse

It wasn't until December 2000 that members of R2K Legal learned about McCaffery's infamous comments at UPenn that past July. News of Vaughan's statement created a flurry of excitement and activity around how to most effectively use it. Ultimately, it would become the focus of a legal strategy aimed at preventing McCaffery from ruling on RNC-related cases by recusing him from the large group trials scheduled in his courtroom. If it worked, the strategy had the potential to stop McCaffery from ruling on dozens of cases.

After meetings between R2K Legal and Defender Association attorneys, a plan was hatched to gather evidence to illustrate McCaffery's prejudice, if not his demonstrated bias. A wealth of evidence was compiled around McCaffery's pro-police persona, but it was Vaughan's statement citing

McCaffery's "preventive detention" comments that was the strongest showing of bias against RNC protesters. The trick was being able to use *all* of the
evidence to build a solid case, both in the courtroom and in the media. The
legal tool for stopping McCaffery was a defense motion to recuse. The plan
was for the Defender Association to file its own recusal motion largely based
on Vaughan's statement. That motion would then be followed by another
filed by *pro se* RNC defendants after more evidence had been gathered.

On January 4, 2001, the Defender Association filed its "Motion for
Recusal," with Ellen Greenlee, Bradley Bridge, Shawn Nolan, and Meg
Flores listed as co-counsel. The motion, filed on behalf of George Ripley
and "others similarly situated," accused McCaffery of impropriety and bias
for saying that "the judges had met and that they had a plan on how to handle the protestors during the upcoming Republican National Convention.
Their plan was to hold any arrested protestors in jail for at least three days
until the convention was over, essentially to incapacitate them."[9]

The Defender Association cited *Commonwealth v. Darush* (1983), in
which the Pennsylvania appellate court ruled that "in order for the integrity of the judiciary to be compromised, we have held that a judge's behavior is not required to rise to a level of actual prejudice, but the appearance
of impropriety is sufficient." That court further stated that "a defendant is
entitled to a trial before a fact finder whose impartiality cannot reasonably
be questioned," a standard the defense claimed to have met. The motion
argued that McCaffery's comments did, in fact, "reasonably suggest that his
impartiality could be questioned." Another Pennsylvania appellate court ruling cited in the motion, *Commonwealth v. Hammer* (1985), addressed the
requirement of recusal "where the actions of the judge suggest bias against
a party." Drawing attention to Vaughan's statement and McCaffery's comments at UPenn, the motion further argued that "any plan to hold arrested
RNC protestors beyond that constitutional limit [of forty-eight hours] would
have been improper, and for a judge to either prepare such a plan or know
of it and do nothing would reasonably call into question the impartiality of a
judge to hear a case involving someone arrested during the RNC."

One of the first problems R2K Legal and the Defender Association
encountered was that, traditionally, the judge being accused of bias is the
same judge who rules on the recusal motion and the chances of success were
remote if McCaffery were to rule on his own recusal motion. In response,
the Defender Association filed its motion with Judge James DeLeon, who
had previously ordered that all RNC pretrial motions be heard in his courtroom. Although the defense was hopeful that DeLeon would rule on the

motion himself, the case law was not very supportive. "Generally, it is the duty of the trial judge to decide whether he or she can hear a case fairly and without prejudice," read the motion. But the defense argued that the motion was nonetheless being sent to DeLeon because "Judge McCaffery might be a necessary witness" to his own recusal. Remarkably, the defense was asking DeLeon to recuse a fellow Municipal Court judge from hearing dozens of cases based on very serious accusations of judicial impropriety. Unsurprisingly, DeLeon punted and set a motions hearing for January 16 in McCaffery's courtroom. DeLeon gave the defense until January 12 to provide the district attorney with information on any witnesses it expected to call.

A flurry of activity ensued between January 4, when the Defender Association motion was filed, and the January 16 hearing. To increase the chance of success, R2K Legal worked feverishly to: (1) gather sufficient evidence of McCaffery's history of bias, (2) use that evidence to develop a second, further incriminating motion to recuse, and (3) find witnesses to McCaffery's infamous comments at UPenn to better substantiate the recusal effort.

Meanwhile, Bradley Bridge tried an additional approach. He wrote to McCaffery on January 9 asking the judge to recuse himself without a hearing. Bridge pointed out that by recusing himself, McCaffery "would not suggest an agreement with Kevin Vaughan's recollection of the events." Rather, "It would simply be a recognition that a judge can recuse him/herself from hearing any matter without stating a reason." Bridge had given McCaffery a back door through which to easily, and quietly exit. The letter went on to request that "if a hearing on the Motion for Recusal is required . . . the matter [should] be reassigned to a judge other than Your Honor." To back up this argument for judicial reassignment, Bridge cited a Pennsylvania Supreme Court ruling, *Municipal Publications v. Court of Common Pleas* (1985), which held that "if a judge has 'personal knowledge of disputed facts' relevant to recusal, that judge cannot also rule on the recusal motion."[10] Neither Bridge nor the Defender Association received a response.

Finding additional witnesses to corroborate Vaughan's statement and his version of events proved more difficult than expected. The brief campaign to find witnesses began with R2K Legal members circulating flyers all over the UPenn campus and the neighboring areas. The legal collective thought that at least one of the students would see a flyer or hear about it and respond, but no one came forward. R2K Legal and the Defender Association together drafted and filed subpoenas on UPenn professors Pletcher and Rostain, the two other speakers and hosts of the July class. Conveniently for McCaffery, they were also acquaintances of his, a factor that would make pursuit of witnesses even more difficult. The subpoenas sought the list of students who attended the class so that R2K Legal could formally invite them to come forward, but the UPenn professors refused to comply on privacy grounds. "We are deeply concerned that we would jeopardize the integrity of this academic activity were we to discuss any-thing about what a guest said to our class," wrote Pletcher and Rostain in response to the subpoenas. Philadelphia District Attorney Lynne Abraham also filed a motion to quash the subpoenas, which succeeded in delaying the process long enough to prevent the list from ever surfacing publicly.[11]

Researching a Pro-police Judge

While R2K Legal was busy trying to locate witnesses, its members also began compiling information to be used in the second recusal motion against McCaffery. The research effort turned out to be fairly easy. McCaffery's connections to the police and their fraternal order lay just beneath the surface. Although it was well known that prior to becoming a judge McCaffery had been a cop for many years, it was less known that his membership in the Fraternal Order of Police (FOP) never lapsed after becoming a Municipal Court judge. Accounts of McCaffery sporting a large FOP ring in court also made their way to R2K Legal.

The FOP had endorsed Governor Bush for president.[12] Meanwhile, its organizational principles were undeniably at odds with what dissidents had been calling for on August 1: an end to the prison industrial complex, to the death penalty, and to police brutality. The FOP characterized itself as "the nation's oldest" police union and "the world's largest organization of sworn law enforcement officers, with more than 318,000 members in more than 2,100 lodges."[13] During an FOP meeting at one of these lodges, McCaffery once acted in his capacity as Municipal Court judge and signed a search warrant for a Philadelphia police officer. This fact was raised in a 1998 court case before Common Pleas Judge Gary S. Glazer, in which Glazer commented that McCaffery's conduct failed to exemplify "a neutral detached magistrate."[14] Glazer further stated in his ruling that McCaffery represented "a judicial problem," and "to have a judge sign a warrant at an FOP meeting . . . [is] a very bad situation, totally inappropriate and it is not going to pass unnoticed."[15] R2K Legal was able to obtain the trial transcript and the ruling in order to use them in the *pro se* motion.

McCaffery was on the Philadelphia police force when Mumia Abu-Jamal was accused of killing Daniel Faulkner, a fellow cop. But it was McCaffery's role as Grand Marshall of the May 2000 "Daniel Faulkner Memorial Motorcycle Run" that best illustrated his pro-cop allegiance and his bias against August 1 protesters. Bikers Allied to Commemorate Uniformed Police, Inc. (BAC-UP) organized the memorial fundraiser.[16] Notably, BAC-UP scheduled its "presentation ceremonies" for August 1, the same day that planned demonstrations were set to occur in support of Mumia Abu-Jamal.

Research by R2K Legal also uncovered a case involving McCaffery and Reverend James Luther Bevel, a one-time aide to Martin Luther King Jr. who had a history of engaging in civil disobedience. In July 1995, Bevel was arrested in Philadelphia "trying to hold a prayer meeting with 40 others for death row inmate Mumia Abu-Jamal in front of Common Pleas Judge Albert F. Sabo's home."[17] McCaffery, who was Bevel's judge, found him and the other civil disobedient protesters guilty of obstruction of justice and criminal conspiracy.[18] After appealing to the Court of Common Pleas, none of McCaffery's convictions against the group were upheld. The legal collective felt that McCaffery's stance toward Bevel and the issue he was protesting underscored his contempt for Abu-Jamal and civil disobedience as a means to foment social change.

As the recusal hearing approached, R2K Legal set out to find RNC defendants who were capable of arguing the motion in a hostile environment. One of the choices was obvious: Danielle Redden. A recent graduate of Villanova University and arrested on August 1, Redden had dedicated much of her life to R2K Legal and the effort to support her fellow defendants. Arrested with dozens of others at 15th and JFK, and scheduled to be tried by McCaffery, Redden was willing to stick her neck out and argue a controversial motion before an inimical judge.

So that Redden would not have to face McCaffery alone, and to improve the odds of squaring off against him, the legal collective set out to find a second *pro se* defendant. Although the selection process was harder than with Redden, the collective eventually settled with confidence on Mark Rifkin. A graduate English student at the time and a member of ACT UP Philadelphia, Rifkin was arrested with Redden at 15th and JFK. Unlike Redden, however, Rifkin's arrest was unplanned and unintentional. A death in the family had prevented Rifkin from being involved in protest organizing efforts, and he hadn't intended to participate in any of the demonstrations. On the afternoon of August 1, he was watching *Oprah*, when the local news interrupted the program to show a scene near City Hall a few blocks from his home. Friends of Rifkin appeared on the screen, as he saw fellow ACT UP members being tackled and assaulted by police.

"I can't just sit here and watch this on fucking TV," Rifkin thought as he grabbed his bag and ran out the door. Imagining his presence as a witness might discourage the police from acting violently, he ended up in a large crowd where he watched demonstrators get arrested.

As the cops pushed the crowd back, Rifkin chose to resist. Frustrated by having to endure cops telling him where he could and couldn't go, Rifkin refused to move. As the cops continued shoving people, they told him that if he didn't move he'd be arrested. In response to his resistance, Rifkin was tackled and dragged away. Rifkin was not made aware of the reason for his arrest until long after his release. Eventually, he was charged with spray-painting public property. In addition to his strongly held political principles, Rifkin was an eloquent writer and an articulate spokesperson, making him an ideal *pro se* candidate.

Redden and Rifkin filed their recusal motion on January 16, the same day that McCaffery was scheduled to hear the Defender Association motion. Legal activists worked furiously until the final hour. Had there been more time, more pressure could have been put on UPenn to supply the names of witnesses. Getting anyone to corroborate Kevin Vaughan's statement was critically important to ensuring media coverage and a solid case against McCaffery. Still, the *pro se* motion included many hard-hitting accusations against McCaffery that not only laid the framework for his recusal but also threatened to damage his reputation. R2K Legal members knew that if they could make the accusations stick, the impact could be significant.

The *pro se* recusal motion included some of the same case law references found in the Defender Association motion. What differentiated the *pro se* motion, however, was the additional evidence showing McCaffery's pro-cop bias. The *pro se* motion stated that "McCaffery's actions in the Disla case [where he signed a warrant at an FOP meeting], his longtime service as a police officer, his tenure as a police officer during both Daniel Faulkner's murder and the trial of Mumia Abu-Jamal, his comments denying the First Amendment rights of RNC protestors in the Matthews case, and his history of questionable convictions of those who participate in civil disobedience together reasonably suggest that he may bear a particular animus against the RNC defendants given the specific nature of their protest and the content of their speech and be incapable of ruling fairly."[19] The motion continued to argue that McCaffery's statements in the Matthews case and his ruling against Reverend Bevel cause him to hear the facts of the RNC cases "within a preexisting prejudice that inhibits his ability to consider these cases on their own merits" and to "suggest a pattern of ruling against those who participate in civil disobedience."

The Recusal Hearing

The morning of January 16, Redden, Rifkin and other members of R2K Legal met to prepare for the hearing that afternoon. Eventually, the determined group made their way to the CJC. But once inside the courthouse, their excitement was replaced with a sense of dread. What was McCaffery going to do? With its sprawling cold marble, the courthouse was designed to intimidate. Inside McCaffery's courtroom, the sense of dread became heightened as police lined the walls. Eventually, however, the defendants and their supporters would far outnumber the cops. Until then, those who had worked long hours on the recusal effort were happy to see their star witness—Kevin Vaughan—ready to testify if necessary.

McCaffery entered the courtroom soon after 3:00 P.M. and immediately began reading from a prepared statement. Not more than a few sentences in, Bradley Bridge interrupted with an objection. In an effort to prevent the judge from shutting down the proceedings, denying the defense a hearing, and getting the only chance to comment on the record, Bridge took control of the proceedings. He explained to McCaffery that he objected to the court providing a statement without the chance to cross-examine him.[20] Bridge also took the opportunity to launch into an explanation of why the defense had been unable to find additional witnesses from the UPenn class to corroborate Vaughan's testimony.

Because the Defender Association was still waiting for a response to its subpoenas for records, Bridge made a request to bifurcate the case (split it in two). The defense wanted to make arguments that day with witness testimony from Vaughan, and hold off on other potential student witnesses so that they could testify on another day. Bridge argued it was only after the January 4 hearing with Judge DeLeon that the defense was able to "subpoena from the university of Pennsylvania a list of the students that were at the session and that is currently pending."[21] He expected to hear back from UPenn within a week or two and wanted to be able to "present the testimony of those students who are not in a position to do so yet."

Bridge then provided the court with Vaughan's statement, curriculum vitae, a letter from UPenn to Vaughan confirming his involvement in the July class, and the letter from Bridge to McCaffery requesting his recusal. Without giving McCaffery time to react, Bridge quickly launched into the basis for the recusal motion and McCaffery's obligation to adhere to the Code of Judicial Conduct. Bridge explained that "the court should uphold the integrity and independence of the judiciary . . . avoid any appearance of impropriety . . . act impartially at all times . . . [and] refrain from any public comment regarding cases." He then underscored a rule that required "disqualification of a Judge in a particular case where the impartiality of the Judge might reasonably be questioned when the Judge has personal knowledge of disputed evidentiary facts."

Bridge argued that the issue before the court was "precisely" disputed evidentiary facts. To support his claims, he stated his intention to not only call Vaughan to testify, but also McCaffery himself. "Your Honor, I would call you as a witness because you obviously have firsthand knowledge." Attempting to limit the impact of the accusations, McCaffery interrupted Bridge to ask whether such disputed evidentiary facts pertained to a case before him. "My question to you," said McCaffery, "do you have any information or any evidence that this fact finder, Judge Seamus Patrick McCaffery, has any information concerning the case that is coming in front of me, specifically?" Bridge did his best to explain that it wasn't the judge's knowledge about specific cases that established his bias or partiality; it was his conduct and bias with regard to protesters and the issues they were protesting. "If you are asking me do you, Judge McCaffery, know anything specifically about any particular case and what a person did or didn't do on August 1st of the year 2000," said Bridge, "no I am not aware of any information regarding that."

Clearly agitated, McCaffery asked Bridge if he had anything more to put on the record, at which point Bridge tried to bring to the judge's attention a *Philadelphia Daily News* article from that day. Embedded in a story completely unrelated to the RNC 2000 protest cases, McCaffery chose to invoke Mumia Abu-Jamal to argue that a defendant before him used "more services in this city than anyone, except Mumia Abu-Jamal."[22] Although McCaffery was clearly not afraid to openly display his contempt for Abu-Jamal as well as RNC protesters, he was less interested in openly discussing his comments or how they could be the basis for prejudicial decisions. McCaffery had heard enough of Bridge's arguments and made clear his unwillingness to hear the recusal motion. "I am not going to allow you to continue," barked the judge. "This is not going to be a hearing." Startled, Bridge exclaimed, "You are not going to give me a hearing on the motion?" Ignoring him, McCaffery began to read from his prepared statement for the record.

This seemed to signal the end of any opportunity for the defense to argue its case. The *pro se* defendants had not even had a chance to raise the arguments they had worked so hard to prepare. Would McCaffery's bias go unchallenged after all? Bridge could not let things end that way. In an attempt to bring the *pro se* defendants and their motion into play, Bridge asked the judge to let him adopt their allegations on behalf of the Defender Association. He explained that Judge DeLeon had sent their motion to McCaffery's court for a hearing that day as well. By drawing Redden and Rifkin into the argument, Bridge was hoping to allow them to make their case before McCaffery had a chance to hijack the proceedings. He pointed to Redden and Rifkin in the courtroom and urged McCaffery to hear their case.

The heated exchange continued with McCaffery repeating his earlier argument, this time against the *pro se* defendants. If no evidence existed of McCaffery's knowledge about facts specific to a case before him, then he would not consider any claim of bias to be valid. Seeing the window of opportunity quickly close before him, Bridge successfully inserted one last argument. "Can I just read one quotation from Commonwealth versus Lamansky?" asked Bridge.[23] "I have afforded you more than an ample opportunity," deflected McCaffery. "Well, then I will just read this once and then I'll stop," responded Bridge. "Lamansky [held that] a party is not limited in his own case in establishing personal bias," and "may show 'temperamental' prejudice on the particular class of litigation involved to support his allegations."

Bridge was cleverly using case law to explain that McCaffery's bias was not limited to a single person's case. *Lamansky* made it seem that McCaffery was on the hook for a lack of impartiality around an entire class of people: dissidents fighting the criminal justice system. Bridge continued, "The allegation I make here is that based upon the RNC, what this Court has said, what is contained in the petition here, comments this Court made in today's paper regarding Mumia Abu-Jamal, the fact that all these protestors were here . . ." McCaffery interrupted, "What was that last one?" To which Bridge replied, "The comment made in today's paper . . . That's what I wanted to quote . . ." But McCaffery cut Bridge off in midsentence, explaining that the court had afforded him the opportunity to read the one sentence he requested. Beginning to read from his prepared statement, McCaffery said, "I have reviewed the recusal motion and the December 22, 2000 statement of Mr. Kevin Vaughn [*sic*]."

> The standards to be used in deciding recusal motions are well settled. As a general rule, a motion for recusal is directed to and decided by the jurists whose impartiality is being challenged. In considering a recusal request a jurist must first

make a conscientious determination of his ability to assess the
case in an impartial manner free of personal bias, of interests
in the outcome. The jurist must then consider whether his or
her continued involvement in the case creates an appearance
of impropriety and/or would tend to undermine public confidence in the judiciary.

That logic seemed to play directly into the hands of the defense, but
McCaffery ignored the standards he had just set forth and delivered an
intellectual slap in the face by citing *Commonwealth v. Mumia Abu-Jamal*
as the reason why the motion should not be heard.[24] "Our Supreme Court
has observed," said McCaffery, "'where fabricated, frivolous and scurrilous charges are raised against the presiding Judge during the course of
the proceeding, the Court may dismiss those objections without a hearing
where the Judge is satisfied that the complaint is fully without foundation.'"
McCaffery claimed that "in light of these standards there is absolutely
no reason for me to recuse myself." Then, in an effort to clear his name,
McCaffery denied making the statements attributed to him by Vaughan.
"Judge, that's exactly why we need an evidentiary hearing," replied Bridge.
"We need to call you as a witness. Now you are testifying as a witness.
You are saying that you didn't make those statements." By denying the
defense a hearing, McCaffery was refusing to review evidence and allow
for cross-examination. In addition, he was able to call Vaughan's claims
"fabricated, frivolous and scurrilous," without giving either Vaughan or the
defense a chance to respond.

Continuing his monologue and quashing any opportunity for rebut-
tal, the judge laid out his alleged innocence. McCaffery claimed he neither
knew about nor spoke of any plan to incarcerate protesters until the conclusion of the convention. "There was no such plan," he said. "On the contrary
what I did address at the University of Pennsylvania class in question were
the arrangements created as a result of a joint agreement between the City
of Philadelphia, the District Attorney's Office, the Defender Association
and the courts to expedite, expedite, not slow down the process of the
summary offenders during the RNC," continued the judge. "Specifically, the
agreement to which the Defender Association was a party called for transportation of defendants charged with summary offenses to Holmesburg
Prison for immediate intake and processing and immediate trial."[25] But
even if there were such an agreement, it was never implemented in the way
that McCaffery had alleged. Instead of charging protesters with summary

offenses, hundreds were charged with multiple misdemeanors and felonies and held without proper access to counsel for days on end.

McCaffery continued by claiming even-handed judgment in the five RNC cases he already tried. That a majority of those cases resulted in conviction mattered less to him than his claim of leniency at sentencing. In the well-known case of Scott Matthews, McCaffery reasoned that jail time was deserved due to the "physical assault on a police officer." Matthews's assault conviction, however, was later overturned by Common Pleas Judge Pamela Dembe who found him guilty of only misdemeanor resisting arrest.[26] McCaffery's final claim of impartiality rested on how he waived the requirement that defendants appear in court. The claims did little to convince those in the courtroom of the judge's neutrality. After accusing Bridge of "the most blatant judge shopping imaginable,"[27] McCaffery wrapped up his commentary by stating that "the public confidence in the judiciary will not be in any way undermined if I preside over additional RNC cases, but it would be undermined if I recuse myself on the basis of unfounded accusations as discussed above." Therefore, barked McCaffery, "your motion is denied."

Pro Se Defendants Demand to Be Heard

Fearful of not getting a chance to present the *pro se* motion at all, Mark Rifkin sprang to his feet to interject. "Excuse me, Your Honor, my name is Mark Rifkin and I'm one of the *pro se* defendants that Mr. Bridge mentioned before." Rifkin went on to explain that McCaffery had just ruled on the Defender Association motion, but not on the *pro se* motion. And since he had not yet heard Redden and Rifkin's case, their motion was still relevant.

In an attempt to beat McCaffery at his own game, Rifkin made the claim that the judge did in fact "have direct knowledge of facts involved in these cases." When asked by the court for clarification, Rifkin explained that McCaffery "knew what it was that we were protesting." Rifkin deftly made the case that McCaffery's knowledge of what was being protested on August 1 was inextricably linked to the judge's bias and the outcome of the RNC criminal cases.

Although Rifkin held McCaffery's attention more than Bridge had managed to do, getting the judge to admit that he had prior knowledge of the protesters' speech turned out to be easier than convincing him he had any more or different information than other judges set to hear RNC protest cases. When asked by McCaffery if it was "reasonable to assume that every judge in the city and county of Philadelphia would also have that same information," Rifkin countered that the substance of the *pro se* motion had to do specifically with his bias as it related to that information. In fact, Rifkin and R2K Legal were not aware of any other judges on the bench at that time who had similar backgrounds, held similar positions, or displayed similar conduct to McCaffery.

Rifkin shot back: "If we had knowledge of other justices' actions and statements," suggesting bias against "the content of what we were protesting we would also be in their courtrooms arguing for a recusal." Rifkin then expounded on the main points in the motion by arguing that "if we had facts including the fact that other justices had been members of the police force, were currently members of the Fraternal Order of Police, had signed warrants at the meetings of the Fraternal Order of Police, had in fact been Grand Marshall in the memorial bike ride for Daniel Faulkner . . . if you have those facts in the case of other justices, yes, absolutely we would be in their courtrooms filing for a recusal."

McCaffery stubbornly fell back on the claim that he knew nothing about facts specific to Rifkin's case. "Absent of anything more specific," McCaffery began to shut down the discussion, "I don't think that your recusal motion . . ." Rifkin interrupted the judge and called him out. "Given the fact that it seems that you have not read or were not aware of our . . . motion and have crafted a response based on a different motion, I would say at least give the respect that our motion deserves. If it needs to be put off to another day, it needs to be put off to another day to receive a response of its own on the facts that we present." It was Rifkin's hope that instead of denying them a hearing entirely, the judge might at least schedule a proper hearing. But, since the Defender Association motion had just been denied without such a hearing, there was no certainty and a low expectation that McCaffery would go for it.

As if on cue, Danielle Redden jumped up to provide the final push: "What we are stating is that in essence, part of our defense; a very important part of our defense is in the message of our speech. And if you could not without bias hear that story as part of our defense . . ." McCaffery interrupted Redden to ask for a copy of the *pro se* motion: "I need to read it." He then called for a brief recess. People in the courtroom had become cautiously optimistic. By the time the judge came back from chambers, his disposition had noticeably changed.

"I have taken your motion in the back along with all of your exhibits," McCaffery told the defendants. "I think out of respect to both of you . . . since you have shown me the courtesy of doing all of your homework

I should at least show you the courtesy of looking through it and giving it the time and effort that it's due." McCaffery's solution was to schedule a special hearing just on the *pro se* motion. This seemed like a momentary victory until the judge said that he would be ruling on just Redden and Rifkin's cases. With McCaffery unwilling to let the *pro se* motion extend to the dozens of RNC defendants scheduled for trial in his courtroom, the plan suddenly looked like it was falling apart. "But it's also to defendants who are similarly situated," said Redden referring to the motion. "No," was McCaffery's only response. At that point, Bridge rejoined the fray in a further attempt to broaden the number of defendants impacted by the motion. But McCaffery insisted that his ruling would apply to their two cases alone, and ended the proceedings by scheduling a recusal hearing for January 30.

Although the recusal motions failed to have the direct effect of removing McCaffery from future RNC-related cases, what did transpire over the next couple of weeks surprised everyone. By placing a spotlight on McCaffery's actions and the recusal issue, R2K Legal was able to achieve unexpected results. Before the January 16 hearing, R2K Legal had issued a press advisory to attract media attention to the recusal motion and the evidence against McCaffery.[28] Scrutiny from journalists benefited dissidents with cases before McCaffery and had an effect on other judges hearing RNC cases too.

Shortly after the recusal effort played out in McCaffery's courtroom, the *Philadelphia City Paper* interviewed Vaughan who "insisted he remembers McCaffery's [UPenn] comments clearly."[29] Vaughan told the *City Paper* about his initial reaction. "I was stunned," he said. The UPenn comments had "made a major impact on me." Vaughan also insisted that McCaffery never mentioned an "expedited plan" for the protesters as he had claimed in court. In the same article, Bradley Bridge complained about how the hearing was "cut off" by McCaffery, a situation he claimed "demonstrates the truth of what [Vaughan] had to say and the animus [McCaffery] holds for RNC protestors." Finally, Bridge said that McCaffery was "wrong to call Vaughn [*sic*] a liar and not allow him to testify in response."

McCaffery's Next Moves

The next group trial in front of McCaffery was held on January 19, 2001, only three days after the recusal hearing. This trial involved twelve defendants arrested at 300 N. 16th Street for allegedly blocking the on-ramp to I-676, the Vine Street Expressway, for more than an hour. The district attorney had video footage of the action depicting many protesters taking part in civil disobedience to block rush-hour traffic and bring attention to the prison industrial complex. Scott Matthews was one of the protesters who took part in the on-ramp blockade and had already been convicted by McCaffery and sentenced to jail time. Needless to say, the defense wasn't confident of an acquittal with McCaffery as the "fact finder."

Dressed in ties fashioned with the letters "R-E-S-I-S-T," defendants and supporters filed into the courtroom with a cynical yet fierce resolve. Most were expecting McCaffery to find the entire group guilty as charged: resisting arrest, obstructing the highway, conspiracy to obstruct the highway, and disorderly conduct. In one sense, that morning's trial was simply a formality; the step before appealing to the Court of Common Pleas and exercising their rights to a jury trial. Yet, in an astonishing turn-around, the judge acquitted the entire group of all charges. According to the *Philadelphia Inquirer*, "McCaffery ruled that although the protesters clearly did block the road, their actions were permissible under the law."[30] In defense of his uncharacteristic acquittals, McCaffery told the *Inquirer* that "the protesters were merely exercising their right to engage in free speech."[31]

Family members, supporters, and activists observing the proceedings were both jubilant and stunned. Many in the courtroom embraced and applauded when McCaffery announced the acquittal. Yet, the celebration was tempered by the reality that the victory—as significant as it was—resulted from a biased judge invoking rights he would normally shun in order to curry favor with the public. "[McCaffery's] newfound appreciation for the First Amendment," the *Boston Phoenix* agreed, was "merely an attempt to salvage his public image."[32] Nevertheless, the acquittals were undoubtedly the result of persistent and creative legal activism.

On January 23, less than a week later, McCaffery tried an RNC case involving a single defendant, a Drexel University student named John Varghese. His crime involved wielding a "fluorescent-green water pistol."[33] Varghese's case was an example of many RNC cases in which activists were brutally arrested by cops then charged with assault to deflect attention from the real abuse that took place.

Varghese's original felony assault charge was dismissed prior to his trial before McCaffery, but his misdemeanor charges of simple assault, reckless endangerment, and resisting arrest remained. Attorney Patrick Artur tried to convince McCaffery that the only assault that occurred that day was by police. "They jumped on him and wrestled him to the ground." Uncharacteristically siding with the defense and chastising Philadelphia cops for overreacting to a water pistol, McCaffery acquitted Varghese of all charges. The acquittal represented another victory attributable to the "failed" recusal hearing.

The next group trial occurred two days after Varghese's acquittal, on January 25. McCaffery was due to try a group of twenty defendants arrested on August 1 at 15th and JFK, the site of a rally organized by Pennsylvania Abolitionists United Against the Death Penalty. The charges were similar to those in the group trial the prior week, with the addition of conspiracy. The packed courtroom waited anxiously for the early morning proceedings to begin. Public defender Shawn Nolan was lead counsel and cautiously optimistic. The question lingering on the minds of defendants, attorneys, and supporters alike was whether McCaffery was going to stick with his newfound appreciation for the First Amendment or revert to his more typical demeanor. Although it was unclear what kind of evidence the district attorney had against any of the defendants facing trial that day, many of them had prepared statements to be read upon conviction or sentencing. They never got the chance.

Before the trial got started, Assistant District Attorney Max Kramer withdrew sixteen of the twenty cases due to the prosecution's inability to adequately identify most of the defendants. Although the four remaining defendants could be identified on video footage committing acts of civil disobedience, McCaffery made clear how he was going to rule. Once again, the judge invoked the First Amendment and found the four "not guilty" on all charges. The celebratory mood among supporters was difficult to suppress; however, the courtroom conduct during the trial compelled some activists to encourage reflection and restraint among their comrades.

RNC defendant Kristin Bricker called for a "set of voluntary 'guidelines' and things to be aware of during trials" to help mitigate bad outcomes and prevent unintentional support for a system that was inherently repressive.[34] Bricker pointed out that when the "audience" or crowd of supporters react to something in court, it can have unintended consequences. For example, "when we laugh at cops on the stand, we are laughing at [McCaffery's] friends," said Bricker in an e-mail exchange with other defendants. "We should be concerned about the copjudge's feelings at these trials not because we actually care if he gets offended or not, but because our sisters' and brothers' futures are in his hands."

Bricker also noted that McCaffery's free speech commentary and verdict were applauded in the last group trial. Some supporters even laughed at his jokes. Bricker pointed out that some people might have felt that "the copjudge was being extremely friendly towards [activists] because he's feeling the heat from that recusal motion." Nevertheless, Bricker reminded the defendants that McCaffery was "the human embodiment of what we were protesting." Without pulling any punches, she called McCaffery "a racist, a sexist, a bigot, a player, a tool, and a puppet in the system we are fighting." Bricker also raised important questions about how to maintain dignity in a repressive system without legitimizing its existence:

> We should not encourage him (McCaffery) or his behavior, despite the fact that he attempted to appease us. We should not let him feel proud that he acquitted a bunch of white activists while he lets black folks rot in jail. He is not our friend. He is not funny. He's an asshole. We do not need to be rude to him, but it was suggested that we not smile at him or laugh at him or clap for him, because we're not buying his bullshit. . . . We may want to consider how we react to not-guilty verdicts so that we can react happily, and let the defendants know that we support them, we love them, and we are happy that they were [found] not guilty, but do it in such a way that we don't let the copjudge think we are happy with his actions and we support him.

One of the defendants in the last group trial, Alex Rae, raised similar concerns by pointing out how the victory with McCaffery "rings hollow" since "he will just return to being the harsh judge he is with the next guy."[35] Needless to say, McCaffery did not prove Rae wrong. That week would signal the decisive end of the "pro–free speech" McCaffery. Yet, the recusal effort had resulted in dismissal or acquittal in thirty-three cases, which was a relief for activists who had been facing serious charges. Less evident, but just as potent, was the sense of empowerment felt by many defendants who became reinvigorated to continue fighting widespread malicious prosecution. It was McCaffery's acquittals that prompted the *Philadelphia Inquirer* to report that "the mounting number of reversals in court have fueled complaints by civil-liberties experts and others that the rights of the protesters were swept aside during the convention in order to ensure a peaceful and prosperous image for the city."[36]

On January 30, the day of the second recusal hearing, the courtroom was filled with nervous tension. Later that week McCaffery would preside over "the van case." Would he refuse to hear the *pro se* recusal motion as he did with the Defender Association motion? What would that mean for

Redden and Rifkin, and what would it mean for the defendants in the van case? Would McCaffery revert back to normal and once again start convicting RNC defendants?

As people filed into court, the surprising news of a dismissal in Danielle Redden's case served to increase everyone's concern. Apparently, the district attorney had dismissed Redden's case the previous day—thus leaving Mark Rifkin as the only defendant to argue the *pro se* recusal motion. Normally, the dismissal of a defendant's case was good news; however, under these circumstances, the *pro se* motion could be hindered by the untimely removal of one of its primary litigants. Before the court was called into session, Redden and public defenders Meg Flores, Bradley Bridge, and Shawn Nolan approached Rifkin with the news. They quickly went into a private room to discuss what would be another significant turn of events. The district attorney had also just dropped Rifkin's case. He was stunned. "That's one of the most fucked up things I've heard in my life!"[37]

The dismissal of Redden and Rifkin's cases meant that the *pro se* recusal motion and the hearing were moot. Because McCaffery had narrowed the scope of the motion to just Redden and Rifkin, denying the involvement of others "similarly situated," the motion no longer had relevance. Despite the positive impact the recusal effort had up to that point, most people left the courtroom that day expecting the worst for the van case defendants and others with trials scheduled before McCaffery. Unfortunately, their instincts proved correct.

The Van Trial

Still angry over being denied the opportunity to argue McCaffery's bias, the van case defendants entered the courtroom the following Friday with a sense of righteousness that muted their fear of conviction. Attempting to create a political climate in McCaffery's otherwise restrained courtroom, defendants, supporters, and attorneys alike made a coordinated political statement by wearing a sticker depicting a U.S. flag upon which corporate logos had replaced the stars and the letters "S-O-L-D" had been emblazoned across the stripes.[38] The theme of a "corporate takeover" of politics had been integral to many of the issues people were protesting during the RNC, and the stickers had also been used during Bush's inauguration just a few weeks earlier.

The van case started with eighteen people accused of numerous misdemeanors, including disorderly conduct, reckless endangerment, criminal mischief, obstructing the highway, obstruction of justice, conspiracy to commit each of the aforementioned offenses, and possession of an instrument of crime (PIC). At a pretrial hearing for the puppet warehouse and van cases, the PIC charge had been dismissed against the warehouse defendants but not the Van defendants. Weeks before the trial, nine of the Van defendants took a plea deal offered by the district attorney, which eventually expunged their arrest and charges after paying a $300 "fine" and spending six months on probation. That left nine activists to fight their charges before McCaffery.

State Trooper Harry Keffer had infiltrated the group and drove the van into custody. He was the prosecution's only witness. Keffer testified extensively during a pretrial hearing two months earlier and, just as he had then, he tried to downplay the political messages that compelled the pro-testers to head downtown on August 1. The trooper focused on a sensa-tionalist statement he said was made by Adam Eidinger, one of the van case defendants. According to Keffer, Eidinger said the protesters were going to "fuck things up" on August 1.[39] McCaffery indicated that he found the testimony to be "pretty striking." In this way, he was persuaded by the city's argument of criminal intent.[40]

The defense countered that the van was filled with political propa-ganda and showed the video depicting such evidence. Although the police failed to produce an accurate record of what was in the van at the time of the arrest, McCaffery and the rest of the courtroom could plainly see from the video footage that it was full of signs, banners, satirical masks and other literature about the death penalty and criminal justice issues. Ignoring arguments made by public defender Shawn Nolan that activ-ists had been targeted for the content of their speech, prosecutor Trevan Borum argued that "the case had nothing to do with the political views held by the protesters."[41] Borum complained that activists did not "have the right to barricade other people and force them to listen to [their] message." Yet, citing the First Amendment, McCaffery had just acquitted numerous activists over the previous two weeks for doing just that.

Once the prosecution rested, the defense moved to dismiss a number of charges, many of which the city willingly withdrew. Only PIC and the conspiracy charges remained. Multiple defense attorneys argued that the PIC charge should not apply based on McCaffery's prior rulings involving lockboxes and street blockades. Representing Alexis Baden-Meyer, R2K Legal attorney Larry Krasner stated that "this court heard a case where peo-ple locked down and blocked an entrance to 676 for an hour and a half and, I believe properly ruled that even though there was inconvenience caused, that

that was reasonable and it was for a legitimate purpose."[42] Public defender
Meg Flores added that the PIC statute "requires an underlying crime to be
committed," but the defendants were no longer being prosecuted for committing a criminal act, only conspiring to do so. "An intellectually consistent
ruling here," said Krasner about the PIC charge, "has to be acquittal."

The defense ended their case with arguments against the conspiracy
counts. "What the Commonwealth must prove is that this conspiracy was
going to come to fruition," said public defender Shawn Nolan. "I suggest
they have not done this." Nolan also argued that prior restraint was at issue
because "These people never did anything." Moreover, Krasner pointed
out, nobody's actions were a certainty. "We cannot simply say that there
was a plan that we have cut off," and there is no way to "know what would
have happened." But without apology, McCaffery swiftly found all nine Van
defendants guilty of four misdemeanors: conspiracy to obstruct justice;
conspiracy to obstruct the highway, conspiracy to commit disorderly conduct; and possession of an instrument of crime. The Van trial represented
a return to business as usual in McCaffery's courtroom.

The main difference between the van case and the other group cases
preceding it—that the Van defendants hadn't done anything yet—should
have worked in favor of the defense. While it may have been true that the
van was transporting lockboxes in addition to signs, banners, and other
political propaganda, the activists had been prevented from engaging
in *any* activity—lawful or not. The court had determined that the activists' intent to commit civil disobedience was enough to convict, thereby
making a "state of mind" assessment of everyone in the van. But how did
McCaffery know that anyone or everyone in the van intended to break the
law? Defendants had little opportunity to make that point, and the arguments that did get made fell on deaf ears.

Another crucial difference between the earlier group cases and the
van case was that it involved police infiltration. If he acquitted the activists, McCaffery would be forced to refute the allegations of Harry Keffer, a
state intelligence officer. It is likely that he did not want to undermine law
enforcement legitimacy, state trooper infiltration, or any aspect of this particular operation. Moreover, since he no longer had to contend with pesky
recusal motions, why bother trying to maintain any semblance of justice,
fairness, or consistency?

McCaffery ended up sentencing the nine activists to time served and
a year of nonreporting parole. All of them vowed to fight their convictions. Seven of the activists decided to file an appeal "de novo," seeking a

new trial, with the right to a jury, in Common Pleas Court. The other two activists decided on a "writ of *certiorari*" appeal, demanding the recusal of McCaffery and arguing that police used prior restraint to deny their constitutional rights. In the end, the van case would turn out to be the longest lasting RNC-related trial.

The Recusal Legacy

Despite its failure to prevent McCaffery from presiding over future RNC trials, the recusal strategy ended up being one of the most empowering aspects of the legal support effort. It was a long-shot legal strategy that became a political success story. While getting cases switched to a more impartial judge was an important goal, it was also a tool to give the public a glimpse into the style of justice that gets meted out every day. Defendants and legal activists were able to expose McCaffery's loyalties and publicly question his impartiality—and not only about RNC-related cases.

Unfortunately, the mainstream media neglected the story. Although the recusal effort got coverage in the *Philadelphia City Paper*, the *Boston Phoenix*, and *The Nation*, the two Philadelphia dailies ignored the story entirely. As a result, a significant portion of the public missed out on the motion and the accusations leveled against McCaffery. Instead, the *Philadelphia Inquirer* published a front page Sunday-edition puff piece called "The Seamus Show" just days prior to the judge's harsh ruling in the van case.[43] With no mention made of the effort to recuse him from RNC cases, the piece was decidedly pro-McCaffery.

As with so many players in Philadelphia's political machine, McCaffery rose quickly through the state court ranks as though allegations of serious judicial misconduct had never been brought against him. A year after the RNC protests, he was appointed administrative judge of Philadelphia's Municipal Court, the fourth largest court in the country at the time. Two years later, McCaffery was elected to the Pennsylvania Superior Court, where he served until he was elected to the State Supreme Court in 2007. But, accusations of even more serious judicial misconduct followed him later in his career. McCaffery was suspended by fellow Supreme Court Justices in 2014 during an ethics investigation of a "pay-to-play" scandal in which law firms paid large referral fees to McCaffery's wife (and judicial aide) in cases brought before him.[44] Rather than face formal misconduct charges and possible impeachment, McCaffery resigned from the court and agreed to a lifetime ban on running for elected office.[45]

CHAPTER 9:
FELONY TRIALS AND LONG-HAUL VICTORIES

B Y THE END OF JANUARY 2001, ONLY TWENTY-EIGHT MISDEMEANOR and fourteen felony trials remained. According to R2K Legal, out of nearly two hundred defendants that went to trial, eighty-one cases had been dismissed, forty-five were acquitted, and the prosecution withdrew six. Only fifteen defendants had been convicted of misdemeanors and eight of summary offenses (equivalent to a traffic ticket). Of those twenty-three convictions, all but three were appealed. Out of an initial forty-three felony defendants, six were offered and took a diversionary plea deal that eventually expunged their records, twelve were reduced to misdemeanors, four had their charges dismissed, four pleaded no contest, three had their charges withdrawn by the prosecution, and one defendant pleaded guilty to a single felony charge with no additional jail time. The thirteen felony defendants who remained were prepared and resolved to go to trial.

Taking stock of the situation, the *Philadelphia Daily News* called the city's "charade" of "mass arrests" and "astronomical" bail "very disturbing."[1] Acknowledging the change in political landscape, the *Daily News* admitted to having been duped by public officials for "taking them at their word." This rare confession stood in stark contrast to the antidissident bias normally displayed by mainstream media. The *Daily News* even called those who believed that rights violations were "an appropriate cost" for hosting political conventions "dead wrong."

In one sense, things were winding down. Most of the cases had been resolved and RNC protesters were gaining further vindication in the court of public opinion. "As the prosecution's cases unravel and the arrest details surface, public opinion has shifted," noted the *Boston Phoenix* at the time.[2] The *Philadelphia Inquirer* published a multipage Sunday edition spread in mid-January in which they took stock of the legal battles thus far. "The reversals in court have added credibility to complaints that the rights of protesters were swept aside in the city's zeal to keep the streets open and peaceful at every corner." The *Inquirer* went on to point out that "widespread violations of civil liberties" were a "steep price" to pay for an undisrupted convention.[3]

But even as activists wanted the hard work to be over, some of the most serious cases had yet to be tried. While less than a third of the original felony cases remained, none of them had gone to trial yet. Several defendants like those in the high-profile Timoney 3 case were charged with assaulting police. Accused of being a protest "ringleader" along with Sellers and McGuckin, Kate Sorensen had also not yet been tried. Despite the victories, then, some of the hardest legal support work still lay ahead.

Amber Amy and Jamie Graham

Before the felony trials began, a high-profile misdemeanor case went to trial involving a National Lawyers Guild (NLG) legal observer who was arrested after witnessing police assault an RNC protester. Amber Amy was with friends the afternoon of August 2. On their way to hear presidential candidate Ralph Nader speak at the Shadow Convention, they were stopped at 12th and Race by police and subjected to unlawful searches. One person in the group who later testified as a defense witness said a cop rummaged through his backpack and, after failing to find anything incriminating, crushed his pack of cigarettes. When Amy objected to the police search and demanded to know their legal grounds, she was violently arrested.[4]

After being alerted to Amy's situation by the NLG, Jamie Graham was dispatched to the scene. While photographing Amy's arrest, Graham soon found himself being assaulted as well. The police knocked the camera from his hand and pushed him to the ground. Graham and Amy were both beaten badly enough to be taken to a nearby hospital before being jailed for nearly three days. On top of a broken rib and a concussion, Graham's face bore tread-shaped marks from the police boot that had stomped his head against the pavement.[5] Amy's mug shots depicted scrapes on her face and an abrasion on her collarbone.[6]

That same afternoon, local activist Jacqueline Ambrosini had been arrested while watching police arrest someone on their way to Nader's address. Ambrosini was charged with a couple misdemeanors, whereas both Amy and Graham were charged with obstruction of justice, failure to disperse, disorderly conduct and obstructing the highway. Amy was additionally charged with conspiracy and resisting arrest. The bulk of their trial took place in January. With cops fabricating reasons for the defendants' injuries to avoid culpability, it would prove to be the most bizarre police testimony that R2K Legal would witness.

According to *Philadelphia City Paper* reporter Gwen Shaffer, Amy's arresting officer Mary Luce said the defendant "dropped to the ground and then self-inflicted wounds on her face by rubbing her forehead and chin against the cement." Several other cops, including Graham's arresting officer Sgt. Dante Coccia, testified that the defendant had intentionally fallen on the ground. Coccia further testified that, a few moments after the arrest, he saw Graham "rubbing his forehead against a cement wall—with the intention of causing abrasions that could later be pinned on the police." To make the story more plausible, Coccia accused Graham of telling the cops he had a good lawsuit as a result of his "self-inflicted" injuries.

When the city's prosecutor began cross-examining Amy's father and questioned the legitimacy of their familial ties because they had different surnames, the audience burst into laughter. This compelled Municipal Court Judge William Meehan to clear the courtroom. As a result, the trial continued in closed session, which emboldened Assistant District Attorney Thomas Malone to attack. When the defense called Angus Love of the local NLG chapter as a character witness for Graham, the prosecution attempted to discredit the decades-old progressive legal organization and called legal observers a fiction invented by protesters to enable them to break the law.[7] On cross-examination, Malone all but accused Love and the NLG of engaging in a criminal conspiracy with the protesters.

Meehan ultimately convicted Amy and Graham at their next trial appearance on February 23, 2001. Both defendants were found guilty of two misdemeanors: failure to disperse and obstructing the highway. Both of them appealed their convictions and, on June 3, 2002, they were given a second trial. But before the trial began, the city offered Amy and Graham a plea bargain for a summary offense and ten hours of community service each. Given that both defendants wanted to move on with their lives and put energy into other important work, they conceded to the deal.

The Van Case Aftermath

By early March 2001, seven of the defendants that McCaffery had found guilty in the initial van trial had filed a *de novo* appeal seeking a new trial before a jury in the Court of Common Pleas. For their part, defendants Amanda Romero and Adam Eidinger appealed by writ of *certiorari*. The writ argued for the suppression of evidence from what the defense considered an illegal stop and search; however, it mainly sought to overturn the convictions based on a recusal of McCaffery and issues of prior restraint. "The United States Supreme Court has described prior restraints on free speech as the most serious and least tolerable infringement on First Amendment Rights," read the writ.[8] "For this reason, the Court has declared that prior restraint by arrest and prosecution for intended acts of symbolic speech that might be punishable under criminal law if they were left to occur is not allowed." The writ went on to cite the U.S. Supreme Court decision in *Southeastern Promotions v. Conrad*:

> The presumption against prior restraints is heavier and the degree of protection broader than that against limits on expression imposed by criminal penalties. Behind the distinction is a theory deeply etched in our law: a free society prefers to punish the few who abuse the rights of speech after they break the law than to throttle them and all others beforehand. It is always difficult to know in advance what an individual will say, and the line between legitimate and illegitimate speech is often so finely drawn that the risks of free-wheeling censorship are formidable.[9]

Granting a "motion to quash" in the case of the six van defendants on a *de novo* appeal (by the time of the trial, Dan Cross had dropped out, choosing to accept a plea bargain instead), Common Pleas Court Judge William J. Mazzola threw out all of their charges on November 21, 2001. During the proceedings, Assistant District Attorney Trevan Borum complained when the judge disagreed that sufficient evidence existed of conspiracy or possession of an instrument of a crime. "Judge, are you kidding?" asked Borum rhetorically.[10] The prosecutor then began arguing with the judge over the evidence and sarcastically commented that maybe the lower court trial had been "conducted in Portuguese." This didn't sit well with Mazzola. "You have remedies, sir, none of which is to show disrespect to the court." While Borum retreated and claimed merely to be "curious," Mazzola angrily accused the prosecutor of "implying I must be out of my mind or I read a totally different transcript."

Despite the loss, the district attorney's office continued to pursue the case—perhaps because of its high profile status and the involvement of a state police infiltrator, or perhaps because it was desperate to gain convictions to improve its damaged reputation. The district attorney appealed the decision, but the case landed back in Mazzola's court. Given the opportunity to clear up the record, Mazzola went through each charge and explained to the prosecution how it had failed to provide the "*prima facie* case*" required to "proceed to trial."[11] Mazzola even called the use of lockboxes "to help express political ideas at the RNC," a "circumstance manifestly appropriate for lawful use of such device." Based on the evidence, the judge concluded it wasn't clear if "the defendants intended to engage in any illegal activity." Mazzola underscored that "to have their views heard" was a "legitimate purpose." "These defendants were never given an opportunity to act criminally, were never given the opportunity to sit in the street, were never given the opportunity to leave, and were never given the right to refuse to leave upon orders from the police authorities. For these reasons intent was unrealized and overt acts in furtherance of this 'conspiracy' were too far removed to withstand a motion to quash, let alone sustain a conviction."[12]

Still unsatisfied, the district attorney appealed to the Superior Court of Pennsylvania. On September 18, 2003, that court ruled the van defendants' charges should not have been thrown out and forced a new trial to occur again in Common Pleas Court.[13] One defendant, Mark DeBrew, appealed the decision, but the Pennsylvania Supreme Court refused to hear his case. By the time the trial began in October 2004, only four *de novo* van defendants remained. One of those defendants was Caleb Arnold, who went to trial representing herself *pro se*. The defendants' aimed to be completely up-front about their plans to block traffic access near the Convention Center, arguing that the obstruction was based in political speech and protected under the First Amendment.[14] All of them testified and—despite being prevented from outlining the rich history of civil disobedience—they convinced the jury of their right to confront authority. The prosecution declared that the defendants were "domestic terrorists" who had descended upon Philadelphia to wreak havoc, but this approach failed to persuade the jury and, on October 20, 2004 (more than four years after the RNC 2000 protests) the four activists were acquitted of all charges.

Common Pleas Court Judge Joyce Kean denied the writ of *certiorari* appeal by Romero and Eidinger in December 2002. They then appealed to the Superior Court, which ruled in 2004 that there was not enough evidence to convict Romero, and dismissed her case outright. Meanwhile, they found that there was enough evidence to validate Judge McCaffery's earlier conviction of Eidinger. For more than four years after the protests, the van case lingered on, outlasting even the Timoney 3 case, which went to trial in April 2004.

Kate Sorensen

The trial of Kate Sorensen was important for many reasons, not least of which was the fanfare surrounding her arrest and detention. Like Sellers and McGuckin, Sorensen was named in the puppet warehouse search warrant affidavit, labeled a protest "ringleader," and held on $1 million bail. But Sorensen was also charged with ten felonies and ten misdemeanors and held in jail for more than a week, much of it in solitary confinement. After her arrest, Sorensen learned that she was the subject of a longer-term surveillance operation before and after the protests. According to legal documents, Sorensen had been followed by undercover FBI agents since April 2000, and the city had gathered her "water and real estate records, bought private data to track her whereabouts as she moved across the country," and even "examined the voter registrations of her friends."[15] The city's Department of Licenses & Inspection (L&I) also harassed Sorensen by repeatedly coming to her house, the site of several PDAG meetings. After Sorensen was released from jail, L&I made weekly visits demanding that everything be up to code, forcing her and her housemates to pay hundreds of dollars in fines and refurbishments. "Every time we'd fix something, they'd find something else," said Sorensen.[16] The week before her trial, L&I badgered her again on three separate occasions, claiming that her West Philadelphia home was on the department's "nuisance list."[17]

Adding to its importance was the fact that Sorensen's was the first RNC-related felony trial. By the time her trial began on March 12, 2001, the number of felony cases had dwindled to ten.[18] All eyes were on Sorensen to see whether the felony trials would fare as well as the misdemeanors had. Hedging their bets, R2K Legal heavily publicized the event, expecting to see a wholesale acquittal and a further erosion of the city's criminal cases. Sorensen had been involved with local and national campaigns for social change for more than twenty years. In the 1980s, as her friends began to die of AIDS, she became involved in the earliest efforts to bring attention to the epidemic. After joining ACT UP Los Angeles in 1986, Sorensen and others used civil disobedience to force the city to establish one of the country's first AIDS wards at L.A. County Hospital. In 1994, she moved to Philadelphia where she continued to work with ACT UP on numerous local, national, and international campaigns. A month before the RNC protests, Sorensen traveled to Durban, South Africa, to participate in the thirteenth International AIDS Conference. As a result of the countless bonds of friendship developed through her years of activism, there was a groundswell of interest in her trial, which in turn gave strength to her legal battle.

On August 1, Sorensen's role was to ensure the safety of dissidents and to help deescalate tense standoffs between protesters and police. She was one of about ten people who were on two-way radio bands in constant communication with medics and the legal team. In fact, Sorensen was arrested while walking through Love Park talking on her Nextel—an "instrument of crime" according to the city.[19] Never told why she was arrested, she was shocked to find out that the police had brought twenty charges (half of them felonies) carrying a sentence of more than twenty years. On top of that, she would not be able to get out of jail because of her prohibitively high bail. The *Philadelphia Gay News* (*PGN*) reported that, nine days after her arrest, Sorensen's bail was lowered to $100,000. In order to justify the city's actions and deny any political motivation, Assistant District Attorney David Desiderio made the incredible assertion that Sorensen was a "risk to the community" and that her high bail "was not necessarily related to the convention."

Despite Sorensen's role as lead organizer of the July 29 march for universal health care and special assistant to Hospital and Health Care Workers Local 1199-C president Henry Nicholas, the city essentially blamed her for orchestrating most of the vandalism that took place on August 1: overturned fences and dumpsters, small fires, and vehicles damaged by slashed tires, broken windows, and spray paint.[20] Because arson and other serious felonies had been dismissed at pretrial hearings, Sorensen was left to go to trial on charges of felony riot, risking a catastrophe, conspiracy, and criminal mischief. Although she had been arrested at least ten times for civil disobedience over the prior twenty years, she had never previously been charged with a felony or crime of violence.[21]

Prosecutors don't typically talk about their cases unless it suits their interests. In this case, the district attorney made a calculated move to publicly sensationalize the accusations against Sorensen by issuing a press release three days before her trial. According to *PGN*, the district attorney said Sorensen was responsible for protesters "damaging city vehicles, setting trash cans on fire and upsetting trash bins and newspaper vending boxes." When you cross the line, Desiderio bombastically told *PGN*, "you have to pay the price," and "Sorensen has to pay the price, not for dissension, but for breaking the law."[22]

Pushing still further, Desiderio maintained that, by breaking the law, Sorensen had also "trample[d] on other people's civil rights." The assistant district attorney then revealed his prosecutorial strategy: undercover

Kate Sorensen's Trial
March 6th - 8th

Philadelphia Criminal Justice Center
1301 Filbert St. (13th& Filbert)
Room 707 9:00am

COURT ROOM STRATEGY

Dear Fellow Activists and Supporters,
This will be the first R2K felony trial. It is important that I win.
My lawyer and I have been working on a court strategy. I welcome your support. Part of the strategy is an understanding that judges and jurors have to get past their first impressions to see justice. I know that it's harsh but please, please wear nice dresses and pants to court. Please pull crazy hairdos back. The charges pressed against me could add up to many years in prison. We need to take this really seriously so I have to ask for no clapping or cat calls. I understand if you are unable to honor these requests and can't come to support me in the court room. Your love, support and solidarity has already been deeply felt that's why I'm having a Win-Lose Trial Reception. Please see the other side of flyer and come.
Courage-
Kate

The Charges:
Riot
Risking Catastrophe
Criminal Mischief
Conspiracy

police who had followed Sorensen would show that she directed as many as seven hundred people by giving commands over a cell phone. Desiderio told *PGN* that "officers watched her and were sometimes able to hear her while she used the phone to direct people who participated in acts of vandalism." Sorensen's attorney, Larry Krasner, countered the city's rhetoric by saying that "the District Attorney must produce evidence that directly points to my client committing a crime."[23] So far, Krasner continued, "the prosecution has only come up with false accusations and outlandish claims." Krasner called Sorensen's case "a fraud and a disgrace to the people of Philadelphia."

As a felony defendant in Common Pleas Court, Sorensen had the choice between a trial by judge or by jury. She chose a jury trial. Sorensen's mother and sister flew in from out-of-state to be witnesses at her trial, which began on March 8 and lasted for three days. Because the risk was so great, Sorensen laid down some ground rules for her supporters. "We had two people at the door who wouldn't let people in if they were wearing jeans," said Sorensen.[24] "No one was allowed to wear black and everyone had to shave." Although she was really conflicted about controlling the presentation of her friends and supporters, Sorensen concluded that "if someone in court was wearing black, the prosecution would start to talk about black-clad anarchists and getting the jury to have disparaging thoughts about the way people dressed." It wasn't really about ideology or actions, she said; "It was all about people's presentation." Throughout her trial, the courtroom was packed with up to forty supporters each day.[25]

As promised, Desiderio attempted to convince the jury that Sorensen was responsible for nearly all of the property destruction that happened on August 1. "She's a leader," he told the jury.[26] Moreover, "It wouldn't make sense to not have someone in charge of a protest," he claimed as he struggled to pin blame on her. Police officers took the stand and testified that Sorensen appeared to be a protest "leader" because she was "often walking at the head of a group of demonstrators and talking 'continually' on a cell phone."[27] But the officers also acknowledged that they never saw her personally destroy any property or obstruct traffic.

Philadelphia police detective Albert Ford testified that Sorensen had pushed a protester into a line of cops, but several defense witnesses contradicted his accusation and said that she had come to their aid. Jessica Piraneo, then a student from Chicago, told the jury that she was "thrown to the ground by a line of police during a demonstration near 18th and Vine Streets."[28] Within seconds, Piraneo said she "found herself surrounded by police on horseback." Sorensen, who happened to be in the area, helped carry Piraneo to safety before calling a medic to take care of her. Fortunately, the R2K Legal evidence working group had located video footage of the incident, which Sorensen later said made a big difference. Other defense witnesses, including Henry Nicholas, praised Sorensen for being "an excellent loyal and dedicated employee."[29] While on the stand, Nicholas also helped to clarify her role as a safety monitor on August 1, and as an organizer of the universal health care march on July 29.

Sorensen herself took the stand and testified for two hours. "My purpose was to let people know what was happening throughout the city," she told the jury.[30] Refuting the prosecution's characterization, Sorensen emphatically stated: "I was not a leader," and "I didn't have a group with me." In the end, the city's accusations didn't stick. As the *Weekly Press* noted in its trial summary, "Desiderio presented no incriminating phone records, no confessions from co-conspirators, and no testimony from informers or insiders."[31] On March 12, after each side had rested, the jury deliberated for five hours. The mood was tense as supporters waited for a verdict to be reached.[32] Finally, the jury returned to acquit Sorensen of all charges—except a single misdemeanor, criminal mischief.

Feelings about the verdict were mixed. On the one hand, Sorensen was happy to be able to go back to organizing without the threat of jail time hanging over her head. To go from twenty charges to a single misdemeanor was also worth celebrating. On the other hand, Sorensen wasn't even guilty of the crime the jury had pinned on her. "If you look, there is no evidence of me doing any criminal mischief," said Sorensen after the trial. Anticipating a verdict on the afternoon of March 12, R2K Legal organized a press conference at the offices of 1199-C. Defiant, Krasner declared that Sorensen "was found guilty of a crime that was not supported by any of the evidence," and that "the conviction will easily be thrown out on appeal."[33] Sorensen, by contrast, was more reflective. "The city was willing to give me 20 years of jail time," she told a group of reporters. "The city was willing to give me a million dollars bail for . . . $1,800 worth of damages I had nothing to do with."[34] Concluding on a positive note, she stated: "I've learned a lot of patience" but "I'm ready to go back to what I'm supposed to be doing, which is being an AIDS activist." About six weeks later, Sorensen was sentenced to probation over the objections of Desiderio, who had asked the court to impose jail time.

Months after her trial, Sorensen had unexpected interactions with two of her jurors.[35] One juror confronted Sorensen in the Friends Center.

A woman who was cleaning the building came up to her and asked her if she'd been in a trial. After responding positively, the woman told Sorensen that she had been on her jury. When asked why they found her guilty, the juror said matter-of-factly, "We had to find you guilty of something." Shortly thereafter, Sorensen was on the phone with the post office and giving personal information to a postal worker who eventually identified herself as another juror. Sorensen asked her the same question, and the worker replied: "You had to be guilty of something." Confounded by the responses she got, Sorensen blamed the justice system. "The trial was so surreal," she said. "It wasn't about justice. It was a competition between the prosecution and the defense and it had nothing to do with me." At the end of the trial, Sorensen said she shook hands with Desiderio. "You played a better game than I did," he said.

Matthew Berghs

On March 14, two days after the Sorensen trial concluded, a nineteen-year-old Bloomington activist and freshman at Indiana University was tried for felony aggravated assault on a police officer and three misdemeanors: simple assault, obstruction of justice, and recklessly endangering another person. After his arrest at 15th and Locust on August 1, Matthew Berghs was held for three days on $50,000 bail.[36] Though Berghs was of slight build and a self-described pacifist, he was accused of hitting Philadelphia police officer Thomas Donahue with a seven-foot bamboo pole.[37] To reinforce Donahue's story, Police Commissioner Timoney unexpectedly testified for the prosecution, making the trial especially noteworthy.

Berghs's attorney Shawn Nolan revealed early on that Berghs himself was the victim of brutality by police and not the other way around. Nolan presented the jury with photographs taken by Berghs's mother five days after his arrest. The pictures showed him with bruises and scrapes on his body, indicating police had beaten him. Nonetheless, Donahue took the stand, testifying that Berghs had hit him with a pole and denying that he had violently arrested the defendant. Reporting for the Philadelphia Independent Media Center, Susan Phillips said Donahue admitted on cross-examination that "he never saw the stick before or after the alleged assault."[38]

Waving the pole around during closing arguments, Nolan referred to the instrument of crime as the "magic stick" and stressed the absurdity of its appearance and reappearance during an incident police claim lasted ten seconds. Implying falsified reports, Nolan questioned why Officer Donahue's story changed twice from arrest to the preliminary hearing to the trial. Donahue's original arrest report had Berghs throwing the stick, then swinging the stick and finally it added a punch in the face of Officer Donahue.

Timoney took the stand as an eyewitness and, although he claimed to have seen the entire incident, acknowledged he did not see Berghs assault Donahue or any other officer.[39] Timoney testified he saw Berghs being chased by Donahue, and confirmed that the officer "got the right guy." Nevertheless, he could not implicate Berghs in any illegal activity, let alone assault on a police officer.[40] Timoney also denied defense allegations that police had beaten Berghs. By the time the prosecution rested, the district attorney had failed to supply fingerprint evidence or other proof beyond Donahue's testimony that Berghs had held the stick and used it to attack the police.

Berghs himself took the stand on the second day of his trial and testified that he was running at the time to get out of Center City where mass arrests were taking place. Berghs and other defense witnesses said that police were acting violently, targeting suspected anarchists and people dressed in black. Because Berghs had worn black that day, he said he was fearful of getting arrested.[41] According to the *Philadelphia City Paper*, Berghs testified that Donahue "grabbed him from behind with a billy club, jamming it across his neck and collarbone," and clubbing him "in the head, near the shoulders and on the calves." Before being arrested, Berghs said, he was thrown to the ground and sustained multiple injuries, some of which still afflicted him.[42]

Despite Police Commissioner Timoney's eyewitness testimony, it took the jury less than two hours to return a verdict of "not guilty" on all counts.[43] The Berghs trial was an embarrassment for the city. Not only was it the second felony trial to be derailed in less than a week, it also made clear that the people of Philadelphia had seen through the police department's lies. Despite his authority, they even refused to believe the testimony of the commissioner.

First Group Felony Trial

On April 9, the first group felony trial took place in the Court of Common Pleas. Four defendants were accused of assaulting multiple police officers and had been charged with numerous felonies, including felony riot, aggravated assault, and conspiracy. One of the defendants, William "Bill" Beckler, was a recent Columbia Law School graduate. He had just taken the New York State Bar Exam less than a month before coming to Philadelphia to act as an NLG legal observer during the RNC 2000 protests. After his arrest, he began to volunteer full-time with the R2K Legal Collective.

The accusations against Beckler and his three co-defendants—Shane Bastien, Andrew Hess, and Daniel Kruk—were as outrageous as the accusations against protesters in other felony cases. On August 1, Beckler had been acting as a legal observer and riding his bicycle around Center City collecting the names of arrestees. That evening, Beckler was bicycling in the vicinity of Rittenhouse Square when he saw co-defendant Shane Bastien being arrested and handcuffed on Latimer Street.[44] When he approached to get Bastien's name, "the cops grabbed me, beat me and arrested me."[45] According to Beckler, "They stood on my body and ground my elbow into the ground."[46] As he was getting handcuffed, Kruk and Hess wandered onto the scene. Hess, who denied any involvement in the protests, had just come from work as a lifeguard and was still wearing swim trunks when he was arrested.[47] Beckler was jailed for six days and held on $60,000 bail.[48]

Beckler told the *Philadelphia Daily News* a couple of months before his trial that he believed he was arrested because he was near the area where Commissioner Timoney had an altercation with protesters a few minutes earlier. During pretrial hearings, however, he learned that he and his co-defendants were being accused of violently attacking the police. According to police reports, Beckler allegedly jumped onto the backs of two police officers. Calling the charges "trumped up," Beckler pointed to his slight build as proof that the allegations were a virtual impossibility.[49] Nevertheless, the specter of years of jail time was a serious concern. Fortunately for Beckler and his co-defendants, most of their charges were thrown out before trial. Still, they were each faced felony riot and misdemeanor disorderly conduct.[50]

In a one-day bench trial with Common Pleas Court Judge Pamela Dembe presiding, the city spun tales of violence and mayhem but failed to convince the court. Arresting officers William Schmidt and Mark Anthony testified that the defendants hurled rocks, threatened them with a "roman candle," and knocked one officer off his bicycle, though no evidence was offered.[51] Schmidt testified that, while on bike patrol on August 1, he "herded" demonstrators southward away from an anti–death penalty rally at City Hall. Schmidt and Anthony further testified that, while following a large group of protesters headed toward Rittenhouse Square, they were "charged" by one of the defendants.[52] According to Anthony, Beckler wrestled with him in an attempt to free his co-defendant. Schmidt testified that another defendant ran at him with an unlit "roman candle," and the fourth defendant allegedly threw objects, possibly rocks, at the two officers. Despite these allegations, however, neither could produce a shred of evidence. Apparently, Schmidt had thrown away the "roman candle," and no rocks were retrieved to substantiate their story.

Needless to say, Judge Dembe was unswayed by Schmidt and Anthony's testimony. At the conclusion of the trial, Dembe swiftly acquitted the four defendants of their felony and misdemeanor charges. For unknown reasons, however, she convicted Bastien and Hess of disorderly conduct. When asked for comment by the *Philadelphia Inquirer*, a spokesperson for the district attorney's office said that "she was not familiar with the case,"[53] an odd response given that it involved the Republican convention protests and accusations of assault against police officers. More likely, the district attorney's office was growing tired of having to "defend" its continued prosecutions in spite of its dismal record.

"My arrest was part of a greater scheme to keep demonstrators off the streets during the Republican National Convention," said Beckler after his acquittal.[54] "I have sat in court and watched numerous police officers lie and get caught lying, including Philadelphia Police Commissioner Timoney." In an e-mail sent to his friends and supporters, Beckler described how his brutal arrest had realigned his beliefs about social change. "Before August 1st, I had not realized that police and government so boldly protect the status quo," he said. Beckler would continue to work with R2K Legal to support activists engaged in criminal defense and civil litigation for more than a year after his trial.

Loose Ends

By mid-April 2001, all of the initial misdemeanor trials had concluded, with only a handful of defendants still awaiting appeal trials. In early May 2001, accused protest "ringleader" Terrence McGuckin had his appeal trial before a jury in the Court of Common Pleas. As with his November 2000 trial, the prosecution's main witness was Angelo Parisi, a detective with the Washington, DC, Metropolitan Police Department. Parisi showed video footage he had taken of McGuckin and testified that he saw the defendant "direct a group of protesters to blockade the corner of 13th and Arch."[55] Parisi's story fell apart, however, when McGuckin's attorney David

Rudovsky presented video evidence on cross-examination that placed his client a mile away from the scene at the time.

Once the prosecution had rested, Common Pleas Court Judge Gary S. Glazer granted a motion to dismiss McGuckin's charges before hearing any defense testimony. Before dismissing his remaining two misdemeanor charges of disorderly conduct and obstructing the highway, Judge Glazer called the city's evidence "underwhelming." Defense attorney Rudovsky called the acquittal "a damning indictment of the Police Department and of the District Attorney's Office, as it showed that Mr. McGuckin did nothing illegal during the Republican convention and that the arrest and detention under $500,000 bail was done simply to punish and incarcerate him for his political views."[56] Rudovsky further noted that, because more than 90 percent of all RNC-related cases had resulted in dismissals or acquittals, "the only conclusion I can draw [is] there was a plan at the highest levels of city government to use the criminal justice system to arrest demonstrators and hold them for the duration of the convention." McGuckin's acquittal cleared the way for him to file a civil lawsuit, which he did in late July 2001 along with John Sellers.

The next felony trial occurred on July 6, 2001, against an elementary school teacher from Tucson, Arizona. Matt Musselwhite had come to Philadelphia to protest, but got a lot more than he bargained for. Like many other activists, he was arrested on August 1 and charged with multiple misdemeanors. Yet after his release from jail and his return to Ashland, Oregon, where he was staying for the summer, Musselwhite found out his case was actually unlike that of any other activist he was arrested with that day.

On September 1, 2000, the *Ashland Daily Tidings* ran a mug shot of Musselwhite under the headline, "Ashland police are asking residents to be on the lookout for a man who allegedly assaulted a Philadelphia police officer." The paper went on to claim that he may be "armed and dangerous."[57] Musselwhite soon found out that the Philadelphia Police Department had issued an arrest warrant and was working collaboratively with other police agencies on a veritable manhunt. Apparently, the district attorney decided to additionally charge the schoolteacher with "attempted murder" for allegedly throwing a cop in front of a moving car.[58] Police reports claimed that the officer, John Livingston, sustained a fractured elbow from being pushed to the ground.

Without any fanfare, Musselwhite voluntarily returned to Philadelphia to face new charges at an October 31 preliminary hearing.

When he appeared at the hearing, however, the city had reduced the attempted murder charge to felony aggravated assault on a police officer, and added misdemeanor obstruction of justice.[59] Without apology, district attorney spokesperson Cathie Abookire said they "dropped the attempted murder charge because it was not the right charge," and that it was "the only fair thing to do." Musselwhite told the *Philadelphia Weekly* at his trial that the police had engaged in numerous intimidation tactics in the year since the RNC protests. "They visited my grandmother and told her I was a terrorist," he said.[60] "They went to my rental agent and told her I was an anarchist."

Common Pleas Court Judge James Lineberger presided over Musselwhite's July 6 jury trial, which began with Assistant District Attorney Pierre LaTour explaining how the defendant "emerged from a crowd of political protesters at the intersection of 15th Street and JFK" and "hoisted [Livingston] and threw him in front of a moving car."[61] Although Livingston testified he didn't see his alleged assailant, two other Philadelphia police officers said they did. Inspector Jeremiah Daley and Officer Joseph Goodwin testified that they chased Musselwhite and caught up with him about fifty feet away in the area of Dilworth Plaza. The problem for the prosecution was that Daley and Goodwin had conflicting accounts of how Musselwhite was dressed.

Because of the inconsistencies in police testimony, Musselwhite's attorney Assistant Defender Shawn Nolan decided that it was unnecessary to put any defense witnesses on the stand. "The prosecution has made our case for us," said Nolan during closing arguments in which he described the case as one of mistaken identity. "Square pegs in round holes," he explained to the jury.[62] "From the beginning, it was absolutely clear they had the wrong guy." Despite the testimony of three police officers, the jury took less than thirty minutes to acquit Musselwhite of all charges.[63]

Steve Swart was the last felony defendant to go to trial until 2004, when the Timoney 3 were finally tried. A longtime and well-respected antiracist and social change activist from Lansing, Michigan, Swart was another defendant charged with aggravated assault on a police officer.[64] Concerned about his trial, which was scheduled for July 16, Swart came to Philadelphia a few days early to prepare. The Sunday before his trial, he and a group of supporters met in West Philadelphia to help deal with last-minute details. As it turned out, Swart was offered a plea bargain by the city on the day of his trial for misdemeanor assault, with two years probation, one hundred hours of community service, and no jail time. Swart accepted the plea deal, which R2K Legal called a "victory," resulting from "the strength and success of our court solidarity campaign to keep folks charged with felonies out of jail."[65] By mid-July 2001, all of the initial RNC-related trials had taken place, with the exception of the high-profile Timoney 3 felony case. Up to that point, RNC defendants had prevailed in 95 percent of their criminal cases.

The Timoney 3 Case

The Timoney 3 defendants—Darby Landy, Eric Steinberg, and Camilo "Camille" Viveiros—didn't know each other before their arrest on August 1. The three were accused of getting into an altercation with police, one of whom was Timoney. Together, they were initially charged with a total of seven felonies and nineteen misdemeanors; however, Viveiros had the most serious charges of first- and second-degree aggravated assault on a police officer.[66] His total of eleven charges also included simple assault, riot, recklessly endangering another person, possessing an instrument of crime, disorderly conduct, resisting arrest, and criminal conspiracy. If convicted, Viveiros faced more than thirty years in prison.[67] Calling their charges "trumped up," the defendants steadfastly denied the city's version of events throughout their years-long prosecution.[68]

According to police testimony, Timoney and two other officers on bicycles encountered a group of people "rocking a parked car" at the corner of 17th and Latimer Streets, near Rittenhouse Square.[69] The way the *Philadelphia Inquirer* described it, Timoney "rammed his bicycle into protesters" and, after attempting to make arrests, a "struggle ensued."[70] Officer Clyde Frasier claimed to have grabbed two people but, while he was trying to cuff them, Steinberg allegedly came at him wielding a police bike. Believing that Steinberg was going to hit him with the bike, Frasier said he punched Steinberg in the chest and knocked him to the ground. Frasier then testified that he saw Viveiros throw a police bike at Timoney and Officer Raymond Felder, who were "both struggling with other people at the time." Timoney testified that he felt a bike hit his back, but didn't see who threw it. He apparently walked away with minor scrapes. Felder (who claimed to have been hit in the head) testified that he suffered a concussion, which kept him out of work for about five weeks.[71]

Shortly after the alleged incident with Viveiros, Timoney said he saw Landy try to steal one of the police bicycles. According to his testimony, the commissioner said he grabbed the bike but that Landy yanked it from his hands and threw it at him.[72] Based on these accusations, Landy was also charged with robbery, theft, and receiving stolen property. All three defendants were kept in jail for more than a week on $450,000 bail each. Landy was held for seventeen days, longer than any other protester.[73]

A soft-spoken, well-liked community organizer and low-income housing activist from southeastern Massachusetts, Viveiros argued his innocence from the beginning. Like his co-defendants, he claimed to have been at the wrong place at the wrong time. "I certainly didn't throw any bike," Viveiros told the *Associated Press*, "and didn't resist the police arresting me."[74] Not only did he deny assaulting Timoney and Felder, he insisted that police had, in fact, attacked him. Viveiros recalled being thrown to the ground, getting his head slammed against the pavement, and blacking out.[75] Witnesses and hospital records strongly reinforced his claims.[76] "It was a very shocking episode in my life," said Viveiros, who had no prior criminal record.[77] "I was actually beaten by the police, and then charged with assaulting police," a fact he would realize at arraignment when Timoney fingered him as the attacker.

What police didn't mention was that, with the large rally against the criminal justice system concluding, protesters like Viveiros were simply attempting to disperse. For his part, Viveiros hadn't even planned on being in Philadelphia that day; he had a grant application to finish in Massachusetts where he lived and worked.[78] By day, he assisted elderly and disabled tenants in working-class communities to find housing and prevent evictions.[79] His friends and comrades could also attest (and did whenever they got the chance) that Viveiros had strongly held views about nonviolent social change, thus making the accusations against him that much more unbelievable. Housing issues brought Viveiros to Philly that summer and, with the encouragement of fellow activists, he decided to stay for the fateful day of direct action. "I came to push for more humane government policies," he said, "and I left worrying about my own freedom."[80] Steinberg was a University of the Arts student living in Philadelphia, who was riding his bicycle observing the protests when he got swept up in the melee.[81] Landy, meanwhile, was an activist from North Carolina. Like Viveiros, both refuted their charges.

Dismissals and Appeals

On October 12, 2000, the Timoney 3 had a pretrial hearing before Common Pleas Court Judge Pamela Dembe. The defendants had filed motions to quash earlier in October. They argued that "the admissible evidence presented at the preliminary hearing (while the protesters were still in jail) failed to establish a *prima facie* case" for most of the charges.[82] Timoney, Frasier, and Felder all testified, but Judge Dembe agreed with the defense and said that the Commonwealth had not succeeded in proving anything more than minor offenses. The defendants were relieved when the judge granted their motion and threw out or reduced their most serious charges.[83] Although Viveiros was still facing up to ten years (he and Steinberg still had felonies), all of Landy's charges were reduced to misdemeanors, and a heavy blow had been dealt to what was one of the city's most important cases.[84] A motion to reconsider was quickly filed by the prosecution, but it was just as abruptly denied on November 2. In response, the city appealed Dembe's dismissal to the Pennsylvania Superior Court, which delayed the case considerably.

Over the next year, legal workers who weren't otherwise completely occupied with more immediate criminal cases helped to scour the activist community for evidence that would exonerate the Timoney 3. A remarkable amount of work went into trying to locate people who witnessed the arrests, including an all-out search for videographers at the scene. An elaborate system of evidence collection was set up by R2K Legal to protect and conceal the body of information being retrieved. Although the search for evidence in the Timoney 3 case continued virtually until the trial, critical footage was uncovered as early as December 2000.[85]

In January 2002, a three-judge panel of the Pennsylvania Superior Court ruled in favor of the city, thus overturning Dembe's dismissals and reinstating all the original felony charges.[86] The defendants appealed to the Pennsylvania Supreme Court, but not before Timoney left Philadelphia to join a private New York "security" firm as a consultant for mass protest policing. While the renewed threat of felony charges hung over the defendants' heads, Timoney had ridden the Republican convention publicity right into the national spotlight. Although he was already known as a "hard-brawling cop from New York,"[87] the *Associated Press* asserted that images of Timoney "dashing about the city on his bike, then appearing at a news conference with a bloody knee, cemented his popularity."[88] It was a career-defining moment for Timoney, who went on to become the architect of the "Miami Model."[89]

Meanwhile, three anxious defendants were left to deal with the fallout from their arrest and prosecution, which continued mainly at Timoney's behest. By July 2002, the Supreme Court had declined to hear their appeal, paving the way for a trial on their original charges in Common Pleas Court.[90] The trial had been set for October 9 but one delay after another prolonged it for nearly two more years. Timoney could not have cared less about Landy, Steinberg, and Viveiros's plight. Even as the Miami police chief, he continued to play up the case in media interviews. Viveiros, on the other hand, struggled to organize tenants with an ominous criminal case looming in the background. At first, Viveiros didn't understand why it was difficult to get people to even attend rallies. Eventually, however, it became clear: "I think some people [were] thinking, 'This could happen to me.'"[91] The state's effort to intimidate dissenters had spread beyond the convention and into the world of community organizing.

Nevertheless, Viveiros continued to fight back against the intimidation, building a formidable network of support on top of his already-impressive list of friends and allied organizations. While Landy and Steinberg chose a more low-key approach and did not work closely with R2K Legal, Viveiros took the spectacle of his case head on in an effort to shift the dynamic in his favor.[92] But because the case involved intricacies that did not factor into other RNC-related cases, he formed a separate support group, which came to be known as "Friends of Camilo" (FoC).[93] Having built a website to guide support efforts, the FoC launched a petition to put pressure on the city. In addition to working with mainstream and independent media, word was spread through newsletters, speaking tours, and solidarity events, as well as through puppetry, poetry, and theater.[94] Fundraisers were held throughout the country to help pay for expensive legal defense costs. As the trial got closer, FoC encouraged individuals, national organizations, community groups, tenant associations, unions, religious congregations, and others to write letters of support to convince the judge of Viveiros's upstanding character and show how much damage his imprisonment would cause to the community.

The Timoney 3 Trial

By the time of the trial, Viveiros had amassed significant and prominent support, including from two members of Congress (Barney Frank and James McGovern), eight members of the Boston City Council, the National Organizers Alliance, the National Coalition for the Homeless, Arthur Miller, Mel King, Howard Zinn, and numerous housing, religious, labor, and social justice organizations. Congressperson Frank, who had worked with Viveiros on housing issues in the past, rejected the accusations of violence and called him "a very decent, low-key person dedicated to poverty issues."[95]

A week before the trial was scheduled to begin, FoC organized a well-attended breakfast press conference at Philadelphia's White Dog Café.[96] More than a mere Timoney slap-down (though it could have been),[97] the idea was to show the level of solidarity enjoyed by Viveiros. It was also meant to reacquaint reporters with a case that was nearly four years old and connect them with relevant spokespeople.[98] A beautiful banner made by local activists adorned the wall behind the speakers and provided a politically symbolic backdrop for the media. Several news outlets attended the breakfast, which set the stage for the Timoney 3 trial the following week.

The trial began on April 5, 2004, and lasted only two days as a result of the defendants' choice to have a bench trial before Common Pleas Judge William Mazzola.[99] Mazzola was the judge who threw out all of the charges against the van case defendants after they had been convicted by Judge McCaffery. The small courtroom was packed and those who couldn't fit inside sat or milled around in the hallways. Other supporters attended a solemn vigil outside the courthouse.

The prosecution started the trial with testimony from several police officers, but the city's star witness, Timoney, testified the next morning. Although Timoney had fingered Viveiros nearly four years ago in a preliminary hearing, the former Philadelphia police commissioner couldn't provide a positive identification of his alleged attacker. "I never saw him," Timoney said, but added, "There is no doubt in my mind he threw the bike at me."[100] After the prosecution rested, the court heard from Viveiros and Steinberg, who both testified in their own defense.[101] Landy, by contrast, chose not to take the witness stand. That afternoon, the defense introduced videotaped evidence taken by a bystander. According to the *Philadelphia Inquirer*, the footage "showed that Viveiros had not struggled with police and showed an officer punching him in the back as he was arrested." The videotape also contradicted the testimony of multiple police officers. One cop had testified that Viveiros was resisting arrest, but the footage showed him face down on the pavement not resisting in any way.[102] Timoney's testimony also conflicted with the taped evidence, thus raising significant doubt about the police version of events.

Once Mazzola had heard from both sides, he quickly acquitted the three defendants of all charges. While acknowledging that a melee had occurred on August 1, and conceding that Felder and Timoney were injured, Mazzola was unconvinced that the defendants were culpable of any crime. After waiting years for this day, the Timoney 3 were finally exonerated. Family and friends wept openly in court when Mazzola announced his verdict. The mood outside the courthouse was both celebratory and reflective as defendants gave interviews. Viveiros told the *Philadelphia Inquirer* that he was greatly relieved, attributing his victory to the "tremendous community support" he had garnered.[103] He commented further that he approached his case with the attitude that "the only way to stop the attempts to criminalize me—and dissent in general—was to organize more effectively than the forces of the state that wanted to shove me into prison."[104] Indeed, it was effective organizing that finally helped to expose "the lies that Timoney threw at us."[105]

Although the van case was technically the last criminal case stemming from the RNC 2000 protests, the acquittal of Landy, Steinberg, and Viveiros represented the closure that many activists in the legal support community had been seeking. If nothing else, it vindicated the scores of activists who put their lives on hold to stand in solidarity with other defendants. Out of 420 people arrested during RNC 2000, approximately 300 were charged with misdemeanors and 43 with felonies.[106] Although 106 people took the district attorney's plea offer of Accelerated Rehabilitative Disposition, a significant 237 people fought back by taking their cases to trial. Out of 43 felony cases, none resulted in a conviction at trial. Ultimately, a scant thirteen people were convicted of misdemeanors and one person took a felony plea bargain. Out of 420 people arrested, only 3 percent were convicted. Of those convicted, no one was sentenced to jail time.

CHAPTER 10:
CIVIL LITIGATION

Street Medics

ORGANIZING TO PROVIDE MEDICAL ATTENTION TO DISSIDENTS at mass political actions in the U.S. began during the civil rights movement. The Medical Presence Project (MPP) was formed out of the Medical Committee for Human Rights (MCHR), the voluntary health corps of the civil rights movement. The MPP then evolved into the early street medic groups, which, "conceived of medicine as self-defense, and believed that anyone could be trained to provide basic care."[1] Street medics of the 1960s and 1970s provided medical support and education within the American Indian Movement, Vietnam Veterans Against the War, and the Black Panther Party. During the post-WTO renaissance of street medic groups, the Colorado StreetMedics (descendants of MCHR) trained thousands of people and became an unmistakable presence at contemporary political demonstrations.[2] The Colorado StreetMedics worked with others in preparation for, and during, the RNC 2000 protests.[3]

Street medics are especially important at times of heightened police violence, as they are trained to care for people injured by chemical agents like pepper spray or tear gas, as well as by projectile weapons, like rubber bullets, bean bags, or pepper balls. Medics are also trained to treat more conventional problems such as sprained ankles, dehydration, and abrasions. Medics can also help deescalate tense and violent situations and provide support to people experiencing trauma. Because medics are almost always clearly identifiable, they stand out and are routinely the targets of police abuse. Such was the case during the RNC 2000 protests.

Less than two weeks after the last Republican had left the First Union Center, and even before the last RNC 2000 protester was released from jail, seven medics from the R2K Medical Collective filed a lawsuit in federal court on seeking compensatory damages, injunctive relief, and attorney's fees. Filed by Pennsylvania ACLU legal director Stefan Presser and R2K Legal attorney David Rudovsky, the August 14 lawsuit named the City of Philadelphia and several known and unknown police officers as defendants. It asserted that the plaintiffs were detained, searched, and harassed by Philadelphia police officers "as part of the Department's campaign to harass the protesters' support organization" and "in violation of rights secured to them by the Fourth Amendment to the United States Constitution."[4] The complaint also alleged that the police destroyed medical supplies and personal items belonging to the volunteer medics. In a press conference held the day the lawsuit was filed, the plaintiffs said they were "verbally abused by officers who illegally searched their bags, threw away bandages and medicine bottles and in one instance poured a bottle of water over a volunteer's head."[5]

The medic lawsuit provided the first postprotest civil response, an offensive around which activists and the R2K Legal Collective could rally. The lawyers working with the R2K Legal Collective came out guns blazing. "This is only the first of what is clearly going to be a series of lawsuits all of which strive to make the point that [the Philadelphia police] department continues to be plagued by an inability to understand that the Fourth Amendment places limits on the conduct of individual officers," said Presser. David Rudovsky, who was dubbed the "czar" of police abuse cases by the *Philadelphia City Paper*, saw the potential for more civil lawsuits based on "numerous grounds," including "false arrest, violation of First Amendment rights, malicious prosecution and excessive detention pending arraignment."[6]

Attorney Complications

With other more obvious and pressing criminal court matters at hand, R2K Legal expressed concern over the lack of coordination between some of the civil attorneys and the broader legal support effort. Without disputing its benefit to the legal and political effort at the time, the medic lawsuit was planned without much involvement of the other attorneys and legal workers. David Rudovsky and his law firm (Kairys Rudovsky Epstein Messing and Rau) was either lead counsel or co-counsel in five out of the six known civil suits.[7] On the one hand, it was helpful to have the expertise of National Lawyers Guild and ACLU-affiliated civil rights attorneys, and on a practical level, to have them help fund the costs incurred from fighting multiple lawsuits. On the other hand, these more recognizable groups tended to overshadow the lawyers from smaller firms or acting as sole practitioners who fought to criminally defend numerous activists arrested during the RNC 2000 protests. As a result, some lawyers felt left out of the civil litigation process.

Further complicating matters was an unresolved dispute between ACLU of Pennsylvania (ACLU-PA) legal director Stefan Presser and many of the RNC arrestees over Presser's extremely harmful comments regarding the targeting of alleged protest "leaders," and his dismissal of arrestee claims of abuse. Because of these comments, many activists involved in the legal fight refused to work with Presser. In a letter to "Defendants of the RNC Demonstrations," dated November 7, 2000, ACLU-PA executive director Larry Frankel responded to the sharp criticism directed toward Presser. He suggested that ACLU-PA general counsel David Rudovsky replace Presser in directing all of its RNC-related civil cases.[8] Many activists found the conciliatory gesture to be insufficient, however. Frankel's plan failed to resolve the impasse, and many activists refused to work with the ACLU-PA at all.

Michael Graves and Susan Ciccantelli

It wasn't until November 2000 that the next civil lawsuit was filed—this time by Michael Graves and Susan Ciccantelli, co-owners of the "puppet warehouse." Graves had been charged with nine misdemeanors and held for approximately four days before being arraigned.[9] Upon his release, Graves found out that his warehouse had been condemned and that the Philadelphia Department of Licenses and Inspection (L&I) had destroyed nearly $10,000 of his property. Even worse, L&I forced Graves to make repairs totaling at least $50,000 to comply with supposed code violations.[10] In addition to the financial burden, Ciccantelli said that the events had been "traumatic" for their entire family.

On January 22, 2001, Paul Messing and David Rudovsky filed a federal lawsuit on behalf of Graves and Ciccantelli, accusing the city of "gross negligence" and arguing that "Michael Graves was subjected to false arrest, lengthy pre-arraignment detention, and malicious prosecution by virtue of a decision by the policy-makers of the City of Philadelphia to chill the exercise of protected First Amendment activity and to detain suspected protesters for the duration of the Republican National Convention in Philadelphia."[11] Graves and Ciccantelli, who sought unspecified compensation for "unlawful arrest, detention and prosecution and for the seizure and destruction of property," named the City of Philadelphia, Mayor John Street, Commissioner John Timoney, and Deputy Commissioner Robert Mitchell as defendants in the lawsuit. The *Graves and Ciccantelli* lawsuit would be the first of many suits filed against the city by those arrested at the warehouse.

Tamara Sisson

A week later, on January 30, 2001, Messing and Rudovsky filed the second puppet warehouse-related lawsuit in federal court, this time on behalf of Tamara Sisson. Sisson had come to Philadelphia to volunteer with Everybody's Kitchen, a traveling bus-based program that has provided food to countless people from the skid row of Los Angeles to disaster-ravaged Louisiana.[12] Everybody's Kitchen also supports the efforts of political dissidents by traveling to cities where mass demonstrations are being planned to provide food to activists and others. Messing claimed that Sisson arrived in Philadelphia the night before her arrest to work with Everybody's Kitchen.[13] While using the bathroom in the puppet warehouse, Sisson was swept up in the police raid and arrested with dozens of others. The lawsuit stated that Sisson was preventively detained and, despite providing her real name and personal information, was held in jail for four days.[14] She was charged with eight misdemeanors and, like Graves, all of them were eventually dismissed.

Puppet Warehouse 4

Unbeknownst to R2K Legal and various attorneys working on RNC-related litigation, Andrew Erba filed a federal lawsuit on March 28, 2001, seeking unspecified monetary damages and injunctive relief on behalf of Traci Franks, Joseph Tedeschi, and Elizabeth Weill Greenberg, who were all arrested in the puppet warehouse raid. The lawsuit was also filed on behalf of Nathan Ackerman, whose political material was destroyed during the raid.[15] An NLG attorney, who worked closely with other R2K Legal attorneys to dismiss the puppet warehouse criminal cases, Erba had failed to notify key people involved in the legal support effort that he was considering civil action. Although all of the puppet warehouse cases had been dismissed by December of 2000, R2K Legal contended that Erba's lawsuit jumped the gun because of the many criminal prosecutions still pending at the time—including those concerning the activists arrested in the van.[16] Regardless, the legal team had a strategic agreement to wait until a majority of RNC-related criminal trials were over before filing civil lawsuits on behalf of protesters.

The *Franks* lawsuit, as it became known, accused the City of Philadelphia, Mayor Street, Police Commissioner Timoney, Deputy Police Commissioner Sylvester Johnson, two Philadelphia police officers, L&I Commissioner Edward McLaughlin, and L&I Deputy Commissioner Dominic Verdi of adopting a policy "to deny the plaintiffs the exercise of their First Amendment Rights by use of an unconstitutional program of prior restraint, which included but was not limited to the false arrest, illegal detention and destruction of the personal, First Amendment and collective property of the plaintiffs . . . in violation of rights guaranteed by the First, Fourth, Fifth, and Fourteenth Amendments to the Constitution of the United States and Article 1, Section 8 of the Pennsylvania Constitution."[17] Malicious prosecution was another cause of action, which highlighted the city's role in bringing meritless criminal cases to court. The complaint further stated that the city "acted with deliberate or reckless indifference, callous disregard, or in an arbitrary and abusive manner as to shock the conscience."

Regarding the pretext for the raid, the *Franks* lawsuit called the puppet warehouse affidavit an "insufficient legal basis for the issuance of the warrant." Moreover, "the factual assertions in the affidavit were false, misleading, inaccurate and otherwise without a proper basis." According to the lawsuit, the arrests of Franks, Tedeschi, and Weill Greenberg arose from a "conspiracy by and between agents and employees of the City of Philadelphia to [restrain] the legitimate First Amendment activity of the plaintiffs" and others arrested in the raid. The complaint argued that the plaintiffs' long prearraignment delay and excessive bail was meant to preventively detain puppet warehouse arrestees and was further evidence of prior restraint. Notably, the *Franks* lawsuit was the first to allege a violation of the city's consent decree[18] by accusing the Pennsylvania State Police of using undercover, surveillance operations with the intent of transmitting that information to the Philadelphia Police Department.[19]

Four months later, and again in discordant fashion, Andrew Erba filed a second lawsuit without coordinating with R2K Legal. The July 27, 2001, suit was filed on behalf of puppet-warehouse arrestees Jacob Fried and Angela Willey less than a week before the anniversary of the mass arrests, the day R2K Legal had been planning to file a much larger and sweeping puppet warehouse lawsuit.[20] Eventually, Erba requested consolidation of the puppet warehouse cases, using Willey as the movant.

John Sellers and Terrence McGuckin

The day before Erba's second lawsuit was filed, two other federal lawsuits were filed by Ruckus Society director John Sellers and local activist Terrence McGuckin, formerly of the Philadelphia Direct Action Group (PDAG).[21] Nearly a year after the protests, most of the criminal cases had ended in dismissal or acquittal. Rudovsky, who represented McGuckin in his criminal case, filed suit about three months after McGuckin's acquittal. Similarly, the *Sellers* lawsuit was filed by Sellers's criminal defense attorney, Larry Krasner. The *Sellers* lawsuit named the City of Philadelphia, Police Commissioner Timoney, Deputy Commissioner Mitchell, and several police officers—including a Washington, DC, officer who had come to Philly to follow and videotape Sellers and McGuckin. Sellers accused the city of unlawfully searching, arresting, and detaining him, as well as unreasonable bail, malicious prosecution, and defamation in violation of his First, Fourth, Fifth, Eighth, and Fourteenth Amendment rights.[22] Unlike the previous lawsuits, Sellers sought injunctive relief as one of his main objectives, attempting to "force changes in police policies toward demonstrators."[23] While the *Sellers* lawsuit did not specify an amount of damages, Krasner told the *Philadelphia Daily News* that his client would be seeking "in excess of $100,000."

Civil Suit Strategy

Much groundwork had already been laid by the time the larger puppet warehouse civil lawsuit was filed on August 1, 2001. The R2K Legal Collective regarded the puppet warehouse lawsuit as a veritable "slam dunk" civil action and was also considering lawsuits related to "four broad categories: denial of medical needs, lack of due process, police brutality in the streets and abuse by correctional officers in prison."[24] As early as January 2001, Marina Sitrin and other R2K Legal members worked to produce a civil suit proposal based on discussions between activists (pro-spective plaintiffs) and key lawyers. Around that time, Sitrin proposed a structure that "maintains plaintiff control over the suits with the legal col-lective helping to facilitate national discussions with as much direct dem-ocratic process as possible."[25] In keeping with democratic process, Sitrin suggested that "ex-defendant and/or potential plaintiff groupings meet in various cities to discuss this proposal."

The civil suit proposal was broken down into two main categories: allegations of civil violations, and the structural relationship between activists, attorneys, and the R2K Legal Collective. The civil violations cat-egory was less a proposal than a laundry list of possible causes of action. It included pre–August 1 violations, as well as abuses that occurred during and after the protests. The pre–August 1 portion of the proposal addressed preemptive disruption and closure of activist spaces, as well as surveil-lance, infiltration, and harassment. The August 1 portion addressed the mass arrests and resulting jail experience, including prior restraint at the puppet warehouse and elsewhere, illegal search and seizure, confiscation and destruction of property, the false arrest of hundreds of people, and the excessive use of force (including "use of clubs, bikes and pepper spray to injure and intimidate on the street and on buses"). The arrest process was followed by abuses in jail, including physical assault, sexual assault, and the denial of medication (HIV drugs in one instance). The proposal hypoth-esized civil action against Holmesburg Prison for its decrepit and inade-quate conditions, then continued with a series of due process violations, including delayed arraignments and a denial of access to attorneys, which dovetailed with "preventive detention" claims of widespread overcharging and excessive bail. Finally, the proposal addressed the issue of malicious prosecution.

The more interesting part of the proposal concerned the way in which activists would work with the attorneys and the legal collective. R2K Legal felt that it was important to "talk through and come to agree-ment on our relationship, because we are attempting to create a new way for activists (both plaintiffs and supporters) and lawyers to work together collectively." To this end, R2K Legal proposed consensus decision-mak-ing between activists and lawyers to ensure that "all those participating in each of the groupings feels the space to discuss all ideas and concerns and is heard as equal to all others." This was important, the proposal asserted, since the lawsuits would likely involve "very sensitive and often painful experiences."

In discussing possible structural options, the R2K Legal civil suit proposal attempted to "strive for balance in all groups from issue groups to the legal team," keeping in mind "race, gender, sexual orientation, transgender issues, education, class, different political backgrounds, etc." The main structural focus was on communication, with the suggested creation of listservs that could accommodate what was expected to be a number of different litigation categories. A spokescouncil model was proposed, such that different groupings of civil suit plaintiffs and attorneys could communicate and make decisions together. Periodic in-person meetings would complement e-mail communication, and R2K Legal would try to smooth "relationships within and between different groups."

In trying to set comprehensive ground rules for collaboration, the civil suit proposal made some attorney-specific suggestions, including an agreement that lawyers "work with the same dedication on cases that are less likely to win and/or are perceived as purely 'political' cases," with the exception of cases that could be considered frivolous. It was the expectation of legal support activists that "direction always comes from the plaintiffs." Regarding how attorneys would deal with any monetary awards and fees, the proposal suggested that the three firms involved at the time "divide the cases equally" and that all monetary awards/fees be divided equally as well.

The Civil Suit Questionnaire and Discussions on Strategy

In the spring of 2001, R2K Legal began canvassing the large group of RNC arrestees to find out who was interested in filing a lawsuit, and whether they had a legal basis for civil action. To facilitate this process, and to help develop a civil litigation strategy, R2K Legal disseminated a lengthy questionnaire requesting personal and factual information and feedback.[26] Like the civil suit proposal that preceded it, the questionnaire addressed everything from arrestees' experiences in the days leading up to the mass arrests on August 1 to their experiences being arrested and prosecuted. "There are many reasons for being involved in filing civil suits," read a letter accompanying the questionnaire.[27] "Instead of having to sit back and watch as cops lie on the stand, lawyers argue about our intentions and judges decide our fate, active involvement in filing civil suits is a way to empower ourselves to expose and fight injustices by cultivating media attention, getting injunctions against future rights' abuses, and winning financial compensation for the many violent and repressive ways the police and authorities illegally organized to smash our dissent."

If additional lawsuits were going to be filed, R2K Legal sought to organize participation on explicitly equitable grounds—not only among activists, but also between attorneys and activists. Like prior RNC solidarity efforts, the collective felt it was important to "ask ourselves serious questions about how and why we are going to participate in on-going solidarity as it pertains to civil suits." R2K Legal boldly envisioned a model of civil-suit participation that connected people to different lawsuits, civil attorneys, other plaintiffs, and the necessary information to work collectively. "It has been months since we marched in the streets together, linked arms and shouted for justice and freedom in the face of those who responded with violent repression," concluded the letter. "Hopefully our successes will discourage other cities and police forces from propagating the oppression and violence we faced in Philly."

A significant effort went into following up with arrestees to confirm they had filled out their questionnaire. This organizing effort also incited discussions about civil litigation strategies in different cities and on various arrestee e-mail lists. Some of the questions raised by RNC arrestees included: Are we trying to make an example out of Philly? Advance our political positions? Or just get revenge and some cash? Why are we working within the system in this instance? What values does this imply that we are endorsing? Will the suit advance free speech? If we win money in these suits, where does that money come from?

An additional question raised was whether civil suits could be used to help those still facing felony charges. R2K Legal believed that such a strategy was possible and that the way to affect the remaining cases was to "discredit the city's handling of all RNC cases" through "political pressure, our press campaign, and educating the public."[28] Another way civil suits could affect felony cases, according to R2K Legal, was by investing some of the monetary award in their legal defense.

Puppet warehouse arrestee Mali Lorenz added that plaintiffs should "publicly pledge to share any [monetary award] . . . where it is most needed."[29] To avoid being accused of "selfishly taking money away from areas where Philadelphia needs it," Lorenz suggested giving any award money "to progressive community efforts" in order to "benefit the city by re-directing its money into grassroots community-building efforts." RNC arrestee Christopher Day argued that civil suits were not necessarily a worthwhile use of the movement's limited resources. "We need to assess what these suits are going to demand from us and weigh that against the likelihood of success and the likely rewards."[30] He noted: "I do not view civil courts as an arena I would choose for political struggle." Nevertheless, Day suggested that the disbursement of award money should be based on "conscious political decisions" and "should go back into the people's struggles."

NLG and R2K Legal attorney Roy Zipris raised the possibility of focusing on injunctive relief.[31] "There may be significant opportunities to get agreements from [the city] about restraints on police abuses and tactics," said Zipris. Given that the city effectively sidestepped restrictions on political spying, some activists wanted to fight for tighter controls. Agreeing with Zipris, one RNC arrestee thought that injunctive relief "should be our primary goal."[32] In December 2000, the *Philadelphia City Paper* reported that RNC arrestees wanted to use civil suits as a way of "barring the city from similar infiltration and surveillance of activists in the future."[33]

R2K Legal established a civil suit committee to compile information from the questionnaires and begin developing a strategy based on arrestee feedback. In a civil suit update from May 2001, it announced that three law firms—represented by Larry Krasner, Paul Hetznecker, and David Rudovsky, who voluntarily undertook some of the more serious criminal cases—agreed to take on the civil suit cases.[34] Remarkably, the update also explained that the lawyers agreed to the unique approach of using "the consensus method and to push for the goals of the collective in their legal strategies."

Civil Suit Agreement

In mid-July, R2K Legal disseminated a draft civil suit agreement for final review. After meeting with lawyers and receiving feedback from prospective plaintiffs, the final version of the contract was sent out to all of the puppet warehouse arrestees. The agreement established a framework for how costs, labor, and monetary awards would be divided.[35] The plan was to spread out litigation costs among the law firms and the collective and, if victorious, the lawyers would get a third of any award, with a predetermined percentage going to an organization of the plaintiffs' choosing. Anything left over would be given to individual plaintiffs.

The final agreement was heavily activist-influenced. In order to avoid common pitfalls like low plaintiff participation and an overly top-down attorney approach, the agreement emphasized the lawsuit's collective and participatory nature. But R2K Legal also stressed that the agreement provided the plaintiffs with "the framework but not the method for . . . collective decision making." In order to ensure that the political aims of the plaintiffs were protected during civil litigation, R2K Legal set out certain "Collective Requirements" to which attorneys were expected to adhere. For example, the agreement required that "at least one representative of each firm . . . remain in the collective process, regularly attending collective meetings," and that "periodic status reports . . . be written by the legal team (in plain English, not legalese) and sent to all plaintiffs."

The Puppet Warehouse Civil Lawsuit

R2K Legal placed its greatest emphasis on the puppet warehouse civil suit. In order to bring attention to the lawsuit, lawyers and activists organized a press conference at City Hall on the day it was filed. The press conference featured plaintiff Matthew Hart, director of the Spiral Q Puppet Theater, as well as R2K Legal attorneys Larry Krasner and Paul Hetznecker.[36] With an expectation that dozens more plaintiffs would come on board over the next couple of weeks, Krasner and Hetznecker filed what was so far the largest RNC 2000–related federal lawsuit on behalf of ten puppet warehouse arrestees and Spiral Q. The suit named the City of Philadelphia, Deputy Police Commissioner Mitchell, the commissioner and deputy commissioner of L&I, and ten unnamed police officers as defendants.[37]

According to the lawsuit, the puppet warehouse plaintiffs were "a group of political activists, community organizers and artists from Philadelphia and elsewhere" who sought unspecified monetary damages and injunctive relief. "Now that well over 95% of the cases against people arrested [at the RNC 2000 protests] have been thrown out," announced an R2K Legal media advisory, the puppet warehouse civil suit "will help activists and others to gain some form of retribution through damages, and more importantly through injunctive relief."[38] As part of the discussions between R2K Legal and RNC arrestees, some ideas for injunctive relief were fleshed out, including better safeguards against surveillance and infiltration, and stricter enforcement of habeas rights and timely arraignments.

Disclosure of the City's Insurance Policy

One of the many legacies of the response to protests in Philadelphia was an insurance policy covering the city against liability for an array of civil rights violations. In early 2000, an umbrella insurance policy was purchased from American International Group (AIG) and a supplemental policy from

Lexington Insurance Company, totaling nearly $900,000.[39] Lexington's supplemental policy covered the city for $3 million and protected the cops from liability for things like false arrest, wrongful detention or imprisonment, malicious prosecution, assault and battery, discrimination, humiliation, violation of civil rights, and defamation, slander, or libel of persons or organizations.[40] Ostensibly a public document, the policy was kept secret for more than a year despite requests from multiple Philadelphia City Council members including the chair of the Public Safety Committee. In September 2001, a copy of the policy was leaked to the *City Paper*— but only after RNC-defendant Bill Beckler had filed a "Right-to-Know" lawsuit and investigative journalist Gwen Shaffer had applied significant pressure.[41] Violently arrested during the protests, Beckler argued that "the city had insurance so they could beat me up!"[42] Knowing that they weren't liable, R2K Legal member Danielle Redden similarly remarked: "The City of Philadelphia and its police conspired to suspend the rights of thousands of people during the convention."[43]

The insurance policy not only emboldened the police, it also enabled the city to hire Hangley Aronchick Segal & Pudlin (Hangley), one of Philadelphia's most prestigious and expensive law firms. This gave it an unfair advantage and allowed it to adopt an aggressive posture when it came to litigating the civil suits. That aggressive posture, and the tactics the city used to "defend" itself, effectively overwhelmed the plaintiffs. NLG attorney Angus Love told the *City Paper* that Philadelphia "usually does a half-assed job of litigating these cases because the typical bureaucrat doesn't have the time or energy" to litigate complicated cases.[44] According to Love, however, Hangley was "a private law firm that is used to a higher level of attack."

Subpoenas, Depositions, and Discovery

The civil litigation discovery process allows each party to request information using subpoenas and depositions (interviews). This period of litigation tends to be the most costly, mainly due to the expense of deposing "witnesses" and transcribing their testimony. But before R2K Legal attorneys had a chance to depose anyone, the city went on the offensive. In fact, it was during this period that the city's law firm adopted its most aggressive position to undermine the civil litigation effort. It appeared that no one was safe from being subpoenaed or deposed, and the city went after activists, nonprofit organizations, and attorneys alike.

Discovery in the cases of Graves and Sisson began before the puppet warehouse lawsuit was filed, but it wasn't until after the *Franks* lawsuit was filed that Hangley went into overdrive, and used the discovery process to subpoena dozens of individuals and organizations in Philadelphia and across the country. Their requests ranged from address books and diary entries to e-mail correspondence and computer hard drives. At least nine attorneys, all affiliated with R2K Legal, were subpoenaed for their records.[45] Many people, including relatives of the plaintiffs, were subpoenaed and deposed despite having nothing to do with the protests. The *City Paper* detailed how Hangley "hired investigators to question ex-wives and flew across the country to interrogate witnesses—all financed by the insurance policy."[46] Hangley not only sought information related to activity that took place long after the RNC had left Philadelphia, but also made inquiries about prominent anarchist activists entirely unrelated to the protests.

Several organizations, including American Friends Service Committee, Kensington Welfare Rights Union, Ruckus Society, R2K Legal Collective, Spiral Q Puppet Theater, Training for Change, the William Way Center, and the Women's International League for Peace and Freedom (WILPF) were subpoenaed for information related to "organizing, planning, conducting, participating in, and/or supporting," the RNC 2000 protests.[47] A subpoena served on the custodian of records at WILPF requested "any written, typed, printed, recorded or graphic matter of any type or description, including with limitation, all e-mails, correspondence, drawings, records, tables, charts, analyses, graphs, schedules, reports, memoranda, notes, lists, calendar and diary entries . . . photographs, photographic negatives, video recordings or motion pictures, phonograph records, tape recordings . . . and all other data compilations from which information can be obtained or translated if necessary." The subpoena also requested information from as early as January 1, 1999, related "in any way to the 2000 Republican National Convention," the "puppet warehouse," and organizations including the R2K Medical Collective, the R2K Legal Collective, the black bloc, the Direct Action Network, the Philadelphia Direct Action Group (PDAG), Training for Change, the Ruckus Society, and Unity 2000. Hangley seemed particularly interested in documents related to the bank accounts of PDAG and R2K Legal.

Epitomizing the excessive nature of the discovery process, local activist and R2K Legal Collective member Jody Dodd was served with a total of four separate subpoenas—one for her work with WILPF, one for conducting trainings with PDAG, and two for her affiliation with the R2K Legal

Collective. One of Dodd's subpoenas requested "any documents mentioning thirty separately named individuals . . . and all documents relating to training of activists prior to the Republican Convention."[48] Hangley's unreasonable posture was also evident in a September 2001 letter to Paul Messing, Sisson's attorney, in which attorney David J. Wolfsohn asked if any relevant e-mail messages had been deleted from the hard drive of Sisson's computer, threatening to seek "the appointment of a computer forensic expert to 'reconstruct' the 'deleted' e-mail."

Despite Hangley's aggressive search for information, several individuals and groups resisted the firm's efforts to compile information. WILPF, which was under heavy surveillance before and during the protests, refused to provide Hangley with any private information and instead handed over materials "of an 'incredibly boring' nature: fliers, pamphlets and other publicly available information."[49] Critical Path AIDS Project, a group that provides internet access to people living with HIV/AIDS, refused to provide Hangley with requested e-mail archives. NLG attorney Roy Zipris, who had trained and organized the dispatch of NLG legal observers during the protests, said he was "subpoenaed for everything—e-mail addresses, names of people trained, manuals."[50] He condemned Hangley's effort to use discovery as "an incredibly broad fishing expedition" and concluded that "little of what they requested was relevant to the puppet warehouse suits." Although they were unsuccessful, Hangley also tried to subpoena client letters from public defender and R2K Legal attorney Bradley Bridge.

For its part, R2K Legal refused to give any information to the city, and some of its members were individually able to fight off subpoenas. Plaintiffs' lawyers successfully quashed subpoenas targeting the collective based on the paralegal status of its membership and attorney-client privilege. Hangley, however, was able to obtain confidential e-mail communication from a private R2K Legal listserv, which was then used in depositions to question people.[51] Repeated attempts to serve a subpoena on R2K Legal member Marina Sitrin "bordered on harassment." According to one of her neighbors, "a man knocked on her door 'for days on end.'"[52] "Hangley also pursued me for my involvement in R2K Legal and inquired into my whereabouts in nearly all of the subpoenas and in many of the depositions." "Frustrated by its inability to track me down, Hangley even attempted to subpoena contact information and e-mail communication from my internet service provider."[53]

Not everyone, however, chose to resist Hangley's demands. According to *the defenestrator*, the Ruckus Society and Training for Change (TFC) both handed over private records, including "meeting notes, outlines of training workshops, handouts, schedules . . . names, phone numbers and other information most activists surely did not expect would be so eagerly handed over to the city."[54] Without a fight, George Lakey of TFC handed over "reams of documents" after consulting with an attorney "who advised them to simply comply with the subpoena." Compliance was also apparently based on Lakey's belief that they had nothing to hide. TFC had played an integral role in training demonstrators and protest organizers. Consequently, its complicity in the subpoena process angered many activists. "Their compliance puts others at risk," said *defenestrator* author Karl Blossfeldt, who pointed out that "the state doesn't care about moral self righteousness of the non-violent activist." According to Blossfeldt, "Lakey and Sellers should have known better" given "their own personal experience of being criminalized." Regardless of one's personal sense of innocence, continued Blossfeldt, "most of these interrogations are not meant to incriminate specifically those being interrogated. They're meant to give the city's prosecutors a deeper understanding of the larger community of anti-capitalists, social-justice advocates and political troublemakers." Downplaying the theory that the city's fishing expedition might harm activists, Hart told the *City Paper* that the case was a "golden goose" that led Hangley "to move as slowly as possible and bill more hours."[55]

The discovery process allowed Hangley to depose activists with no connection to the puppet warehouse raid.[56] A November 2, 2001, video deposition of New York-based activist Eric Laursen—who worked with the R2K Media Collective, but was not arrested and was nowhere near the warehouse at the time of the raid—gave a clear picture of the firm's motivations.[57] Laursen was asked about jail solidarity, the R2K Legal Collective, and information on known anarchist organizers. Hangley spent very little time on questions about Laursen's role as a media worker focused on publicizing the political issues surrounding the protests. Similarly, Traci Franks was deposed for three hours and asked about her political affiliations. "It seemed as though he hoped to prove I was an anarchist," recalled Franks, as though that would make it "legitimate for police to arrest me."[58] Jody Dodd was deposed for her involvement as a trainer with PDAG, as well as her work with the American Friends Service Committee, WILPF, and the R2K Legal Collective.[59] Although Dodd had no direct connection to the puppet warehouse or the police raid, Hangley deposed her for more than four hours and also asked her questions about jail solidarity and the R2K Legal Collective.

City Tries to Depose Plaintiffs' Counsel

In an unusual move, Hangley attempted to depose several lawyers connected to the RNC 2000 legal support effort, whether or not they were involved in the civil litigation. Hangley accused R2K Legal attorneys of "advocating jail solidarity and other disruptive tactics," and being "deeply enmeshed" in the "plan to engage in illegal activity" by helping to train and prepare large numbers of people to engage in civil disobedience.[60] R2K Legal attorneys called the tactic "an attempt to deflect attention away from the merits of the case by attacking plaintiff's counsel." Federal case law has condemned the tactic of taking the deposition of opposing counsel, saying it "not only disrupts the adversarial system and lowers the standards of the profession, but it also adds to the already burdensome time and costs of litigation."[61]

On December 17, 2001, the city filed a motion to depose six lawyers—Jules Epstein, Andrew Erba, Paul Hetznecker, Larry Krasner, Paul Messing and David Rudovsky—who called the motion "frivolous" and "based on materially false factual representations, innuendo, and unsubstantiated charges of criminal conduct." Outrageously, Hangley asserted that plaintiffs' counsel had "trained, directed and assisted protesters in illegal activities and, as active participants in preparation for . . . illegal protest activities," were "at 'the heart' of a broad criminal conspiracy." The city further asserted that plaintiffs' lawyers had "prepared activists to get arrested" and "planned for jail solidarity," helping "inmates engage in it." Although the city's motion to depose counsel of record was denied by Judge Norma Shapiro, multiple attorneys were deposed, including R2K Legal attorney Larry Krasner, public defender Bradley Bridge, and NLG attorneys Roy Zipris and Angus Love. Zipris was deposed for nearly four hours, ostensibly for his role in training NLG legal observers prior to the protests and for his involvement in the R2K Legal Collective.

By Spring 2002, plaintiffs, activists, and attorneys alike were exhausted and ready for the civil litigation effort to be over. The legal struggle against the city was difficult enough without the city's aggressive campaign and virtually unlimited resources. Hangley was billing the city's insurance company at least $250 per hour every time the firm conducted depositions or filed briefs, motions, and subpoenas.[62] Though it was difficult to know exactly how many hours Hangley billed, R2K Legal estimated an amount well over $1 million. By the time the cases were settled, however, that estimate rose to more than $1.5 million. Meanwhile, R2K Legal attorneys worked with a fraction of the city's legal budget. Consequently, they were in a more defensive and vulnerable position. Although legal support activists and attorneys continued to work on the puppet warehouse suit, which eventually grew to twenty-four plaintiffs, much of the focus and energy had dissipated.

Settling

The financial windfall that civil litigation represented for Hangley provided little incentive for the firm to settle. According to R2K Legal, despite routine settlement offers made in similar civil cases, Hangley simply refused to negotiate.[63] In the *Franks* case, the court itself had to step in and force the city to make a settlement offer.[64] Because of city gag orders on all settlement agreements, the civil briefs and details of the settlements themselves were kept secret. And while R2K Legal objected to the gag orders, they were ill-prepared to challenge the secrecy. According to the civil case dockets, it appears that the medic lawsuit was settled in March 2002 and the *Graves* and *Sisson* lawsuits were settled in April 2002. The settlement dates of the *Sellers, McGuckin,* and *Franks* lawsuits are less clear, but likely occurred in the summer of 2002. None of the settlement agreements or the amount of the plaintiffs' awards was ever made public. R2K Legal accused the city of hiding the settlement agreements "to deflect any potential fallout" and called them "another attempt to . . . shield any criticism of wrongdoing."[65]

Despite the city's attempt to keep these details secret, however, the *Philadelphia Daily News* obtained a transcript from a closed hearing, which was inadvertently filed as part of the public record. The document disclosed details about the puppet warehouse settlement agreement. On July 5, 2002, the *Daily News* reported on a "proposed settlement [award] of $72,000," equivalent to $3,000 for each of the twenty-four plaintiffs.[66] The award money came from the city's insurance policy (instead of the city or its taxpayers) and was not earmarked to go to the plaintiffs. Part of it went to attorneys' fees and the rest was split between two local organizations selected by the plaintiffs but approved by the city (which refused to agree to certain groups). Spiral Q was one of the beneficiaries and received the largest sum. The anarchist prisoner-focused group Books Through Bars was listed as the other beneficiary.

Statute of Limitations

Despite an expectation that many more civil actions would follow, the civil litigation effort culminated with the puppet warehouse lawsuit. Some members of the R2K Legal Collective wanted to help people pursue civil actions around violations that occurred in jail, especially in instances where people were physically and sexually abused or denied life-saving medicine. The legal pushback from the city, however, discouraged further lawsuits. By June 2002, only eleven criminal cases remained, but the specter of the Timoney 3 case still loomed large. A little more than a month before the second anniversary of mass arrests, R2K Legal issued a message about the upcoming statute of limitations on filing civil lawsuits and acknowledged the collective's inability to provide the same level of support as it had previously.[67]

While assuring arrestees that it would continue to work on the remaining criminal cases, the collective noted that it could no longer "perform civil suit support in the same way." It explained that Larry Krasner and Paul Hetznecker, the two attorneys putting in most of the civil litigation work, did "not have the capacity to file any more civil suits." Based on the "possibility that further civil suit litigation may leave all of us subject to harassment again," R2K Legal questioned whether filing additional civil suits would be "the most constructive, movement-building tactic." One of the tragedies of the civil litigation effort was that no one who endured physical abuse or was denied needs during the arrest and incarceration period ever filed suit. Unfortunately, despite a strong desire by some to move forward with civil litigation, attorneys had become reluctant to take on additional cases regardless of their merit.

High expectations had become disappointment. Neither substantial monetary awards nor injunctive relief were ever obtained. The city had accomplished its objective by using the insurance policy and virtually unlimited resources to overwhelm those with valid civil rights claims. Then-director of Spiral Q Puppet Theater Mattyboy Hart lamented that the organization's political work had been undermined by the RNC 2000's legacy. "In spite of the amazing work we do," said Hart in a *City Paper* article, "it's still boiled down to this absurd moment when our civil rights were violated."[68] R2K Legal member Jody Dodd was relieved by the decision to settle. "I'd like to see these cases go away," she said. "As an activist, this sucks up time and energy and I doubt if the political benefits are enough to make it worthwhile."

SECTION III
LEGACIES & LESSONS

Photo © Brad Kayal

CHAPTER 11:
SUCCESS AND FAILURE OF CIVIL LITIGATION

O N RARE OCCASION CIVIL LITIGATION HAS ESTABLISHED HELP-
ful case law and provided injunctive relief to curtail antidissident law enforcement activity. Sometimes it has even resulted
in financially significant awards for activists, political organizations, and
their attorneys. As a result of blowback against the repressive counterintelligence tactics used by the FBI, a small wave of reform took place in the
U.S. in the mid-to-late 1970s. These included congressional legislation that
made intelligence committees permanent in both houses and executive
orders issued by presidents Ford and Carter restricting certain intelligence
operations. In the mid 1980s, the federal courts granted injunctions in a
couple of important cases—*Alliance to End Repression v. City of Chicago*
(1984) and *Handschu v. Special Services Division* (1985)—that attempted
to limit surveillance activity by local police.[1] Resulting from a 1974 lawsuit
in which the Alliance to End Repression and the ACLU accused Chicago
and its police of engaging in decades of political spying, disruption, and
sabotage, the *Alliance* case helped establish the 1981 "Red Squad" consent
decree.

In 1971, National Lawyers Guild (NLG) attorney Barbara Handschu
and others filed a lawsuit stemming from similar COINTELPRO-era
police tactics. The *Handschu* plaintiffs—including Abbie Hoffman
and members of the War Resisters League, the Gay Liberation Front,
Computer People for Peace, the Black Panther Party, and others—accused
the New York City Police Department (NYPD) of "[deterring] them from
First Amendment activity by using informers, infiltration, interrogation,

surveillance, summary punishment, and by creating a fearful atmosphere at public gatherings."[2] As part of a 1980 settlement agreement, which involved a plaintiff class of millions of people, a consent decree was later established in 1986 implementing court-ordered guidelines that "prohibited [police] from investigating political activity" unless there was evidence of current or planned crimes and "prohibited creation of files on groups or individuals based solely on their political, religious, sexual or economic preference." The *Handschu* consent decree also established an "Authority" within the NYPD to oversee the police Intelligence Division activities.

Citing the time, money and other resources necessary to win such battles, many political activists reject and abhor strategies that rely on gaining victories through civil litigation. Meanwhile, the question of whether injunctions and monetary awards actually make a difference cannot be ignored. Many dissidents argue that the energy put into civil litigation is better expended on political organizing. Furthermore, hard-fought legal victories are often impermanent. Indeed, the gains achieved in both *Alliance* and *Handschu* have since been muted. In 1997, Chicago mayor Richard Daley sought to modify the "Red Squad" decree by claiming that "it was impeding investigations of gang activity." At the same time, the city "asked permission to return to the practice of videotaping and spying on street demonstrations." After being denied by the District Court, Mayor Daley appealed to the Seventh Circuit Court of Appeals. Then, in January 2001, and signaling a shift toward intelligence gathering, the appeals court eviscerated the 1981 "Red Squad" consent decree—the only thing standing in the way of Chicago police spying on or disrupting protest activities. Federal Circuit Court Judge Richard A. Posner held that the decree had "rendered the police helpless to do anything to protect the public."[3] Further missing the mark, Judge Posner asserted, "The culture that created and nourished the Red Squad has evaporated. The consent decree has done its job."

Even before the court changed its mind on *Handschu*, police simply ignored the injunction. A couple of months before the RNC 2000, a crowd of activists at a May Day demonstration in New York were subjected to police surveillance.[4] After 9/11, *Handschu* met its fate. In 2002, the police requested modification of the *Handschu* Guidelines on the basis that it would inhibit efforts to fight terrorism. Despite the lack of specific instances in which criminal investigations had been curtailed, the NYPD requested a virtual repeal of the guidelines. Federal District

Court Judge Charles Haight ultimately agreed and, in early 2003, relaxed the guidelines and further weakened the 1985 decree.[5] Whereas the original guidelines authorized investigations only with evidence of "specific information" that a crime was about to be committed, the new guidelines merely require "reasonable indication" of a future crime.[6] The Court also eliminated the requirement that police get approval for intelligence gathering from the *Handschu* Authority, a three-member panel consisting of two high-level police officials and one civilian appointed by the mayor.[7]

No group has been more affected by the evisceration of the *Handschu* consent decree than the Muslim community. In August 2011, the *Associated Press* published a Pulitzer Prize–winning series exposing the vast domestic spying network developed by the NYPD since 2001.[8] The massive multistate operation was aimed at the surveillance, mapping, and infiltration of Muslim groups, from recording information like where they pray and eat to manufacturing criminal activity in an effort to entrap them.[9] As indefensible as the spying operation was, New York Police Commissioner Ray Kelly claimed it violated no laws and was "within the framework of the modified [*Handschu*] consent decree."[10]

Just as the relaxed *Handschu* Guidelines signaled a green light for spying on the Muslim community, the NYPD has also used the new intelligence landscape to spy on political groups. Internal police reports made public in 2006 showed that, as early as 2002, NYPD had used "proactive arrests," covert surveillance, and psychological tactics at political demonstrations. Claiming success, the police reports recommended that such tactics be used at future political demonstrations.[11] The modified decree also allowed for the widespread surveillance and infiltration of political groups in the lead-up to the 2004 Republican convention. Indeed, the *New York Times* reported in 2007 that the NYPD had "spied broadly" before the convention, traveling to "cities across the country, Canada and Europe to conduct covert observations of people who planned to protest at the convention, according to police records and interviews."[12] Arguably, dissidents and other targeted groups have never been completely protected from police harassment, surveillance, and interference, or from arbitrary and mass arrest. Nevertheless, activists deprived of their rights in such an injurious way are inclined to seek retribution. And, because of relatively limited options, activists often defer to litigation.

Civil Litigation Methodology

As the Philadelphia example makes clear, civil lawsuits can take signifi-cant amounts of time and energy and may not reap the "benefits" sought by activist plaintiffs. Even when gains are made (as in *Handschu* and the Chicago Red Squad consent decree), these gains can easily be eviscer-ated. Nevertheless, civil actions continue to be used as a tool for estab-lishing or affirming certain rights. Without a doubt, some progress has been made.

Most of the protest-related civil lawsuits over the past decade have been filed in federal court. The obvious reason is that such civil actions commonly involve violations of the U.S. Constitution. Although cases alleging state or federal constitutional violations can certainly be litigated in state court, the legal remedies are far fewer and the cases routinely get moved to federal court anyway. Otherwise known as the Ku Klux Klan Act, the Civil Rights Act of 1871 was adopted a few years after the U.S. Civil War ostensibly to provide southern Blacks with some form of protection against the Klan.[13] The act was later codified as 42 U.S.C. § 1983, "Civil action for deprivation of rights," to ensure that local and state officials did not violate the U.S. Constitution with impunity.[14] The Supreme Court then identified two of the principal policies embodied in § 1983 as "deterrence" and "compensation,"[15] thereby providing "a remedy to parties deprived of constitutional rights"[16] and serving as "a deterrent against future constitu-tional deprivations."[17]

Another reason to bring constitutional claims into federal court stems from the ruling in *Monell v. Department of Social Services of New York*, where the court established direct municipal liability for constitu-tional violations by policy, practice, or custom.[18] *Monell* and subsequent Supreme Court cases further established that such policies, practices, or customs could either be written, de facto, or a single act carried out by local officials like police officers and mayors. "In cases where the accused official has committed a constitutional violation but is immune from suit, a *Monell* claim against the municipality may be the only actionable claim," suggests longtime civil rights and NLG attorney G. Flint Taylor.[19] "A *Monell* claim gives plaintiffs' lawyers in serious [police] brutality cases a direct path to the municipality, which is often important for purposes of discovery, settlement, trial, and collection." Taylor argued that the main reason to "establish municipal liability was . . . to reach a deep pocket in circumstances where the municipality did not willingly indemnify its police." However, "A *Monell* claim also permits wider discovery, broadens the scope of admissibility at trial, facilitates holding supervisory and command officials responsible, and allows plaintiffs' litigators to properly apportion the blame between the individual officers and the municipality." Taylor concludes by noting that "in some instances, aggressive discovery and litigation of such claims can also positively affect pertinent police policies and practices, as well as increase the value of the case for settlement or at trial."

Shhh … City trying to settle protester suits

But why secrecy on cases related to convention?

By **JIM SMITH**
smithjm@phillynews.com

The city is secretly trying to settle federal civil-rights lawsuits filed on behalf of protesters who were jailed during the Republican National Convention nearly two years ago.

The Police Department was widely praised for controlling demonstrations during the convention. Many demonstrators, however, believe that the rights of some protesters were violated by police actions to curtail protests. The city maintains there was no wrongdoing by police officers or prosecutors.

It's unclear why the city appears determined to keep the settlements secret. An $800,000 liability-insurance policy specifically covers civil-rights claims against the city and state.

Some civil-rights lawyers predicted last year that the lawsuits that flowed from the convention could cost the city and its insurer millions. But that doesn't appear to be the case.

In photo from December 2000, people arrested at 'puppet warehouse' in West Philly during GOP convention hold press conference outside City Hall.

Inquirer photo

For the purpose of analysis, one way to categorize contemporary civil lawsuits is by rights violations that occur either before or during the protests, though many civil actions incorporate both types of violations into a single lawsuit. Types of preprotest rights violations can include the denial of demonstration permits, the establishment of anti-protest or anti–free speech laws, aggressive surveillance, police infiltration, pretextual searches, and preemptive raids of activist spaces by police. Types of rights violations that typically occur during mass protests can include police use of weapons and violence against protesters, media, and others, unlawful crowd control techniques, various forms of physical abuse in jail, abuse of due process (timely arraignment, access to counsel, excessive bail, etc.), and malicious prosecution.

In Advance of Mass Mobilizations

While activists have made little headway in challenging constitutional violations that occur in advance of mass mobilizations, some progress has been achieved. Litigation is commonly used to challenge denial of protest permits or unconstitutional permit schemes (e.g., "free speech zones") as well as administrative searches and preemptive raids. Unfortunately, police tactics have arguably worsened over the years, supported by the immense and steadily increasing "security" budgets for large-scale political events. While civil lawsuits continue to be used to stem rights violations that occur in advance of mass mobilizations, even the victories have failed to prevent subsequent violations.

The ACLU achieved an early victory against the City of Philadelphia's effort to deny protest permits for the RNC 2000; however, local attorneys failed to challenge the city's permit scheme as unconstitutional. Because of this, permits were later denied in May 2001, when activists commemorated the anniversary of the MOVE bombing with a two-day anti–death penalty and pro-Mumia demonstration at Dilworth Plaza near City Hall. This time, a lawsuit filed by the NLG and the Partnership for Civil Justice (PCJ) forced the city to grant the permit. Refusing to stop there, the NLG and PCJ pursued a permanent injunction.[20] On the eve of trial in July 2003, Mayor John Street agreed to no longer enforce the city's discretionary permitting scheme.[21] The Los Angeles NLG chapter was also successful at striking down the city's parade-permit ordinance and park-permit regulations, as well as the restrictive "free-speech zone" established for the DNC 2000 protests. According to former NLG executive director Heidi Boghosian, the lawsuit resulted in "an injunction striking down a secure zone of more than eight million square feet around the convention site, striking down the City's parade-permit ordinance, and striking down the City's park-permit regulations," including "[barring] the city from requiring liability insurance or assessing . . . service charges for parades or other demonstrations."[22]

Protesters must also contend with unconstitutional and chilling antiprotest ordinances adopted in the days before a mass mobilization. In the lead-up to demonstrations against the 2003 Free Trade Area of the Americas (FTAA) meeting in Miami, the city adopted laws severely limiting free speech activity, which resulted in the arrest of countless protesters. In February 2004, the NLG, Southern Legal Counsel, and others filed *Lake Worth for Global Justice v. City of Miami*, a lawsuit that ultimately forced the City Council to repeal its restrictive assembly laws and revise its flawed permit scheme.[23] Yet, despite this victory, cities continue to selectively refuse protest permits and—even when they're granted—rally locations and march routes are commonly dictated by local or federal officials. For example, the route of the main march during the RNC 2008 protests in St. Paul was imposed and, for many blocks, constrained by ten-foot-high fencing patrolled by riot cops with guns and dogs.

Although the U.S. Supreme Court has held that administrative searches like fire and building inspections should not be used as pretexts for criminal investigations or raids, the state has used such tactics with relative impunity. Determined to prevent similar raids in the lead-up to the DNC 2000, the NLG and several other groups filed suit against police chief Bernard Parks and the City of Los Angeles, which resulted in an injunction inhibiting police and other city agencies from conducting administrative searches before and during the protests.[24] Despite this victory, administrative searches have been used to disrupt or shut down protest convergence spaces in Lake Worth (2003), St. Paul (2008), and elsewhere.

In 1996, the NLG won an important victory against "preventive punishment," or the banning of First Amendment activity because similar activity resulted in instances of violence in the past.[25] In the landmark case *Collins v. Jordan*, brought by Guild attorney Rachel Lederman, the Ninth Circuit held that "the proper response to potential and actual violence is for the government to ensure an adequate police presence and to arrest those who actually engage in such conduct rather than to suppress legitimate First Amendment conduct as a prophylactic measure."[26] Still, and especially since the 1999 WTO protests, cities have used exaggerated concerns about "violent anarchists" along with images of property destruction and billowing tear gas to instill fear and justify police violence and mass arrests.

Challenging Rights Violations

Lawsuits that accuse local, state, or federal governments of violating dissidents' rights during or directly after mass political demonstrations are typically filed long after the protests mainly to avoid conflict with unresolved criminal cases. In *Punishing Protest*, Boghosian noted that "police misconduct litigation around the country has resulted in several settlements to help restrain over-reaching law enforcement." Some of the places where successful contemporary police misconduct litigation has occurred include Seattle, Washington, DC, Oakland, Los Angeles, and New York.

Since the turn of the century, several victories have been achieved (with monetary awards totaling more than $50 million) by legally challenging mass arrests and police abuse at political demonstrations in the U.S.[27]

Mass protest in U.S.	Year	City	Civil Suit Settlement Amount
World Trade Organization	1999	Seattle	$1,800,000
DNC	2000	Los Angeles	$4,100,000
IMF/World Bank	2000	Washington, DC	$13,700,000
IMF/World Bank/ Iraq War	2002	Washington, DC	$8,630,000
Iraq War	2003	Chicago	$11,000,000
Iraq War	2003	Oakland	$1,500,000
Free Trade Area of the Americas	2003	Miami	$1,500,000
RNC	2004	New York	$18,000,000
May Day	2007	Los Angeles	$12,800,000

As a result of litigation filed shortly after the 1999 World Trade Organization protests in Seattle, activists represented by Trial Lawyers for Public Justice (now Public Justice) won a class action lawsuit against the city for wrongfully arresting nearly two hundred protesters outside of a "no protest zone."[28] In January 2007, a jury found that the City of Seattle had violated protesters' Fourth Amendment rights and, two months later, agreed to a settlement of $1 million and the overhaul of its police department training manual.[29] The city also paid another $800,000 to settle police misconduct cases stemming from the WTO protest response.[30]

On April 15, 2000, police used similar tactics at the protests against the IMF/World Bank in Washington, DC, to arrest nearly seven hundred people participating in a march against the prison industrial complex. In a lawsuit that took many years to litigate, PCJ reached a settlement agreement in November 2009 with monetary awards in excess of $13 million.[31] When Federal Judge Paul Friedman issued final approval, he called the class action settlement "historic" and an achievement for "future generations."[32] The agreement also required "enhanced training" for "D.C. police assigned to demonstrations" including a prohibition on the use of police lines to encircle or "trap and detain" political protests.[33] PCJ called the settlement award "the largest amount ever paid in the U.S. to compensate protesters who were wrongfully arrested."[34] PCJ attorney Mara Verheyden-Hilliard further declared that the award "sends a message to every city and every law enforcement officer that there is going to be a steep price to pay for violating protesters' First Amendment rights."

Legal challenges to police violence against protesters can be more difficult to achieve. In a violent attack on an antiwar picket at the Oakland docks on April 7, 2003, police fired a range of so-called "less-lethal" weapons at protesters. According to the NLG, "Nearly 60 people, including dockworkers from Local 10, ILWU, were hit by wooden bullets, sting ball grenades and shot filled bean bags, resulting in numerous injuries" including broken bones. Police fired projectile weapons directly at people's heads despite the warnings on projectile shell casings that doing so may cause "serious injury or death." Class action litigation brought by the NLG, ACLU of Northern California, and several civil rights attorneys, compelled a settlement in November 2004. As a result, Oakland became the first city in the country to forbid "the indiscriminate use of wooden bullets, rubber bullets, tasers, bean bags, pepper spray and police motorcycles to control or disperse crowds or demonstrations."[35] NLG attorney Rachel Lederman, who helped litigate the case, said that "OPD agreed to overhaul its crowd control protocols" as a result of the settlement, "and we worked with the police to write a detailed, comprehensive new Crowd Control and Crowd Management Policy."[36] According to the ACLU of Northern California, the adoption of a new Crowd Management Policy "strictly limits the use of force, and mandates that a primary goal of the Oakland Police Department in their planning for and management of demonstrations must be the protection of the right to assemble and demonstrate." Eventually, the City of Oakland was forced to pay over $2 million in damages, fees, and costs to fifty-eight injured demonstrators and dockworkers.[37] Yet, despite the city's monetary and policy concessions, Oakland police have repeatedly violated their own crowd control policy, sometimes by brutally arresting protesters.[38]

A few months after the Oakland docks incident, Miami police engaged in a level of violence against FTAA protesters that made the police violence in Oakland pale in comparison. The AFL-CIO, Florida Alliance of Retired Americans, and individual members of those groups who were attacked by police, filed a lawsuit alleging that police "advanced without warning, firing at this group from close range with 'less lethal' ordnance, including projectiles, 'beanbags,' 'pepper-spray balls,' and attacking some of them with batons."[39] The first settlement arising from the police response to the 2003 FTAA protests was $180,000 paid by the City of Miami to an independent filmmaker who was seriously injured when police fired a beanbag projectile at his head.[40] But the largest settlement—totaling more than $500,000—came from a lawsuit filed by the NLG on behalf of twenty anti-FTAA protesters who were unlawfully arrested.[41] In September 2006, an Eleventh Circuit ruling compelled a settlement after denying qualified immunity to several police officers and putting them on the hook for rights violations found at trial.[42] Nevertheless, despite less-than-favorable independent reviews on police behavior and nearly $1.5 million in lawsuit settlements, the "Miami Model" has continued to be widely used at political protests.

NLG member and academic Dave Saldana was shot with a rubber bullet during the Los Angeles DNC 2000 protests. He was, therefore, not surprised to see police "beat peaceful demonstrators at the Immigrant Rights march" on May Day 2007.[43] "Disregard for the demonstrators' rights seems to be ingrained in the LAPD, no matter how much settlements, consent decrees or court judgments cost them," said Saldana. "They'll do it again." Despite paying out over $5 million to settle eleven lawsuits stemming from excessive use of force and disruption of lawful assemblies during the DNC 2000 (including a 2005 settlement agreement that caused changes to the LAPD crowd control policy and was supposed to restrict the use of less-lethal weapons), they did indeed do it again.[44] In response to more than six thousand people gathered for a permitted rally in Macarthur Park, "three platoons of officers with the [LAPD] Metro Division suddenly charged the crowd, striking people with batons and shooting them with less-lethal weapons."[45]

During what became known as the May Day Melee, hundreds of people sustained injuries. Carol Sobel, the Los Angeles NLG chapter president, called it "nothing short of a police riot." The NLG and attorneys from the Mexican American Legal Defense and Educational Fund (MALDEF) filed a federal class action lawsuit on behalf of several community groups that helped organize the demonstration. Just over a year later, *MIWON v. City of Los Angeles* resulted in another landmark police misconduct settlement worth nearly $13 million—one of the most expensive payouts in the city's history.[46] Police Chief William Bratton announced "plans to suspend 11 lower-ranking officers and called for the termination of four others for excessive use of force, failing to rein in other officers or lying to investigators during the inquiry." The LAPD also "retrained all its officers in basic crowd control tactics and overhauled the way it prepares for and manages protests and other major events."

These cases all involved difficulties; however, civil litigation victories based on denials of needs and due process or prosecutorial misconduct are even harder to achieve. It's rare for an arrestee to be successful at holding police and other officials accountable for denying access to medical treatment, legal counsel, timely arraignments, or food and water. One of those rare examples, however, occurred during the RNC 2004 protests in New York. The NLG and Legal Aid Society filed habeas corpus writs to seek the release of arrestees whose processing, they argued, had been "deliberately delayed" for "up to two days during the RNC until President Bush had left the Convention."[47] Although New York State Supreme Court Judge John Cataldo issued release orders for 560 arrestees, the city failed to comply. Under threat of contempt, the city eventually settled in April 2005, agreeing to pay $230,000 in attorneys' fees and fines to the arrestees. In other lawsuits stemming from the RNC 2004, the City of New York was forced to pay out nearly $18 million in awards and attorneys' fees—the largest mass protest-based settlement in U.S. history.[48]

Many are hopeful that the policy reforms coming from such civil litigation and large monetary awards like those obtained from DC, Los Angeles, and New York will be enough to change police behavior. But given repeated rights violations, there are grounds to be pessimistic. It has mattered little that excessive police force is prohibited by the International Covenant on Civil and Political Rights ratified by the U.S. in 1992, or that similar protections exist in the Convention against Torture and Other Cruel, Inhuman or Degrading Treatment or Punishment ratified in 1994. The U.N. Commission on Human Rights condemned the use of weapons by Oakland police in 2003, as did an independent review panel investigating police misconduct at the Miami FTAA protests.[49] But not only has the police reaction to subsequent mass political demonstrations belied this scrutiny, the response to the 2008 Republican convention protests in St. Paul would become one of the most calculated, violent, and politically repressive in years. Meanwhile, the lawsuits filed after the RNC 2008 achieved no known policy changes and resulted in less than $200,000 in settlement awards.

CHAPTER 12:
THE LEGACY OF AUGUST 1

WHAT ASSESSMENT CAN BE MADE OF THE EVENTS SURROUND-
ing August 1? On the one hand, the lives of hundreds, if not
thousands, of people were disrupted. "Many small activist
groups whose members were tried and found innocent or had charges
dropped were forced to suspend their political work for months to deal
with the trials," read an FoC press release in advance of the Timoney 3
trial.[1] "Months and years of legal wrangling also disrupted the lives of the
students, social workers, union organizers, and others who were rounded
up during the convention." In its coverage, the *Boston Phoenix* also detailed
how defendants' lives were "forever changed" even if their cases were dismissed. "They've wasted hundreds of hours worrying about their defense,"
they wrote.[2] "They've spent thousands of dollars traveling to and from
Philly to appear in court," and "Some felony defendants have also been
forced to spend thousands more hiring private lawyers."

On the other hand, the solidarity experience was unlike anything else
and holds important lessons for activists organizing in a country that regularly tries to stifle dissent. "The importance of collective action cannot be
stressed enough, and it is a principle that is hard to explain," reflected RNC
defendant and R2K Legal member Bill Beckler more than a year after the
protests.[3] According to Beckler, victory in the courts was "a direct result
of collective action by defendants and supporters." While recognizing the
skilled attorneys who worked with R2K Legal, Beckler argued that the collective action was "outside the realm of our lawyers' toolkits" and "tran-
scended the legal solutions."

The reason no RNC protesters are in jail right now in Philadelphia is the sacrifice made by those defendants who went to trial against their own interests. Our lawyers were at times baffled and horrified by those decisions. The project we embarked upon was outside anybody's experience. Nobody had any idea if and how we were going to succeed. We operated on one consistent principle: collective action. . . . We relied on each other to host defendants arriving for trials. We relied on each other to track down witnesses. We relied on each other to educate ourselves about the legal process and to become wise defendants. We worked together to fund our project, and we used those funds to make sure every single case was victorious.[4]

Arguably, it is in the realm between the legal world and the world of political organizing where, when boundaries are pushed, unexpected results can occur. The successes of R2K Legal came from a combination of legal and political strategies developed by activists and defendants. Whether fighting to overcome hostile judges or defending the Timoney 3, the political element was crucial. It can be found not only in criminal defense efforts, but also in public campaigns to garner community support and pressure key officials. Indeed, without the community support efforts to call out Police Commissioner Timoney, District Attorney Abraham, and Mayor Street, the Timoney 3 and other targeted RNC defendants might not have prevailed. According to Beckler, "Lawyers must learn these stories, because through this high level of cooperation and mutual aid, defendants have accomplished victories that would not have been possible any other way." Yet the lesson applies equally to social change activists who, but for a better understanding of solidarity, could more effectively achieve their goals.

The events surrounding the RNC 2000 protests were neither unique nor exceptional in terms of planning, participation, police surveillance, infiltration, preemptive raids, police brutality, and mass arrests. Yet, there were unique and exceptional aspects, like overcharging (pinning more than ten charges each on scores of people arrested for sitting in the street) and exorbitant bail amounts (starting at $10,000 and going all the way up to $1 million). The vehemence of the district attorney was also exceptional. But the events in Philadelphia are notable for other reasons too—like the birth of a more coordinated and financially invested state response to mass political protest and the waning of the Global Justice movement. These trends, combined with the initiation of the so-called "War on Terror," an increase in coordinated counterintelligence, and the relaxation of restrictions on political policing, have produced serious problems for dissidents in the U.S.

Meanwhile, resistance in the streets has been inconsistent and wavering in intensity. While dissident movements struggle to develop solidarity and collective strength, the state has assembled a formidable "security" apparatus to respond to mass political action. Chip Berlet of Political Research Associates heralded the events in Philadelphia as a turning point. "In Philadelphia, we saw the return of overt government repression of dissent," he told the *Boston Phoenix*, "which works fine for a police state, but not at all for the free-speech principles of democracy."[5] While mass political actions continued in the years following the RNC 2000 protests, and while jail and court solidarity efforts helped to strengthen some activists' resolve, many have felt stunted by the state's increased repression against dissent.

Local activist and RNC felony defendant Dave Onion felt like Philadelphia's activist community went "backwards" as a result of the police reaction in 2000.[6] "We got our asses kicked," he said. It wasn't so much the two-week jail experience as it was the subsequent collective depression, or the "hangover," as he called it. At the same time, Onion pointed to several good things that came out of the experience. "A lot of networking happened," he said, "and a lot of relationships were built, which has been super valuable." In addition to the growth of the Philadelphia Independent Media Center (IMC), the RNC 2000 protests also spurred the creation of the Lancaster Avenue Autonomous (LAVA) space, a radical community center in West Philadelphia. Initially, LAVA housed groups like the Philly IMC and *the defenestrator*. According to Onion, LAVA was the result of "networks we built from the RNC" and "discussions about the need for the antiglobalization movement to engage more in community organizing." Philly activist Jodi Netzer told the *City Paper* in 2002 that "the local activist movement is stronger than it was two years ago."[7] Netzer claimed that, after hearing about the protests, activists flocked to the city. "Some came to deal with their arrests, others were attracted to the highly publicized anarchist community, and still others saw opportunities for 'coalition building' in Philadelphia." Today, the IMC is still very active and LAVA is thriving.

Jail Solidarity since R2K

Can jail solidarity continue to work in the face of powerful state opposition? With our robust prison industrial complex, the state has ample space to detain people for longer periods of time. While strain can still be placed on the penal system, many more jail cells exist today than did twenty years ago. "We don't have the same pressure points we had," said Jody Dodd.[8] "I think that makes jail solidarity . . . much more difficult." Dodd recalled how well the tactic worked in the 1980s at the Nevada nuclear test site. "When hundreds of people got arrested and there was only a small town jail with three cells in it, what are you going to do with everyone?" Dodd argued that the police there didn't have the resources—the space, the food, the health care, the people-power—to meet certain legal standards. In Philadelphia, "they cleared out the jails in anticipation of being able to hold people for significant periods of time." Before the RNC 2000 protests, activists were told that arrestees with summary offenses would be processed in the defunct Holmesburg Prison. Similarly, New York City opened the old Chelsea bus terminal during the RNC 2004 protests to absorb an overflow of nearly two thousand arrestees.

Despite these obstacles, many activists have been unwilling to abandon jail solidarity. The cooperation, friendship, and strength that come from solidarity efforts continue to inspire jailed dissidents. The protection of those who are singled out and bargaining for equitable low-level charges are still considered to be achievable goals. Although people's expectations of jail solidarity dropped precipitously after the RNC 2000, the positive impact of the experience cannot be denied. After RNC 2000 arrestee and SLAM member Zosera Imaana was released from jail, she spoke at a press conference about coming "face to face" with a "racist" prison system made up of mostly poor Latinos and African Americans. "You do not know the truth of America or the reality of its lies until you've been in our prisons."[9] Dave Onion concurred. "Having that imminent experience of state repression is important for people who work on criminal justice and Prison Industrial Complex–related issues." He thought it was interesting to see "people who had been locked up for the first time, be really shaken by that."[10] According to Onion, the jail experience really "deepened their understanding." Danielle Redden said her jail experience "radicalized me a little more."[11] She even convinced her conservative family to go to court with her so that they could see the abusive legal system firsthand. Kate Sorensen affirmed Redden's experience. "Four hundred hard-core prison activists have been born, and that's all I have to say," said Sorensen upon her release from jail.[12] In addition to prison activism, the jail experience also spurred interest in the legal activist community.

Other less obvious effects of jail solidarity include police dread at having to deal with hundreds of political dissidents acting collaboratively in detention. According to Jamie Graham, Philly cops seemed reluctant to repeat the RNC protest experience. He noted that a couple of years later, during protests against the Iraq war, "the police seemed to be going out of their way to avoid mass arrests."[13]

> They never officially acknowledged a different strategy, but in talking to Civil Affairs officers, they wanted to avoid the experience from the RNC of having police authority undermined, both in terms of dealing with hundreds of people engaged in jail solidarity, creating a huge strain on the system, and in terms of court solidarity, winning acquittal after acquittal. They just didn't want to go through all that again. . . . I think there are probably hundreds of people that would have been arrested in protests against the war in Philadelphia in the following years who weren't arrested because the police just didn't want to deal with another RNC-like situation.

Since the RNC 2000 protests, the use of jail solidarity has generally been abandoned. One exception occurred during the 2000 DNC demonstrations in Los Angeles. On August 16, several hundred people marched from Macarthur Park to the Rampart police station to protest the police abuse and murders that had made national headlines. Thirty-eight activists were arrested on the station steps and participated in preplanned jail solidarity. After six days in jail, the group was able to negotiate with the prosecutor to drop their charges.[14]

Despite that victory, however, jail solidarity remained rare in the following years. Graham, who went on to work with Up Against the Law, claimed that "Philadelphia was the last time I witnessed the widespread use of jail solidarity."[15] The tactic was certainly not used during the next two Republican conventions. Despite a high number of arrests at both conventions (more than 1,800 in New York in 2004 and more than 800 in St. Paul and Minneapolis in 2008), protest organizers and legal support activists opted not to promote the tactic. At the RNC 2008 protests, a network of radical, queer activists called Bash Back! urged arrestees to withhold their identities by using the name "Jesse Sparkles." Although some employed this tactic, not enough used it to clog up the jail.

While the use of jail solidarity has been impacted by state aggression, it is also indexed to the movement's awareness of the tactics themselves. The decision to use solidarity tactics can be heavily influenced by legal workers who play an integral role in educating activists. Although strong arguments can be made for the need to develop more creative ways of using collective action to avoid rigorous legal battles, a sense of ambiguity about those methods continues to persist among protest organizers. Adding to the ambiguity, the legal support community has also been split on this issue. Legal support fatigue and a lack of "faith" in jail solidarity has diminished its use in recent years, but the split has less to do with whether solidarity tactics might work and more to do with how the legal community should engage with the broader movements it supports. Should legal teams take a proactive role by training dissidents in the use of solidarity tactics or should they remain neutral and only support whatever decisions political organizers make? Because of ongoing rights violations in jail, these questions are extremely important. According to movement author and activist Starhawk, "We may need to focus more on preparation for surviving jail, for resisting intimidation and being prepared for interrogation, than on the classic jail solidarity tactics we've used in the U.S."[16]

The Legacy of Court Solidarity

Since the aftermath of the RNC 2000 protests, court solidarity tactics have rarely been used in the U.S. Since 2000, movements for social change and legal support groups have de-emphasized their use. Far less preprotest training has focused on the history and benefits of collective action in jail and court, resulting in decreased levels of legal coordination among groups during and after the protests. In turn, this has led to a form of amnesia around the use of solidarity tactics. In the case of the 2004 Republican convention demonstrations in New York City, the nearly two thousand people who were arrested—more than most other contemporary political protests—could have been a significant bloc of resistance. But not only was solidarity downplayed, the legal team adamantly and publicly refused to support such tactics. While it's unclear whether the thousands arrested at political protests in the U.S. since the RNC 2000 would have fared any better by using solidarity tactics, political repression has increased while collective resistance seems to have waned.

It wasn't until 2008 that tactics of court solidarity were used again in a significant way. After the Republican convention protests in Minneapolis–St. Paul, a sustained, arrestee-driven legal support structure was formed. The Community RNC Arrestee Support Structure, or CRASS (a tip of the hat to the punk band), was the Twin Cities' response to the prosecution of hundreds of people, including activists, medics, legal observers, journalists, and bystanders. CRASS adopted a similar structure to the one used by R2K Legal. The support from CRASS, and the solidarity that it built among RNC 2008 arrestees, was unquestionably valuable. "We suffered some losses and lost some battles, for sure," summarized CRASS in a zine published in 2010.[17] "But, we have all gained so much more than we've lost since the RNC." According to CRASS, acts of solidarity and mutual aid "are things that strengthen us and our communities, helping us to be stronger." But despite its close similarity to R2K Legal and its various courtroom victories, RNC 2008 arrestees endured dozens of convictions and were unable to prevent the state from imposing punitive sentences and fines.

One of the differences between Minneapolis–St. Paul and Philadelphia arose from the former's decreased emphasis on jail solidarity. Although a number of activists protesting at the RNC 2008 refused to give their identities to jail authorities, jail solidarity tactics were not widely used. And though jail solidarity does not necessarily have to precede an effective court solidarity strategy, the bonds built by collective action in jail can be invaluable to subsequent legal campaigns. This was one of the most significant lessons learned in Philadelphia.

Because bonds of solidarity had not been adequately fostered before everyone was released from jail, CRASS was forced to create relationships among arrestees long after many people had left the area. According to Twin Cities activist and CRASS member Jude Ortiz, "We had a lot of success with aspects of court solidarity, such as a strong 'courtwatch' program that tracked the progress and outcome of criminal cases."[18] Ortiz also pointed out that the RNC 8 (a group of activists charged with conspiracy) and the RNC 8 Defense Committee "developed a joint legal defense strategy, at the same time as mounting a political campaign that included packing the courtroom and staging protests outside the courthouse for two years of hearings." At the same time, Ortiz said, "The vast majority of cases were declined for prosecution, which greatly reduced the leverage available for court solidarity." Although CRASS pushed for court solidarity and established a travel fund to help arrestees come back and fight their charges, Ortiz lamented that "most defendants took an individualized approach and pleaded guilty or accepted an offer of probation or community service in lieu of a conviction."

Another significant difference between CRASS and R2K Legal was that R2K Legal adopted the strategy of taking misdemeanor cases to trial to use them as leverage in undermining the felony and high-level misdemeanor prosecutions. In Philly, the conviction rate was very low and no one served jail time whereas, in the Twin Cities, there was a higher conviction rate and several activists sustained significant fines and jail time. Although a direct connection between the use of jail solidarity and the subsequent effect of court solidarity may be difficult to prove, the adverse legal results in Minneapolis–St. Paul are still noteworthy and deserve reflection in the context of future legal support efforts.

Domestic Terrorism Laws

Following 9/11, the increased ferocity with which the state responded to mass demonstrations was complemented by the enactment of domestic terrorism laws. The passage of the Patriot Act in 2001 and formation of the Cabinet-level Department of Homeland Security (DHS) in 2002 amounted to an unprecedented consolidation of state authority and erosion of civil liberties. Absorbing and restructuring twenty-two federal agencies, DHS was the largest government reorganization since the creation of the Department of Defense fifty years prior. President Bush appointed Pennsylvania governor Tom Ridge to head the DHS and its newly subsidiary agencies, including the Transportation Security Administration (TSA), Immigration & Customs Enforcement (ICE), the U.S. Secret Service, Federal Emergency Management Administration (FEMA), and the U.S. Coast Guard.[19] The rise of the Patriot Act and DHS were predicated on lessons learned from the 1996 Antiterrorism and Effective Death Penalty Act, as well as recommendations from the Council on Foreign Relations (CFR) and the 1998 Clinton-appointed Hart-Rudman Commission.[20] The Commission's report, issued in January 2001, called for a "National Homeland Security Agency" and outlined a domestic security blueprint strikingly similar to the Patriot Act. A majority of the supposedly bipartisan Commission was made up of members of CFR, a highly influential right-wing think tank that even the John Birch Society called a "semi-secret, private organization that serves as the most visible element of the Internationalist Power Elite."[21]

In addition to a reorganization of law enforcement and emergency management under the DHS, which allowed for greater information-sharing and cooperation between agencies, some of the laws that were created or impacted by the Patriot Act included: the creation of a new crime category called "domestic terrorism" (defined as "dangerous" criminal acts intended "to intimidate or coerce a civilian population" or "to influence the policy of a government by intimidation or coercion"); an expanded ability to conduct secret wiretap, internet, and e-mail surveillance; the use of "no-fly" lists at domestic airports; access to library and bookstore records; "sneak and peek" searches; and FBI monitoring of "privileged" attorney-client communication.[22] Despite the Patriot Act's broad wiretapping provisions, President G.W. Bush consistently violated its minimal constraints. The act also expanded the availability of National Security Letters, which according to the Center for Constitutional Rights (CCR) "allow the FBI and many other agencies to subpoena almost any personal information from a variety of institutions, including banks, internet service providers, credit card companies, telephone companies, and even libraries" without probable cause or judicial oversight.[23] Perhaps the most troubling aspect of new terrorism laws, however, has been the blurred line between political protests or common criminal acts and what the state considers "terrorism." The term "terrorism" has been defined so broadly that people engaged in traditional forms of protest or civil disobedience are at risk of investigation, interference, and arrest.

The Patriot Act's reclassification of radical activists as domestic terrorists coincided with the passage of state and federal laws that also defined acts of First Amendment–protected political dissent as "terrorism." These laws employed new and harsher penalties to target environmental and animal liberation activists for crimes typically covered by other criminal statutes. The passage of draconian laws targeting radical activists is largely the result of behind-the-scenes public-private partnerships like that of the American Legislative Exchange Council (ALEC).[24] A lobby made up of stakeholders from local, state, and federal law enforcement (including the FBI, DHS, and hundreds of corporations), ALEC worked to pass laws such as the "Animal Enterprise Terrorism Act" (AETA) in 2006.[25] The AETA amended the Animal Enterprise Protection Act (AEPA) of 1992 and increased the penalties for arson and other acts of sabotage related to "animal enterprises." According to CCR, the AETA "deters protests, leafleting, boycotts, and joining animal rights organizations by using broad language that induces fear of being labeled a 'terrorist,' and federalizes penalties for civil disobedience–type actions that were previously classified as minor crimes and prosecuted under state law."[26] The AETA also broadened the definition of what constitutes a crime to include forms of free speech that impact the financial bottom-line of certain businesses. The AETA was pushed through Congress without discussion or debate at a time when the Bush administration was prosecuting dozens of radical environmental and animal liberation activists.[27]

In May 2005, FBI Deputy Assistant Director John Lewis testified before a U.S. Senate Committee and stated, remarkably, that radical environmental and animal liberation activists represented "One of today's most serious domestic terrorism threats."[28] The coordinated legal attack that became known as the "Green Scare" resulted in the prosecution of numerous activists. Under Operation Backfire, activists charged with crimes of arson and other forms of sabotage were prosecuted as terrorists despite no one ever being physically harmed.[29] After obtaining convictions, the Justice Department has used "terrorism enhancements" to seek prolonged prison sentences. One activist received a sentence of more than twenty years for two crimes of arson. In a New Jersey case against members of Stop Huntingdon Animal Cruelty (SHAC), several activists were convicted and sentenced to years in prison for maintaining a website.[30] The RNC 8, a group of activists arrested in advance of the 2008 Republican convention protests, were originally charged as terrorists under Minnesota's version of the Patriot Act, though their terrorism-related charges were eventually dropped due to public pressure.

Relaxing the FBI Guidelines

Accompanying the passage of domestic terrorism laws and the creation of DHS was the repeated relaxation of the 1976 Attorney General's Guidelines on FBI surveillance. A few months after 9/11 and for the first time in nearly thirty years, Attorney General John Ashcroft revised the guidelines in 2002 to grant the FBI broad authority to conduct domestic surveillance and searches without evidence of suspicious behavior.[31] According to CCR, the revisions allowed for "wholesale political spying on dissenters."[32] Gone were the restrictions barring the FBI from "attending political meetings and houses of worship to spy on activities and individuals not suspected [or] accused of any crimes." Consequently, "the Ashcroft guidelines instituted massive surveillance of political meetings and rallies, religious gatherings, Internet sites and bulletin boards, and other purely expressive activities explicitly protected by the First Amendment." At the end of the Bush administration in 2008, Attorney General Michael Mukasey adopted new guidelines that, once again, vastly expanded the investigative authority of FBI agents. According to the Defending Dissent Foundation, the new guidelines "authorize a number of intrusive investigative techniques" including "pretext interviews, interviewing members of the public, recruiting and tasking informants, physical surveillance not requiring a court order, grand jury subpoenas for telephone or electronic mail subscriber information, and more."[33]

CCR described the Mukasey guidelines as an expansion of the FBI's mandate "well beyond its traditional role of dealing with violations of the law." With greater authority and responsibility to investigate "threats to the national security," CCR found that the FBI was turned into "a kind of political police." Many of the investigative methods authorized by the Mukasey guidelines are permitted without a court order, including "opening and reading mail, physical searches of personal or real property without a warrant under certain circumstances . . . electronic surveillance, closed-circuit television surveillance, use of global positioning and other monitoring devices, National Security Letters, and more." Not only do the 2008 guidelines grant the FBI the authority to use and retain records on millions of people in the U.S., they also encourage the Bureau to make aggressive use of informants and, according to CCR, "authorize undercover operations, involving the infiltration of a group by an FBI agent, without any need for a criminal predicate."

Despite the new relaxed guidelines, the FBI has been accused several times over the past decade of violating even these protocols. During the mid-to-late 2000s, the Justice Department's Inspector General (IG) issued at least three different reports on illegal and improper collection of information by the FBI.[34] In one report, the IG found that the FBI had frequently misused National Security Letters. The IG also found that the FBI had illegally collected thousands of telephone records over a four-year period.[35] In 2007, FBI director Robert Mueller was called before the Senate Judiciary Committee to account for the abuse. ACLU Executive Director Anthony D. Romero condemned the FBI abuse and pointed to Attorney General Gonzales as "part of the problem." Remarkably, Gonzales's successor Mukasey further relaxed the FBI guidelines the following year.[36]

Another significant revelation occurred in 2010, when then–inspector general Glenn A. Fine issued a 209-page report that found between 2001–2006, the FBI had improperly spied on several individuals and political groups, including Greenpeace, People for the Ethical Treatment of Animals (PETA), the Thomas Merton Center, and the Catholic Worker. Though engaged in First Amendment-protected activity, political activists were subjects of investigations based on "factually weak" or even "speculative" reasons.[37] Fine also revealed that the FBI made false and misleading statements to Congress and the public to avert criticism for its unlawful surveillance activities. In an attempt to justify its surveillance of a 2002 antiwar rally in Pittsburgh, the Bureau falsely claimed the investigation was linked to an unrelated FBI terrorism investigation. Perhaps most egregiously, the FBI considered civil disobedience activity by Catholic Workers to be tantamount to "terrorism." Meanwhile, several Greenpeace activists were improperly placed on a terrorist watch list. Fine pointed out that the low investigational standards set by the 2002 Attorney General's Guidelines on FBI surveillance contributed to the problem.

The Ever-Expanding Intelligence and Policing Apparatus

Coincident with the passage of the Patriot Act and the relaxation of FBI political policing guidelines has been the build-up of a political intelligence apparatus and enhanced coordination between the intelligence community and local, state, and federal law enforcement. Although the roots of coordinated, multi-agency policing and intelligence gathering existed long before 9/11, the attacks enabled an unprecedented expansion of that apparatus. The first post-COINTELPRO attempt to coordinate local, state and federal law enforcement efforts with the intelligence community was the Joint Terrorism Task Force (JTTF). First established in New York City in 1980, the JTTF became a model used in thirty-five cities by September 2001. Then, with the relaxation of the Attorney General's Guidelines in 2002, the strength and coordination of the JTTFs grew precipitously despite evidence of agents spying on nonviolent political groups.[38] A classified FBI memorandum sent to more than fifteen thousand local law enforcement organizations days before demonstrations were to be held in Washington, DC, and San Francisco in 2003 encouraged police to report certain protester activity—like using video recorders and wearing bandanas—to the FBI Joint Terrorism Task Force.[39] The memo boasted that the Bureau had collected detailed information on the tactics, training, and organization of antiwar demonstrators. That same year, the FBI issued an internal newsletter that encouraged agents to step up interviews with antiwar activists "for plenty of reasons, chief of which it will enhance the paranoia endemic in such circles and will further serve to get the point across that there is an FBI agent behind every mailbox."[40] By 2011, there were more than one hundred JTTFs operating across the U.S., with at least one in each of the FBI's fifty-six field offices, excepting Portland, Oregon. According to DHS and FBI, "More than 600 state and local agencies participate in JTTFs nationwide," including "representatives from the U.S. Intelligence Community, the Departments of Homeland Security, Defense, Justice, Treasury, Transportation, Commerce, Energy, State, and Interior, among others."[41]

In 2002, to complement the work of the JTTFs and other intelligence-gathering entities, the federal government established a database called TALON (Threat and Local Observation Notice), which was intended to collect information on potential threats to U.S. military personnel and civilian workers, at home and abroad. In 2005, however, it was revealed that the database was tracking antiwar groups and other political activists and included hundreds of "wrongly added" or improperly stored entries.[42] Amid controversy, the government supposedly shut TALON down in 2007. Although the Pentagon admitted some officials may have used the system improperly, it said that TALON was shut down because its "analytical value had declined" and not because of public criticism. Notably, the government said it was developing "a new reporting system to replace Talon."[43] If the closure of TALON was a reaction to controversy, the intelligence community certainly didn't suffer any serious financial setback. That year, the government claimed to have spent more than $43 billion on its National Intelligence Program,[44] which included 16 different agencies and did not count the $10 billion spent on military intelligence and $35 billion spent on DHS.[45]

Although the JTTF model is still used today, local and state intelligence officials have since 9/11 sought to improve their coordination with the federal government and expand their objectives beyond terrorism investigations (though JTTFs were arguably already doing this). Beginning in about 2003, local and state agencies started working with DHS to form "Fusion Centers" to "integrate information from the Central Intelligence Agency (CIA), the FBI, the Pentagon, the Department of Defense . . . and other [agencies]."[46] Ostensibly started with a focus on terrorist investigations, Fusion Centers soon expanded their mission to cover "all crimes and all hazards."[47]According to David L. Carter, director of the Michigan State University Intelligence Program, coinciding with the state's preemptive actions against dissidents, the fusion process "proactively seeks to identify threats . . . to stop them before they occur." Carter added that "prevention is the essence of the intelligence process."[48]

In 2004, Congress passed the Intelligence Reform and Terrorism Prevention Act, which required information sharing between local, state, and federal agencies, as well as the private sector.[49] Then, in 2006, the Departments of Justice and Homeland Security issued Fusion Center guidelines for "Developing and Sharing Information and Intelligence in a New Era."[50] The federal government defined Fusion Centers as a "collaborative effort of two or more agencies that provide resources, expertise, and information to the center with the goal of maximizing their ability to detect, prevent, investigate, and respond to criminal and terrorist activity." A year later, as many as forty-three Fusion Centers were operating in the U.S., with only two focused exclusively on terrorism. By 2009, DHS recognized the existence of at least seventy-two Fusion Centers. According to the ACLU, "The types of information they seek for analysis has also broadened over time to include not just criminal intelligence, but public and private sector data, and participation in these centers has grown to include not just law enforcement, but other government entities, the military and even select members of the private sector."[51]

Significant public concern has surrounded Fusion Centers, based mainly on recent and historical examples of political repression carried out by local, state, and federal law enforcement agencies. Unfortunately, because the centers are shrouded in secrecy, it's next to impossible to maintain public oversight or easily detect and overcome abuse. News accounts have indicated overzealous intelligence gathering, the expansion of uncontrolled access to data, hostility to open government laws, and inadequate protections against invasions of privacy.[52] According to the ACLU, ambiguous lines of authority and the participation of agencies from multiple jurisdictions allow Fusion Centers to "manipulate differences in federal, state and local laws to maximize information collection while evading accountability and oversight." One Fusion Center analyst even said officials were free to "use a variety of technologies before 'politics' catches up and limits options." Another serious concern with the centers is the involvement of entities other than law enforcement, including public safety personnel like firefighters and sanitation workers, and even the private sector. Given that one of the goals of Fusion Centers is to protect the nation's "critical infrastructure" (owned predominantly by private interests), it is no surprise that corporations have become an extension of the surveillance state. Meanwhile, the U.S. devotes roughly 70 percent of its intelligence budget to private contractors, some of whom store and analyze Fusion Center data.[53] Some suggest that these private sector partnerships—involving banks, universities, hotels, telecommunication companies, health care providers, and private security firms—provide opportunities for the government to mask illicit activities. An example of public-private intelligence abuse was revealed in 2006, when it was discovered that the National Security Agency unlawfully obtained customer data from major telecommunications companies. The practice was subsequently made legal in 2008 when the decades-old Foreign Intelligence Surveillance Act was overhauled.

As with JTTFs and other counterintelligence efforts, Fusion Centers have also conspired to suppress dissent. By blurring the lines between terrorism and political protest, Fusion Centers can easily deviate from the "reasonable suspicion" standard. In fact, the standards are so relaxed that local police departments often collect "suspicious activity reports" on individuals and share them with Fusion Centers without the burden of first proving "reasonable suspicion." The Los Angeles Police Department, for instance, requires officers to report activities such as "taking pictures or video footage with no apparent esthetic value," "taking notes," or "espousing extremist views." With more than eight hundred thousand local and state law enforcement officials across the country acting as the loosely regulated "eyes and ears" of the federal intelligence community, free speech violations and political repression are inevitable. Fusion Centers have been used for several mass political actions including the RNC 2004 in New York City, the DNC 2008 in Denver, the RNC 2008 in St. Paul, and the 2009 G-20, at which police brutalized and arrested thousands of people. In 2009, activists from the Olympia-based, antiwar group Port Militarization Resistance (PMR) discovered through a Freedom of Information Act request that they were under surveillance and being infiltrated by agents connected to a Fusion Center.[54] When confronted by activists, John Towery (one of the infiltrators and a member of the U.S. Army Force Protection Service at Fort Lewis) admitted to extensive surveillance and infiltration of PMR and other political groups in Olympia and Tacoma. Towery also admitted that police had installed a video camera across the street from an anarchist infoshop in Tacoma with plans to raid it and the homes of activists in the area.

Towery's surveillance efforts and his participation in Fusion Center information sharing represent a disturbing trend in domestic counterintelligence. The Posse Comitatus Act of 1878 was supposed to prevent the military from acting in a law enforcement capacity on U.S. soil. But the direct involvement of military personnel in Fusion Centers contradicts that objective and, according to the ACLU, has seen "little [public] debate about the legality of this activity or the potential effects this may have on our society." Admittedly, the military has not recently broken up labor strikes, imprisoned workers, or denied them *habeas corpus* rights as it did in the early twentieth century.[55] But by deploying military personnel and using military intelligence at political demonstrations, they have defied Posse Comitatus to suppress dissent. Prior to the June 2004 protests against the G-8 in Sea Island, Georgia, then-governor Sonny Perdue declared a "state of emergency" and deployed soldiers all over coastal Georgia.[56] There was even "a military checkpoint on the way to the candlelight peace vigil on Georgia's St. Simons Island."[57] In 2006, without much fanfare or publicity, the Insurrection Act[58] was amended to allow the president to declare a "public emergency," deploy military troops and equipment across the country, and seize control of state-based National Guard units to "suppress public disorder."[59] Then, the ACLU discovered from documents released in January 2007 that the Pentagon's domestic surveillance program had monitored nearly two hundred antiwar protests in the U.S. under the authority of the Department of Defense.[60] Perhaps the most insidious violation of Posse Comitatus, however, has been the use of military-developed and designed weaponry against U.S. dissidents, a vivid manifestation of militarized policing and "war brought home."[61]

In September 2010, the Pennsylvania office of homeland security (a state agency modeled on the federal department with the same name) accidentally leaked evidence that it had illegally spied on political and apolitical groups. In a leaked e-mail, agency director James Powers stated that he wanted to protect "natural gas stakeholders" from those "fomenting dissent."[62] Out of more than a hundred intelligence bulletins disseminated by the Pennsylvania Office of Homeland Security to police and private corporations, many were focused on environmental activists. Amy Goodman reported that "groups opposed to the environmentally destructive extraction of natural gas . . . were referred to as 'environmental extremists.'"[63] Environmentalists weren't the only targets, however. In a no-bid contract, Powers hired a private Philadelphia-based organization called the Institute of Terrorism Research and Response (ITRR) for $125,000 to conduct surveillance on lawful political protests, including antiwar demonstrations, support for Mumia Abu-Jamal, antideportation rallies in Philadelphia, and resistance to mountaintop-removal in West Virginia.[64] According to the *Associated Press*, some of the bulletins also focused on what the agency referred to as "anarchists and Black Power radicals." When the news first broke, Pennsylvania Governor Ed Rendell's office showed support for the program, but quickly changed its tune.[65] In a public apology, Rendell called the surveillance "ludicrous" and tantamount to trampling on people's constitutional rights. He called for the program to be halted immediately, but rejected calls to fire Powers.[66]

Most recently, a private membership-based organization came to light after its involvement in coordinating a crackdown on Occupy Wall Street encampments across the U.S. in late 2011. According to the *San Francisco Bay Guardian*, the Police Executive Research Forum (PERF)—an "international non-governmental organization with ties to law enforcement and the U.S. Department of Homeland Security"—was "coordinating conference calls with major metropolitan mayors and police chiefs to advise them on policing matters and discuss response to the Occupy movement."[67] Notably, the *Bay Guardian* called PERF's current and former directors "a who's who of police chiefs involved in crackdowns on anti-globalization and political convention protesters resulting in thousands of arrests, hundreds of injuries, and millions of dollars paid out in police brutality and wrongful arrest lawsuits." Notably, Philadelphia police commissioner and former Washington, DC, metro police chief Charles Ramsey—well known for his repressive response to the April 2000 IMF/World Bank and other political protests in the early-to-mid 2000s—was chair of the PERF board of directors in 2011.[68] Ramsey's predecessor was none other than John Timoney, who went on to train Iraqi police in Kirkuk, evaluate the U.S. detention facilities in Guantanamo Bay,[69] and became an advisor to Bahrain's Interior Minister during the Arab Spring. According to *Miami New Times*, Timoney was brought to Bahrain supposedly to "lead a group of police advisors from the U.S. and Britain" and retrain the Bahraini police force, which has been accused of using torture and excessive force against prodemocracy protesters.[70] Hiring the architect of the "Miami Model," however, may not have been the best decision for the Middle Eastern country if its objective was to bring accountability to its policing.

The state's insatiable thirst for politically related information is not balanced by any reasonable oversight. Looking into police abuse during the 2003 FTAA protests, the Civilian Investigative Panel (CIP) was denied access to the "Operational Plan" developed by Timoney and the Miami Police Department (MPD) along with Homeland Security and the FBI.[71] Though the plan was repeatedly referenced in the MPD "after action report," the city refused to turn it over. Using the excuse that divulging the information could jeopardize future security operations in Miami and around the country, the city also refused to comply with requests made by several civil litigants engaged in legal battles with the city. As recently as 2010, the federal Court of Appeals for the Second Circuit agreed that revealing police records that detailed political surveillance and tactical strategy in advance of protests "could undermine the safety of law enforcement personnel and would likely undermine the ability of a law enforcement agency to conduct future investigations."[72]

National Special Security Event Designation

In order to focus attention and financial investment on responding to mass political protest under the guise of national security and counterterrorism, President Clinton established the "National Special Security Event" (NSSE) designation in 1998. It became law in December 2000.[73] The Presidential Threat Protection Act and NSSEs covered certain national and international events held in the United States and placed security under the purview of the U.S. Secret Service.[74] Events such as the Free Trade Area of the Americas meetings in Miami, the Republican and Democratic conventions (including the RNC 2000) and the G-20 meetings in Pittsburgh have all been designated as NSSEs. According to the National Lawyers Guild (NLG), factors contributing to NSSE designation include "the attendance of foreign dignitaries and United States officials, the expected number of attendees, and its political or historic significance."[75] While the Secret Service is authorized as the lead agency in charge of security for NSSEs, the FBI is in charge of counterintelligence, counterterrorism, and criminal investigations. Both the Secret Service and FBI work with local law enforcement and military personnel to develop plans for security. According to the NLG, "heavy police presence and restrictions at [NSSEs] can include canine units, sharpshooters, surveillance, road closures, rail and air travel restrictions and United States Coast Guard patrols." Documents released by WikiLeaks in November 2008 outlined the NSSE security apparatus for the RNC earlier that year, confirming the involvement of the military and Northern Command (NORTHCOM) personnel, arguably in violation of the Posse Comitatus Act.[76]

Under the guise of fighting terrorism, the "NSSE" designation can give the state political cover while suppressing dissent. Through state-imposed "rules of engagement," police have employed increasingly repressive tactics to mitigate mass political protest. According to Heidi Boghosian, over the past decade, tactics such as "less-lethal munitions on passive crowds, pre-event raids of homes and meeting spaces of organizers, confiscation of journalists' cameras, video equipment and recorded images, unlawful containment of crowds and mass arrests without probable cause typify modern policing of protesters."[77] Other elements of contemporary policing at NSSEs and other political meetings have included: screening checkpoints, at which all bags are subject to search; the imposition of "no speech zones" and restricted march routes; and corralling or trapping protesters with the use of police lines, motorcycles, bicycles, and horses. Based on so-called "antiterrorism" laws and selective prosecution practices, dissidents are now more seriously charged and more aggressively prosecuted than in the past.

In an elaborate ruse, "the government targets leaders of social and political movements . . . stigmatizes groups of activists, and uses the mass media to denigrate demonstrators, reinforce negative stereotypes or publicize high-profile arrests on charges which are frequently later dropped for lack of evidence," noted the NLG. Part of this effort includes labeling protesters as "outside agitators," or "anarchists" prone to violence and mayhem, enabling police to use repressive security measures and excessive force in an indiscriminate, widespread manner. When it fails to convince the public, the state often fabricates evidence. According to the NLG, uncorroborated statements by informants were used during the RNC 2008 "to obtain arrest warrants by alleging that, among other things, activists sought to kidnap delegates to the RNC, assault police officers with firebombs and explosives, and sabotage airports in St. Paul." For their part, Seattle officials acknowledged that the police response to protests against the NSSE-designated 1999 WTO meetings was a "laboratory for how American cities will address mass protests," and recognized it as "a vivid demonstration of what not to do."

State Resources Used to Suppress Dissent

In response to the mass political protests against the WTO, IMF/World Bank, RNC and DNC 2000, the federal government began to increase its investment in policing and weaponry. Resources allocated for the policing of mass political protests has steadily increased over the years, jumping from just over $10 million in 2000 to $44 million at the World Economic Forum held in New York in February 2002.[78] Subsequent policing efforts required similarly high sums, such as nearly $37 million for the G-8 meeting in Sea Island, Georgia, and $76 million for the RNC 2004 in New York.

It was estimated that more than $1 billion was spent on policing the 2010 G-8 and G-20 protests in Toronto, Canada—ten times as much as the policing budget for the previous year's G-20 meeting held in Pittsburgh.[79] Sometimes this increased investment has gone to procure weaponry (i.e., tasers, projectile, chemical, and electrical weapons, as well as other high-tech weapons including the Long Range Acoustic Device), which is later used on civilians living in the host city. Funding for "security" has also been used to increase police presence with the aim of overshadowing protesters. According to author and activist Gan Golan, the ratio of police to protesters during the G-8 meeting in Sea Island, Georgia was 66:1.[80]

Mass protest in U.S.	Year	Amount spent on "security"	# of police deployed	# of law enforcement agencies
World Trade Organization	1999	$11,200,000	1,100	28
IMF/World Bank	2000	$10,000,000	1,400	-
RNC	2000	$13,300,000	7,000	-
World Economic Forum	2002	$44,000,000	4,000	-
Free Trade Area of the Americas	2003	$23,900,000	2,500	40
G-8 Sea Island	2004	$37,000,000	20,000	136
RNC	2004	$76,000,000	36,000	66
Bush inauguration	2005	-	13,000	60+
RNC	2008	$50,000,000	3,500	100+
G-20 Toronto	2010	$100,000,000	6,000	-

In most cases, this increased investment in "security" resulted in police-instigated riots, heavy surveillance and infiltration, countless injuries, mass arrests, and the wholesale chilling of dissent. At the same time, the normalization of police violence has meant that the public has asked fewer questions and come to expect that such violence is inevitable. During mass protests, author and journalist Naomi Klein reported encountering several activists "who carried the requisite protective gear of swimming goggles and bandanas soaked in vinegar," not because they were planning to attack a Starbucks, but because "they've come to expect that getting gassed is what happens when you express your political views."[81]

State Reactions to Mass Political Protest since 2000

Countless mass demonstrations have taken place since the RNC 2000 and many of them have been met with police tactics similar to those used in Philadelphia. Over the years, police have repeatedly used preemptive raids and "proactive" arrests with little to no consequence. Especially disturbing has been the recurrent use of excessive force. During the November 2003 Free Trade Area of the Americas (FTAA) protests in Miami, Timoney and his coordinated "security" apparatus shot at, gassed, tasered, pepper-sprayed, clubbed, and beat thousands of protesters. For longtime activist Jody Dodd, it was "the emergence of urban tanks and the synchronized militarism" that was "so stunning, horrible and traumatizing."[82] Dodd and other legal workers deliberately formed the law collective Miami Activist Defense to deal with the numerous rights violations and the criminal cases of more than two hundred people arrested during the FTAA protests. Nearly all of the cases were ultimately dismissed. Circuit Judge Richard Margolius publicly condemned the police response. Margolius, who apparently observed some of the protests himself, called the police response "disgraceful" and said that he saw "no less than 20 felonies committed by police officers."[83] In September 2007, activists achieved a bittersweet victory when a federal court ruled that the actions of the MPD violated protesters' First Amendment rights but that those violations were not the result of a conspiracy between the MPD and other law enforcement agencies—a claim made by activists and their NLG attorneys.[84]

Less than a year later, at least thirty-six thousand police were deployed during the RNC 2004 in New York. In a bizarre attempt to keep tens of thousands of people from protesting during the convention, the city denied a permit for a rally on the Great Lawn of Central Park. Police ended up arresting more than 1,800 people during the protests. It was a contemporary high-water mark for mass wrongful arrests, with 91 percent of the cases dismissed or acquitted at trial. Later, it was revealed that the NYPD had "spied broadly" for at least a year prior to the Republican convention, traveling to more than fifteen U.S. cities, as well as to Canada and Europe.[85] Police reports obtained by the *New York Times* revealed that teams of undercover officers "attended meetings of political groups, posing as sympathizers or fellow activists" in order to gather information, which they shared with other law enforcement agencies. A month before the March 2007 *New York Times* story, a federal judge recognized *Handschu* and found that police must have "some indication of unlawful activity on the part of the individual or organization to be investigated." Nevertheless, the *Times* concluded after reviewing hundreds of reports stamped "NYPD Secret," the police Intelligence Division "chronicled the views and plans of people who had no apparent intention of breaking the law," including "members of street theater companies, church groups and antiwar organizations, as well as environmentalists and people opposed to the death penalty, globalization and other government policies." Footage taken by I-Witness Video during the RNC 2004 also indicated that the NYPD was using undercover police to infiltrate the protests.[86]

At the RNC 2008 in St. Paul, police and responded with a level of violence and political repression similar to that experienced by FTAA protesters in Miami. Not only were people harassed, searched, and arrested in the lead-up to the demonstrations, informants and infiltrators were also used to spy on activist groups and to act as *agents provocateurs*. Police used heavy surveillance and infiltration to preemptively raid the RNC Welcoming Committee's convergence space, where they detained dozens of people and confiscated personal belongings, computers, and political propaganda. With assault rifles drawn, police also preemptively raided the houses of several organizers in Minneapolis and St. Paul—including activists later charged with conspiracy in a high-profile case that became known as the "RNC 8." Although St. Paul Mayor Chris Coleman called the protests "one of the most coordinated, orchestrated efforts in the history of this country to try to create chaos in a community and to shut down political dialogue," it was in fact the police who engaged in widespread violence and political repression.[87] With taxpayer money, they purchased millions of dollars in surveillance equipment and weaponry, much of which is still in use today.[88] To quell dissent, the state used tear gas, pepper spray, stun grenades, rubber bullets, and other projectiles. Ultimately, they arrested more than eight hundred people.

A year after the RNC 2008 protests, the Courtwatch Working Group of CRASS reported that at least ten people were convicted by a jury (two felony and eight misdemeanor cases), three people were acquitted by a jury, and more than forty people pleaded guilty to criminal charges (eight felony and thirty-three misdemeanor cases).[89] Eight defendants dubbed the "RNC 8" were charged with conspiracy to riot for helping to organize protests at which other individuals unknown to them were arrested. They also became the first to be charged with terrorism enhancements under Minnesota's own "Patriot Act." After sustaining ongoing public pressure, however, Ramsey County Attorney Susan Gaertner dropped the terrorism enhancements, and dismissed all of the charges against three of them. The remaining activists took noncooperating plea bargains, which included pleading guilty to gross misdemeanors conspiracy to riot or conspiracy to damage property.[90] Four of the five who pleaded guilty were sentenced to time served with up to two years' probation. The other defendant took ninety-one days in jail with no probation. The remainder of the state cases were either never prosecuted or dismissed. A couple of other state court convictions resulted in jail time, and some people convicted of property destruction were forced to pay thousands of dollars in restitution.[91] Two women accused of throwing a traffic sign over a bridge pleaded guilty to misdemeanors resulting in seven years of probation, nearly two hundred hours of community service, and restitution.[92] According to CRASS, the vast majority of prosecutions were against people who lived outside of the Twin Cities in the hope that they would take plea deals rather than returning to St. Paul at considerable time and expense. "Most of the people who took plea deals were guilty of nothing whatsoever, they simply couldn't continue to fight the legal system," read an August 2009 CRASS newsletter. "Most of the people who fought their charges won."

Three out-of-town activists who came to the Twin Cities to protest at the RNC were targets of the FBI and set up by paid federal informants. Bradley Crowder, Matt DePalma and David McKay were arrested and accused of making Molotov cocktails. In an effort to characterize activists as violent, the FBI paid Brandon Darby—an activist-turned-informant—to encourage illegal activity. DePalma and Crowder took plea deals to avoid the potential of longer sentences. DePalma was sentenced in March 2009 to forty-two months in prison followed by three years of supervised release. Crowder received a fifteen-month sentence from a plea agreement in a separate RNC-related state case and an additional two years for his federal conviction. McKay, who chose to go to trial to fight the charges, argued that the federal government had entrapped him. The trial ended in a hung jury, but the government decided to try him again. McKay ultimately took a plea deal to keep federal pressure from being placed on Crowder—a long-time friend of his—to testify against him.[93] McKay was sentenced in May 2009 to four years in federal prison followed by three years of supervised release.

To be fair, the legal impact of the RNC 2008 protests had less to do with deficiencies in legal support and more to do with the state's determination. As in Philadelphia, the Republican host committee gave the City of St. Paul an insurance policy to help it avoid accountability for civil rights violations. Without a sufficient backlash, insurance policies will continue to be used as a defense against civil action. To make matters worse, the federal and state courts have generally refused to recognize underlying law enforcement conspiracies, thereby enabling them to continue with relative impunity. The lack of public outcry is often frustrating for dissidents, but understandable given the immense resources the state dedicates to dominating the discourse and instilling fear and intimidation in the public.

Critique and Analysis

Ten years after 9/11, several journalists offered retrospectives on the impact of the U.S. Global Justice movement. "For a moment," said *Dissent Magazine* contributor Bhaskar Sunkara, "radical politics appeared pregnant with possibility."[94] *Truthout* journalist Daniel Denvir added that "a rapid-fire series of mass demonstrations forced secretive financial institutions, corporations (and political parties) to make their case to the American people for the first time in a very long time, and there was a sense of incredible optimism and power."[95] Freelance journalist Mark Engler also pointed out that young activists were "exposed to critiques of neoliberalism, to campaigns targeting multinational corporations as dominant actors on the world stage, and to challenges to the . . . acceptance of a new 'free trade' orthodoxy."[96] There's little doubt that the tens of thousands of activists who shut down the WTO meetings in 1999 inspired further actions and hindered progress on international trade for years afterward. However, that's not the entire story.

After the brutal state response to the RNC 2000 protests, many groups went through a reflective process focused on strategy and tactics but also on race and the direction of the movement. "Building multiracial unity . . . is the most important and most difficult task facing white people interested in fighting for social justice," said Christopher Day, an activist and white member of SLAM.[97] "Generally, white progressives have paid lip service to this without prioritizing concrete anti-racist work in practice." Day shared his thoughts about the impact of RNC 2000 protest planning with groups like the Direct Action Network (DAN) in New York:

> The August 1st action's success or failure as an action cannot be separated from the internal struggles that DAN and others had to go thru to make it happen. The fights around racism internally did divert energy from tasks that could well have

affected the outcome of the action. Not being adequately
prepared for the police was probably, in part, a consequence
of not being able to give the fullest attention to all the practical tasks involved in preparing for the hostility of the state.
But we shouldn't draw the conclusion that it's a mistake to
struggle around these issues—until we have these struggles,
we're going to be hampered in our work.

Day further emphasized that "the work around August 1st has
strengthened the embryonic development of a direct action trend among
young activists of color." For Day, however, that didn't necessarily translate into "people of color joining DAN, nor perhaps should it, but DAN's
resources, experience and expertise actually made a contribution to building the kind of multiracial movement we need." Kazembe Balagun, another
SLAM member, offered his take on the fallout from the RNC 2000 protests. "A lot of folks went through a lot of trauma," he recalled, and "people
in SLAM got really reflective."[98] Balagun derived the following lessons:

> (1) direct action is so central to the work of dismantling the
> state and capitalism; (2) direct action, done correctly, can fos-
> ter solidarity across racial and gender lines, and that's some-
> thing we definitely learned; and (3) we really need to main-
> tain this sense of communication and national network, and
> be really innovative in terms of strategy. We consistently go
> back to Seattle, but the world has changed since Seattle, and
> the police state's learning curve has increased since Seattle.
> What are we going to do in terms of re-imagining our tactics?

"Out of R2K also came the birth of Critical Resistance East and all
this other great prison abolitionist work," continued Balagun. "R2K did
help foster regional and national conversations on race and incarceration." Underscoring the ongoing importance of prison issues, Balagun
pointed out that "when you're talking about prison abolition and restor-
ative justice, you're really talking about, 'How do we provide solutions to
this society?'"

In *Black Bloc, White Riot*, social theorist A.K. Thompson wrote that
the antiglobalization movement was "gripped by a series of confusing tensions . . . expressed abstractly through antithetical pairs like 'violence' and
'non-violence,' 'summit hopping' and 'local organizing,' and 'direct' and

'mass' action."[99] Often failing to address the underlying problems brought on by these tensions, much of the post-RNC 2000 political discourse was focused on whether the same protest tactics were still useful. Covering the RNC protests in Philadelphia, journalist Ana Nogueira noted that "although the strategies of the activists often proved successful, police were well-informed enough to be able to respond immediately."[100] Indeed, ever-increasing budgets for the policing of political protests has convinced some that the success of the Seattle WTO protests won't happen again. "Far too much expectation is being placed on these protests," claimed Naomi Klein in a June 2000 article for *The Nation*.[101] "The organizers of the DC demo [against the IMF], for instance, announced they would literally 'shut down' two $30 billion transnational institutions, at the same time as they attempted to convey sophisticated ideas about the fallacies of neoliberal economics to the stock-happy public." Klein argued that they simply couldn't do it: "Seattle's direct-action tactics worked because they took the police by surprise." John Sellers echoed Klein when he noted that, after the success of Seattle, "we gave up the element of surprise."

Not all dissidents agree with this analysis, however. A key organizer of the Seattle WTO protests, David Solnit disagrees wholeheartedly with the conclusions drawn by Sellers, Klein, and others. In *The Battle of the Story of the Battle of Seattle*, he argued that the notion that Seattle's success was based largely on surprise "ignores the lessons learned there."[102] Solnit pointed to the 2003 antiwar shutdown of San Francisco as evidence that "at key moments, when we are well organized, strategic, and learn lessons, we can be amazingly effective." Despite a much tighter timeline than for Seattle, Bay Area activists (many of whom helped organize the WTO protests) set out to "'create a social, economic and political cost' if the US invaded Iraq, by shutting down the largest corporate and financial center in the Western United States." As planned, on March 20, 2003, "20,000 Bay Area and regional residents brought San Francisco's Financial District streets to a standstill, and blockaded war-related corporations, government offices, and financial institutions." A local cop even agreed that dissidents had succeeded in shutting down the city. "They are highly organized, but they are totally spontaneous," said officer Drew Cohen. "The protesters are always one step ahead of us."

To help further develop and spread some of the strategic principles used in Seattle, Solnit and other organizers got together to reflect on "the key elements that made the successful one-day mass urban action." As a result, Solnit offered the following principles:

- "Clear What-and-Why Logic," establishing a simple rationale for the mass action that makes sense to people;
- "Broadly Publicized," including lead-up actions, press conferences, print and web-based outreach, as well as regional road shows;
- "Mass Training and Mass Organization," through broad-based and diverse networks;
- "Decentralization," in order to increase flexibility, allow for quick decision-making, and respond easily to changes;
- "Action Agreements," which frame the goals, strategies and tactics;
- "Open Organizing," to reduce vulnerability and repression at the same time as attracting and involving greater numbers of people; and
- "Media and Framing," that will plainly communicate the issues and the aim of the protests to participants, movements, and the public.

In her own seven-point plan for *Organizing in the Face of Increased Repression*, author, activist, and WTO arrestee Starhawk suggested that the greatest restraint to police violence "is the organizing and alliance building we've done before the action ever happens."[103] Starhawk further argued that "we need to counter their disinformation campaigns with our own community outreach, to leaflet, to talk to people, to go door to door, to explain to the community what we're doing and why long before we do it." Starhawk also recommended more flexible and creative tactics. "The more we can plan for orchestrated spontaneity, the harder we'll be to stop." Stressing the obvious need for "building a broader, larger movement," she suggested finding ways to "encourage participation at varied levels of risk, to support a wide variety of forms of protest that can mobilize different groups of people" while confronting the dynamics of racism, sexism, classism, and other forms of oppression. Most of all, Starhawk said, "we need to clarify our vision of the world we want to create, so we can mobilize people's hopes and desires as well as their outrage."

For her part, Rebecca Solnit underscored the importance of organizing in affinity groups and making decisions democratically by spokescouncil. She also pointed out that public and open organizing is "less vulnerable to government infiltrators or informants and its plans are not ruined if they are found out." Furthermore, Solnit argued that "keeping planning secret goes against the need to attract and involve large numbers of people, to have open democratic decision-making." The element of surprise comes from the ability of each affinity group and cluster to make autonomous tactical decisions. Regarding media, Solnit said that "too often, a healthy, radical critique of the corporate media leads to groups deciding to not even try to engage with them, standing by while they get beaten up in the mainstream press, and sometimes not even making the effort to communicate through independent media or directly through their own media and outreach."

In "a pushback against the rigidity of 'nonviolence,'" some activist groups have strongly promoted a "diversity of tactics" framework. But Solnit lamented that when this approach has replaced concrete action agreements, activists tend to receive less public support and become more vulnerable to repression. In response, activists familiar with the state's propensity to exploit divisions developed the "St. Paul Principles," to subvert the false dichotomy between "good protesters" and "bad protesters." Widely discussed and adopted in advance of the 2008 Republican convention, the principles stand as a contemporary standard.[104] The St. Paul principles were based on "respect for a diversity of tactics and the plans of other groups," the need to "maintain a separation of time or space" for different protest actions and tactics, and to keep debates or criticisms internal to the movement, "avoiding any public or media denunciations of fellow activists and events." The principles explicitly opposed "state repression of dissent, including surveillance, infiltration, disruption and violence," and included the refusal to "assist law enforcement actions against activists and others."

After the November 2003 FTAA protests in Miami, political activist and organizer Ryan Harvey began what he called "a long reflective process," which illuminated for him how unconnected street actions were from "any real strategy to achieve change" with "no goals" other than "to ruin the party for the bigwigs."[105] In an open letter to fellow anarchists issued directly after the 2009 G-8 protests in Pittsburgh, Harvey asked "Are We Addicted to Rioting?" In this way, he tried to create a dialog about the effectiveness of "militant street protests." In the letter, Harvey conceded that he and his friends were "pretty much addicted to these intense street situations" and searching for the "mythological 'next Seattle.'"

Miami changed things for Harvey, who was next to a woman when she was shot in the face with a rubber bullet. "Something clicked when the blood poured out of this woman's mouth," he recalled. "This is for real. I am really here and we are really getting the shit kicked out of us." Harvey pointed out that anarchists and street militants get to engage in "roles that we don't get to enact in our everyday lives, heroism, bravery, sacrifice, quick thinking, fear-testing, and some forms of solidarity." However, "We also get to experience prison, pain, and life-changing trauma." Admitting that "all of this is well worth it," Harvey stipulated that we must also "have our eyes on the prize" and be "fully aware of the risks, reasons, and responsibilities of these types of actions. . . . There's too much at stake to waste our time and energy preparing for and executing these theater-like confrontations. . . . We have a lot of work to do, and most of it is not going to get done in the streets. It's going to get done on the doorsteps, the libraries, the churches, the labor halls, the schools, the military bases, the parks, the prisons, the abortion clinics, the neighborhood associations, the PTAs."

Adding to this sentiment, RNC 2000 arrestee and labor organizer Chris White recalled that, the RNC protest organizing "made me realize that we had to be more serious about building a popular base and winning real demands, building real power, and not being stuck in our identity as part of the fringe."[106] According to White, "doing direct action with my own white community and getting my ass kicked" taught him certain lessons that later helped him organize successful labor actions where no one got beaten up or arrested.

That Harvey, White, and others experienced strategic revelations is significant; however, according to A.K. Thompson, the turn from "summit" actions to "local organizing" was still "fraught with theoretical and practical difficulties."[107] As the "abstract antithesis to a universalized 'global,'" Thompson argued that "local organizing" against global capital "remained opaque" and that "activists were often thwarted by a conception of 'the local' that was itself inadequate to the task they hoped to accomplish." Specifically, Thompson pointed to a failure on the part of white activists to "see 'the local' in their own neighborhoods, schools, or places of work." In the post-RNC 2000 and post-9/11 climate, Camilo Viveiros of the Timoney 3 offered ideas for overcoming that failure. Being strategic involves "making a plan on how to achieve goals and monitoring your success along the way."[108] Moreover, "It means learning from mistakes and thinking carefully about how to outwit—and out-organize—your enemy." Paradoxically, that style of community organizing, found in models promoted by groups like the Alinsky-inspired Midwest Academy, has been around for decades. But while the Academy focuses on important questions like "Who has the power to give you what you want?" and "What power do you have over them?," these efforts are often supplanted by the tactical mechanics of militant confrontation.[109]

In 2001, veteran organizer Taj James founded the Oakland-based Movement Strategy Center (MSC) to "help transform the common challenges" faced by movements for racial justice.[110] His formula can easily be applied to social change movements aimed at uniting people through "shared strategy, shared principles and shared goals." Refuting the common misconception that movements occur spontaneously, James concedes that it can be easier to see the impacts of movements than the nuts and bolts that went into making them. For this reason, the MSC developed a "blueprint" to help movements be "more strategic, collaborative and sustainable." Philadelphia-based Training for Change is another activist resource. Like MSC, Training for Change (TFC) also emphasizes a strategic approach to political organizing. According to TFC, some of the ingredients of social change campaigns include: (1) understanding the elements of building a strategy, (2) visioning and identifying specific objectives, (3) identifying allies to reach out to, and (4) finding a framing or message to appeal to allies.[111] Their strategy workshop focuses on empowerment, uses specific exercises to "help people think more strategically" and to deal with "feelings of failure or resistance to strategizing." The group also underscores that there is no single answer—no "magic bullet"—to strategy.

Even members of the anarchist collective CrimethInc. (some of whom seek "a total break with domination and hierarchy in all their forms, involving an armed uprising if need be") emphasize the need to develop skills and broaden participation.[112] Considering a series of "recurring clashes" in the Fall 2009 issue of *Rolling Thunder*, CrimethInc. asked how to ensure that such confrontations "strengthen us more than our enemies." They ask, "What else do we have to do to make our efforts effective?" CrimethInc. pointed to "a small current" in U.S. anarchist circles that prioritized "insurrection and social conflict" with some emphasizing "confrontation for its own sake, rather than as a means of achieving reforms," and others framing revolt as "a means of building the power of the oppressed outside static organizations." In conclusion, they note that "by interrupting the apparent consensus and social peace, confrontations make injustice visible and legitimize the rage others feel as well." In *Black Bloc, White Riot*, A.K. Thompson argued that the "anti-globalization riot," while "not always tactically efficacious," broke with representational politics "by not advancing particular demands, by *not asking for anything*."[113] At the same time, if the force of an insurrection is social and not military (which, according to CrimethInc.

is a long established tenet of insurrectionists), why is it so frequently forgotten in practice, with activists "unconsciously adopting the military logic of one's enemies?" Harvey claimed to have engaged in what he called "combat scenarios" and "mini-war scenes," at mass mobilizations.[114] But, as CrimethInc. accurately pointed out, "the state is often more prepared and vigilant, rendering successful attacks more difficult from a purely military point of view."[115]

Shortly after the WTO protests in Seattle, a section of the N30 black bloc called the ACME Collective issued a public communiqué explaining the black bloc tactic and the rationale for property destruction. "When we smash a window, we aim to destroy the thin veneer of legitimacy that surrounds private property rights," read the communiqué.[116] "At the same time, we exorcise that set of violent and destructive social relationships which has been imbued in almost everything around us." By "destroying" private property, the ACME Collective said, "we convert its limited exchange value into an expanded use value." Ten years later, CrimethInc. had a chance to reflect on N30 and what has transpired since then:

> Much has changed since the communiqué from the ACME collective following the black bloc at the WTO protests in Seattle. In 1999, the ACME statement was widely read and debated, influencing the politics of a new generation that saw more sense in opposing corporate power with crowbars than with signs or lockboxes. A decade later, black-clad anarchists are miraculously still finding ways to smash windows, despite ever-increasing surveillance and repression—but the communiqué, if not the action itself, seems to be directed only to those who understand and approve of the tactic. . . . Symbolic clashes can help develop the capacity to fight for more concrete objectives, but not if they are so costly that they drain their social base out of existence.[117]

Harvey and CrimethInc. appear to agree that spreading skills and practices may be more pressing for anarchists than secretive military strikes. "There is no substitute," observed CrimethInc., "for participatory activities that offer points of entry for new people and opportunities for existing groups to connect." While many dissidents avoid visible organizing because of a repressive political environment, CrimethInc. wisely argued that "the chief dangers of visibility are not posed by the police, after all, but by the possibility of being absorbed into the spectacle, performing for the cameras until one comes to mistake representations for reality."

> In the US, militant struggle means taking on the most power-
> ful state in the history of the world. It demands a strategy that
> takes into account the repression, legal support, and prison
> sentences that will inevitably result, and somehow turns
> them to our advantage. The absence of such a strategy is per-
> haps the most significant structural flaw in insurrectionist
> projects today. We have to engage with the issue of repres-
> sion beyond the usual security culture, limited prisoner sup-
> port, occasional solidarity actions, and wishful thinking.[118]

Furthermore, if social force is "a matter of culture, values, alle-
giances, priorities . . . influenced by but distinct from the physical terrain
of actual confrontations," we may need to analyze our strategies and base
our approaches on a different set of criteria than those used for military
confrontations. The questions posed by CrimethInc. included: "How many
people will support you in a conflict? How many will join in themselves?
If you go to prison, will your grandmother support you? Will her community?" The state understands social war and will not solely use force to
overcome movements for social change. "It is significantly more cost-ef-
fective for them to intimidate, isolate, or discredit radicals," CrimethInc.
noted. "We should recognize this intimidation and isolation as their top
priority, and defend our relationships and our connections to others
accordingly." *Rolling Thunder* provided the following, helpful "Social Skills
for Social War":

- Decision-making structures and cultural conventions that encourage horizontal power dynamics
- Accountability processes to address internal domination
- Conflict resolution, both internally and with potential allies
- The ability to provide for material, social, and emotional needs
- The capability to reproduce the social forms of resistance faster than they are destroyed
- The means to communicate beyond a single subculture
- The flexibility to adjust according to context, rather than remaining caught in ritual

"The most effective insurrectionist actions not only open up the fault lines that run through society, they also compel the undecided to take sides." The outcome of revolutionary struggle, said CrimethInc., "is not decided by revolutionaries or autocrats so much as by those who sit on the fence between them." Thus, "there are no shortcuts in social war." The challenge in confronting the massive resources of the state is not to ignore the violent consequences of police retaliation, but to plan accordingly and take such aggression into account. The state's blatant disregard for popular movements, coupled with an increasing intolerance to political protest, calls out for a radical response that adequately exposes and alters the existing political paradigm.

CHAPTER 13:
A New Dawn for Radical Legal Activism

I N OPPOSITION TO THE RISE OF STATE REPRESSION THAT BEGAN IN Philadelphia at the turn of the century, there has been a formidable legal response. While civil litigation based on constitutional rights violations has resulted in monetary awards and injunctive relief, it has not been the only way of using the legal system to fight back. Although millions of dollars in civil awards have been granted in such civil cases, often with the help of the National Lawyers Guild (NLG), the money and periodic changes in police policy have been insufficient to end the attack on dissent. As a result, other forms of legal resistance have developed over the past decade that build on historical examples of radical legal support and blur the lines between the legal and the political.

The New Legal Collective Renaissance

The Global Justice movement prompted a legal collective renaissance in North America. While embracing many of the principles and tactics of the past, contemporary legal support groups also discovered new ways to "monkeywrench" the legal system. At the forefront of this renaissance were the Direct Action Network (DAN) Legal Team and the Midnight Special Law Collective.[1] One of the founding members of DAN Legal and Midnight Special was attorney Katya Komisaruk, who had been involved in the antinuclear movement in the early 1980s.[2] The importance of the link that Komisaruk provided to that historical movement and its use of solidarity tactics cannot be overstated. In 1999, the Direct Action Network helped organize protests against the WTO in Seattle. Because of an expectation that police might react harshly to the protests, the DAN Legal Team was formed. Consisting of law students, legal workers, and other activists, DAN Legal would help coordinate the legal strategy for more than six hundred arrested activists. Influenced by Komisaruk, DAN Legal arguably repopularized the use of jail and court solidarity in the context of mass political demonstrations.

Once it became clear that the collective leverage of jail solidarity had failed to pressure the city to negotiate, DAN Legal switched to a court solidarity strategy. But the members of DAN Legal never anticipated that the aftermath from the protests would last for months or take such an enormous amount of work. According to Midnight Special cofounding member Paul Marini, "two weeks after folks got arrested, almost everyone in the legal team had to leave."[3] Marini said that Komisaruk basically put her life on hold to help coordinate the legal support effort in the weeks and months following the WTO protests. In an article written for *Earth First! Journal*, members of Midnight Special detailed their role in Seattle and the magnitude of work they undertook: "Working with local lawyers, [Midnight Special] did legal research, outlined motions, created tools for jury selection, created courtroom displays and coordinated a team of jury analysts. In addition to attorney support, they supported defendants directly by designing a database to keep track of all arrestees and their court dates. This enabled them to draw public awareness to the political prosecutions by writing press releases, organizing rallies and gathering supporters to pack the courtrooms."[4]

Whereas jail solidarity failed to get rid of the charges levied against hundreds of protesters, court solidarity was a huge success. Because protesters demanded their right to a speedy trial and a court appointed attorney, Marini said the city was forced to try hundreds of cases within ninety days. "Now they don't try 600 people in a year in Seattle," Marini said. After a handful of trial acquittals, the city began to quietly dismiss hundreds of cases. In the end, out of the hundreds that were arrested, only a handful accepted plea bargains and only six went to trial, resulting in just one conviction.[5] Soon after the resolution of misdemeanor cases in Seattle (the felony cases took longer to litigate), the newly formed Midnight Special left for Washington, DC, to help with legal support for the IMF/World Bank protests in April 2000.

In addition to staffing a legal office in DC and coordinating several Know Your Rights and jail solidarity trainings, Midnight Special played a critical role as mediator between the city and hundreds of jailed protesters. With more than a thousand activists engaged in jail solidarity, sufficient leverage was created for Midnight Special to negotiate an acceptable agreement. Protesters used group meetings in jail to arrive at their demands, which were communicated to Midnight Special and used in its negotiations with the city. After five days, an agreement was reached that resulted in the release of all remaining IMF/World Bank protesters with nothing more than an infraction (e.g., a parking ticket) and a small fine, paid for by Midnight Special. The deal applied to almost all of the more than 1,200 people arrested, with the exception of a handful of people charged with felonies. Just as in Seattle, the felony cases were dealt with separately, thereby limiting the solidarity strategy to the misdemeanor defendants. Nonetheless, the success of jail solidarity in DC provided Midnight Special and more than a thousand protesters with what is considered the single biggest collective bargaining victory in recent history. If the events in Seattle were successful at shining a light on the importance of legal support, the experience in DC underscored the benefits of jail solidarity and the collective bargaining process.

Combined, the legal victories in Seattle and DC—largely facilitated by the work of Midnight Special—helped to inspire a new generation of activists. Conceding that no amount of legal expertise can replace a strong movement, Midnight Special members argued that "by deepening our collective understanding of the legal system, spreading the tools to fight it and keeping decision-making power in the hands of the people affected by those decisions, activist-based law collectives are helping to strengthen the movement."[6] Mac Scott, a legal worker formerly with the New York City People's Law Collective and Common Front Legal in Toronto, Canada agreed. "We don't believe the law can be used to create justice," Scott said.[7] "We believe that justice, that social change, revolution, is created on the street," and "what we can do as legal activists is to help protect movements and people in movements, while they go about the real business of creating change." Scott understood the importance of being able to manipulate the legal system as a tool of resistance to political repression. Likewise, Midnight Special members wrote that "the ability to monkeywrench the legal system is a valuable tool that belongs in the hands of everyone facing it. By understanding the points of intervention in the legal system we can and have effectively turned the machine on itself, with stunning results." It was these stunning results that were likely responsible for the subsequent proliferation of legal collectives across the North American continent.

Although they didn't always have the same objectives, most of the nascent legal collectives of the early 2000s shared similar principles to those held by Midnight Special. For their part, Midnight Special described contemporary law collectives as "community-based activist organizations familiar with the law and the politics of the legal system," which are "organized on the affinity group model and use democratic decision-making processes."[8] Many law collectives have since folded, including Midnight Special itself. The following collectives had been active at one time or another over the past decade, or are still active:

> **Midnight Special Law Collective, Oakland, CA:** An independent non-profit organization dedicated to providing legal trainings and accessible, relevant, democratic and accountable legal support to a wide range of activists participating in the struggle for social change.[9]
>
> **Just Cause Law Collective, Oakland, CA:** A law firm that represents criminal defendants, as well as victims of police misconduct, and provides educational workshops and materials on the law and your rights.[10]
>
> **R2K Legal Collective, Philadelphia, PA:** A loose-knit collective of over four hundred defendants, activists, and attorneys stemming from the Republican National Convention protests in 2000.[11]
>
> **Up Against the Law, Philadelphia, PA:** A collective committed to standing up to the criminal legal system—by taking collective action to eliminate the structural barriers to social and political equality that the legal system upholds. Up Against the Law empowered ex-offenders to take their own legal action and to reclaim rights and services to which they are entitled.[12]
>
> **New York City People's Law Collective, New York, NY:** A collective founded after the RNC 2000 on the principles of liberation, solidarity and mutual aid, consensus process and critical use of the law. Its members were anarchist, antiracist, anti-sexist, and anti-capitalist. As part of the movements with which they worked, they provided legal support, training, and education to people and groups engaged in radical action.[13]
>
> **JustUs Legal Collective, New York, NY:** A collective providing legal information and support for at-risk communities to address inequalities in the legal system and promote self-sustainable community

development in the greater New York area. Specifically, it provides Know Your Rights trainings, Jail Support, post-arrest criminal and civil procedural information and on-line legal resources.[14]

Justice & Solidarity Collective, Washington, DC: A tightly knit collective of activists, legal workers, and lawyers with radical political ideologies. Justice & Solidarity combined its resources with those of the existing progressive legal community to: act as a clearinghouse of information, provide or arrange for relevant and/or requested trainings, and support the empowerment of activists planning actions in DC, arrested individuals, and community members.[15]

Portland Law Collective, Portland, OR: A collectively run law firm providing legal services to progressive activist groups and which represents individuals in civil rights, labor, and criminal defense matters. The Portland Law Collective strives to provide legal representation while furthering its values of egalitarianism, tolerance, and sustainability in its own workplace, in the legal system, and in society more broadly.[16]

Cincinnati People's Law Collective, Cincinnati, OH: A Collective that worked with the local activist community and in support of the Coalition for a Just Cincinnati's boycott of downtown Cincinnati following the 2001 killing of Timothy Thomas, an unarmed nineteen-year-old African American.[17]

Austin People's Law Collective, Austin, TX: A group of activists committed to providing legal trainings (Know Your Rights, jail/court solidarity, etc.), legal observing, and support for the Austin community. Austin People's Law Collective was a dynamic group centered upon nonhierachical power-sharing and consensus process. Its members were not lawyers, but did work with lawyers to provide legal support that was responsive to the needs of the people.[18]

Coldsnap Legal Collective, Minneapolis, MN: An autonomous collective formed in advance of the RNC 2008 protests whose purpose is to work in solidarity with other groups or individuals in order to educate, empower, and support the radical community by sharing knowledge, raising awareness, and developing a network of legal support and solidarity.[19]

Libertas Legal Collective, Québec City, QC: A non-profit, volunteer organized legal collective, formed prior to the Summit of the Americas protest in Québec City in April 2001. Libertas was composed of law students and other volunteers who worked together with a team of lawyers initially to help ensure access to all necessary legal information before the demonstrations, then to organize legal defense for more than four hundred arrestees.[20]

Common Front Legal Collective, Toronto, ON: A collective that provided legal support for demonstrations by the Ontario Coalition Against Poverty (OCAP). As non-attorneys, members of Common Front Legal were involved in direct action social work, including representing undocumented immigrants and assisting people in obtaining government benefits.[21]

Movement Defence Committee, Toronto, ON: An autonomous working group of the Law Union of Ontario made up of legal workers, law students, activists and lawyers, which provides legal support to progressive organizations and activists in Toronto. The Movement Defence Committee recognizes that members of oppressed groups are at higher risk when they encounter the law and we work to provide information and support that is specific to these groups.[22]

Sylvia Rivera Law Project, New York, NY: Soon after getting arrested at the February 2002 World Economic Forum protests in New York City, Dean Spade founded a legal collective run by and for the transgender community. In addition to providing free legal services for people of color and low-income, SRLP has won precedent-setting lawsuits, represented hundreds of people, and trained numerous government organizations, community service providers, schools, and local organizations.[23]

In the early-to-mid 2000s, Midnight Special and others organized conferences for North American legal collectives in order "to share skills and provide resources for each other, to discuss different legal support strategies, and to build the foundations for a network of radical legal support."[24] These informal conferences were held for four consecutive years and involved several law collectives and legal workers from across the United States, Canada, and occasionally Mexico. The first conference was held in Philadelphia in 2002 when the R2K Legal Collective was still active. In 2003, the Libertas Legal Collective hosted the conference in Montreal during the same weekend that more than nine million people took to the streets globally to protest the imminent U.S. war with Iraq. The Austin People's Law Collective hosted the conference in 2004 and the Common Front Legal Collective hosted it in Toronto in 2005. Law collectives and other legal support activists have also met, strategized, and shared information at annual conventions held by the National Lawyers Guild, which has a legal worker committee and dedicates much of its resources to empowering non-lawyer legal activists.

It's worth noting that, while this renaissance of radical legal support has certain similarities to the law collectives of the 1960s and 1970s, it also has many differences. Mutual aid, consensus-based decision-making, and an egalitarian approach to work can all be considered common principles among historical and contemporary law collectives. Yet law collectives from the past tended to be attorney-focused, institutional in nature, and engaged in legal representation like a traditional law firm. San Francisco Community Law Collective cofounder Paul Harris tried to shake this stereotype by forming a collective law office, which he felt sent a message to the client that "lawyers were people . . . and that the law was a tool to be used, not a mysterious force to be feared or idealized."[25] But as Harris also lamented, some aspects of being a lawyer remain inescapable: "Lawyers play the role of priests, translating experience into legal dogma instead of piercing the legal mystique. The lawyer, like the priest, suffers the initiation rights [sic] of his calling, wears its vestments, legitimizes its authority, speaks its language, partakes of its rituals, and maintains a monopoly over its mystery."

While attorneys can be hindered by legal ritual and an obligatory adherence to the system, law collectives play a critically important role in "sharing information and refusing to allow the legal system to separate and silence us."[26] Midnight Special claimed that, by "creating bridges between the activist community and the legal community, demystifying the law, [and] spreading valuable skills,"[27] law collectives have helped to "assert everyone's right to access and everyone's ability to understand the law."[28] Midnight Special also argued against the notion that special training is necessary to understand the law, a myth "perpetuated in order to keep power in the hands of the privileged."[29] Contemporary law collectives have tended to be more issue-specific and rooted in the movements they're supporting. This dynamic has been crucial to building a level of trust and rapport—important to effective legal work but often unattainable for many in the legal community. Midnight Special described "accountable, activist-driven legal support structures" as follows:

> A dedicated legal support group can keep the case politically focused, create propaganda and work with the media in ways that most lawyers can't. They can assist attorneys

so that the same local lawyers don't always get burned out.
The support group can provide legal trainings and help the
community enforce its rights. . . . Over-reliance on lawyers
(who are by definition part of the system) or groups like the
American Civil Liberties Union (whose behavior ranges from
quite helpful to politically abhorrent) . . . disempowers our
community.[30]

One of the features that most distinguishes contemporary law collectives from their historical counterparts is that most of the newer organizations are composed entirely of activists and legal workers, purposely
excluding attorneys. And while law collectives certainly don't obviate the
need for lawyers or ignore the benefits of collaboration, the tension caused
by competing interests can often be counterproductive. The source of at
least some of this tension comes from the discord between the legal interests of the "individual activist" and the considerations of the greater movement of which she or he is part. Criminal defense attorneys are bound by
oath to prioritize their individual client's interests regardless of the broader
legal implications, the impact on other activists, or the consequences for
the greater political movement. Law collectives don't begrudge individual
interests as much as they lament the system that creates divisions between
comrades. Attempts to balance these interests have been met with derision
even from some of the most left-leaning attorneys.

But while integrating legal strategies with protest organizing goals
has been attempted over the last fifteen years, it remains rare. If effective
integration occurs, it is usually aimed at addressing legal issues (such as
Know Your Rights trainings, the denial of permits, police harassment,
etc.) before a demonstration begins. Legal groups and dissidents also
work fairly well together during mass mobilizations by deploying trained
legal observers to document arrests and police abuse, staffing an office
and hotline, collecting evidence, defending arrestees at arraignment and
bail hearings, and providing support to people being released from jail.
Still, there is tension during this chaotic period, and opportunities to use
political or legal leverage have been repeatedly been missed. The period
of greatest discord between legal and political groups, however, usually
occurs in the aftermath of mass mobilizations. Despite years of inten-
sified policing at protests, activists and the legal community are often
caught off-guard in the weeks and months following the protests. How
can broad-based political support and public sympathy be generated?

How can large numbers of arrestees work to overcome charges and politicize the legal process? Unfortunately, these questions are routinely only asked *after* protests, when the ability to develop strategy is far more limited.

Working Together?

Compounding the problem of integration between legal and political groups is the tendency to think of legal support as a service. Legal collectives have become fairly adept at carrying out critical legal tasks, but their routine and specialized nature has caused activists to view them as little more than "service providers." This perception fails to empower activists to take control of their own legal predicament. It can also inhibit activists from seeing their legal fight as a political fight too. While the "service provider" dynamic has affected some support efforts more adversely than others, it has prevented many activists from achieving their legal and political objectives and from overcoming the repressive actions of the state. The dynamic between legal and political activists was enough of a concern to warrant discussion at multiple legal collective conferences held in the U.S. and Canada during the early 2000s. Participants raised concerns about:

- Centralized legal support wielding too much power and control
- Activists taking centralized legal support for granted
- Activists not engaging enough in their legal struggle
- Limited financial and human resources being available for legal support
- Wanting greater engagement with activists/movements being supported
- Goals of legal support often being unclear
- Legal support efforts being predominantly temporary, failing to build power in their greater communities, and having a limited capacity to overcome political repression

In response, legal workers felt they needed to better assess the power dynamic between their legal communities and the broader movements they supported. After all, if movement advancement is the paramount objective, and if combining legal and political strategies is ultimately additive, some legal workers suggested that it might make sense to take advantage of a more integrated and intentional relationship. Without seeking to dominate or direct movements for social change, legal workers wanted to work more effectively with them. Some legal workers thought they could avoid the "service provider" trap and simultaneously build political strength by eliminating any elitist power dynamics arising from the concentration of information and by better strategizing with dissidents to exploit points of legal and political leverage. They thought this invigorated relationship should be based on mutual participation, consideration, and responsibility. Forms of increased engagement between legal and political activists can include:

- Decentralizing much of the legal support effort to the affinity group level
- Forming legal worker affinity groups for peer participation in spokescouncils
- Training political activists and legal workers in advance of mass political actions
- Interactive legal worker involvement in political (strategic and tactical) decision-making
- Making strategic use of civil litigation in advance of and during the protests
- Working with arrestees to make best use of their collective legal and political leverage

Political and Legal Leverage

In addition to being more engaged with protest organizers, legal workers can focus attention on how to make the most of collective action by arrestees and the broader movement. If mass arrests occur, it's in everyone's interest in the long run to dispense with criminal cases. By evacuating the streets and subduing political speech with threats of prosecution, the state certainly benefits in the short term; however, in the long term, the state and everyone else (protesters, entire movements, the public) is affected by the financial and psychic toll of long-winded, largely symbolic, and occasionally punitive prosecutions. And while there may be little chance of avoiding mass arrests, there are ways to achieve short-term objectives beneficial to everyone. There are several points of leverage that legal support teams and activists have focused on in the past, which have yielded successful outcomes, including: (1) civil litigation in advance of and during the demonstrations, (2) the use of jail solidarity to collectively bargain the lowest-penalty, most-equitable release conditions for arrestees, (3) placing community pressure on key decision-makers to make that happen, and (4) making use of mainstream and independent media to broadcast a narrative counter to that of the state and for the purpose of achieving short and long-term, as well as both legal and political, objectives.

In response to permit denials, heavy surveillance, infiltration, and police raids in advance of demonstrations, a combined legal and political campaign can successfully push back and get the public discussing protest issues. While still a tool of the dysfunctional justice system, civil litigation can be used to gain concessions and force the state to tolerate planned protest activity. It can also be used to keep police out of convergence spaces, and to overturn unconstitutional ordinances before they're used against activists. Once mass arrests have occurred, collective bargaining is another powerful tool for confronting the repressive actions of the state. The effectiveness of collective bargaining depends on many different factors, not least of which is the willingness of local officials to negotiate. While arrestees negotiated the terms of their release in Washington, DC, in 2000, negotiations posed insurmountable problems in Philadelphia. Effective collective bargaining also heavily depends on the level of activist and legal-team preparation and whether there is a clear sense of the power that can be wielded by hundreds of unified arrestees. By identifying key officials like the district attorney or state prosecutor and the mayor, pressure can be applied to better negotiate the terms of release. It is also important to identify legal team members who can be trusted to deliver arrestees' demands to key decision-makers. This strategy is greatly facilitated by creating lines of communication in advance of the protests to make it easier to discuss issues when the situation becomes critical.

At the end of the day, the likelihood of the state conceding to protester demands depends on the amount of political pressure that movements can muster. This requires that we investigate points of state vulnerability (jail capacity and conditions, unconstitutional criminal statutes, detention practices, historical reactions to dissent, and even the political pursuits of key decision-makers) and determine ways to exploit them. Unexpected points of leverage may also arise as a result of how events unfold. Without sufficient pressure, however, a state's attorney or mayor will refuse to concede to protester demands. Indeed, grassroots political pressure from call-ins, fax and e-mail campaigns, ongoing demonstrations, and effective media strategies have successfully embarrassed public officials who, on occasion, have buckled. Use of media in a legal context cannot be overstated, but care should be taken not to lose sight of the reasons that people took to the streets. Because the mainstream media is known for being sensationalist, distorting the facts, and using a biased approach to covering political protests, many activists refuse to engage it. Nevertheless, the media can be a powerful tool for legal workers, dissidents, and movements for social change. If used with forethought and strategic purpose, the media can help expose preemptive state tactics, mitigate police brutality, keep activists out of jail, and reduce the physical harm of incarceration and legal harm of prosecution by providing accurate information and by building public support to oppose the state's actions.

The ability of political arrestees to collectively bargain and negotiate desirable terms of release has often made the difference between a movement's need for short-term or long-term legal support. In the weeks after release, additional opportunities exist to collectively bargain. Arrestees have successfully used court solidarity strategies to plead "not guilty" en masse, refuse plea bargain offers by the state, and demand speedy trials. Cities faced with the prospect of having to prosecute hundreds of cases have been known to blink and dismiss all or most of the charges. This was not the case in Philadelphia, however. In the absence of collective will by arrestees, sufficient political pressure, or responsive public officials, a more long-term legal support effort may be needed.

Long-Term Legal Support

R2K Legal and CRASS stand as contemporary examples of long-term, single-issue, arrestee-led legal support. They are important case studies for a number of reasons including their emphasis on the strength of solidarity and mutual aid. In both Philly and the Twin Cities, people naturally came together to support those facing charges, and especially for those with felonies or who were still incarcerated after the protests. Each legal support model had unique qualities, but both embodied many of the same principles. So broad-based were these efforts that they far outgrew the preprotest legal teams from which they evolved. In the summer of 2008, meetings of arrestees, activists, and legal workers were held with the aim of continuing the legal support effort in the Twin Cities. According to CRASS, the meetings were "designed to share information, provide an opportunity for people to connect with each other, and create collective bargaining demands."[31]

Out of this, CRASS became a coalition of arrestees, activists, and community groups, with arrestees making up the group's core membership. Although CRASS was formed primarily to help activists and others fight their charges and build solidarity around court cases, it was also dedicated to providing support regardless of the severity of charges or whether arrestees were local, could afford an attorney, or even wanted to fight their charges. "By standing in solidarity with one another," read a CRASS statement included in a 2010 zine, "we felt we would be in the best position to use the strength of our numbers to pressure the system into dropping the charges, or at least to help protect the most vulnerable among us." Including groups such as the Anti-War Committee, the Coalition to March on the RNC and Stop the War, Communities United Against Police Brutality, North Star Health Collective, the RNC Welcoming Committee, and Twin Cities Indymedia, CRASS hoped its coalition would involve "a broad, decentralized spectrum of those affected by state repression, rather than a narrow or particularly vocal subsection of the activist community."

In its zine, CRASS described how it "operated out of a fundamentally anarchist/antiauthoritarian framework."[32] Like R2K Legal, CRASS employed a horizontal committee structure with no leadership and a consensus decision-making process, which meant that "participating individuals determined the direction" of the group and "all voices were accorded equal weight." CRASS overtly rejected what it called the "cult of expertise" or the a tendency to give deference to "professionals." Instead, members of CRASS tried to educate defendants on the law, encouraged them to get involved in their case, and helped balance the sometimes competing priorities of solidarity and legal utility. One of the most unique aspects of CRASS was its public attempt to deal with forms of oppression that became evident within the group. "When conflicts based on oppressive power structures arose, we tried to tackle them," read the CRASS zine. "This was an unusual step to take for some . . . but it strengthened the group even as it challenged individuals . . . and made some of us aware of power and privilege in unexpected ways."

A Federated Working Group Structure

Both R2K Legal and CRASS were autonomous groups, which had similar working group structures that operated semiautonomously and adapted over time to account for changes in strategy or capacity. To ensure that everyone involved was sufficiently heard, CRASS organized spokescouncils for raising and discussing proposals, and making overarching decisions affecting the group. Both collectives had working groups for outreach, media, felony support, fundraising, and civil litigation; however, CRASS also had working groups for applying pressure to public officials, tracking the outcome of court appearances, and providing hospitality to out-of-town defendants. Both groups directly supported defendants by helping to pay their travel and by finding housing when they came to town for court appearances. R2K Legal also provided significant funds for lawyers' fees stemming from criminal defense in high-profile cases.

Attempts to build public support and place pressure on key officials by strategically using media stunts and public confrontation grew organically from both legal support efforts. The campaign to get the charges against RNC 2008 protesters dropped included putting pressure on Ramsey County Sheriff Bob Fletcher, Minneapolis Mayor R.T. Rybak, St. Paul Mayor Chris Coleman, and St. Paul City Prosecutor John Choi by showing up at campaign appearances, crashing their press conferences, and staging targeted call-in days. CRASS also worked with the RNC 8 Defense Committee to put pressure on the prosecutor, Ramsey County Attorney Susan Gaertner. Like R2K Legal, CRASS used a media working group to aid in the effort to pressure public officials. Both issued press releases, held press conferences, conducted interviews, submitted opinion pieces, and wrote letters to the editor.

One of the most important working groups common to both R2K Legal and CRASS was "felony support," which typically supported felony defendants as well as other high-risk cases involving people facing immigration and citizenship issues, transgender folks, and those with high-level misdemeanors. Though fewer in number, these cases often take greater care and attention. Felony support working groups can provide direct, practical support for defendants including attending their court appearances, keeping them up-to-date, and finding them housing as needed. They can also be helpful in developing legal strategies. Because of concerns over police infiltration, felony support working groups should be structurally isolated from other working groups, while still striving to be accountable to the larger legal support effort.

Complications

In Philadelphia and the Twin Cities, this legal support model was effective for maintaining communication with hundreds of arrestees, updating them on their cases, coordinating their involvement in court solidarity efforts, and discussing ways to take political action. In its zine, CRASS argued that "The court system is designed to isolate and intimidate people," which is why solidarity and legal support work is so important. Yet, as invaluable as structures like R2K Legal and CRASS were, they still struggled against a number of pitfalls, which must also be considered. The CRASS felony working group is a good case in point. Although the vast majority of the hundreds arrested during the RNC 2008 protests had their charges withdrawn, dismissed, or acquitted, most of the nearly two dozen felony defendants pleaded guilty. And though some members of CRASS claimed that pretrial plea agreements were often a defendant's best option, others disagreed. An analysis of the felony support effort laid out in the CRASS zine helps to illuminate a number of problems within the working group that affected its ability to collaborate with defendants, attorneys, and the greater coalition.

First, people were unprepared for the number of felony cases and, as a result, support was stretched thin. According to CRASS, the felony support working group wasn't really set up to help defendants on a long-term basis. As a result, "the group had largely disintegrated by the time these cases went to trial." The semiclosed nature of the group also impeded legal workers and other supporters from getting involved. Second, because most felony defendants did not live in the Twin Cities or were still in jail, they were unable to participate in CRASS meetings. This made communication and strategizing that much more difficult. In spite of a buddy system set up to support each of the felony defendants, many of them "often didn't know what they needed or how they could be helped." According to CRASS, this left the working group without direction. Without adequate communication and information about their legal options, people charged with felonies bonded out of jail before their bail hearings, thus paying out more money to the state than they otherwise might have. Similarly, some felony defendants pleaded guilty without a plea agreement in place, leaving them no ability to negotiate the terms of their sentence. Third, the relationship between the working group and attorneys who represented felony defendants became strained because of conflicting interests and ideological differences. Criminal defense attorneys are motivated by what's "best" for their individual clients. Meanwhile, working group members were focused on felony support not just because of the consequences, but also because the cases were politically charged.

That said, many felony defendants "did not wish to have their names or stories associated with activist or anarchist support." According to

CRASS, this cost them support and allowed the state to use its own narrative when discussing the cases. Some attorneys encouraged their clients to accept plea bargains over pursuing political trials and discouraged their clients from associating with other felony defendants and their supporters. Attempting to dispel the myth that defendants can benefit from political isolation, CRASS argued that it rarely worked since activists who took such advice in the Twin Cities still ended up with felonies on their records. In retrospect, some members of CRASS felt "it would have been better to push the defendants to meet with people aside from their lawyers to get other perspectives about how to handle their cases and to think about media, fundraising, and other support needs." CRASS said that just reminding defendants of the support system and the prosecutor's burden of proving their guilt "may be enough to convince a person to fight their charges when they might otherwise just accept a deal." But because of suffering serious losses in the form of felony convictions and jail time for several RNC 2008 protesters, some CRASS members questioned whether their support had made a positive difference to the legal outcome.

While serious accusations leveled against defendants by the state failed to deter the support efforts of R2K Legal and CRASS, they can sometimes have an impact on the level of public support, even if the accusations are unfounded. By highlighting the trumped-up nature of all the charges, R2K Legal was able to use the wholesale dismissal of misdemeanor cases to gain public support for the felony defendants too. In the Twin Cities, this was more difficult—perhaps because a greater number of activists were charged with vandalism or property destruction, making it more difficult to gain public support. But rather than create an abstract division between "good" and "bad" protesters in order to define the parameters of legal support, it's important to consider at least three things: (1) all of the arrests, from infraction to felony, are political in nature, (2) people are supposed to be considered innocent until proven guilty, and (3) vilifying some participants tends to undermine the entire movement. CRASS considered its unconditional support to be "super relevant" under conditions where we are "increasingly criminalized."

Where to from Here?

As the evidence of repeated rights violations against dissidents at contemporary mass political demonstrations makes clear, the state is willing to pay the price of suppressing dissent—either with taxpayer dollars or insurance policies that allow police to violate rights with impunity. Such policies were used in Philadelphia, the Twin Cities, and during the 2012 demonstrations against NATO in Chicago. Police are thus emboldened to use excessive force and make indiscriminate, mass arrests with the expectation that insurance money will pay for a high-powered law firm to defend their actions. Civil suit monetary awards have also been paid for by insurance.

From a legal and constitutional rights-based perspective, things are looking pretty bleak. Contemporary civil litigation has been relatively impotent in curtailing police abuses despite the multi-million-dollar awards they've often yielded. The post-9/11 relaxation of police consent decrees in New York and Chicago, and the weakening of the Attorney General's Guidelines to give sweeping surveillance authority to federal agencies have contributed to a new level of violence against protesters. Are social change activists in the U.S. destined to be repressed by an ever-encroaching National Security State, or can we devise better ways of pushing back against police surveillance, mass arrests, and malicious prosecutions? Can civil litigation be used to achieve more meaningful and widespread changes in these areas or are other methods required?

By placing greater attention on the way legal support efforts are integrated with organizing efforts, we can better help advance movements for social change. The break-up of Midnight Special—one of the few radical institutions that dedicated itself to building power in the legal support community—has created a vacuum. For years, Midnight Special trained legal support activists and legal workers across the U.S. With its passing, the collective has given us an opportunity to design what's next. What will radical legal support efforts look like in a post–Midnight Special era? How will the legal community engage with its political counterparts? And how will legal workers collaborate with political comrades and attorneys to develop creative means of keeping dissent alive and thriving?

While the RNC 2000 case study mainly applies to mass mobilizations in which hundreds of arrests occur, it is still invaluable for understanding the motivations of contemporary political policing and for developing the means to challenge today's National Security State. We cannot let the state continue to interfere with our efforts to bring about social change. We must counter the state's repression by strengthening our bonds, by spurning efforts to instill distrust and suspicion, and by developing more creative forms of militant resistance. By using a more integrated approach, legal workers and political organizers can help dissidents use the legal system against itself and empower those who are otherwise under its control. It can also equip social change movements with the tools required to vanquish state repression. For these reasons, the lessons learned from the R2K Legal experience must be recognized, heeded, and put into practice. Only then can we be certain to achieve more than incremental social change in the years ahead.

Pigs are successfully cloned

Headline taken from an August 17, 2000, *Philadelphia Inquirer* story.

NOTES

Introduction

1. Amy Goodman, "Glenn Greenwald: The NSA Can 'Literally Watch Every Keystroke You Make,'" *Democracy Now!*, December 30, 2013, http://www.democracynow.org/2013/12/30/glenn_greenwald_the_nsa_can_literally.
2. Mark Larabee, "Police Role in Terror Task Force Criticized," *Oregonian*, December 6, 2000.
3. Clark McPhail, David Schweingruber, and John D. McCarthy, "Policing Protest in the United States: 1960–1995," in *Policing Protest: The Control of Mass Demonstrations in Western Democracies*, eds. Donatella della Porta et al. (Minneapolis: University of Minnesota Press, 1998), 50–54.
4. Patrick Gillham and John Noakes, "Aspects of the New Penology in the Police Response to Major Political Protests in the United States, 1999–2000," in *The Policing of Transnational Protest after Seattle*, eds. Donatella della Porta et al. (Ashgate, 2006), 111–13.
5. John King, "Philadelphia Will Host 2000 Republican National Convention," *CNN*, November 5, 1998, http://www.cnn.com/ALLPOLITICS/stories/1998/11/05/gop.convention.
6. The last Republican mayor of Philadelphia, Bernard Samuel, held office from 1941 to 1952. See: "Mayors of the City of Philadelphia: 1691–2000," City of Philadelphia, http://www.phila.gov/PHILS/Mayortxt.htm.
7. John King, "Philadelphia Will Host 2000 Republican National Convention," *CNN*, November 5, 1998.
8. In 1978, the City of Philadelphia laid siege to a MOVE home in West Philadelphia. Unprovoked, police fired repeatedly on the home, resulting in the death of a police officer. In 1985, the City of Philadelphia dropped a bomb on another MOVE home, with police shooting and killing eleven men, women, and children trying to flee the burning building.
9. There are numerous examples of law enforcement trainings in the early 2000s, following the WTO protests in Seattle. For example, in February 2000, a

conference was held at the FBI Academy in Virginia for police commanders from around the country, including Las Vegas, San Diego, Minneapolis, Tulsa, and Washington, DC, to study the Seattle protests and how to prepare for similar events. See: "Nation Looks to Learn Lessons from Seattle's WTO Problems," *Seattle Post-Intelligencer*, February 29, 2000, http://seattlepi.nwsource.com/national/trai29.shtml (as of December 2007), and Shannon Jones, "Police Build Up Anti-riot Forces in U.S. Cities," World Socialist Web Site, March 14, 2000, http://www.wsws.org/articles/2000/mar2000/poli-m14.shtml.

10. Kristen Lombardi, "Rough Justice," *Boston Phoenix*, January 18, 2001, http://www.bostonphoenix.com/boston/news_features/top/documents/00289134.htm.

11. "Miami Protests of Free-Trade Talks Stay Peaceful So Far," *Miami Herald*, November 19, 2003.

12. "National Special Security Events," United States Secret Service, http://www.secretservice.gov/nsse.shtml.

13. "Planning and Managing Security for Major Special Events," U.S. Justice Department, March 2007, http://www.cops.usdoj.gov/Publications/e07071299_web.pdf.

14. Amy Goodman and Juan Gonzalez, "NSA Whistleblower Kirk Wiebe Details Gov't Retaliation after Helping Expose 'Gross Mismanagement,'" *Democracy Now!*, December 19, 2013, http://www.democracynow.org/2013/12/19/nsa_whistleblower_kirk_wiebe_details_govt.

15. "Report on the existence of a global system for the interception of private and commercial communications (ECHELON interception system)," European Parliament, July 11, 2001: 11, http://www.fas.org/irp/program/process/rapport_echelon_en.pdf, and Steve Kroft, "Echelon," *60 Minutes*, February 22, 2000, http://cryptome.org/echelon-60min.htm.

16. Martin Asser, "Echelon: Big Brother without a Cause?" *BBC News*, July 6, 2000, http://news.bbc.co.uk/1/hi/world/europe/820758.stm.

17. From an interview with John Viola conducted on February 25, 2012.

Chapter 1

1. Robert Helms, "Philly Police against Dissent & Free Speech: A Chronology," Philadelphia Independent Media Center, August 8, 2000, http://www.phillyimc.org/en/node/33770.

2. In 1978, after nearly a year of twenty-four-hour police surveillance of the West Philadelphia MOVE home, the city—under the leadership of Mayor Frank Rizzo—obtained a court order to deprive the inhabitants of water, gas, and electricity for almost two months. Then, on August 8, 1978, the Philadelphia police fired repeatedly on the MOVE home, an incident that resulted in the death of a police officer. Instead of investigating the crime scene for evidence, the city used bulldozers in defiance of a court order to destroy the house, its foundations, and the trees in the yard. With the help of the Civil Affairs Unit, the city succeeded in convicting nine MOVE members in absentia, who all received sentences of thirty to one hundred years. Another attack on the MOVE organization occurred in 1985 under the leadership of Mayor Wilson

Goode. After evacuating the entire block of 6200 Osage Avenue on May 13, 1985, the city used tear gas, water cannons, shotguns, automatic rifles, a 20mm antitank gun, and a 50-caliber machine gun in order to force MOVE members from their home. According to MOVE, the police fired ten thousand rounds of ammunition and used military explosives to blast through the walls. Eventually, a bomb was dropped by helicopter on the house, and as MOVE members attempted to flee the burning building, police shot at them, killing eleven men, women, and children. See: "25 Years on the Move," MOVE, May 1996.

3. After years of political and legal pressure, in March 2008 the U.S. Court of Appeals for the Third Circuit vacated Abu-Jamal's death sentence, a decision that was reaffirmed three years later.

4. Dave Onion, "A History of Civil Affairs," *the defenestrator*, July 2000.

5. See: Pledge of Resistance v. We the People 200, Inc., 665 F. Supp. 414 (1987).

6. Linda K. Harris, Craig R. McCoy, and Thomas Ginsberg, "State Police Infiltrated Protest Groups, Documents Show," *Philadelphia Inquirer*, September 7, 2000, http://articles.philly.com/2000-09-07/news/25582916, and Kit Konolige, "Managing Director Must OK Police Spying," *Philadelphia Daily News*, September 16, 1987.

7. Robert Helms, "Philly Police against Dissent & Free Speech: A Chronology," Philadelphia Independent Media Center, August 8, 2000.

8. According to U.S. Census data from 2000, Philadelphia had a 43.2 percent African American population. See: http://www.census.gov.

9. "Philadelphia NAACP Plans Civil Rights Suit in Police Beating," *CNN*, July 14, 2000, http://cnn.com/2000/US/07/14/police.beating.03/index.html (as of December 2004).

10. Larry Miller, "Losing a Generation?" *Philadelphia Tribune*, September 5, 2006, http://www.phila-tribune.com/channel/inthenews/090506/behindbarsP1.asp (as of October 2009).

11. Tina Rosenberg, "Deadliest D.A.," *New York Times Magazine*, July 16, 1995.

12. The Blanketman, "Who Watches the Watchmen: Why the DA's Office Can't Be Trusted to Police the Police," *the defenestrator*, May 2000.

13. Rosenberg, "Deadliest D.A." At the time of the RNC 2000, Abraham oversaw the country's third largest death-row population, composed of the highest percentage of African Americans.

14. "About Our Mayor," The City of Philadelphia, http://www.phila.gov/mayor (as of February 2007); Christopher McDougall, "Philly Is Not Easy Street," *George Magazine*, August 2000.

15. Ibid.

16. "Police Prepare for Republican Convention Protests," *Reuters*, July 2, 2000.

17. Ibid.

18. Common Struggle, "End of Year Communique from NEFAC: Solidarity with Protesters against Neoliberalism," North-East Federation of Anarchist Communists, January 1, 2004, http://www.nefac.net/node/910.

19. In 1995, a former president of the Philadelphia FOP and its treasurer were convicted of racketeering, mail fraud, and bribery, and sentenced to several years in jail.

20. Robert Moran, "Panel Says Timoney Stymies Its Work," *Philadelphia Inquirer*, November 17, 2000, http://articles.philly.com/2000-11-17/news/25614246.

21. According to right-wing think tank Maldon Institute, "Assistance was provided to Philadelphia from neighboring police jurisdictions; the Pennsylvania, New Jersey and Delaware State Police; and the federal law enforcement community including the Department of Justice and the Federal Bureau of Investigation, and the Treasury's US Secret Service and Bureau of Alcohol, Tobacco and Firearms." Furthermore, Maldon added, "In the control and coordination of these law enforcement groups, the prime responsibility for enforcing the law rested with Commissioner Timoney." See: "R2K: Philadelphia's Convention Protests," The Maldon Institute, August 17, 2000.

22. See: http://www.phila.gov/mdo/.

23. Liz Theoharis, ed., "Battle for Broad: Educational Supplement," University of the Poor, 2000, http://www.povertyontrial.org/resources/educationals/Battle4Broad-educ.pdf

24. Erin Einhorn, "It'll Be Mask Hysteria," *Philadelphia Daily News*, June 13, 2000, http://articles.philly.com/2000-06-13/news/25602063.

25. Gwen Shaffer, "Masker Raid," *Philadelphia City Paper*, June 29, 2000, http://archives.citypaper.net/articles/062900/cb.conwatch.shtml.

26. Ibid.

27. Laura Smith, "Mask Ban in Bureaucratic Limbo," *The Unconvention* 1, Philadelphia Independent Media Center, July 29, 2000, http://phillyimc.org/en/node/33165.

28. Thomas Ginsberg, "All-Out Security Effort for GOP Convention," *Philadelphia Inquirer*, May 26, 2000, http://articles.philly.com/2000-05-26/news/25617930.

29. Jane M. Von Bergen, "Philadelphia Spent over $1 Million to Reel in Political Convention," *Philadelphia Inquirer*, February 10, 2000, http://articles.philly.com/2000-02-10/business/25576420.

30. Jane M. Von Bergen and Josh Goldstein, "Republican Convention Fundraisers Rake In Millions from Philadelphia," *Philadelphia Inquirer*, April 24, 2000.

31. Tom Bishop, "Philadelphia Tense with Preparations Under Way for Republican National Convention," World Socialist Web Site, July 10, 2000, http://www.wsws.org/articles/2000/jul2000/phil-j10.shtml.

32. "Biography of David L. Cohen," Executive Vice President, Comcast Corporation, http://www.comcast.com/corporate/about/pressroom/corporateoverview/corporateexecutives/davidcohen.html.

33. Jeff Blumenthal, "Philadelphia Lawyers Help Prepare for GOP," *The Legal Intelligencer*, July 27, 2000.

34. Ron Goldwyn, "Conventional Legal Fallout," *Philadelphia Daily News*, February 15, 2001, http://articles.philly.com/2001-02-15/news/25318980.

35. Ibid.

36. "Political Parties to Protesters: Stay Home," American Civil Liberties Union, July 21, 2000 http://www.aclu.org/features/f072100a.html (as of February 2005).

37. "Protest Groups, City Agree on Rallies During GOP Convention," *The Associated Press*, April 28, 2000.

38. Dave Lindorff, "Marching On," *In These Times*, June 12, 2000, http://www.inthesetimes.com/issue/24/14/lindorff2414a.html.

39. "Protest Groups, City Agree on Rallies during GOP Convention."

40. "Memorandum in Support of Motion for Preliminary Injunction," Unity 2000 v. City of Philadelphia (Civil Action No. 00-CV-1790), See: http://www.acluutah.org/00fall.htm.

41. Blumenthal, "Philadelphia Lawyers Help Prepare for GOP"; and Dave Lindorff, "Marching On," *In These Times*, June 12, 2000.

42. "Protest Groups, City Agree on Rallies during GOP Convention."

43. Theoharis, ed., "Battle for Broad."

44. "Pre-convention Coverage Whitewashes Police Violence, Distorts Activists' Agendas," Action Alert, Fairness & Accuracy in Reporting, July 25, 2000, http://fair.org/take-action/action-alerts/pre-convention-coverage-whitewashes-police-violence-distorts-activists-agendas.

45. "Nation Looks to Learn Lessons from Seattle's WTO Problems," *Seattle Post-Intelligencer*, February 29, 2000, http://seattlepi.nwsource.com/national/trai29.shtml (as of December 2007).

46. Shannon Jones, "Police Build Up Anti-riot Forces in U.S. Cities," World Socialist Web Site, March 14, 2000, http://www.wsws.org/articles/2000/mar2000/poli-m14.shtml.

47. "Nation Looks to Learn Lessons from Seattle's WTO Problems."

48. Jones, "Police Build Up Anti-riot Forces in U.S. Cities."

49. "Anti-terror Exercise Held in Philadelphia," *Associated Press*, April 20, 2000.

50. John Way Jennings and Alicia A. Caldwell, "Region's Police Prepare for Civil Unrest during Convention," *Philadelphia Inquirer*, July 8, 2000, http://articles.philly.com/2000-07-08/news/25608290.

51. "Harassment of Phila Anarchists," *the defenestrator*, May 2000; and from my observations as an organizer of the Philadelphia IMF/World Bank teach-in.

52. Robert Moran, "Philadelphia Looks at D.C. Protests to Plan for Republican Convention," *Philadelphia Inquirer*, April 19, 2000.

53. Abby Scher, "The Crackdown on Dissent," *The Nation*, January 30, 2001, http://www.thenation.com/article/crackdown-dissent.

54. See: Handschu v. Special Services Division, 605 F Supp 1384 (SDNY 1985).

55. John Marzulli and Joanne Wasserman, "Pa. Police Were Spies at N.Y. May Day Rally," *New York Daily News*, July 13, 2000, http://articles.nydailynews.com/2000-07-13/news/18151467.

56. "Anti-terror Exercise Held in Philadelphia."

57. Thomas Ginsberg, "Philadelphia Political Activists Under a Mysterious Gaze," *Philadelphia Inquirer*, July 6, 2000.

58. Thomas Ginsberg, "All-Out Security Effort for GOP Convention," *Philadelphia Inquirer*, May 26, 2000.

59. Shannon, "Police Arrest and Harass Suspected Anti-RNC Activists," *the defenestrator*, May 2000.

60. Ibid.

61. "Today's Weather: Harassment of Activists, Threats, Surveillance up the Wazoo," *the defenestrator*, July 2000.

62. Gwen Shaffer, "Do You Look Weird?" *Philadelphia City Paper*, July 20, 2000, http://archives.citypaper.net/articles/072000/cb.citybeat.weird.shtml.

63. Thomas Ginsberg and Craig R. McCoy, "Philadelphia Police Admit Spying on Activists," *Philadelphia Inquirer*, July 21, 2000.

64. Ginsberg, "All-Out Security Effort for GOP Convention."

65. "Police Prepare for Republican Convention Protests," *Reuters*, July 2, 2000.

66. Ginsberg, "All-Out Security Effort for GOP Convention."

67. Harry L. Helms, *Inside the Shadow Government: National Emergencies and the Cult of Secrecy* (Los Angeles: Feral House, 2003), 55.

68. "Federal Response Plan: July 31–August 3, 2000," Federal Emergency Management Agency, undated.

69. Ginsberg, "All-Out Security Effort for GOP Convention."

70. "Federal Response Plan: July 31–August 3, 2000."

71. Jane M. Von Bergen and Josh Goldstein, "Republican Convention Price Tag Will Top $60 Million," *Philadelphia Inquirer*, October 4, 2000, http://articles.philly.com/2000-10-04/news/25588687, and Jane M. Von Bergen, "Philadelphia Committee's Report on GOP Convention Tells a $66 Million Story," *Philadelphia Inquirer*, October 22, 2000.

72. Jane M. Von Bergen and Josh Goldstein, "Republican Convention Fundraisers Rake in Millions from Philadelphia," *Philadelphia Inquirer*, April 24, 2000.

73. "Activist Sues City to Disclose RNC Insurance Policy against Civil Rights Abuses," press release, R2K Legal Collective, August 23, 2001, http://r2klegal.protestarchive.org/r2klegal/press/pr-082301.html.

74. Von Bergen and Goldstein, "Republican Convention Fundraisers Rake in Millions from Philadelphia."

75. Von Bergen, "Philadelphia Committee's Report on GOP Convention Tells a $66 Million Story."

76. Ron Goldwyn, "Conventional Legal Fallout," *Philadelphia Daily News*, February 15, 2001.

77. "Law Enforcement Professional Liability" insurance policy, Lexington Insurance Company, purchased January 11, 2000 http://r2klegal.protestarchive.org/r2klegal/ins-1stpolicy01.html.

78. From an e-mail announcement made by the Philadelphia Direct Action Group, June 29, 2000.

79. A sampling of groups in the coalition included: ACT UP Philadelphia, Black Radical Congress, Critical Resistance, Direct Action Network (DAN), Drexel University TV, Earth First!, International Concerned Family & Friends of Mumia Abu-Jamal, International Wages for Housework Campaign, Jobs with Justice, Kensington Welfare Rights Union (KWRU), National Organization for Women (NOW), Pennsylvania Citizen Action Network (PCAN), Pennsylvania Abolitionists United Against the Death Penalty, Public Citizen's Global Trade Watch, Rainforest Action Network (RAN), School of the Americas (SOA) Watch, United Students Against Sweatshops (USAS), and Women's International League for Peace and Freedom (WILPF).

80. The "R2K" abbreviation of "Republican National Convention 2000" was a riff on "Y2K" and was also used in conjunction with protests against the

Democratic National Convention in Los Angeles, similarly called "D2K."

81. Eric Odell, ed., "Direct Action," R2K/D2K Broadsheet, August 1st Direct Action Coalition, Continental Direct Action Network, NY Free Mumia Abu-Jamal Coalition, Student Liberation Action Movement, July 2000.

82. Kerul Dyer, "Activists Drop Banner at Lord & Taylor," *The Unconvention* 3, Philadelphia Independent Media Center, July 31, 2000, http://www.phillyimc.org/es/node/34043.

83. Thomas Ginsberg, Angela Couloumbis, and Melanie Burney, "A Calm Start for Protesters," *Philadelphia Inquirer*, July 30, 2000, http://articles.philly.com/2000-07-30/news/25611284.

84. Ian Christopher McCaleb, "All Roads Lead to Philadelphia for Candidates, Delegates, as Convention Kick-off Nears," *CNN*, July 29, 2000, http://cnn.com/2000/ALLPOLITICS/stories/07/29/convention.wrap (as of December 2006).

85. See: http://www.silentmarch.org (as of February 2005).

86. "Corpzilla" was created by the Washington Action Group (WAG), a Washington, DC–based organization. WAG also made use of the infiltrating State Troopers by putting them to work on building "Corpzilla" in the puppet warehouse.

87. "Frequently Asked Questions," Shadow Conventions 2000, http://www.shadowconventions.com/faq.htm (as of February 2003).

88. Jennifer Bleyer, "Shadow Convention Highlights Failures of Drug War," *The Unconvention* 5, Philadelphia Independent Media Center, August 22, 2000, http://www.phillyimc.org/en/node/34045.

89. Based on my firsthand account as ground support for the banner drop action.

90. "AIDS activists take over billboard with giant banner," press release, ACT UP Philadelphia, July 31, 2000, http://www.healthgap.org/press_releases/00/073100_AU_PR_REPUB_CONV.html.

91. John Tarleton, "8 SOA Watch Activists Arrested," *The Unconvention* 3, Philadelphia Independent Media Center, July 31, 2000. Father Roy Bourgeois founded the SOA Watch in 1990 after soldiers trained at the School murdered six Jesuit priests in El Salvador. Each year, thousands of protesters cross over the perimeter of the School to be arrested in a symbolic statement of resistance. In an attempt to address growing attention being paid to the SOA, the U.S. government renamed the school in 2001 to the Western Hemisphere Institute for Security Cooperation. See: http://www.soaw.org.

92. See: http://www.kwru.org.

93. "March for Economic Human Rights Fact Sheet," Poor People's Economic Human Rights Campaign, 2000.

94. Theoharis, ed., "Battle for Broad."

95. Jennifer Bleyer, "Delegates Will Miss Neglected Side of Philly," *The Unconvention* 3, Philadelphia Independent Media Center, July 31, 2000.

96. David Montgomery and Debbie Goldberg, "Thousands Risk Arrest in Poverty Protest," *Washington Post*, August 1, 2000.

97. Theoharis, ed., "Battle for Broad."

98. Dave Lindorff, "The Battle of Philadelphia," *In These Times*, September 4, 2000, http://www.inthesetimes.com/issue/24/20/lindorff2420.html.

99. The coalition's call had widespread support from dozens of organizations, but was led in large part by a contingent of groups from New York, including the Student Liberation Action Movement, the local chapter of the Direct Action Network (one of the few remaining chapters at the time), the Prison Moratorium Project, the Free Mumia Abu-Jamal Coalition, and the Coalition Against Anti Asian Violence. Other groups that endorsed the call for direct action included Campaign to End the Death Penalty, International Action Center, International Concerned Family & Friends of Mumia Abu-Jamal, International Longshore and Warehouse Union, Local 10, International Socialist Organization, Mothers Organized Against Police Terrorism, National Lawyers Guild, Pennsylvania Abolitionists United Against the Death Penalty, Philadelphia Direct Action Group, and Refuse & Resist!

100. Suzy Subways, ed., *"We Shut the City Down": Six Former Student Liberation Action Movement (SLAM) Members Reflect on the Mass Direct Actions against the 2000 RNC in Philadelphia*, SLAM Herstory Project, December 2, 2010, http://slamherstory.wordpress.com.

101. Texas Governor Rick Perry exceeded then-governor George W. Bush's record by executing well over two hundred death row prisoners during his tenure. See: Richard Dawkins, *The God Delusion* (London: Bantam Press, 2006), 291.

102. David C. Fathi, "Texas Increasingly out of Step on Death Penalty," Human Rights Watch, May 23, 2009, http://www.hrw.org/news/2009/05/23/texas-increasingly-out-step-death-penalty.

103. Amadee Braxton, "Activists of Color in the New Movement: Lessons from RNC Organizing," Colours of Resistance, July 1, 2000.

104. "A Call for Non-violent Direct Action against the Criminal Justice System at the Republican National Convention, Philadelphia, Pennsylvania, Tuesday, August 1, 2000," flyer, August 1st Direct Action Coalition, July 2000, http://www.coloursofresistance.org/490/activists-of-color-in-the-new-movement-lessons-from-rnc-organizing/.

Chapter 2

1. Jennifer Gonnerman, "Hell-Raising in Philly: An Activist's Guide to Protests Outside the Republican Convention," *Village Voice*, July 25, 2000, http://www.villagevoice.com/2000-07-25/news/hell-raising-in-philly.

2. Thomas Ginsberg, "Widespread Clashes Disrupt Center City," *Philadelphia Inquirer*, August 2, 2000, http://articles.philly.com/2000-08-02/news/25595640.

3. Angela Couloumbis, Maria Panaritis, and Diane Mastrull, "With No Warning, Clashes Begin," *Philadelphia Inquirer*, August 2, 2000, http://articles.philly.com/2000-08-02/news/25593371.

4. A "hard block" is considered to be a human blockade aided by physical instruments such as lockboxes used to obstruct or prevent passage of vehicles or people, and a "soft block" is a barrier of people, sometimes with interlocked

arms, meant to slow down the expected onset of police or others, but able to disperse quickly and easily, often avoiding arrest.

5. Josie Foo and John Tarleton, "Lockdowns," *The Unconvention* 5, Philadelphia Independent Media Center, August 2, 2000, http://phillyimc.org/en/node/34045.
6. Ibid.
7. Philadelphia Radical Surrealist Front, "They're Not Just Dirty Anarchists, Dammit!" *The Unconvention* 7, Philadelphia Independent Media Center, August 23, 2000, http://phillyimc.org/en/node/34047.
8. Suzy Subways, ed., *"We Shut the City Down": Six Former Student Liberation Action Movement (SLAM) Members Reflect on the Mass Direct Actions against the 2000 RNC in Philadelphia*, SLAM Herstory Project, December 2, 2010, http://slamherstory.wordpress.com.
9. Amy Hammersmith, "North of Market: Black Bloc," *The Unconvention* 5, Philadelphia Independent Media Center, August 2, 2000.
10. Ginsberg, "Widespread Clashes Disrupt Center City."
11. Hammersmith, "North of Market: Black Bloc."
12. Michael Schreiber, "Thousands Protest Republicans," *Socialist Action*, August 2000, http://www.socialistaction.org/news/200008/republican.html.
13. Josie Foo, "Civil Disobedience and Confusion: Three Snapshots of Tuesday Actions," *The Unconvention* 5, Philadelphia Independent Media Center, August 2, 2000.
14. Amy Goodman and Juan Gonzalez, "Police Step Up Crackdown on Activists," *Democracy Now!*, August 3, 2000, http://www.democracynow.org/2000/8/3/police_step_up_crackdown_on_activists.
15. Sarah Ferguson, "A Black Bloc Mama Says She Took a Beating from Cops on the Streets of Philadelphia," *Village Voice*, August 3, 2000, http://www.villagevoice.com/2000-08-01/news/they-were-kicking-me.
16. Dave Lindorff, "The Battle of Philadelphia," *In These Times*, September 4, 2000, http://www.inthesetimes.com/issue/24/20/lindorff2420.html.
17. Joseph Rogers, "My Arrest," ca. August 5, 2000, http://www.actupny.org/reports/rnc-updates.html.
18. From an interview with Danielle Redden conducted on April 23, 2012.
19. Couloumbis, Panaritis, and Mastrull, "With No Warning, Clashes Begin."
20. "'Timoney Three' Acquitted on All Charges," Philadelphia Independent Media Center, April 9, 2004.
21. Ginsberg, "Widespread Clashes Disrupt Center City."
22. The criminal cases against Kate Sorensen and Terrence McGuckin were based at least in part on this allegation.
23. Heidi Boghosian, *The Assault on Free Speech, Public Assembly, and Dissent: A National Lawyers Guild Report on Government Violations of First Amendment Rights in the United States* (Great Barrington, MA: North River Press, 2004), 72, 79, http://www.nlg.org/wp-content/files_flutter/1269018699DissentBookWeb.pdf, Michael Schreiber, "Thousands Protest Republicans," *Socialist Action*, August 2000, and Thomas C. Greene, "'Hacktivist' Bail Reduced, Finally," *The Register*, August 9, 2000, http://www.theregister.co.uk/2000/08/09/hacktivist_bail_reduced_finally.
24. From an interview with Jody Dodd conducted on December 23, 2011.
25. From a report provided by Jamie Graham to R2K Legal, August 6, 2000.

26. From an interview with Jacqueline Ambrosini conducted on July 12, 2012.

27. John F. Timoney, "'Well, Let Me Tell You Something, We're Not Having Any Jokes Here,'" *Philadelphia Inquirer*, January 14, 2001.

28. Kristen Lombardi, "Rough Justice," *Boston Phoenix*, January 18, 2001, http://www.bostonphoenix.com/boston/news_features/top/documents/00289134.htm.

29. From arrestee and other reports provided to the R2K Legal Collective, ca. August 2000.

30. Ibid.

31. Ana Nogueira, "Free Speech Falls Victim to Police Crackdown," *The Unconvention* 5, Philadelphia Independent Media Center, August 2, 2000.

32. Several local and out-of-town activists reported to R2K Legal that they had been assaulted by police on August 1 then charged with felonies. Needless to say, the police in Philadelphia and elsewhere often use the tactic of "cover" arrests by charging people with assault or battery on a police officer (and sometimes lesser crimes like disorderly conduct, refusing to obey an officer, or resisting arrest) in order to avoid incrimination and divert attention from their own brutality. From records compiled by R2K Legal.

33. Christy E. Lopez, "Disorderly (mis)Conduct: The Problem with 'Contempt of Cop' Arrests," *American Constitution Society* (June 2010): 6, https://www.acslaw.org/publications/issue-briefs/disorderly-misconduct-the-problem-with-"contempt-of-cop"-arrests.

34. From an interview with Jody Dodd conducted on December 23, 2011.

35. Harold H. Martin, "Philadelphia Officials Defend Arrests," *United Press International*, August 4, 2000.

36. Linda K. Harris, Linda Loyd, and Robert Moran, "Lawyers Call Protests a 'Civil-Rights Disaster,'" *Philadelphia Inquirer*, August 9, 2000, http://articles.philly.com/2000-08-09/news/25594255.

37. Editorial, "Civil Disobedience: It's a Commitment, Not a Spring-Break Romp," *Philadelphia Inquirer*, September 9, 2000, http://articles.philly.com/2000-09-19/news/25583652.

38. From an interview with Jody Dodd conducted on December 23, 2011.

39. From an interview with Kate Sorensen conducted on January 19, 2012.

40. The FOP rally was later used by R2K Legal defense attorneys to seek the dismissal of activists' charges based on selective prosecution. See: Linda K. Harris, "5 Protesters Cleared in GOP Rally," *Philadelphia Inquirer*, October 31, 2000, http://articles.philly.com/2000-10-31/news/25588231.

Chapter 3

1. "The Great Puppet Caper" was the title of a November 13, 2000, editorial by the *Philadelphia Inquirer*.

2. Ibid, 191.

3. See: http://www.spiralq.org/aboutQ.html.

4. Morgan F.P. Andrews, "When Magic Confronts Authority: The Rise of Protest Puppetry in N. America," in *Realizing the Impossible: Art Against Authority*, eds. Josh MacPhee and Erik Reuland (Oakland: AK Press, 2007), 207.

5. Ibid., 203.

6. See: New York v. Burger, 482 US 691 (1987).

7. Transcript of motions hearing in Commonwealth v. Mammarella, Philadel-
    phia Municipal Court Judge James DeLeon presiding, November 29, 2000
    (morning session).

8. Gwen Shaffer, "Once a Cop . . ." Philadelphia City Paper, September 21, 2000,
    http://archives.citypaper.net/articles/092100/cs.covside.puppet.shtml.

9. Ibid.

10. Thomas Ginsberg, "City Closes Activists' Studio," Philadelphia Inquirer, July
    22, 2000.

11. Amy Goodman and Juan Gonzalez, "Police Step Up Crackdown on Activists,"
    Democracy Now!, August 3, 2000: http://www.democracynow.org/2000/8/3/
    police_step_up_crackdown_on_activists.

12. Linda K. Harris and Craig R. McCoy, "'Puppet Warehouse' Owner Recalls
    Raid during GOP Convention," Philadelphia Inquirer, September 29, 2000.

13. Andrews, "When Magic Confronts Authority," 202.

14. Ibid, 181.

15. From an interview with Jodi Netzer conducted on September 28, 2011.

16. Susan Platt, "Art and Activism Then and Now," Lecture presented at the College
    Art Association, Chicago, March 1, 2001, http://www.artandpoliticsnow.com.

17. "General Investigation Report," State Trooper Gregory Thomas, Bureau of
    Criminal Investigation, Pennsylvania State Police, July 26, 2000.

18. "General Investigation Report," State Trooper Karina Betz, Bureau of Criminal
    Investigation, Pennsylvania State Police, August 1, 2000.

19. "General Investigation Report," State Trooper Raymond Cook, Bureau of
    Criminal Investigation, Pennsylvania State Police, July 27, 2000.

20. "General Investigation Report," State Trooper Karina Betz, Bureau of Criminal
    Investigation, Pennsylvania State Police, August 2, 2000.

21. From an interview with Jodi Netzer conducted on September 28, 2011.

22. Written report provided to R2K Legal by "Stripling," ca. August 2000.

23. From an interview with Jody Dodd conducted on December 23, 2011.

24. Gwen Shaffer, "Bully Puppet," Philadelphia City Paper, August 15, 2002,
    http://archives.citypaper.net/articles/2002-08-15/cover.shtml.

25. From an interview with Jodi Netzer conducted on September 28, 2011.

26. "Newswire," Philadelphia Independent Media Center, August 1, 2000.

27. "General Investigation Report," State Trooper Karina Betz, Bureau of Criminal
    Investigation, Pennsylvania State Police, August 2, 2000.

28. Shaffer, "Bully Puppet"; and "Newswire," Philadelphia Independent Media
    Center, August 1, 2000.

29. Andrews, "When Magic Confronts Authority," 181.

30. Craig R. McCoy, Thomas Ginsberg, and Emilie Lounsberry, "Protest Leaders
    Were Earmarked by Police," Philadelphia Inquirer, August 4, 2000, http://
    articles.philly.com/2000-08-04/news/25594576.

31. The Texas vehicle code allows proof of registration to be displayed on the vehi-
    cle's front windshield, which it was at the time.

32. Transcript of motions hearing in Commonwealth v. Mammarella, Municipal

Court Judge James DeLeon presiding, November 29, 2000 (afternoon session).

33. Jacqueline Soteropoulos and Craig R. McCoy, "No Break for Protesters, Street Vows," *Philadelphia Inquirer*, August 5, 2000, http://articles.philly.com/2000-08-05/news/25595028.

34. Linda K. Harris, Craig R. McCoy, and Thomas Ginsberg, "State Police Infiltrated Protest Groups, Documents Show," *Philadelphia Inquirer*, September 7, 2000.

35. See: Statement by Maria Danielson, September 20, 2000 (provided to R2K Legal and used with permission).

36. See: Laird v. Tatum, 408 U.S. 1 (1972); Handschu v. Special Services Division, 349 F.Supp. 766, 76–70 (S.D.N.Y. 1972); and Philadelphia Yearly Meeting of Religious Society of Friends v. Tate, 519 F. 2d 1335, 1338 (3rd Cir. 1975)

37. Harris, McCoy, and Ginsberg, "State Police Infiltrated Protest Groups, Documents Show."

38. Tim Ream, "Unrestrained Stories: False Police Claims of Protestor Violence," Los Angeles Independent Media Center, August 10, 2000, http://www.redandgreen.org/Information/display.php3.

39. Francis X. Clines, "Demonstrators Nearly Steal the Spotlight at Convention," *New York Times*, August 2, 2000, http://www.nytimes.com/library/politics/camp/080200gop-protesters.html.

40. David Zucchino, "Philadelphia Police Brace for Possibility of More Protests," *Philadelphia Inquirer*, August 2, 2000.

41. Destroying crime scenes is a familiar tactic in Philadelphia. In 1978, police bulldozed the MOVE house after a raid in which a cop was shot and killed. Despite the city's intentional destruction of the crime scene and the lack of direct evidence linking any MOVE members to the bullet that killed the cop, nine MOVE members were accused and convicted of the death.

42. Carla Anderson, "Where Have All the Puppets Gone?" *Philadelphia Daily News*, August 25, 2000.

43. Andrews, "When Magic Confronts Authority," 181.

44. John Tarleton, "Police Destroy Puppets; Shock and Dismay Widespread," Philadelphia Independent Media Center, August 3, 2000, http://www.phillyimc.org/en/node/33470.

45. From an interview with Jodi Netzer conducted on September 28, 2011.

46. Clines, "Demonstrators Nearly Steal the Spotlight at Convention."

47. Zucchino, "Philadelphia Police Brace for Possibility of More Protests."

48. Andrews, "When Magic Confronts Authority," 181.

49. The Affidavit of Probable Cause was signed and enforced on August 1, 2000, but not unsealed until September 6, 2000. See: Gwen Shaffer, "Spy in the Ointment," *Philadelphia City Paper*, September 14, 2000, http://archives.citypaper.net/articles/091400/cb.hallmonitor1.shtml.

50. Craig R. McCoy and Linda K. Harris, "State Police: Troopers Were Arrested at Protests," *Philadelphia Inquirer*, November 16, 2000, http://articles.philly.com/2000-11-16/news/25613281.

51. Editorial, "Rock-a-Bye, Constitutional Rights," *Philadelphia Daily News*, November 15, 2000, http://articles.philly.com/2000-11-16/news/25613771.

52. Craig R. McCoy and Linda K. Harris, "Engaged in an Endless Pursuit of Dissenters," *Philadelphia Inquirer*, October 26, 2000, http://articles.philly.com/2000-10-26/news/25586741.

53. "Spring Rites Return: Protests against the IMF/World Bank," The Maldon Institute, April 7, 2000.

54. "Affidavit of Probable Cause in Support, Search and Seizure Warrant, no. 97823," Philadelphia Police Department, August 1, 2000.

55. Andrews, "When Magic Confronts Authority," 203.

56. McCoy and Harris, "Engaged in an Endless Pursuit of Dissenters."

57. Tom Bishop, "Police Targeted Protesters at Republican National Convention for their Political Views," World Socialist Web Site, September 12, 2000, http://www.wsws.org/articles/2000/sep2000/rnc-s12.shtml.

58. McCoy and Harris, "Engaged in an Endless Pursuit of Dissenters."

59. "R2K: Philadelphia's Convention Protests," The Maldon Institute, August 17, 2000.

Chapter 4

1. "What Is Jail/Court Solidarity?" flyer, Mass Nonviolent Direct Action Packet, 1999.

2. To "cite out" means to accept a citation in order to get released on one's own recognizance, with the expectation of returning for future court dates.

3. "Nonviolent Action Handbook," War Resisters League, undated.

4. By using "action names," protesters can maintain a level of anonymity so as to protect their identity from police and undercover agents, especially when engaging in jail solidarity.

5. Hundreds of arrestees who refused to provide identification to jail authorities during the April 2000 IMF/World Bank protests in Washington, DC, succeeded in negotiating the terms of their release.

6. From an interview with Jamie Graham conducted on July 6, 2009.

7. Michael Jordan, *Hush Hush: The Dark Secrets of Scientific Research* (Buffalo, NY: Firefly Books, 2003), 176. Two months after RNC protesters were detained at Holmesburg, in October 2000, nearly three hundred former prisoners filed a lawsuit over "experiments" unwillingly conducted on them. Defendants in the lawsuit included the City of Philadelphia and the University of Pennsylvania, as well as Johnson & Johnson and Dow Chemical, whose products were allegedly used on prisoners.

8. From an interview with Jamie Graham conducted on July 6, 2009.

9. See: Letter from Jules Epstein of R2K Legal to Louis Presenza, President Judge of the Municipal Court of Philadelphia, and Bradford Richman, counsel for the Police Commissioner, re: Counsel Observers at RNC Summary Proceedings, July 25, 2000.

10. David Zucchino, "Philadelphia Police Brace for Possibility of More Protests," *Philadelphia Inquirer*, August 2, 2000.

11. Eula Holmes and Tom Bishop, "Over 450 Arrested during Republican Convention in Philadelphia," World Socialist Web Site, August 4, 2000, http://

www.wsws.org/articles/2000/aug2000/prot-a04.shtml, and based on reports from RNC arrestees, compiled by the R2K Legal Collective, August 2000.

12. Dave Bailey, "Puppetistas Sever Court's Strings," *Lumpen*, February 2001, http://www.lumpen.com/magazine/81/puppetistas.shtml.

13. John Tarleton, "Protesters Endure Holmesburg Blues," *The Unconvention* 7, Philadelphia Independent Media Center, August 4, 2000, http://phillyimc.org/en/node/34047.

14. Suzy Subways, ed., *"We Shut the City Down": Six Former Student Liberation Action Movement (SLAM) Members Reflect on the Mass Direct Actions against the 2000 RNC in Philadelphia*, SLAM Herstory Project, December 2, 2010, http://slamherstory.wordpress.com.

15. From an interview with Danielle Redden conducted on July 9, 2009.

16. Handcuffs of arrestees are routinely over-tightened by police so as to cut off circulation, thereby causing inconspicuous injury.

17. Mali Lorenz, "10 Days as a Political Prisoner," Philadelphia Independent Media Center, August 31, 2000, http://www.phillyimc.org/en/node/34087.

18. "Uncle Mike" was the "action name" used by Kate Sorensen, arrested on high-level charges and a bail of $1 million.

19. From an interview with Kate Sorensen conducted on January 19, 2012.

20. From an interview with Joshua Stephens conducted on July 6, 2012.

21. Lorenz, "10 Days as a Political Prisoner."

22. Zucchino, "Philadelphia Police Brace for Possibility of More Protests."

23. Francis X. Clines, "Convention Demonstrators Are Held on Very High Bail," *New York Times*, August 5, 2000, http://www.nytimes.com/2000/08/05/us/convention-demonstrators-are-held-on-very-high-bail.html.

24. Zucchino, "Philadelphia Police Brace for Possibility of More Protests."

25. Jacqueline Soteropoulos and Craig R. McCoy, "No Break for Protesters, Street Vows," *Philadelphia Inquirer*, August 5, 2000, http://articles.philly.com/2000-08-05/news/25595028.

26. Harold H. Martin, "Philadelphia Officials Defend Arrests," *United Press International*, August 4, 2000.

27. Dave Bailey, "Puppetistas Sever Court's Strings," *Lumpen*, February 2001.

28. Amethyst, "Torturous Conditions in Philly Jails," Philadelphia Independent Media Center, August 6, 2000, http://www.phillyimc.org/en/node/33726.

29. "Letter Sent to the Inquirer," e-mail message, Philadelphia Direct Action Group, August 10, 2000.

30. Lorenz, "10 Days as a Political Prisoner."

31. Amethyst, "Tortuous Conditions in Philly Jails."

32. Stacey Burling, "Newly Released Protesters Focusing on Jail Conditions," *Philadelphia Inquirer*, August 16, 2000, http://articles.philly.com/2000-08-16/news/25593856. Most accounts were reported directly to the medics or R2K Legal, which were then broadcast over the internet.

33. "Update from R2K Legal," e-mail message, R2K Legal Collective, August 7, 2000, http://www.actupny.org/reports/rnc-updates5.html.

34. From reports provided to R2K Legal in the days after protesters were released from jail.

35. Clines, "Convention Demonstrators Are Held on Very High Bail."
36. "Convention Protesters Claim Abuse," *Associated Press*, August 5, 2000.
37. It would be another four years before Facebook was founded, and six years before Twitter.
38. "Update from R2K Legal," e-mail message, R2K Legal Collective, August 6, 2000.
39. Morgan F.P. Andrews, "When Magic Confronts Authority: The Rise of Protest Puppetry in N. America," in *Realizing the Impossible: Art Against Authority*, eds. Josh MacPhee and Erik Reuland (Oakland: AK Press, 2007), 203.
40. Zucchino, "Philadelphia Police Brace for Possibility of More Protests."
41. Craig R. McCoy, Thomas Ginsberg, and Emilie Lounsberry, "Protester Leaders Were Earmarked by Police," *Philadelphia Inquirer*, August 4, 2000, http://articles.philly.com/2000-08-04/news/25594576.
42. Amy L. Dalton, "ACLU Action and Inaction Proves Pivotal for Protestors in Philadelphia and Los Angeles," *The Unconvention*, Postconvention issue, Philadelphia Independent Media Center, November 29, 2000, http://www.phillyimc.org/es/comment/reply/34337.
43. From a "Fax Transmission" sent by ACLU of Pennsylvania Legal Director Stefan Presser to Philadelphia City Solicitor Kenneth Trujillo, August 4, 2000, and see: Pledge of Resistance v. We The People 200, Inc., 665 F. Supp. 414 (1987).
44. Soteropoulos, "No Break for Protesters, Street Vows."
45. "Update from R2K Legal," e-mail message, R2K Legal Collective, August 6, 2000.
46. Monica Yant Kinney and Linda Loyd, "Bail Reduced for a Leader of GOP Convention Protests," *Philadelphia Inquirer*, August 8, 2000, http://articles.philly.com/2000-08-08/news/25595641.
47. See: Letter from Jules Epstein of R2K Legal to Louis Presenza, President Judge of the Municipal Court of Philadelphia, and Bradford Richman, Counsel for the Police Commissioner, re: Counsel Observers at RNC Summary Proceedings, July 25, 2000.
48. Linda K. Harris, Linda Loyd, and Robert Moran, "Lawyers Call Protests a 'Civil-Rights Disaster,'" *Philadelphia Inquirer*, August 9, 2000, http://articles.philly.com/2000-08-09/news/25594255.
49. "Prominent Lawyers from around the Country Join Forces to Challenge Constitutional and Civil Rights Violations following RNC Protests," press release, R2K Legal Collective, August 8, 2000, http://r2klegal.protestarchive.org/r2klegal/press/pr-080700.html.
50. Harris, Loyd, and Moran, "Lawyers Call Protests a 'Civil-Rights Disaster.'"
51. "Labor, Civil Rights Activists, Elected Officials Meet at City Hall to Object to Timoney Treatment of Philadelphia Arrestees," Press Advisory, ACT UP New York and Student Liberation Action Movement, August 9, 2000.
52. "Female Protesters Embark on Water Strike," press release, R2K Network, August 9, 2000.
53. From reports provided by RNC arrestees to R2K Legal.
54. Rabbi Arthur Waskow, "URGENT/Please Help Jailed & Brutalized Protesters in Phila," widely circulated e-mail message, August 7, 2000.

55. "Rabbis, Jewish Community Leaders Support RNC Protesters," media advisory, R2K Legal Collective, August 9, 2000, http://r2klegal.protestarchive.org/r2klegal/press/pr-080900.html.

56. "Delegation of Interfaith Clergy Will Attempt to Visit Prisoners," news advisory, Training for Change, August 10, 2000.

57. Julie Stoiber and Linda Loyd, "Clergy Question Treatment of Protesters," *Philadelphia Inquirer*, August 12, 2000, http://articles.philly.com/2000-08-12/news/25593238.

58. Soteropoulos, "No Break for Protesters, Street Vows."

59. Harold H. Martin, "Philadelphia Officials Defend Arrests," *United Press International*, August 4, 2000.

60. Gwen Shaffer, "Civil Engineering: Activists Arrested during the RNC May Seek Big Bucks via Civil Suits," *Philadelphia City Paper*, December 21, 2000, http://archives.citypaper.net/articles/122100/cb.citybeat.protest.shtml.

61. Francis X. Clines, "Bail Reduced for Man Accused of Leading Philadelphia Protests," *New York Times*, August 8, 2000, http://www.nytimes.com/2000/08/08/us/bail-reduced-for-man-accused-of-leading-philadelphia-protests.html.

62. Kinney and Loyd, "Bail Reduced for a Leader of GOP Convention Protests."

63. From reports provided by RNC arrestees to R2K Legal.

64. See: Deposition of Maralee Sisson in Sisson v. City of Philadelphia, November 31, 2001.

65. See: Pennsylvania Rules of Criminal Procedure, Rule 518(A) and County of Riverside v. McLaughlin, 500 U.S. 44, 56–57 (1991).

66. From reports provided by RNC arrestees to R2K Legal.

67. Dave Bailey, "Puppetistas Sever Court's Strings," *Lumpen*, February 2001.

68. Beverly Yuen Thompson, "Jane WTO: Jail Solidarity, Law Collectives, and the Global Justice Movement," dissertation, PhD in philosophy, New School, Political and Social Science, October 2005, 92, https://snakegrrl.files.wordpress.com/2010/02/dissertation.pdf.

69. Ibid, 101.

70. "Letter from John Does Currently Being Held at CFCF," CFCF John Does (24), August 6, 2000, http://www.phillyimc.org/es/node/33707.

71. Bailey, "Puppetistas Sever Court's Strings."

72. Tom Bishop, "Over 200 Republican Convention Protesters Remain in Philadelphia Jails," World Socialist Web Site, August 12, 2009, http://www.wsws.org/articles/2000/aug2000/phil-a12.shtml.

73. Jon Elliston, "Local Activist Cleared of Philadelphia RNC Charges," *Independent Weekly*, April 14, 2004, http://www.indyweek.com/gyrobase/Content?oid=oid%3A21446.

74. From an interview with Kate Sorensen conducted on January 19, 2012.

Chapter 5

1. Harold H. Martin, "Philadelphia Officials Defend Arrests," *United Press International*, August 4, 2000.

2. From an interview with Jamie Graham conducted on July 6, 2009.

3. From an interview with Jody Dodd conducted on December 23, 2011.

4. From an interview with Kate Sorensen conducted on January 19, 2012.

5. Many young activists also received travel grants from the Rosenberg Fund for Children.

6. Francis X. Clines, "Convention Demonstrators Are Held on Very High Bail," *New York Times*, August 5, 2000, http://www.nytimes.com/2000/08/05/us/convention-demonstrators-are-held-on-very-high-bail.html, "Convention Protesters Claim Abuse," *Associated Press*, August 5, 2000; Monica Yant Kinney and Linda Loyd, "Bail Reduced for a Leader of GOP Convention Protests," *Philadelphia Inquirer*, August 8, 2000, http://articles.philly.com/2000-08-08/news/25595641, and Dana DiFilippo, "Let Them Out! Protest Backers Present Demands to Authorities," *Philadelphia Daily News*, August 9, 2000, http://articles.philly.com/2000-08-09/news/25594135.

7. See: Letter from Amnesty International U.S. Program Director Javier Zúñiga to Mayor John Street, Police Commissioner John Timoney, and District Attorney Lynne Abraham, August 14, 2000.

8. See: Letter from Human Rights Watch to Philadelphia Mayor John Street, August 22, 2000, http://www.hrw.org/news/2000/08/21/hrw-letter-philadelphia-mayor-john-street.

9. While the Amnesty International and HRW letters undoubtedly helped draw attention to the abuses going on in Philadelphia and put pressure on the city to investigate, they ultimately went unanswered.

10. Francis X. Clines, "Bail Reduced for Man Accused of Leading Philadelphia Protests," *New York Times*, August 8, 2000, http://www.nytimes.com/2000/08/08/us/bail-reduced-for-man-accused-of-leading-philadelphia-protests.html.

11. Linda Loyd and Monica Yant Kinney, "Trial Is Set in Timoney Scuffle," *Philadelphia Inquirer*, August 10, 2000, http://articles.philly.com/2000-08-10/news/25593037.

12. Linda K. Harris, Linda Loyd, and Robert Moran, "Lawyers Call Protests a 'Civil-Rights Disaster,'" *Philadelphia Inquirer*, August 9, 2000, http://articles.philly.com/2000-08-09/news/25594255.

13. A surety is the person responsible for an arrestee complying with their bail conditions, and also the person to whom the courts return the bail (minus fees) once a criminal case is resolved.

14. From an R2K Network meeting held on May 25, 2000.

15. From an interview with Emily Nepon conducted on October 3, 2011.

16. "Brutal Treatment Continues against Jailed Protesters," press release, R2K Network, August 4, 2000.

17. Clines, "Convention Demonstrators Are Held on Very High Bail."

18. Craig R. McCoy, Thomas Ginsberg, and Emilie Lounsberry, "Protester Leaders Were Earmarked by Police," *Philadelphia Inquirer*, August 4, 2000, http://articles.philly.com/2000-08-04/news/25594576.

19. "Convention Protesters Claim Abuse," *Associated Press*, August 5, 2000.

20. "ACLU Criticizes Police Commissioner and District Attorney for Overreacting to Convention Related Disruptions," press release, ACLU of Pennsylvania, August 7, 2000.

21. Amy L. Dalton, "ACLU Action and Inaction Proves Pivotal for Protestors in Philadelphia and Los Angeles," *The Unconvention*, Postconvention issue, Philadelphia Independent Media Center, November 29, 2000, http://www.phillyimc.org/es/comment/reply/34337.

22. See: Letter from Defendants of the Republican National Convention demonstrations to American Civil Liberties Union of Pennsylvania, October 5, 2000.

23. See: Letter from ACLU of Pennsylvania Executive Director Larry Frankel to Defendants of the Republican National Convention demonstrations, November 7, 2000.

24. "Prominent Lawyers from around the Country Join Forces to Challenge Constitutional and Civil Rights Violations following RNC Protests," press release, R2K Legal Collective, August 8, 2000, http://r2klegal.protestarchive.org/r2klegal/press/pr-080700.html.

25. Harris, Loyd, and Moran, "Lawyers Call Protests a 'Civil-Rights Disaster.'"

26. William Goodman, "Statement of the Center for Constitutional Rights," Center for Constitutional Rights, August 8, 2000.

27. Harris, Loyd, and Moran, "Lawyers Call Protests a 'Civil-Rights Disaster.'"

28. From an interview with Dave Onion conducted on December 14, 2011.

29. From an interview with Jody Dodd conducted on December 23, 2011.

30. "Dear Videographer," letter from R2K Legal Collective, August 14, 2000.

31. Ron Goldwyn, "Conventional Legal Fallout," *Philadelphia Daily News*, February 15, 2001.

32. From an interview with Jody Dodd conducted on December 23, 2011.

33. "Philly: Town Meeting on RNC Protests," meeting notice, ACT UP Philadelphia and the Brown Collective, August 16, 2000.

34. The Brown Collective was a multiracial, intergenerational collective working to highlight the racism and inhumanity of the criminal justice system.

35. See: http://the-aspace.org.

36. See: http://whitedogcafe.com.

37. Julie Davids, "Philadelphia Police and District Attorney Out of Control: Demand that City Council Investigate," briefing paper, September 12, 2000.

38. Council member Angel Ortiz was arrested for civil disobedience and quickly released just weeks prior to the RNC protests.

39. See: Transcript of City Council hearing on September 14, 2000, e-mail message from Michael Decker of the Philadelphia City Clerk's Office, September 22, 2000.

40. "Organizing and Outreach Min. 10/4," e-mail message, R2K Legal Collective, October 6, 2000.

41. Kris Hermes, "An Attempt to Criminalize Dissent," op-ed, *Philadelphia Inquirer*, October 6, 2000.

42. Sara Marcus, "A Demonstrator's View," op-ed, *Philadelphia Inquirer*, December 2, 2000, http://articles.philly.com/2000-12-02/news/25577580.

43. Judy Wicks, "Corporate Abuses Have to Be Tamed," op-ed, *Philadelphia Daily News*, December 12, 2000, http://articles.philly.com/2000-12-12/

news/25580342, Michael Morrill, "We Were Right: Get the Money out of Politics," *Philadelphia Daily News*, December 12, 2000, http://articles.philly.com/2000-12-12/news/25580633, Matt Ruben, "Despite Press Reports, It Was about Human Needs, Not Property Damage," op-ed, *Philadelphia Daily News*, December 12, 2000, http://articles.philly.com/2000-12-12/news/25578829.

44. See: http://phillyimc.org.

45. See: http://www.defenestrator.org, http://www.2600.com/news/view/archive/08-2000, http://wbai.org, and http://fsrn.org.

46. See: http://btlonline.org.

47. Howard Zinn, "The Role of Civil Disobedience in Promoting US Democracy," *Peacework* 292, February 1, 1999.

48. See: Letter from Members of Congress to Philadelphia Mayor John Street, October 19, 2000, http://r2klegal.protestarchive.org/support/ltr-congress01.html.

49. See: Letter from Local Labor Leadership to Philadelphia District Attorney Lynne Abraham, October 5, 2000 http://r2klegal.protestarchive.org/support/ltr-afscme01.html.

50. See: Letter from American Postal Workers Union Local President Arthur T. Doherty to District Attorney Lynne Abraham, October 6, 2000, http://r2klegal.protestarchive.org/support/ltr-apwu01.html.

51. See: Joint Letter from Labor and Religious Leadership to District Attorney Lynne Abraham, October 10, 2000, http://r2klegal.protestarchive.org/support/ltr-unitarian01.html.

52. Ibid.

53. See: Letter from More Than Eighty Local and National Organizations to Philadelphia Mayor John Street and District Attorney Lynne Abraham, October 24, 2000, http://r2klegal.protestarchive.org/support/ltr-org01.html.

54. "Pressure on D.A. Mounts as RNC Trials Begin," press release, R2K Legal Collective, October 24, 2000, http://r2klegal.protestarchive.org/r2klegal/press/pr-102300.html.

55. "10/24 Press Conference Update," widely circulated e-mail message from me, October 26, 2000.

56. From an interview with Jody Dodd conducted on December 23, 2011.

57. "Timeline of the Republican Convention Arrests: A Civil Rights Catastrophe," R2K Legal Collective, February 2001, http://r2klegal.protestarchive.org/r2klegal/timeline.html.

58. The "week of solidarity" was held February 19–25, 2001. Numerous cities across the U.S. took part in educating the public on criminal justice issues and the RNC protest debacle, urging the public to take action.

59. From an e-mail interview between independent journalist John Tarleton and R2K Legal member and RNC arrestee Bill Beckler, May 9, 2001.

Chapter 6

1. Harold H. Martin, "Philadelphia Officials Defend Arrests," *United Press International*, August 4, 2000.

2. Kristen Lombardi, "Rough Justice," *Boston Phoenix*, January 18, 2001, http://www.bostonphoenix.com/boston/news_features/top/documents/00289134.htm.

3. Thomas Ginsberg, "Suit Says Aides at Protest Harassed," *Philadelphia Inquirer*, August 15, 2000, http://articles.philly.com/2000-08-15/news/25593705.

4. Linda K. Harris, Craig R. McCoy, and Thomas Ginsberg, "State Police Infiltrated Protest Groups, Documents Show," *Philadelphia Inquirer*, September 7, 2000, http://articles.philly.com/2000-09-07/news/25582916.

5. Craig R. McCoy and Linda K. Harris, "Rumors Had Troopers Seeing Reds During the GOP Convention," *Philadelphia Inquirer*, September 10, 2000, Linda K. Harris and Craig R. McCoy, "Protest Arrest Irks Lawmaker in Conn.," *Philadelphia Inquirer*, September 14, 2000, http://articles.philly.com/2000-09-14/news/25581288, Larry Frankel, "'Secret' Police Do Not Belong in America," op-ed, *Philadelphia Inquirer*, October 3, 2000, http://articles.philly.com/2000-10-03/news/25585137; editorial, "Rock-a-Bye, Constitutional Rights?," *Philadelphia Daily News*, November 15, 2000, http://articles.philly.com/2000-11-16/news/25613771; and editorial, "Costly Preemptive Strike," *Philadelphia Inquirer*, November 16, 2000, http://articles.philly.com/2000-11-16/news/25613752.

6. "Frequently Asked Legal Questions," R2K Legal Collective, September 12, 2000, http://r2klegal.protestarchive.org/r2klegal/a1-faq.html.

7. Ibid.

8. While these large group meetings were extremely helpful in facilitating mass consensus-based decision-making on important issues, e-mail listserv communication was also invaluable for involving people in distant places and those not connected to a larger community of activists.

9. "Legal Update from *the defenestrator*," October 25, 2000, http://r2klegal.protestarchive.org/r2klegal/def-102500.html.

10. "Week's Update," e-mail message, R2K Legal Collective, September 3, 2000.

11. Statement provided to R2K Legal Collective by Washington, DC–area RNC arrestees, August 24, 2000.

12. "Goals of the Court Solidarity Campaign," R2K Legal Collective, September 6, 2000.

13. Harold H. Martin, "Philadelphia Officials Defend Arrests," *United Press International*, August 4, 2000.

14. Linda K. Harris, "In Court, Protesters Reject Fine, Seek Trials," *Philadelphia Inquirer*, September 24, 2000, http://articles.philly.com/2000-09-24/news/25583292; and Linda K. Harris, "128 Request Trials in GOP Protests," *Philadelphia Inquirer*, October 1, 2000, http://articles.philly.com/2000-10-01/news/25587995.

15. Harris, "In Court, Protesters Reject Fine, Seek Trials."

16. Harris, "128 Request Trials in GOP Protests."

17. Jamie "Bork" Loughner, *Going Pro Se: Representing Yourself without a Lawyer* (Breaking Glass Press, Undated), http://www.infoshop.org/breakingglasspress/ProSe.pdf.

18. See: http://fija.org.

19. Lombardi, "Rough Justice."

20. Onion and The Blanketman, "Update on the Status of RNC Legal Defendants," *the defenestrator*, March 1, 2001, http://www.phillyimc.org/en/node/34403.

Chapter 7

1. Linda K. Harris, "Charges Dropped against 2 Arrested in Protest Group," *Philadelphia Inquirer*, October 6, 2000, http://articles.philly.com/2000-10-06/news/25585217.
2. Linda K. Harris, "Most Charges against 3 Protesters Thrown Out," *Philadelphia Inquirer*, October 13, 2000, http://articles.philly.com/2000-10-13/news/25584986.
3. "R2K Update," e-mail message, R2K Legal Collective, October 24, 2000.
4. See: "Omnibus Motion for Pre-trial Relief Pursuant to Rule 306," filed by Defender Association of Philadelphia on October 6, 2000, http://r2klegal.protestarchive.org/r2klegal/billofp.html.
5. Most defendants had more than five charges each and dozens of defendants had more than ten charges.
6. Harris, "Most Charges against 3 Protesters Thrown Out."
7. "Legal Update from *the defenestrator*," October 25, 2000, http://r2klegal.protestarchive.org/r2klegal/def-102500.html.
8. From statements made by State Troopers Harry Keffer III, Joseph Thompson, George Garris, and Thomas Bachman by Detective Peterman and Sergeant Nodiff of the Philadelphia Police Department, Homicide Division, October 11, 2000.
9. Linda K. Harris, "5 Protesters Cleared in GOP Rally," *Philadelphia Inquirer*, October 31, 2000, http://articles.philly.com/2000-10-31/news/25588231.
10. See: Ruling granting motion to dismiss in Commonwealth of Pennsylvania v. Panetta, Municipal Court Judge James DeLeon, October 30, 2000, http://r2klegal.protestarchive.org/r2klegal/jud-103000-01.html.
11. "Legal Update," R2K Legal Collective, October 31, 2000, http://r2klegal.protestarchive.org/r2klegal/r2k-103100.html, and Linda K. Harris, "One Protester Gets Jail; 5 Others Go Free," *Philadelphia Inquirer*, November 2, 2000, http://articles.philly.com/2000-11-02/news/25613285.
12. "Legal Update," R2K Legal Collective, November 10, 2000, http://r2klegal.protestarchive.org/r2klegal/r2k-111000.html.
13. Ibid.
14. Kristen Lombardi, "Rough Justice," *Boston Phoenix*, January 18, 2001, http://www.bostonphoenix.com/boston/news_features/top/documents/00289134.htm.
15. While the editorial pages of mainstream newspapers are not necessarily considered a direct reflection of public sentiment, editorial boards were strongly in favor of ending the prosecution of RNC defendants.
16. Linda K. Harris and Craig R. McCoy, "Accused Protest Leader Is Cleared of All Charges," *Philadelphia Inquirer*, November 15, 2000, http://articles.philly.com/2000-11-15/news/25612175.
17. Debbie Goldberg, "Many Summer Protesters Cleared: Charges Dropped in Dozens of GOP Convention Cases," *Washington Post*, November 30, 2000.
18. "McGuckin Ducks It!," *Philadelphia Weekly*, May 9, 2001.

19. "Press Conference Tuesday, November 14th at 4pm with John Sellers of the Ruckus Society and Terrence McGuckin of the Philadelphia Direct Action Group," media advisory, R2K Legal Collective, November 13, 2000, http://r2klegal.protestarchive.org/r2klegal/press/pr-111300.html.

20. "Charges against Alleged 'Ringleaders' of the RNC Protests Withdrawn and Dismissed," press release, R2K Legal Collective, November 14, 2000; http://r2klegal.protestarchive.org/r2klegal/press/pr-111400.html.

21. Linda K. Harris, "An Activist Wins Appeal of Protest Convictions," *Philadelphia Inquirer*, May 5, 2001, http://articles.philly.com/2001-05-05/news/25301102.

22. Debbie Goldberg, "Many Summer Protesters Cleared," *Washington Post*, November 30, 2000.

23. Lombardi, "Rough Justice."

24. Editorial, "Rock-a-Bye, Constitutional Rights," *Philadelphia Daily News*, November 15, 2000, http://articles.philly.com/2000-11-16/news/25613771; editorial, "Costly Preemptive Strike the Goal," *Philadelphia Inquirer*, November 16, 2000, http://articles.philly.com/2000-11-16/news/25613752.

25. "Pennsylvania State Troopers Pose as RNC Activists," press release, R2K Legal Collective, November 16, 2000, http://r2klegal.protestarchive.org/r2klegal/press/pr-111600.html.

26. Josie Foo with John Tarleton, "Lockdowns," *The Unconvention* 5, Philadelphia Independent Media Center, August 2, 2000, http://phillyimc.org/en/node/34045.

27. Craig R. McCoy and Linda K. Harris, "State Police: Troopers Were Arrested at Protests," *Philadelphia Inquirer*, November 16, 2000, http://articles.philly.com/2000-11-16/news/25613281.

28. Craig R. McCoy and Linda K. Harris, "Story on Infiltration of Protesters Could Be Sorted Out in Court," *Philadelphia Inquirer*, September 9, 2000, http://articles.philly.com/2000-09-09/news/25581884.

29. "R2K: Philadelphia's Convention Protests," The Maldon Institute, August 17, 2000.

30. McCoy and Harris, "Story on Infiltration of Protesters Could Be Sorted Out in Court."

31. McCoy and Harris, "State Police: Troopers Were Arrested at Protests."

32. "Pennsylvania State Troopers Pose as RNC Activists."

33. Craig R. McCoy, "Raid Notes Must Become Public, City Judge Orders," *Philadelphia Inquirer*, November 9, 2000, http://articles.philly.com/2000-11-09/news/25611710.

34. See: Order in *Re: Walter Stanezack*, Philadelphia Municipal Court Judge James DeLeon, November 8, 2000.

35. McCoy, "Raid Notes Must Become Public, City Judge Orders."

36. "Orders/Directions Given to Undercover Intelligence Officers—Republican National Convention," memorandum, Pennsylvania State Police Lt. George Bivens, November 13, 2000.

37. Transcript of motions hearing in Commonwealth v. Protesters, Municipal Court Judge James DeLeon presiding, November 28, 2000.

38. Transcript of motions hearing in Commonwealth v. Mammarella, Municipal Court Judge James DeLeon presiding, November 21, 2000.

39. "PA State Police Refuse to Turn Over Information on Undercover Infiltration Officers Arrested During the RNC," press release, R2K Legal Collective, November 21, 2000, http://r2klegal.protestarchive.org/r2klegal/press/pr-112100.html.

40. "Legal Update," R2K Legal Collective, November 27, 2000, http://r2klegal.protestarchive.org/r2klegal/r2k-112700.html.

41. Linda K. Harris, "Cases Dropped against 38 Protesters," *Philadelphia Inquirer*, November 28, 2000, http://articles.philly.com/2000-11-28/news/25615108.

42. Peter Cantrell is a pseudonym.

43. "Law Enforcement Losing War on Dissent," press release, R2K Legal Collective, November 28, 2000, http://r2klegal.protestarchive.org/r2klegal/press/pr-112800.html.

44. Gwen Shaffer, "Puppet Theater of the Absurd," *Philadelphia City Paper*, December 7, 2000, http://archives.citypaper.net/articles/120700/cb.citybeat.protest.shtml.

45. Linda K. Harris, "Charges against 46 Protesters Are Upheld," *Philadelphia Inquirer*, December 2, 2000, http://articles.philly.com/2000-12-02/news/25577861.

46. Transcript of motions hearing in Commonwealth v. Mammarella, Municipal Court Judge James DeLeon presiding, November 29, 2000 (morning session).

47. Transcript of motions hearing in Commonwealth v. Mammarella, Municipal Court Judge James DeLeon presiding, November 29, 2000 (afternoon session).

48. Transcript of motions hearing in Commonwealth v. Mammarella, Municipal Court Judge James DeLeon presiding, November 29, 2000 (morning session).

49. Transcript of motions hearing in Commonwealth v. Mammarella, Municipal Court Judge James DeLeon presiding, November 29, 2000 (afternoon session).

50. Transcript of motions hearing in Commonwealth v. Protesters, Municipal Court Judge James DeLeon presiding, November 28, 2000.

51. Transcript of motions hearing in Commonwealth v. Mammarella, Municipal Court Judge James DeLeon presiding, November 29, 2000 (morning session).

52. Gwen Shaffer, "Puppet Theater of the Absurd," *Philadelphia City Paper*, December 7, 2000.

53. Transcript of motions hearing in Commonwealth v. Mammarella, Municipal Court Judge James DeLeon presiding, November 29, 2000 (morning session).

54. Transcript of motions hearing in Commonwealth v. Mammarella, Municipal Court Judge James DeLeon presiding, November 29, 2000 (afternoon session).

55. Linda K. Harris, "Warehouse Owner's Charges Dropped," *Philadelphia Inquirer*, November 30, 2000, http://articles.philly.com/2000-11-30/news/25612053.

56. Linda K. Harris and Craig R. McCoy, "'Puppet Warehouse' Owner Recalls Raid during GOP Convention," *Philadelphia Inquirer*, November 30, 2000.

57. Gwen Shaffer, "Bully Puppet," *Philadelphia City Paper*, August 15, 2002, http://archives.citypaper.net/articles/2002-08-15/cover.shtml.

58. Harris, "Warehouse Owner's Charges Dropped."

59. Transcript of motions hearing in Commonwealth v. Protesters, Municipal Court Judge James DeLeon presiding, November 28, 2000.

60. Ibid.
61. Transcript of motions hearing in Commonwealth v. Mammarella, Municipal Court Judge James DeLeon presiding, November 30, 2000.
62. Transcript of motions hearing in Commonwealth v. Protesters, Municipal Court Judge James DeLeon presiding, November 28, 2000.
63. Transcript of motions hearing in Commonwealth v. Mammarella, Municipal Court Judge James DeLeon presiding, November 30, 2000.
64. Transcript of motions hearing in Commonwealth v. Protesters, Municipal Court Judge James DeLeon presiding, November 28, 2000.
65. "Death Penalty Opponents Plan Day of Protest," press release, Pennsylvania Abolitionists United Against the Death Penalty, July 31, 2000, http://www.cuadp.org/pressrel14.html.
66. Transcript of motions hearing in Commonwealth v. Protesters, Municipal Court Judge James DeLeon presiding, November 28, 2000.
67. Transcript of motions hearing in Commonwealth v. Mammarella, Municipal Court Judge James DeLeon presiding, November 30, 2000.
68. Shaffer, "Puppet Theater of the Absurd."
69. Transcript of motions hearing in Commonwealth v. Mammarella, Municipal Court Judge James DeLeon presiding, November 30, 2000.
70. Harris, "Charges against 46 Protesters Are Upheld."
71. Transcript of motions hearing in Commonwealth v. Mammarella, Municipal Court Judge James DeLeon presiding, November 30, 2000.
72. "Court Update 12/01: Motions Decisions," e-mail message, R2K Legal Collective, December 1, 2000.
73. This number of defendants was lower than the actual number of people arrested in the warehouse because a handful of defendants chose to accept the district attorney's plea offer a few weeks earlier.
74. "Many Charges Are Dismissed in GOP Convention Protests," New York Times, December 10, 2000, http://www.nytimes.com/2000/12/10/politics/10PHIL.html.
75. Linda K. Harris and Craig R. McCoy, "Troopers Fail to ID Convention Protesters," Philadelphia Inquirer, December 7, 2000, http://articles.philly.com/2000-12-07/news/25579604.
76. Editorial, "Tyranny's Puppets: Raid Had Police Dancing to a Troubling Tune," Philadelphia Inquirer, December 8, 2000, http://articles.philly.com/2000-12-08/news/25579256.
77. Linda K. Harris and Craig R. McCoy, "Prosecutors Pardon the Final Puppeteers," Philadelphia Inquirer, December 14, 2000, http://articles.philly.com/2000-12-14/news/25578387.
78. "RNC Puppetista Press Conference," media advisory, R2K Legal Collective, December 11, 2000, http://r2klegal.protestarchive.org/r2klegal/press/pr-121100.html.
79. "Remaining RNC Puppet Warehouse Defendants Cleared of All Charges," press release, R2K Legal Collective, December 13, 2000, http://r2klegal.protestarchive.org/r2klegal/press/pr-121300.html.
80. McCoy and Harris, "State Police: Troopers Were Arrested at Protests."
81. "Rock-a-Bye, Constitutional Rights?"

82. "Tyranny's Puppets: Raid Had Police Dancing to a Troubling Tune."

83. Editorial, "'Enhanced Image' or a City's Shame?" *Philadelphia Daily News*, December 11, 2000, http://articles.philly.com/2000-12-11/news/25580139.

84. Editorial, "Putting a Damper on Dissent," *St. Petersburg Times*, January 6, 2001, http://www.sptimes.com/News/010601/Opinion/Putting_a_damper_on_d.shtml.

85. Bill Beckler, "Statement on RNC Mass Defense," e-mail message, September 26, 2001.

86. From an interview with Jody Dodd conducted on December 23, 2011.

87. "Legal Update," R2K Legal Collective, January 13, 2001, http://r2klegal. protestarchive.org/r2klegal/r2k-011301.html.

Chapter 8

1. From a statement by Kevin Vaughan made to the Defender Association of Philadelphia, December 22, 2000.

2. L. Stuart Ditzen, "Now in Session: The 'Seamus Show,'" *Philadelphia Inquirer*, January 28, 2001, http://articles.philly.com/2001-01-28/news/25310603.

3. McCaffery was also elected to the Court of Common Pleas in 2003 before becoming a Pennsylvania Supreme Court Justice.

4. "Bustleton Judge Is Tops in Municipal Court," *Northeast Times*, October 24, 2001, http://www.northeasttimes.com/2001/1024/bustleton.html, (as of February 2005).

5. From trial transcript in Commonwealth v. Matthews, October 25, 2000.

6. "'When I Was Out There, Trust Me, That Young Man Right There, He'd Still Be in the Hospital,'" *Philadelphia Inquirer*, January 14, 2001, http://articles. philly.com/2001-01-14/news/25310902.

7. Matthews appealed his conviction and, on January 17, 2001, Common Pleas Court Judge Pamela Dembe found him guilty of one misdemeanor resisting arrest and sentenced him to eighteen months of nonreporting probation and one hundred hours of community service.

8. The Philadelphia Municipal Court only allows for trial by judge (bench trial). Elimination of a jury for misdemeanor trials allows the court to save time and money and, in so doing, limits the rights of defendants. Persons convicted at their bench trial have the right to appeal the ruling and demand a second trial, by either judge or jury, in the Court of Common Pleas.

9. From the Motion for Recusal filed on behalf of George Ripley and others similarly situated, Defender Association of Philadelphia, January 4, 2001.

10. See: Letter from attorney Bradley Bridge of the Defender Association of Philadelphia to Municipal Court Judge Seamus McCaffery, January 9, 2001.

11. Greg Richards, "Judge's Comments at Penn Coming Back to Haunt Him," *Daily Pennsylvanian*, January 18, 2001, http://www.dailypennsylvanian.com/ node/22126.

12. "Governor Bush Accepts Fraternal Order of Police Endorsement in Philadelphia," news release, Fraternal Order of Police, September 20, 2000, http://www.grandlodgefop.org/press/pr000920a.html (as of January 2006).

13. See: http://www.grandlodgefop.org.

14. From hearing transcript in Commonwealth v. Disla, November 11, 1998.
15. From ruling by Common Pleas Court Judge Gary S. Glazer in Commonwealth v. Disla, November 13, 1998.
16. "Bikers Donate $40 G to Nonprofit Organizations That Support Police," press release, Bikers Allied to Commemorate Uniformed Police, Inc., prior to August 1, 2000 (date unknown).
17. "Minister Arrested," *Associated Press*, July 17,1995.
18. See: Commonwealth v. Bevel, (PA, MC# 9507-1663 and PA, CP# 9601-0915)
19. See: Motion for Recusal in Commonwealth of Pennsylvania v. Mark Rifkin, Danielle Redden, January 16, 2001.
20. From notes taken by R2K Legal members during court proceeding, January 16, 2001.
21. From notes taken by R2K Legal members and excerpts from transcript of court proceeding on motions to recuse in Commonwealth v. Mark Rifkin, Danielle Redden, George Ripley and others similarly situated, January 16, 2001.
22. "A Neighborhood Nightmare," *Philadelphia Daily News*, January 16, 2001.
23. See: Commonwealth v. Lamansky, 365 Pa. 332, A.2nd 1085. (No date or copy held.)
24. See: Commonwealth v. Mumia Abu-Jamal; 553 Pa. 485, 720 A.2nd 79 78 (1998).
25. Holmesburg Prison was a condemned facility, which was closed in 1995, but it was reopened by the City of Philadelphia to deal with what they expected to be a large number of arrestees from the RNC protests. Numerous activists who were held there reported extensively on the prison's abominable, inhumane conditions.
26. Linda K. Harris, "Courts Dispose of 2 Dozen More GOP Convention Cases," *Philadelphia Inquirer*, January 27, 2001, http://articles.philly.com/2001-01-27/news/25310440.
27. Gwen Shaffer, "Partial Fraction: Judge Seamus McCaffery Squashes an Effort to Remove Him from Presiding over RNC Protester Trials," *Philadelphia City Paper*, January 18, 2001, http://archives.citypaper.net/articles/011801/cb.citybeat.mccaffery.shtml.
28. "Biased Judge Refuses to Relinquish RNC Cases," press release, R2K Legal Collective, January 16, 2001, http://r2klegal.protestarchive.org/r2klegal/press/pr-011601.html.
29. Shaffer, "Partial Fraction."
30. "12 Acquitted in Protest That Closed Highway Entrance," *Philadelphia Inquirer*, January 20, 2001.
31. L. Stuart Ditzen, "Now in Session: The 'Seamus Show,'" *Philadelphia Inquirer*, January 28, 2001.
32. Kristen Lombardi, "First Amendment Triumphs in Philly," *Boston Phoenix*, February 1, 2001, http://www.bostonphoenix.com/boston/news_features/this_just_in/documents/00422996.htm.
33. Harris, "Courts Dispose of 2 Dozen More GOP Convention Cases."
34. Kristin Bricker, "Courtroom Etiquette," e-mail message, January 28, 2001.
35. Lombardi, "First Amendment Triumphs in Philly."
36. Harris, "Courts Dispose of 2 Dozen More GOP Convention Cases."

37. From an interview with Mark Rifkin conducted on January 4, 2005.

38. The design for the sticker came from the U.S. corporate logo flag created by Adbusters Media Foundation. See: http://www.adbusters.org.

39. Gwen Shaffer, "Ninny Van," *Philadelphia City Paper*, February 8, 2001, http://archives.citypaper.net/articles/020801/cb.hallmon1.shtml.

40. Transcript of van trial in Commonwealth v. Arnold, et al, Municipal Court Judge Seamus McCaffery presiding, February 2, 2001.

41. Shaffer, "Ninny Van."

42. Transcript of van trial in Commonwealth v. Arnold, et al.

43. L. Stuart Ditzen, "Now in Session: The 'Seamus Show,'" *Philadelphia Inquirer*, January 28, 2001.

44. Craig R. McCoy, "New documents: McCaffery had role in referral fees," *Philadelphia Inquirer*, March 16, 2015, http://articles.philly.com/2015-03-16/news/60141849_1_mccaffery-and-rapaport-rassias-dion-g.

45. Craig R. McCoy and Dylan Purcell, "In stepping down, McCaffery moved to save pension, avoid ethics inquiry," *Philadelphia Inquirer*, October 28, 2014, http://articles.philly.com/2014-10-28/news/55525989_1_mccaffery-lawyer-lise-rapaport-ethics-investigation.

Chapter 9

1. Editorial, "Bust 'Em Now, Pay Later: Keeping GOP Conclave Peaceful May Prove Costly," *Philadelphia Daily News*, July 30, 2001, http://articles.philly.com/2001-07-30/news/25315615.

2. Kristen Lombardi, "Rough Justice," *Boston Phoenix*, January 18, 2001, http://www.bostonphoenix.com/boston/news_features/top/documents/00289134.htm.

3. Craig R. McCoy and Linda K. Harris, "Experts: City's Push for Peace at Convention Harmed Rights," *Philadelphia Inquirer*, January 14, 2001.

4. Gwen Shaffer, "Trial Run," *Philadelphia City Paper*, January 18, 2001, http://archives.citypaper.net/articles/011801/cb.hallmon2.shtml.

5. From an interview with Jamie Graham conducted on July 6, 2009.

6. Shaffer, "Trial Run."

7. Onion and The Blanketman, "Update on the Status of RNC Legal Defendants," *the defenestrator*, March 1, 2001, http://www.phillyimc.org/en/node/34403.

8. See: Petition for Writ of *Certiorari* in Re: Adam Eidinger, filed by Assistant Defender Bradley Bridge, March 2001.

9. Southeastern Promotions v. Conrad, 420 U.S. 546, 558–59, 95 S. Ct. 1239 (1975).

10. Transcript of appeal trial in Commonwealth v. Osher et al., Common Pleas Court Judge William J. Mazzola presiding, November 21, 2001.

11. See: Ruling from appeal hearing in Commonwealth v. Osher et al., Common Pleas Court Judge William J. Mazzola presiding, June 28, 2002.

12. Ibid.

13. See: Commonwealth v. Ripley, 2003 PA Super 352.

14. From an interview with Caleb Arnold conducted on January 9, 2005.

15. McCoy and Harris, "Experts."

16. From an interview with Kate Sorensen conducted on January 19, 2012.

17. Gwen Shaffer, "Wrong Number," *Philadelphia City Paper*, March 15, 2001, http://archives.citypaper.net/articles/031501/cb.citybeat.protest.shtml.
18. "RNC Defendant and Accused 'Ringleader' Kate Sorensen Acquitted of Felony Charges," press release, R2K Legal Collective, March 13, 2001, http://r2klegal. protestarchive.org/r2klegal/press/pr-031301.html.
19. Sorensen and others were charged with possessing an instrument of crime for using their cell phones.
20. Dave Racher, "Protester Wins & Loses," *Philadelphia Daily News*, March 13, 2001, http://articles.philly.com/2001-03-13/news/25328540.
21. McCoy and Harris, "Experts."
22. Karen M. Goulart, "Felony RNC Case Heads to Trial," *Philadelphia Gay News*, March 9, 2001.
23. "Felony Trials for GOP Protesters Begin with Kate Sorensen—Accused 'Ringleader,'" media advisory, R2K Legal Collective, March 2, 2001, http:// r2klegal.protestarchive.org/r2klegal/press/pr-030201.html.
24. From an interview with Kate Sorensen conducted on January 19, 2012.
25. Linda K. Harris and Craig R. McCoy, "Jury Finds Phila. Activist Guilty of One Misdemeanor," *Philadelphia Inquirer*, March 13, 2001, http://articles.philly. com/2001-03-13/news/25327683.
26. Bill Hangley Jr., "Kate Sorensen: Riot, Conspiracy, and Risking Catastrophe . . . NOT!" *Weekly Press*, March 14, 2001.
27. Harris and McCoy, "Jury Finds Phila. Activist Guilty of One Misdemeanor."
28. Shaffer, "Wrong Number."
29. Racher, "Protester Wins & Loses."
30. Harris and McCoy, "Jury Finds Phila. Activist Guilty of One Misdemeanor."
31. Hangley Jr., "Kate Sorensen: Riot, Conspiracy, and Risking Catastrophe . . . NOT!"
32. Harris and McCoy, "Jury Finds Phila. Activist Guilty of One Misdemeanor."
33. "RNC Defendant and Accused 'Ringleader' Kate Sorensen Acquitted of Felony Charges."
34. Racher, "Protester Wins & Loses."
35. From an interview with Kate Sorensen conducted on January 19, 2012.
36. Gwen Shaffer, "Stickin' It Out," *Philadelphia City Paper*, March 22, 2001, http://archives.citypaper.net/articles/032201/cb.hallmonitor4.shtml.
37. "Second RNC Felony Defendant Acquitted of All Charges," press release, R2K Legal Collective, March 15, 2001, http://r2klegal.protestarchive.org/r2klegal/ press/pr-031501.html.
38. Susan Phillips, "Police Misconduct No Surprise to Protesters," Philadelphia Independent Media Center, April 3, 2001.
39. "Second RNC Felony Defendant Acquitted of All Charges," press release, R2K Legal Collective, March 15, 2001, and Gwen Shaffer, "Stickin' It Out," *Philadelphia City Paper*, March 22, 2001.
40. Phillips, "Police Misconduct No Surprise to Protesters."
41. Shaffer, "Stickin' It Out."
42. Phillips, "Police Misconduct No Surprise to Protesters."
43. "Jury Acquits an Activist of Convention-Related Assault," *Philadelphia Inquirer*, March 16, 2001.

44. Ron Goldwyn, "Conventional Legal Fallout," *Philadelphia Daily News*, February 15, 2001, http://articles.philly.com/2001-02-15/news/25318980.

45. Phillips, "Police Misconduct No Surprise to Protesters."

46. Goldwyn, "Conventional Legal Fallout."

47. Gwen Shaffer, "No Protest Here," *Philadelphia City Paper*, April 12, 2001, http://archives.citypaper.net/articles/041201/cb.hallmonitor3.shtml.

48. "Four More RNC Defendants Acquitted of Felony Charges," press release, R2K Legal Collective, April 9, 2001, http://r2klegal.protestarchive.org/r2klegal/press/pr-040901.html.

49. Goldwyn, "Conventional Legal Fallout."

50. "Four Acquitted of Riot Charges from GOP Convention Protest," *Philadelphia Inquirer*, April 10, 2001.

51. Shaffer, "No Protest Here."

52. "Four More RNC Defendants Acquitted of Felony Charges," press release, R2K Legal Collective, April 9, 2001.

53. "Four Acquitted of Riot Charges from GOP Convention Protest."

54. Bill Beckler "My Life and Trial," e-mail message, April 3, 2001.

55. "McGuckin Ducks It!" *Philadelphia Weekly*, May 9, 2001.

56. Linda K. Harris, "An Activist Wins Appeal of Protest Convictions," *Philadelphia Inquirer*, May 5, 2001, http://articles.philly.com/2001-05-05/news/25301102.

57. Gwen Shaffer, "Redshirt-ed," *Philadelphia City Paper*, July 12, 2001, http://archives.citypaper.net/articles/071201/news.hallmon2.shtml.

58. "RNC Protest Defendant Acquitted of All Charges," press release, R2K Legal Collective, July 6, 2001, http://r2klegal.protestarchive.org/r2klegal/press/pr-070601.html.

59. Shaffer, "Redshirt-ed."

60. Susan Phillips, "Did Someone Call the Fashion Police?" *Philadelphia Weekly*, July 11, 2001, http://www.philadelphiaweekly.com/news-and-opinion/city-38353729.html.

61. Shaffer, "Redshirt-ed."

62. Phillips, "Did Someone Call the Fashion Police?"

63. "RNC Protest Defendant Acquitted of All Charges."

64. "Legal Update," R2K Legal Collective, July 17, 2001, http://r2klegal.protestarchive.org/r2klegal/r2k-071701.html.

65. Ibid.

66. Jon Elliston, "Local Activist Cleared of Philadelphia RNC Charges," *Independent Weekly*, April 14, 2004, http://www.indyweek.com/indyweek/local-activist-cleared-of-philadelphia-rnc-charges.

67. "Community Organizer Faces Decades in Prison," action alert, Friends of Camilo, March 2004.

68. Kristen Lombardi, "Rough Justice," *Boston Phoenix*, January 18, 2001.

69. See: Brief for Appellee in Commonwealth v. Viveiros, Superior Court of Pennsylvania Eastern District, July 3, 2001.

70. Thomas Ginsberg, "Widespread Clashes Disrupt Center City," *Philadelphia Inquirer*, August 2, 2000, http://articles.philly.com/2000-08-02/news/25595640.

71. Frank Rubino, "Victim of Circumstances?" *Philadelphia Weekly*, February 19, 2003, http://www.philadelphiaweekly.com/news-and-opinion/victim_of_circumstances-38364929.html.

72. Linda Loyd and Monica Yant Kinney, "Trial Is Set in Timoney Scuffle," *Philadelphia Inquirer*, August 10, 2000, http://articles.philly.com/2000-08-10/news/25593037.

73. Jon Elliston, "Local Activist Cleared of Philadelphia RNC Charges," *Independent Weekly*, April 14, 2004.

74. David B. Caruso, "With Political Conventions Looming, Charges Linger from 2000," *Associated Press*, April 1, 2004, http://jacksonville.com/tu-online/apnews/stories/040104/D81MA8V80.shtml.

75. Michael Blanding, "A Warning for Miami," *The Nation*, December 1, 2003, http://www.thenation.com/article/warning-miami.

76. "Community Organizer Faces Decades in Prison," action alert, Friends of Camilo, March 2004.

77. Susan Phillips, "Republican National Convention Protesters Acquitted of All Charges," *Weekly Press*, April 14, 2004.

78. Lombardi, "Rough Justice."

79. "White Dog Café's Judy Wicks, Philadelphia Leaders Support Camilo Viveiros, Republican National Convention Defendant from 2000," press release, Friends of Camilo, March 30, 2004.

80. Phillips, "Republican National Convention Protesters Acquitted of All Charges."

81. Linda K. Harris, "Trial of GOP Convention Protesters Begins," *Philadelphia Inquirer*, April 6, 2004, http://articles.philly.com/2004-04-06/news/25364449.

82. See: Brief for Appellee in Commonwealth v. Viveiros, Superior Court of Pennsylvania Eastern District, July 3, 2001.

83. Onion and The Blanketman, "Update on the Status of RNC Legal Defendants," *the defenestrator*, March 1, 2001.

84. Lombardi, "Rough Justice."

85. From an interview with xtn hansen conducted on July 5, 2012.

86. "Legal Update," R2K Legal Collective, January 17, 2002, http://r2klegal.protestarchive.org/r2klegal/r2k-011702.html.

87. Michael Blanding, "A Warning for Miami," *The Nation*, December 1, 2003.

88. Caruso, "With Political Conventions Looming, Charges Linger from 2000."

89. Timoney's sheen would begin to fade after public condemnation of his police department's response to demonstrations against the Free Trade Area of the Americas in November 2003. Considered to have been one of the most violent police reactions to mass protest in recent U.S. history, Timoney used an array of weaponry and brute force against thousands of activists, medics, legal workers, reporters, and bystanders. This time, the criticism was harder to shrug off than it had been in Philadelphia. In response to the treatment of union workers and protesters, both the AFL-CIO and the United Steelworkers of America demanded Timoney's resignation. Miami Mayor Manny Diaz did his best to deflect the bad PR by calling Timoney's response to the demonstrations a "model for homeland defense." But multiple independent investigations concluded that the "Miami Model" was akin to a "police state," in which "civil rights were trampled," with "unrestrained and disproportionate use of force."

90. Gwen Shaffer, "Run-on Sentence," *Philadelphia City Paper*, August 15, 2002, http://archives.citypaper.net/articles/2002-08-15/cover2.shtml.

91. Caruso, "With Political Conventions Looming, Charges Linger from 2000."

92. "Legal Update," R2K Legal Collective, June 21, 2002, http://r2klegal.protestarchive.org/r2klegal/r2k-062102.html.

93. See: http://www.friendsofcamilo.org.

94. "Community Organizer Faces Decades in Prison."

95. Michael Blanding, "A Warning for Miami," *The Nation*, December 1, 2003.

96. "White Dog Café's Judy Wicks, Philadelphia Leaders Support Camilo Viveiros, Republican National Convention defendant from 2000."

97. At that time, some of the cases from the November 2003 Free Trade Area of the Americas protests in Miami were about to go to trial. The resultant mass dismissals and acquittals in the Miami criminal cases would further discredit Timoney's record.

98. Speakers at the breakfast included White Dog Café owner Judy Wicks, Shalom Center Director Rabbi Arthur Waskow, Action Alliance for Senior Citizens Director Pedro Rodriguez, AFSCME District Council 47 representative and Philadelphia Coalition of Labor Union Women President Kathy Black, Philadelphia City Council member David Cohen's staff Shoshana Bricklan, and Training for Change Director George Lakey.

99. Linda K. Harris, "Three Protesters Are Acquitted of Criminal Charges," *Philadelphia Inquirer*, April 7, 2004, http://articles.philly.com/2004-04-07/news/25364749.

100. Oscar Corral, "Timoney Testifies in Philadelphia," *Miami Herald*, April 7, 2004.

101. Harris, "Three Protesters Are Acquitted of Criminal Charges."

102. Phillips, "Republican National Convention Protesters Acquitted of All Charges."

103. Harris, "Three Protesters Are Acquitted of Criminal Charges."

104. Camilo Viveiros, "Ten Lessons from the Criminalization of Dissent," *Earth First! Journal*, April 2006, http://www.earthfirstjournal.org/article.php?id=190.

105. Jim DeFede, "The Truth Is Out, Says Man Cleared in Timoney Case," *Miami Herald*, April 11, 2004.

106. Not everyone arrested was charged with a crime.

107. "Legal Statistics," R2K Legal Collective, April 6, 2004, http://r2klegal.protestarchive.org/r2klegal/stats.html.

Chapter 10

1. See: http://medic.wikia.com/wiki/Street_medic.

2. See: http://streetmedic.wordpress.com.

3. Approximately fifty people, who received one-day training seminars, volunteered as street medics during the RNC 2000 protests. See: Dana DiFilippo, "Volunteer Medics Sue City," *Philadelphia Daily News*, August 15, 2000, http://articles.philly.com/2000-08-15/news/25594281.

4. See: Complaint in Schiavone v. City of Philadelphia, August 14, 2000, http://r2klegal.protestarchive.org/docs/Complaint_Medics.pdf.

5.   "Medics at Protest Suing Phila.," *Associated Press*, August 15, 2000.

6.   Gwen Shaffer, "Civil Engineering: Activists Arrested during the RNC May Seek Big Bucks via Civil Suits," *Philadelphia City Paper*, December 21, 2000, http://archives.citypaper.net/articles/122100/cb.citybeat.protest.shtml.

7.   The law firm is now known as Kairys Rudovsky Messing and Feinberg. See: http://www.krlawphila.com.

8.   See: Letter from ACLU of Pennsylvania Executive Director Larry Frankel to Defendants of the Republican National Convention Demonstrations, November 7, 2000.

9.   See: Complaint in Graves v. City of Philadelphia, January 22, 2001, http://r2klegal.protestarchive.org/docs/Complaint_Graves.pdf.

10. Linda K. Harris and Craig R. McCoy, "'Puppet Warehouse' Owner Recalls Raid during GOP Convention," *Philadelphia Inquirer*, September 29, 2000.

11. See: Complaint in Graves v. City of Philadelphia, January 22, 2001.

12. Bill Sasser, "'Everybody's Kitchen' Delivers Meals in Louisiana Bayou Country," *Christian Science Monitor*, November 26, 2008, http://www.csmonitor.com/The-Culture/2008/1126/everybody-s-kitchen-delivers-meals-in-louisiana-bayou-country.

13. Joseph A. Slobodzian, "Volunteer Sues Phila, Police over Her Arrest," *Philadelphia Inquirer*, January 31, 2001, http://articles.philly.com/2001-01-31/news/25311413.

14. See: Complaint in Sisson v. City of Philadelphia, January 30, 2001, http://r2klegal.protestarchive.org/docs/Complaint_Sisson.pdf.

15. See: Complaint in Franks v. City of Philadelphia, March 28, 2001, http://r2klegal.protestarchive.org/docs/Complaint_Franks.pdf.

16. In the *Franks* complaint, Erba details the infiltration and arrest of people in the van as connected to the puppet warehouse raid, even though criminal charges were still pending at the time against several people from the van case.

17. See: Complaint in Franks v. City of Philadelphia, March 28, 2001.

18. The City of Philadelphia settled a lawsuit in 1987, which resulted in a mayoral directive restricting political-based infiltration by the Philadelphia Police Department. See: Linda K. Harris, Craig R. McCoy, and Thomas Ginsberg, "State Police Infiltrated Protest Groups, Documents Show," *Philadelphia Inquirer*, September 7, 2000, http://articles.philly.com/2000-09-07/news/25582916.

19. See: Complaint in Franks v. City of Philadelphia, March 28, 2001.

20. See: Complaint in Fried v. City of Philadelphia, 2:01-cv-03804-LP.

21. Ron Goldwyn, "RNC Protesters Set to Sue City," *Philadelphia Daily News*, July 26, 2001.

22. See: Complaint in Sellers v. Police Commissioner Timoney, July 26, 2001, http://r2klegal.protestarchive.org/docs/Complaint_Sellers.pdf.

23. Goldwyn, "RNC Protesters Set to Sue City."

24. Gwen Shaffer, "Warm-Up Suit," *Philadelphia City Paper*, April 5, 2001.

25. "Civil Suit Proposal," e-mail message, R2K Legal Collective, January 29, 2001.

26. "R2K Civil Suit Questionnaire," R2K Legal Collective, February 2001.

27. From a letter that accompanied the R2K Legal civil suit questionnaire sent to RNC arrestees in the spring of 2001.

28. "Important: Civil Suits," e-mail message, R2K Legal Collective, October 23, 2001.

29. Mali Lorenz, "Civil Suits, Proposal for Money Use," e-mail message, December 13, 2000.

30. Christopher Day, "Re: Civil Suits, Proposal for Money Use," e-mail message, December 14, 2000.

31. Roy Zipris, "Re: Civil Law Suits," e-mail message, December 14, 2000.

32. "Re: Civil Law Suits," e-mail message, December 15, 2000.

33. Gwen Shaffer, "Civil Engineering: Activists Arrested during the RNC May Seek Big Bucks via Civil Suits," *Philadelphia City Paper*, December 21, 2000.

34. "R2K Legal Newsletter," R2K Legal Collective, May 2001, http://r2klegal. protestarchive.org/docs/R2K_Legal_Newsletter_May_2001.pdf.

35. "Final Draft of Civil Suit Contract," e-mail message, R2K Legal Collective, July 11, 2001.

36. John F. Morrison, "RNC Protesters Celebrate Last Year's Arrests by Suing the City," *Philadelphia Daily News*, August 2, 2001.

37. See: Complaint in Spiral Q Puppet Theater v. City of Philadelphia, August 1, 2001, http://r2klegal.protestarchive.org/docs/Complaint_Puppet_Warehouse.pdf.

38. "Press Conference—Wednesday, August 1st at Noon," media advisory, R2K Legal Collective, August 1, 2000, http://r2klegal.protestarchive.org/r2klegal/ press/pr-080101a.html.

39. Gwen Shaffer, "Insurance Assurance," *Philadelphia City Paper*, September 27, 2001, http://archives.citypaper.net/articles/092701/news.hallmon4.shtml.

40. "Law Enforcement Professional Liability" insurance policy, Lexington Insurance Company, purchased January 11, 2000, http://r2klegal. protestarchive.org/docs/Insurance_Policy.pdf.

41. "Activist Sues City to Disclose RNC Insurance Policy against Civil Right Abuses," press release, R2K Legal Collective, August 23, 2001, http://r2klegal. protestarchive.org/r2klegal/press/pr-082301.html.

42. Ibid.

43. "Continued Prosecution and Harassment of Activists Two Years after Mass Arrests at RNC Protests," press release, R2K Legal Collective, July 31, 2002.

44. Gwen Shaffer, "Bully Puppet," *Philadelphia City Paper*, August 15, 2002, http://archives.citypaper.net/articles/2002-08-15/cover.shtml.

45. Karl Blossfeldt, "The Ghost of R2K: A Strange Tale of Subpoenas, Compliance and Their Joyful Negation," *the defenestrator*, May 21, 2001, http://www. indybay.org/newsitems/2002/06/19/1337121.php.

46. Shaffer, "Bully Puppet.",

47. See: Subpoena by Hangley Aronchick Segal & Pudlin to the Custodian of Records for the Women's International League for Peace and Freedom, September 10, 2001.

48. Shaffer, "Bully Puppet."

49. Blossfeldt, "The Ghost of R2K."

50. Shaffer, "Bully Puppet."

51. Blossfeldt, "The Ghost of R2K."

52. Shaffer, "Bully Puppet."

53. Based on several subpoenas and deposition transcripts.

54. Blossfeldt, "The Ghost of R2K."

55. Shaffer, "Bully Puppet."
56. For example, DC-based activist Adam Eidinger, who had helped work on art inside the warehouse, was deposed on July 17, 2001.
57. Transcript of deposition of Eric Laursen re: Sisson, Graves and Franks, November 2, 2001.
58. Shaffer, "Bully Puppet."
59. Transcript of deposition of Jody Dodd re: Sisson, Graves and Franks, November 26, 2001.
60. "Plaintiff's Memorandum of Law in Opposition to Motion for Leave to Take Depositions of Counsel," in Graves v. City of Philadelphia, filed December 31, 2001.
61. See: Shelton v. American Motors Corp., 805 F.2d 1323 (8th Cir.1986).
62. Shaffer, "Bully Puppet."
63. "RNC Debacle Continues as 2nd Anniversary Approaches," e-mail message, R2K Legal Collective, July 26, 2002.
64. In June 2002, federal District Judge Louis Pollak forced Hangley to prepare and submit a draft settlement within six days.
65. "RNC Debacle Continues as 2nd Anniversary Approaches"; and "Continued Prosecution and Harassment of Activists Two Years After Mass Arrests at RNC Protests," press release, R2K Legal Collective, July 31, 2002, http://r2klegal.protestarchive.org/r2klegal/press/pr-073102.html.
66. Jim Smith, "Shhh . . . City Trying to Settle Protester Suits," *Philadelphia Daily News*, July 5, 2002.
67. "IMPORTANT: Time Is Running Out to File Further Civil Suits," e-mail message, R2K Legal Collective, June 22, 2002.
68. Shaffer, "Bully Puppet."

Chapter 11

1. See: Alliance to End Repression v. City of Chicago, 742 F. 2d 1007 (7th Cir. 1984); and Handschu v. Special Services Division, 605 F. Supp. 1384 (SDNY 1985).
2. Heidi Boghosian, *Punishing Protest: Government Tactics That Suppress Free Speech* (National Lawyers Guild, 2007), 59.
3. See: Alliance to End Repression v. City of Chicago, 237 F. 3d 799 (7th Cir. 2001).
4. Abby Scher, "The Crackdown on Dissent," *The Nation*, January 30, 2001, http://www.thenation.com/article/crackdown-dissent.
5. See: Handschu v. Special Services Division, 273 F. Supp. 2d 327 (SDNY 2003).
6. Chris Hawley, "In NYPD Spying, a Yippie Legal Battle Echoes Again," *Associated Press*, November 17, 2011, http://apnews.excite.com/article/20111117/D9R2G7L81.html.
7. Justin Elliott, "Did the NYPD's Spying on Muslims Violate the Law?," *ProPublica*, July 11, 2012, http://www.propublica.org/article/nypd-surveillance-on-muslims-qa.
8. See: http://www.ap.org/media-center/nypd/investigation.
9. Center for Human Rights and Global Justice, "Targeted and Entrapped: Manufacturing the 'Homegrown Threat' in the United States" (NYU

School of Law, 2011) http://chrgj.org/documents/targeted-and-entrapped-manufacturing-the-homegrown-threat-in-the-united-states.

10. Hawley, "In NYPD Spying, a Yippie Legal Battle Echoes Again."

11. Jim Dwyer, "Police Memos Say Arrest Tactics Calmed Protest," *New York Times*, March 17, 2006, http://www.nytimes.com/2006/03/17/nyregion/17police.html.

12. Jim Dwyer, "City Police Spied Broadly Before G.O.P. Convention," *New York Times*, March 25, 2007, http://www.nytimes.com/2007/03/25/nyregion/25infiltrate.html.

13. See: Chapter 31, 17 Stat. 13, April 1871.

14. See: 42 U.S.C. § 1983.

15. See: Board of Regents of University of State of New York v. Tomanio, 446 U.S. 478, 448 (1980).

16. See: Monroe v. Pape, 365 U.S. 167, 172 (1961).

17. See: Owen v. City of Independence, 445 U.S. 662, 651 (1980).

18. See: Monell v. Department of Social Services of New York, 436 U.S. 658 (1978).

19. G. Flint Taylor, "A Litigator's View of Discovery and Proof in Police Misconduct Policy and Practice Cases," *DePaul Law Review* (Spring 1999), http://www.nlg-npap.org/reports/litigators-view-discovery-and-proof-police-misconduct-policy-and-practice-cases.

20. See: International Action Center v. City of Philadelphia, et al.

21. Jim Smith, "Philadelphia Agrees to Abandon March Permit Process," *Philadelphia Daily News*, July 8, 2003.

22. Heidi Boghosian, *Punishing Protest: Government Tactics That Suppress Free Speech* (National Lawyers Guild, 2007), 26.

23. Carolyn Salazar, "Miami Commissioners Repeal Protest Law," *Associated Press*, March 11, 2004.

24. See: "Complaint for Injunctive Relief, Declaratory Relief and Damages," in D2K Convention Planning Coalition v. City of Los Angeles, National Lawyers Guild, Los Angeles Chapter, August 9, 2000, http://www.nlg-la.org/index_files/LAPDLawsuit/complaint.htm.

25. Heidi Boghosian, *The Policing of Political Speech: Constraints on Mass Dissent in the U.S.* (National Lawyers Guild, 2010), 11, http://www.nlg.org/wp-content/files_flutter/1286308219bodyfinal.pdf.

26. See: Collins v. Jordan, 110 F.3d 1363 (1996).

27. Stansfield Smith, "The Cost of US Police Brutality During Protests," Toward Freedom, August 12, 2011, http://www.towardfreedom.com/29-archives/activism/2428-the-cost-of-us-police-brutality-during-protests.

28. See: Complaint in Hickey v. City of Seattle, filed October 2, 2000, http://www.publicjustice.net/sites/default/files/downloads/wto_amended_complaint.pdf.

29. "WTO Westlake Arrestees Settle With the City of Seattle for $1 Million," Seattle Indymedia Center, April 2, 2007, http://news.infoshop.org/article.php?story=20070406102652306.

30. Smith, "The Cost of US Police Brutality During Protests."

31. See: Becker, et al. v. District of Columbia, et al., Case No. 01-CV-811 (Class Action), http://www2.justiceonline.org/site/PageServer?pagename=a15.

32. Boghosian, *The Policing of Political Speech*, 51.

33. Sarah Karush, "DC Agrees to Pay $13M over Arrests of Protesters," *Associated Press*, November 23, 2009.

34. Jordan Weissmann, "City to Settle Mass Arrest Class Action for $13.7 Million," *Legal Times*, November 23, 2009.

35. "In Landmark Agreement, Oakland Prohibits Less Lethal Weapons for Crowd Control," press release, ACLU of Northern California, November 9, 2004.

36. Rachel Lederman and Bobbie Stein, "SF Bay Area Chapter Files Class Action Suit against Oakland Police," Guild Notes, National Lawyers Guild, Summer/Fall 2011, http://www.nlg.org/wp-content/files_flutter/1317229924GNSummerFall2011.pdf.

37. Smith, "The Cost of US Police Brutality During Protests."

38. In October 2011, the Oakland Police Department (OPD) violated their crowd control policy and were subsequently sued by veteran Scott Olsen, who was shot at close range with a "less-lethal" projectile and suffered a traumatic brain injury. Olsen was awarded $4.5 million in March 2014, and additional restrictions were imposed on OPD.

39. Matthew Rothschild, "AFL-CIO Sues Miami over FTAA," *The Progressive*, December 4, 2007, http://www.progressive.org/mag_mc120407.

40. Michael Vasquez, "Miami Approves Payout to FTAA Protesters," *Miami Herald*, October 11, 2007.

41. Tamara Lush, "FTAA Settlement Reached," *Miami New Times*, October 4, 2007.

42. See: Eleventh Circuit Ruling in Killmon v. City of Miami, September 27, 2006, http://docs.justia.com/cases/federal/appellate-courts/ca11/06-11208/200611208-2011-02-28.pdf, and "Protesters Unlawfully Arrested at FTAA Demonstrations Win Victory," press release, National Lawyers Guild, September 27, 2006.

43. Boghosian, *Punishing Protest*, 53.

44. Smith, "The Cost of US Police Brutality During Protests."

45. Boghosian, *The Policing of Political Speech*.

46. Joel Rubin, "L.A. to Pay Nearly $13 Million over May Day Melee, Sources Say," *Los Angeles Times*, November 20, 2008.

47. "City of New York to Pay $230,000 to Settle Republican National Convention Contempt Proceeding," press release, National Lawyers Guild, New York chapter, April 15, 2005.

48. Benjamin Weiser, "New York City to Pay $18 Million over Convention Arrests," *New York Times*, January 15, 2014, http://www.nytimes.com/2014/01/16/nyregion/city-to-pay-18-million-over-convention-arrests.html.

49. Boghosian, *Punishing Protest*, 38.

Chapter 12

1. "White Dog Café's Judy Wicks, Philadelphia Leaders Support Camilo Viveiros, Republican National Convention Defendant from 2000," press release, Friends of Camilo, March 30, 2004.

2. Kristen Lombardi, "Rough Justice," *Boston Phoenix*, January 18, 2001.

3. Bill Beckler, "Statement on RNC Mass Defense," e-mail message, September 26, 2001.
4. Ibid.
5. Lombardi, "Rough Justice."
6. From an interview with Dave Onion conducted on December 14, 2011.
7. Gwen Shaffer, "Bully Puppet," *Philadelphia City Paper*, August 15, 2002, http://archives.citypaper.net/articles/2002-08-15/cover.shtml.
8. From an interview with Jody Dodd conducted on December 23, 2011.
9. Stacey Burling, "Newly Released Protesters Focusing on Jail Conditions," *Philadelphia Inquirer*, August 16, 2000.
10. From an interview with Dave Onion conducted on December 14, 2011.
11. Ron Goldwyn, "Conventional Legal Fallout," *Philadelphia Daily News*, February 15, 2001, http://articles.philly.com/2001-02-15/news/25318980.
12. Burling, "Newly Released Protesters Focusing on Jail Conditions."
13. From an interview with Jamie Graham conducted on July 6, 2009.
14. Beverly Yuen Thompson, "Jane WTO: Jail Solidarity, Law Collectives, and the Global Justice Movement," dissertation, PhD in philosophy, New School, Political and Social Science, October 2005, 98, https://snakegrrl.files.wordpress.com/2010/02/dissertation.pdf.
15. From an interview with Jamie Graham conducted on July 6, 2009.
16. Starhawk, "Organizing in the Face of Increased Repression," in *Waging War on Dissent*, eds. Seattle National Lawyers Guild WTO Legal Group (Seattle: Seattle National Lawyers Guild, 2000), 22.
17. "Untitled, or What to Do When Everyone Gets Arrested: A CRASS Course in Providing Arrestee Support," zine, Community RNC Arrestee Support Structure, 2010, http://rnc08report.org/CRASS-zine.
18. From an interview with Jude Ortiz conducted on October 28, 2012.
19. See: http://www.dhs.gov/xabout/history/editorial_0133.shtm.
20. Jennifer Van Bergen, "Homeland Security Act: The Rise of the American Police State," *Truthout*, September 2002.
21. William F. Jasper, "Rise of the Garrison State," The New American, John Birch Society, July 15, 2002, http://www.jbs.org/node/846 (as of April 2008).
22. "USA Patriot Act," Department of Homeland Security Exposed Citizens Committee for Constitutional Protection, http://www.departmentofhomelandsecurityexposed.com/patriot_act.php (as of May 2009).
23. Michael Ratner and Margaret Ratner Kunstler, *Hell No: Your Right to Dissent in Twenty-First-Century America* (New York: The New Press, 2011), 18.
24. See: http://www.alec.org.
25. See 18 U.S.C. Section 43, http://assembler.law.cornell.edu/uscode/html/uscode18/usc_sec_18_00000043----000-.html.
26. Ratner and Kunstler, *Hell No*, 9.
27. Heidi Boghosian, *Punishing Protest: Government Tactics That Suppress Free Speech* (National Lawyers Guild, 2007), 14, http://www.nationallawyersguild.org/NLG_Punishing_Protest_2007.pdf.
28. See: "Statement of John E. Lewis, Deputy Assistant Director, Counterterrorism Division, Federal Bureau of Investigation,

Before the Senate Committee on Environment and Public Works," May 18, 2005, http://www.fbi.gov/news/testimony/addressing-the-threat-of-animal-rights-extremism-and-eco-terrorism.

29. See: http://www.fbiwitchhunt.com (as of July 2007).

30. See: http://www.shac7.com.

31. See: Analysis of the Attorney General's Guidelines by the Electronic Privacy Information Center, http://epic.org/privacy/fbi.

32. Ratner and Kunstler, *Hell No*, 87.

33. "FBI Domestic Intelligence Guidelines: Attorney General's Guidelines," Defending Dissent Foundation, undated, http://www.defendingdissent.org/program/dissent.html#guidelines.

34. "The New COINTELPRO," Defending Dissent, undated, http://www.defendingdissent.org/program/dissent.html.

35. Charlie Savage, "F.B.I. Agents Get Leeway to Push Privacy Bounds," *New York Times*, June 12, 2011, http://www.nytimes.com/2011/06/13/us/13fbi.html.

36. David Stout, "F.B.I. Head Admits Mistakes in Use of Security Act," *New York Times*, March 10, 2007, http://www.nytimes.com/2007/03/10/washington/10fbi.html.

37. "FBI Improperly Spied on Activists, Says Justice Department Inspector General," press release, American Civil Liberties Union, September 20, 2010, http://www.aclu.org/free-speech-national-security/fbi-improperly-spied-activists-says-justice-department-inspector-gener, and "A Review of the FBI's Investigations of Certain Domestic Advocacy Groups," Office of the Inspector General, U.S. Department of Justice, September 2010, http://www.justice.gov/oig/special/s1009r.pdf.

38. "Presenting Documentary Evidence of FBI Political Spying, ACLU Files FOIA Request on Behalf of 16 Organizations and 10 Individuals," American Civil Liberties Union, December 2, 2004, http://aclu-co.org/news/presenting-documentary-evidence-of-fbi-political-spying-aclu-files-foia-request-on-behalf-of-16; and Amy Goodman, "Peace Group Infiltrated By Government Agent," *Democracy Now!*, October 9, 2003, http://www.democracynow.org/2003/10/9/peace_group_infiltrated_by_government_agent.

39. Eric Lichtblau, "F.B.I. Scrutinizes Antiwar Rallies," *New York Times*, November 23, 2003, http://www.nytimes.com/2003/11/23/us/fbi-scrutinizes-antiwar-rallies.html.

40. James Bovard, "Quarantining Dissent: How the Secret Service Protects Bush from Free Speech," *San Francisco Chronicle*, January 4, 2004, http://www.sfgate.com/opinion/article/Quarantining-dissent-How-the-Secret-Service-2816927.php.

41. "Intelligence Guide for First Responders," Interagency Threat Assessment and Coordination Group, 2nd Edition, March 2011, http://www.nctc.gov/docs/ITACG_Guide_for_First_Responders_2011.pdf.

42. "Pentagon to Shut Down Controversial Database," *Associated Press*, August 21, 2007, http://www.msnbc.msn.com/id/20375361/ns/us_news-security/t/pentagon-shut-down-controversial-database.

43. "Defense Department to Close Talon System," American Forces Press Service,

U.S. Department of Defense, August 21, 2007, http://www.defense.gov/news/newsarticle.aspx?id=47127.

44. "DNI Releases Budget Figure for National Intelligence Program," news release, Office of the Director of National Intelligence, October 30, 2007, http://www.dni.gov/press_releases/20071030_release.pdf.

45. "$43 Billion Spent on Spying in '07," *Associated Press*, October 31, 2007.

46. Torin Monahan and Neal A. Palmer, "The Emerging Politics of DHS Fusion Centers," Department of Human & Organizational Development, Vanderbilt University, (SAGE Publications 2009), http://torinmonahan.com/papers/FC-SD.pdf.

47. Michael German and Jay Stanley, "What's Wrong with Fusion Centers?" American Civil Liberties Union, December 2007, http://www.aclu.org/pdfs/privacy/fusioncenter_20071212.pdf.

48. David L. Carter, Ph.D., "The Intelligence Fusion Process for State, Local and Tribal Law Enforcement," white paper, Michigan State University Intelligence Program, January 2007, http://www.cops.usdoj.gov/files/ric/CDROMs/LEIntelGuide/pubs/IntelligenceFusionProcessWhitePaperv3.5.pdf.

49. See: http://news.findlaw.com/usatoday/docs/terrorism/irtpa2004.pdf.

50. "Fusion Center Guidelines: Developing and Sharing Information and Intelligence in a New Era," Departments of Justice and Homeland Security, August 2008, http://it.ojp.gov/documents/fusion_center_guidelines.pdf.

51. Michael German and Jay Stanley, "What's Wrong with Fusion Centers?"

52. Michael German and Jay Stanley, "Fusion Center Update," American Civil Liberties Union, July 2008, http://www.aclu.org/pdfs/privacy/fusion_update_20080729.pdf.

53. Monahan and Palmer, "The Emerging Politics of DHS Fusion Centers."

54. Amy Goodman and Anjali Kamat, "Declassified Docs Reveal Military Operative Spied on WA Peace Groups," *Democracy Now!*, July 28, 2009, http://www.democracynow.org/2009/7/28/broadcast_exclusive_declassified_docs_reveal_military.

55. Grover Furr, "Protest, Rebellion, Commitment: Then and Now," *CounterPunch*, April 26, 2004, http://www.counterpunch.org/furr04262004.html.

56. See: http://www.gov.state.ga.us/ExOrders/05_07_04_01.pdf.

57. Michelle Goldberg, "Georgia When It Fizzles," *Salon*, June 11, 2004, http://archive.salon.com/news/feature/2004/06/11/protests/index_np.html.

58. See: The Insurrection Act of 1807, 10 U.S. Code, Sections 331–35.

59. Frank Morales, "Bush Moves Toward Martial Law," Global Research, October 26, 2006, and see: HR5122, the John Warner Defense Authorization Act of 2007 (Public Law 109-364).

60. Aaron Glantz, "U.S. Military Spied on Hundreds of Antiwar Demos," OneWorld.net, January 25, 2007, http://us.oneworld.net/article/view/145395/1/4536 (as of February 2007); and "ACLU Report Shows Widespread Pentagon Surveillance of Peace Activists," press release, American Civil Liberties Union, January 17, 2007, http://www.aclu.org/national-security/aclu-report-shows-widespread-pentagon-surveillance-peace-activists.

61. Heather Wokusch, "Rumsfeld's Guinea Pigs: US Citizens at Risk for Military-Weapons Testing," *Common Dreams*, September 20, 2006, http://www.commondreams.org/views06/0920-31.htm.

62. Will Potter, "PA Homeland Security Bulletin Warned of Extremist 'Recruitment' at Carriage Horse Protest," Green is the New Red, September 30, 2010, http://www.greenisthenewred.com/blog/pa-homeland-security-bulletin-carriage-horse-protest/3185.

63. Amy Goodman and Denis Moynihan, "FBI Raids and the Criminalization of Dissent," *Democracy Now!*, September 29, 2010, http://www.democracynow.org/blog/2010/9/29/fbi_raids_and_the_criminalization_of_dissent.

64. "Pa. Governor Shuts Down State Reports on Protests," *Associated Press*, September 15, 2010.

65. Marcy Wheeler (a.k.a. emptywheel), "When Political Activism Gets Treated as Potential Terrorism," Firedoglake, September 15, 2010, http://emptywheel.firedoglake.com/2010/09/15/when-political-activism-gets-treated-as-potential-terrorism.

66. Patrick Martin, "Report Whitewashes FBI Political Spying," World Socialist Web Site, September 22, 2010, http://www.wsws.org/articles/2010/sep2010/fbir-s22.shtml.

67. Shawn Gaynor, "The Cop Group Coordinating the Occupy Crackdowns," *San Francisco Bay Guardian*, November 18, 2011, http://www.sfbg.com/politics/2011/11/18/cop-group-coordinating-occupy-crackdowns.

68. See: http://www.policeforum.org.

69. Michael Blanding, "A Warning for Miami," *The Nation*, December 1, 2003, http://www.thenation.com/article/warning-miami.

70. Kyle Munzenrieder, "John Timoney, Former Miami Police Chief, to Train Police in Middle East Kingdom of Bahrain," *Miami New Times*, December 1, 2011, http://blogs.miaminewtimes.com/riptide/2011/12/john_timoney_former_miami_poli.php.

71. Cyril Mychalejko, "Revisiting the 'Miami Model,'" *Z Magazine*, November 2006, http://zmagsite.zmag.org/Nov2006/mychalejko1106.html (as of September 2007).

72. Al Baker, "Court Lets City Withhold Data of Surveillance," *New York Times*, June 9, 2010, http://www.nytimes.com/2010/06/10/nyregion/10rnc.html, and See: *In re City of New York* (2010), http://caselaw.findlaw.com/us-2nd-circuit/1526751.html.

73. "National Special Security Events," United States Secret Service, http://www.secretservice.gov/nsse.shtml.

74. "Planning and Managing Security for Major Special Events," U.S. Justice Department, March 2007, http://www.cops.usdoj.gov/Publications/e07071299_web.pdf.

75. Heidi Boghosian, *The Policing of Political Speech: Constraints on Mass Dissent in the U.S.* (National Lawyers Guild, 2010), 25, http://www.nlg.org/wp-content/files_flutter/1286308219bodyfinal.pdf, 25.

76. "National Special Security Events," U.S. Northern Command and Federal Bureau of Investigation, March 4, 2008, http://rnc08report.org/engine/uploads/1/Day-2-Breakout-2-NSSE-Carillo-Lowry-Lumley.pdf.

77. Boghosian, *The Policing of Political Speech*, introduction.
78. Gan Golan, "Closing the Gateways of Democracy: Cities and the Militarization of Protest Policing," Massachusetts Institute of Technology, 2005, http://protestarchive.org/files/Dissertation_Gan_Golan.pdf.
79. Amy Goodman, "Fortress Toronto: Massive Security Clampdown for G8/G20 Meetings Most Expensive in Canadian History," *Democracy Now!*, June 25, 2010, http://www.democracynow.org/2010/6/25/fortress_toronto_massive_security_clampdown_for.
80. Golan, "Closing the Gateways of Democracy."
81. Naomi Klein, *Fences and Windows: Dispatches from the Front Lines of the Globalization Debate* (New York: Picador, 2002), 122.
82. From an interview with Jody Dodd conducted on December 23, 2011.
83. "Judge Questions Officers' Actions," *Associated Press*, December 21, 2003, http://www.heraldtribune.com/article/20031221/NEWS/312210384.
84. See: Killmon v. City of Miami, Case No. 06-11208.
85. Jim Dwyer, "City Police Spied Broadly Before G.O.P. Convention," *New York Times*, March 25, 2007, http://www.nytimes.com/2007/03/25/nyregion/25infiltrate.html.
86. See: http://iwitnessvideo.info.
87. "Untitled, or What to Do When Everyone Gets Arrested: A CRASS Course in Providing Arrestee Support," zine, Community RNC Arrestee Support Structure, 2010, http://rnc08report.org/CRASS-zine.
88. For example, the St. Paul Police Department purchased at least 230 additional tasers so that none of their officers would be without one. Those tasers are still being used against the people of St. Paul today. See: Cyril Mychalejko, "RNC: Exporting the 'Miami Model' to St. Paul," Twin Cities Indymedia, August 20, 2008, http://twincities.indymedia.org/2008/aug/rnc-exporting-miami-model-st-paul.
89. "THE RNC800! Newsletter," Community RNC Arrestee Support Structure (CRASS), August 24, 2009, http://rnc08arrestees.files.wordpress.com/2009/01/rnc800_082409.pdf.
90. Urmila Ramakrishnan, "Last of RNC8 accept plea bargain, avoid jail," *Minnesota Daily*, October 20, 2010, http://www.mndaily.com/2010/10/20/last-rnc8-accept-plea-bargain-avoid-jail, and Madeleine Baran, "Charges dismissed against three of RNC 8 suspects," *Minnesota Public Radio*, September 16, 2010, http://minnesota.publicradio.org/display/web/2010/09/16/rnc-charges-dismissed.
91. Emily Gurnon, "California Man Gets 60 Days for Breaking U.S. Bank Windows during GOP Convention," *St. Paul Pioneer Press*, February 6, 2009.
92. "THE RNC800! Newsletter," Community RNC Arrestee Support Structure (CRASS), November 13, 2009, http://rnc08arrestees.files.wordpress.com/2009/01/rnc800_111309.pdf.
93. *Better This World*, DVD produced by Katie Galloway, Kelly Duanne de la Vega, and Mike Nicholson (Loteria Films/Independent Television Service, 2011).
94. Bhaskar Sunkara, "Ten Years Later: The History of Possibility," *Dissent Magazine*, September 8, 2011, http://dissentmagazine.org/online.php?id=540.

95. Daniel Denvir, "A Political Casualty of 9/11: The Anti-corporate Globalization Movement," *Truthout*, September 15, 2011, http://truth-out.org/political-casualty-911-anti-corporate-globalization-movement/1316099319.
96. Mark Engler, "Elbowed Out of Spotlight by 9/11, Anti-globalization Movement Endures," Focal Points, Foreign Policy in Focus, September 21, 2011, http://www.fpif.org/blog/elbowed_out_of_spotlight_by_911_anti-globalization_movement_endures.
97. Christopher Day, "Some thoughts on DAN's role in the August 1st action," Notes, October 28, 2000.
98. Suzy Subways, ed., *"We Shut the City Down": Six Former Student Liberation Action Movement (SLAM) Members Reflect on the Mass Direct Actions against the 2000 RNC in Philadelphia*, SLAM Herstory Project, December 2, 2010, http://slamherstory.wordpress.com.
99. A.K. Thompson, *Black Bloc, White Riot: Anti-globalization and the Genealogy of Dissent* (Oakland: AK Press, 2010), 18.
100. Ana Nogueira, "Free Speech Falls Victim to Police Crackdown," *The Unconvention* 5, Philadelphia Independent Media Center, August 2, 2000.
101. Naomi Klein, "The Vision Thing," *The Nation*, June 22, 2000, http://www.thenation.com/article/vision-thing.
102. Rebecca and David Solnit, *The Battle of the Story of the Battle of Seattle* (Oakland: AK Press, 2009), 24.
103. Starhawk, "Organizing in the Face of Increased Repression," in *Waging War on Dissent*, eds. Seattle National Lawyers Guild WTO Legal Group, Winter 2000, 22.
104. See: http://rnc08report.org/archive/224.shtml.
105. Ryan Harvey, "Are We Addicted to Rioting?," Open letter, September 24, 2009, http://news.infoshop.org/article.php?story=2009092714272755.
106. Chris White, "Re: Inquirer story," e-mail message, August 2, 2010.
107. Thompson, *Black Bloc, White Riot*, 81.
108. Camilo Viveiros, "Ten Lessons from the Criminalization of Dissent," *Earth First! Journal*, April 2006, http://www.earthfirstjournal.org/article.php?id=190.
109. "Strategy Chart," Midwest Academy, undated, http://www.tcsg.org/sfelp/toolkit/MidwestAcademy_01.pdf.
110. See: http://www.movementstrategy.org.
111. "Strategy Is Possible," Training for Change, undated, http://www.trainingforchange.org/strategy_is_possible.
112. CrimethInc., "Say You Want an Insurrection," *Rolling Thunder*, Fall 2009, http://www.crimethinc.com/texts/rollingthunder/insurrection.php.
113. Thompson, *Black Bloc, White Riot*, 123.
114. Ryan Harvey, "Are We Addicted to Rioting?," open letter, September 24, 2009.
115. CrimethInc., "Say You Want an Insurrection."
116. "N30 Black Bloc Communiqué," ACME Collective, December 4, 1999, http://theanarchistlibrary.org/HTML/ACME_Collective__N30_Black_Bloc_Communique.html.
117. CrimethInc., "Say You Want an Insurrection."
118. Ibid.

Chapter 13

1. See: http://www.midnightspecial.net.
2. Beverly Yuen Thompson, "Jane WTO: Jail Solidarity, Law Collectives, and the Global Justice Movement," dissertation, PhD in philosophy, New School, Political and Social Science, October 2005, 115, http://snakegrrl.files. wordpress.com/2010/02/dissertation.pdf.
3. Ibid, 117.
4. Phaedra Travis, Sarah Coffey and Paul Marini, "Wrenching the Bench: People's Law Collectives and the Movement," *Earth First! Journal*, 2002, http://www. earthfirstjournal.org/article.php?id=123.
5. "On the Road," Midnight Special Law Collective, http://midnightspecial.net/ history.html.
6. Travis, Coffey, and Marini, "Wrenching the Bench."
7. Thompson, "Jane WTO," 114.
8. Travis, Coffey, and Marini, "Wrenching the Bench."
9. See: http://midnightspecial.net.
10. See: http://www.lawcollective.org.
11. See: http://r2klegal.protestarchive.org/r2klegal.
12. http://upagainstthelaw.org.
13. Thompson, "Jane WTO."
14. http://justusnyc.org.
15. http://www.justiceandsolidarity.org (as of January 2010).
16. http://portlandlawcollective.com.
17. Travis, Coffey, and Marini, "Wrenching the Bench."
18. http://piano.geo.utexas.edu/fing/aplc (as of January 2009).
19. http://coldsnaplegal.wordpress.com.
20. http://libertas.taktic.org/english/navigation-en.html (as of February 2005).
21. http://nyc.indymedia.org/media/application/3/efj_blank_wall_2.doc.
22. http://movementdefence.org.
23. http://srlp.org.
24. "Past Projects," Midnight Special Law Collective, http://www.midnightspecial. net/projects/pastprojects.html.
25. Ritchie Eppink, "Law Collectives," *Ritchie Eppink's Blog*, November 5, 2006, http://usefulinfo.org/journal/archives/40.
26. See: http://www.midnightspecial.net.
27. Travis, Coffey, and Marini, "Wrenching the Bench."
28. See: http://www.midnightspecial.net.
29. Travis, Coffey, and Marini, "Wrenching the Bench."
30. Ibid.
31. "Untitled, or What to Do When Everyone Gets Arrested: A CRASS Course in Providing Arrestee Support," Zine, Community RNC Arrestee Support Structure, 2010, http://rnc08report.org/CRASS-zine.
32. Ibid.

AFTERWORD

I TRIPPED UP THE STAIRS TO SEEK REFUGE IN A STRANGER'S APART-
ment. A uniformed police officer with a raised nightstick was chasing
me and a few other people I'd run into the building with. His baton
struck the door as it slammed shut behind us.

A few hours earlier, working for a community newspaper, I had
gone to observe local residents protesting imposition of a 1:00 A.M. park
curfew in Tompkins Square Park in Manhattan's East Village. But when
I arrived, instead of finding a gathering of concerned neighbors, I saw
mounted police galloping north on Avenue A. Within minutes, hundreds
of riot-clad officers with badges covered or removed converged from
several directions, wreaking mayhem and grabbing at passersby. They
charged the streets wielding indiscriminate force: a billy club caught a
journalist in the neck. He went down. Officers dragged a pregnant woman
from a restaurant. The next day these and other images of police brutality headlined the international news.

It was August 7, 1988, and the *New York Times* proclaimed the
melee a police riot—a violent confrontation initiated and sustained by
law enforcement officers against members of the public with the aim of
political repression. The officer in charge of these actions by the New
York City Police Department (NYPD) that night was Deputy Inspector
John F. Timoney.

The term "police riot" entered the public lexicon just two decades
earlier with issuance of the Walker Report, named after a commission
of over 200 members formed to investigate unrestrained police violence
against approximately 10,000 protesters in Chicago's Grant Park at the
1968 Democratic National Convention. The Commission interviewed

more than 1,400 witnesses and examined FBI reports and film of confrontations between police and protesters. It deemed the convention violence a "police riot" and recommended prosecuting the offenders, stressing that failure to prosecute those law enforcement officers would erode public confidence in the police.

Parks and political conventions are natural places for protesters and police to converge. As Kris Hermes has detailed in these pages, although violent police tactics have been routinely used against dissenters in this country, the 2000 Republican National Convention marked the beginning of a well-financed and finely tuned state response to mass political assemblies. The election of George W. Bush, the 2001 plane hijackings, and the government's War on Terror coalesced to institutionalize this response. As the balance between civil liberties and law enforcement tilted in favor of the police—accelerated by a conservative Supreme Court and corporate-friendly policies—guidelines enacted in the 1970s to curb FBI monitoring of dissenters were all but eviscerated. Now, the very actions that shocked the public at police riots such as those in Chicago and New York are standard operating crowd control procedures.

The new policing paradigm involves studying the character, behaviors and technology of activists. Just as environmentalists, animal rights activists and others learned important lessons in Philadelphia—about the value of acting in solidarity to resist unjust charges—so did Timoney closely observe their tactics in order to disrupt them. Modern hallmarks of American policing have treated people bringing anti-globalization and other messages to the streets as invading foreigners or prospective terrorists. Twentieth century policing is preemptive and closely resembles acts of counterintelligence. It involves unlawful infiltration tactics, surveillance, negative stereotyping and raising the specter of fear among residents and merchants that Americans who peaceably assemble in public spaces are disruptive lawbreakers.

Of all the individuals who have worked during and since the 2000 RNC to suppress lawful dissent, John Timoney—author of *Beat Cop to Top Cop: A Tale of Three Cities*—stands out as the lead architect of the new policing model. Despite having accumulated nearly seventy department NYPD medals including the Medal of Valor, his brash tactics earned him the disdain of citizens and other law enforcement officials alike.

Timoney did something in Philadelphia that no other police chief had done. He put himself in the middle of his adversaries. He got on a bicycle and rode with activists through the streets of Philadelphia at the height of the RNC protests. And as Kris Hermes documents, a year before, under his leadership the Philadelphia Police Department (PPD) traveled to the World Trade Organization Ministerial Conference in Seattle to study protesters' methods in advance of the RNC. Timoney also sought funding to bolster the department's resources. Amplifying threat assessments in advance of specific events to secure funding from the Department of Homeland Security is now commonplace among police departments. Under Timoney, the PPD was the first to tactically control demonstrations and protest parades on bicycles when his officers policed the 2000 RNC. (When Timoney became Police Chief in Miami, he grew the bike patrol in size and prestige. Officers learned techniques to apprehend subjects, to wield bicycles as weapons and as barricades to control crowds, and to use them as protective shields.)

Such flagrant abuse of police power poses a danger to civil society. We elect civilian governments and in no circumstance should a parallel structure of police authority exist that operates without civilian oversight. Timoney's denial that police engaged in infiltration at the RNC—even though documents show that undercover state police posed as demonstrators to infiltrate activist groups planning the protests—is but one example of the flaunting of this authority. The use of state troopers as undercover operatives occurred in bold defiance of a mayoral directive forbidding the city from using its own officers for infiltration without the permission of the mayor, the managing director, and the police commissioner.

The result of the carefully crafted Timoney campaign is evident in the policies and practices used across the nation following the 2000 RNC. To garner wide support for his aggressive policing campaign the notorious "tough cop" put forth a false narrative that violent anarchists were descending on cities as he alleged they had at the Seattle WTO protests. Before the 2003 FTAA Ministerial Meeting in Miami, he showed police an edited videotape suggesting that protesters in Seattle had injured or even killed police who were shown lying on the ground. As other municipalities now frequently do, Timoney exploited the press to instill fear into local residents and business owners. He did this despite the findings of several independent review panels blaming Seattle police for their handling of the 1999 protests.

As a rash of law enforcement killings of Black men captured the attention of the country, from Ferguson, Missouri to Baltimore, so too has a wave of righteous anger over police brutality ignited peoples' uprisings across the nation. Ordinary people are taking to the streets en masse to shift the dialogue around issues of racism, impunity for police departments, and political dissent. Coverage on network news and the front pages of tabloids exposes graphic images of excessive policing for the world to see. Signaling a shift in the public consciousness, the New York Times' front page published still frames of the video of South Carolina murder by a police officer of Walter Scott, an indication that as *Crashing the Party* went to press, events were unfolding that signal hope that the imbalance of police power may be changing in radical ways. The Baltimore state's attorney charged eight six police officers in the killing of Freddie Gray, the Department of Justice released a report on the Philadelphia Police Department's use of deadly force, and the California state Senate passed a bill prohibiting grand juries from investigating police shootings in cases where an individual dies from excessive force during an arrest.

The routine killing by police of young African American men makes it increasingly important—as Kris Hermes details in *Crashing the Party*—to challenge the modern policing model.

The more individuals experience firsthand the hallmarks of a police state, the more they will come to realize that those calling to "crash the party" are not domestic terrorists or enemies of the state. They are among society's bravest individuals willing to risk abuse at the hands of law enforcement to remind us that the streets and parks belong to we the people to use, without fear of recrimination or reprisal, for public assembly and the constitutionally protected exercise of free speech.

INDEX

Page numbers in *italic* refer to illustrations. "Passim" (literally "scattered") indicates intermittent discussion of a topic over a cluster of pages.

ABOUT THE CONTRIBUTORS

Kris Hermes is a Bay Area–based activist who has worked for nearly thirty years on social justice issues. Organizing with ACT UP Philadelphia in the late 1990s spurred his interest in legal support work and led to his years-long involvement with R2K Legal. Since 2000, Hermes has been an active, award-winning legal worker-member of the National Lawyers Guild and has been a part of numerous law collectives and legal support efforts over the years. In this capacity, he has organized dozens of press conference and spoken at numerous community meetings, political conferences, book fairs, and other similar events across the U.S. Hermes has written extensively in his professional career as a media worker and as a legal activist.

Marina Sitrin is a writer, lawyer, teacher, organizer, and dreamer. She is the editor of *Horizontalism: Voices of Popular Power in Argentina*, author of *Everyday Revolutions: Horizontalism & Autonomy in Argentina* and coauthor of *They Can't Represent US! Reinventing Democracy from Greece to Occupy*. She has a JD in International Women's Human Rights from CUNY Law School and a PhD in Global Sociology from Stony Brook University.

Heidi Boghosian is the executive director of the A.J. Muste Memorial Institute and former executive director of the National Lawyers Guild. She is the cohost of the weekly civil liberties radio show *Law and Disorder* on Pacifica's WBAI in New York and over forty national affiliates. She received her JD from Temple Law School where she was the editor in chief of the *Temple Political & Civil Rights Law Review*. She also holds an MS from Boston University and a BA from Brown University. She is the author of *Spying on Democracy: Government Surveillance, Corporate Power, and Public Resistance*.

About PM Press

PM Press was founded at the end of 2007 by a small collection of folks with decades of publishing, media, and organizing experience. PM Press co-conspirators have published and distributed hundreds of books, pamphlets, CDs, and DVDs. Members of PM have founded enduring book fairs, spearheaded victorious tenant organizing campaigns, and worked closely with bookstores, academic conferences, and even rock bands to deliver political and challenging ideas to all walks of life. We're old enough to know what we're doing and young enough to know what's at stake.

Contact us for direct ordering and questions about all PM Press releases, as well as manuscript submissions, review copy requests, foreign rights sales, author interviews, to book an author for an event, and to have PM Press attend your bookfair:

PM Press ✦ PO Box 23912 ✦ Oakland, CA 94623
510-658-3906 ✦ info@pmpress.org

Buy books and stay on top of what we are doing at:

www.pmpress.org

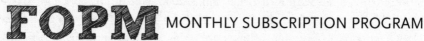 MONTHLY SUBSCRIPTION PROGRAM

These are indisputably momentous times—the financial system is melting down globally and the Empire is stumbling. Now more than ever there is a vital need for radical ideas.

In the eight years since its founding—and on a mere shoestring—PM Press has risen to the formidable challenge of publishing and distributing knowledge and entertainment for the struggles ahead. With hundreds of releases to date, we have published an impressive and stimulating array of literature, art, music, politics, and culture. Using every available medium, we've succeeded in connecting those hungry for ideas and information to those putting them into practice.

Friends of PM allows you to directly help impact, amplify, and revitalize the discourse and actions of radical writers, filmmakers, and artists. It provides us with a stable foundation from which we can build upon our early successes and provides a much-needed subsidy for the materials that can't necessarily pay their own way. You can help make that happen—and receive every new title automatically delivered to your door once a month—by joining as a Friend of PM Press. And, we'll throw in a free T-Shirt when you sign up.

Here are your options (all include a 50% discount on all webstore purchases):
  ✦ $30 a month: Get all books and pamphlets
  ✦ $40 a month: Get all PM Press releases (including CDs and DVDs)
  ✦ $100 a month: Superstar—Everything plus PM merchandise, free downloads

For those who can't afford $30 or more a month, we're introducing *Sustainer Rates* at $15, $10, and $5. Sustainers get a free PM Press T-shirt and a 50% discount on all purchases from our website.

Your Visa or Mastercard will be billed once a month, until you tell us to stop. Or until our efforts succeed in bringing the revolution around. Or the financial meltdown of Capital makes plastic redundant. Whichever comes first.